D0301720

Letters from the Desert

The Correspondence of Flinders and Hilda Petrie

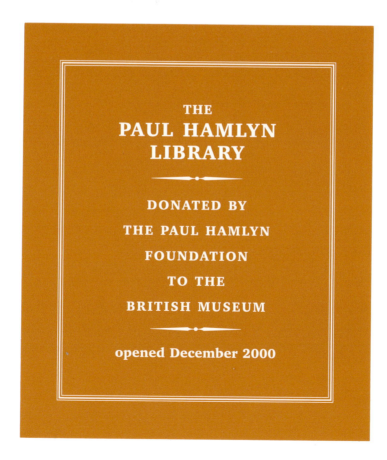

THE
**PAUL HAMLYN
LIBRARY**

DONATED BY

THE PAUL HAMLYN

FOUNDATION

TO THE

BRITISH MUSEUM

opened December 2000

Sir William Matthew Flinders Petrie

Letters from the Desert

The Correspondence
of Flinders and Hilda Petrie

edited by
Margaret Drower

Aris and Phillips

Aris & Phillips is an
imprint of Oxbow Books
Park End Place, Oxford

© Margaret Drower 2004

0-85668-748-0

This book is available from

Oxbow Books, Park End Place, Oxford OX1 1HN
Email: oxbow@oxbowbooks.com

and

The David Brown Book Co.
PO Box 511, Oakville, CT 06779
Tel: (860) 945–9329; Fax: (860) 945–9468
Email: david.brown.bk.co@snet.net

and via the website
www.oxbowbooks.com

Printed in Great Britain at
The Short Run Press, Exeter

THE BRITISH MUSEUM
THE PAUL HAMLYN LIBRARY
WITHDRAWN

930.1092 PET

Contents

Foreword

During the latter part of the nineteenth century the Middle East, in particular Egypt and Palestine, became for the first time more easily accessible to travellers from Europe. John Murray's first handbook for Egypt was published in 1835, and in 1869 Thomas Cook's steamers made their appearance on the Nile. From then on, visitors attracted to Egypt by the climate, the antiquities and the natural scenery of the valley could view them with comparative ease and comfort. On board they enjoyed the comfort of a hotel and the congenial company of their fellow-travellers; their cabins were comfortable, their meals were cooked by chefs; when they landed near a temple or tomb, they were provided with transport and escorted by a dragoman or guide. In Luxor and Assuan they found shops selling western goods; dealers in antiquities offered them valuable souvenirs of their visit. They had little contact with the people of the country, saw the villages and towns they passed through only from a distance, and had no contact with the fellahin in the fields.

The archaeologist who spends the winter months, perhaps from October or November till April, excavating a town site or cemetery, has a very different view of the country and its people. He often has to build his own house on the edge of the desert, beyond the cultivated land. He is on friendly terms with the villagers of his neighbourhood, some of which he will be employing as labourers on his 'dig'; the men and children he takes on as diggers are known to him by their names and rewarded weekly for their work; when injured or sick they come to the 'mudir' for bandages and medicines. The letters of Flinders and Hilda Petrie, written for their friends and relatives back in England and sent regularly throughout the season, throw light on little-known aspects of rural life in Egypt and in Palestine. For the scientific results of the excavations, the reader is referred to the volumes of Petrie's archaeological discoveries.

Editorial Foreword

The following letters and journal entries have been selected for the light they throw on Petrie, his life while excavating in Egypt, and his times. They are specifically not selected for their scientific interest or for the discoveries they describe as these are amply covered by the numerous publications which he produced with commendable speed after his excavations were completed. His bibliography compiled by E.P. Uphill contains over 100 books and more than 1,000 items. After his marriage in 1897 the letters of his wife Hilda prove equally fascinating and she is also responsible for a number of entries in the journals after this date. It is remarkable that this Victorian lady was able to adapt so quickly to the austere conditions of a Petrie dig.

Letters from the Desert is arranged chronologically and does not contain a continuous narrative as this would have produced a book many times the length of the present volume. It has been compiled from the transcriptions made from Petrie's letters, diaries and notes for my biography *Flinders Petrie – A Life in Archaeology* (Victor Gollancz 1985) published in paperback by the University of Wisconsin in 1995. Readers should consult this work for a detailed bibliography of Petrie's publications and further reading.

Petrie's letters from Egypt were usually circulated among his family and friends, and those who supported his work financially. There is a long list of recipients at the beginning of most letters; this list has been omitted. From 1905 onwards, when he was financed by the British School of Archaeology in Egypt, his letters went to the Committee. Hilda Petrie's letters were written to her parents and one or other of her women friends. Letters from 1905 onwards are addressed to their children; letters from Palestine were sent to John and Ann, or in the form of reports to the British School.

The extracts presented here should be assumed to have been written by Flinders Petrie unless stated otherwise; they are unedited. Small amounts of editorial comment are given where explanations or background information are deemed necessary or appropriate.

I have to thank Dr. Jaromir Malek, the Archivist of the Griffith Institute, Oxford, for providing me with Xerox copies of Petrie's letters and for permission to reproduce them. Most of the Petrie's letters to their children are in the possession of Dr. Lisette Petrie, their grandaughter. I am grateful to her for letting me reproduce some of the couple's watercolour sketches in her possession.

Margaret Drower

Preface

Sir William Matthew Flinders Petrie (1853-1942), the Egyptian and Palestinian archaeologist, was one of the most extraordinary of the great polymaths of his period. His countenance, with his broad, high forehead, luxuriant hair, moustache and beard, initially black but later white, his prominent eyebrows and piercing eyes, fits the popular stereotype of an eminent Victorian. But Petrie was a very unconventional and unusual man by the standards of his own or any age, and his genius, though brilliant and wide-ranging, was visionary, idiosyncratic and dogmatic.

He was the son of William Petrie, a devout fundamentalist and a surveyor and inventor of undoubted talent, who had neither the means nor the know-how to market his varied clever electrical and chemical inventions, and of Anne Flinders, daughter of the explorer and sea-captain Matthew Flinders, who discovered much of the Queensland coast and is revered in Australia as a founding father. Flinders Petrie exhibited a precocious intellectual curiosity, demanding explanations of everything even in infancy; but at the age of four he fell seriously ill with bronchitis and only narrowly survived. Thereafter he had to be confined indoors in winter and could not be sent to school. He thus had an extremely irregular education, at first with his mother and under a series of governesses, but later educating himself, with only sporadic and desultory lessons from his father. At the age of ten he was already reading his mother's editions of classical literature in translation and Gibbons's *Decline and Fall of the Roman Empire*, collecting coins, searching the countryside for minerals and fossils, and visiting auction sales to purchase coins and antiquities. This led him to the British Museum, where the Department of Coins and Medals encouraged him to bring in his purchases for identification and occasional acquisition. He became rapt in wonder at the collections, and soon knew the exhibits of all the departments off by heart. He qualified for a Reader's ticket at 21, whereafter the Reading Room became his university. Meanwhile, he had started, with the occasional help of his father, to survey the Prehistoric earthworks and stone circles of southern England, of which there were then no accurately surveyed plans; and in 1877 he deposited with the British Museum completed plans of forty monuments, including full plans of Stonehenge measured to one-tenth of an inch.

Back in 1866 Petrie had bought Piazzi Smyth's book, *Our Inheritance in the*

Great Pyramid, and his father and he became deeply intrigued with Smyth's idea, derived from John Taylor, that the measurements of the Great Pyramid at Giza contained divine messages to mankind, though they did not share Smyth's British Israelite convictions. Flinders Petrie started his own mathematical calculations and published his first book, *Researches on the Great Pyramid* in support of Piazzi Smyth's theory in 1874. This led to controversy, and eventually Petrie and his father decided that they must go to Egypt to make their own accurate surveys of the Great Pyramid in order to test the theory. His father's enthusiasm was, however, sporadic, and in 1880 Flinders Petrie set off for Egypt on his own. Over the next two years, living alone on minimal supplies in an empty rock-cut tomb on the Giza plateau, he made complete triangulations of all the Giza pyramids, demonstrating the inaccuracy of Piazzi Smyth's data and calculations. While in Egypt he contrived even on his exiguous means to visit a number of ancient sites by camel or donkey or on foot. He was both enthralled by their richness and appalled at the constant and callous destruction to which they were then exposed, and he became totally committed to their study and rescue. So began his sixty year career in Egyptian and Palestininian archaeology.

Petrie's early surveys and excavations on Delta sites took place under the aegis of the Egypt Exploration Society, which had recently been founded mainly through the efforts of Miss Amelia B. Edwards and R. S. Poole of the British Museum. The Society was, however, then principally concerned with tracing the route of the Exodus and with obtaining art objects and Hieroglyphic inscriptions for the British Museum. Petrie soon came into conflict with the Committee over aims, methods and financial administration and resigned. Miss Edwards, had, however, formed a great admiration for his scientific methods, his attention to detail and his economy of means, and found a backer, Jesse Haworth, who enabled him to work independently, which he did until 1892. In that year Miss Edwards died, and left a capital endowment to University College London to provide an annual income of £140 to found a Professorship of Egyptian Archaeology and Philology. In accordance with her known wishes, Petrie was appointed to this chair, with the special condition that he should have leave in the second term of each session to pursue research and excavate in Egypt. Thereafter, apart from one further short period of work for the Egypt Exploration Society in the 1990s, Petrie worked for the Egyptian Research Account, funded by Haworth and many other donors, including Museums, and for its successor the British School of Archaeology in Egypt, based on the Department of Egyptology at University College London. With the exception of the years of the First World War, he worked in Egypt virtually every winter until 1926, often on more than one site, returning to England each spring to lecture, to prepare his annual publication of results, and to exhibit and distribute his finds in order to raise funds for the following season. Many of the antiquities he was working on, and those suitable for building up archaeological type series, he retained in his own collection, which in 1913 passed to University College, where it forms the nucleus of the Petrie Museum, now one of the most important Egyptological collections in Britain.

Petrie's lonely childhood and lack of formal school training, his unfamiliarity with and distaste for society and his passion for intellectual and scientific pursuits set him wholly apart from the majority of the resident British community in Egypt at that time, whether diplomatic, military or commercial, and from privileged visitors on the grand tour. He had, even after his appointment at UCL, very little money of his own. He lived on his sites, in empty tombs, vacated mud-brick hovels or under canvas with the most frugal economy imaginable. Hardened by his British surveys, he walked almost everywhere, thinking nothing of tramping fifteen miles a day to and from his sites, and eschewing for the most part even the hire of a camel or donkey. Frequently ill, and prone to fevers and bronchitis, he slept on average only three to five hours a night, and was often up before sunrise, sorting potsherds, setting up his pin-hole camera or writing reports, and was generally off to work at first light. His overriding concern was to save every fragment of evidence that could throw light on the course of man's development, whether physical, technological or cultural, in ancient times. To him, in contrast to his contemporaries, bones, potsherds, flints, tools, coins, weights, fragments of minerals, metals, textiles and every form of artifact were as important as the finest work of art or the most splendid standing monument, for from them he could hope to reconstruct the daily lives of the ancient Egyptians and the outlines of their social and economic history. He was, in this sense, the first 'modern' archaeologist to excavate in Egypt, a man far in advance of his time; and to his work he brought his brilliant surveying and mathematical skills and encyclopaediac first-hand knowledge of ancient artifacts, rather than the perspectives of a classical education. To give but one example of his original genius, he was working out his famous sequence-dating for the Predynastic Naqada culture of Upper Egypt on principles of mathematical seriation in the 1890s, at a time when many intellectually-inclined people were still seriously debating Archbishop Usher's dating of the creation of the world in 4004 BC.

It is no wonder, then, that he shunned the social and diplomatic round of Cairo, and went in to towns and cities only to purchase stores and to negotiate with the authorities of the Government Antiquities Service, who were in those times predominantly French. With them he had an ambiguous and sometimes stormy relationship; for though many of them were fine

Egyptologists in the textual and historical fields, few of them had seen with their own eyes the destruction of the ancient urban and cemetery sites or regarded their protection with Petrie's passionate zeal, for their main focus was upon standing monuments and inscriptions. Moreover, as officials of the Khedivial government, it was their decision what antiquities the excavator should be allowed to take out of the country. As Petrie was dependent upon having antiquities to distribute in order to raise funds for his work, the terms of his permissions to dig and the subsequent divisions of antiquities resulted in many tussles, culminating in the justified change in the Antiquities Law after the find of the tomb of Tutankhamun, which eventually resulted in Petrie shifting his work to Palestine in 1926.

Thus Petrie seemed doomed to continue to bear the full weight of his archaeological crusade himself. However, in July 1896, when he was already 43, a fair-haired, blue-eyed young woman visited his exhibition at University College of his recent discoveries at Thebes, and immediately attracted his attention. Her name was Hilda Urlin; he found that she was working in the College on drawings of classical ornament for a family friend, the Pre-Raphaelite painter Henry Holiday, who had already used her, well chaperoned of course, as a model for his painting of Dante and Beatrice (now in the Leeds Art Gallery). She professed an interest in ancient Egypt, and Petrie encouraged her by giving her scarabs to draw for him and by lending her books and giving her lecture-tickets. She too proved to be an unconventional spirit, fascinated with nature, history, antiquities and the arts, but with little taste for society and none for domestic pursuits. Throughout the following winter in Egypt he corresponded with her, and decided to propose to her on his return in May. At first she rebuffed him on grounds of their slight acquaintance, and he wrote her a tempestuous letter, vowing that, if she continued to reject him, he would leave England, resign his chair and live in Syria permanently. She relented, and on her mother's advice he visited her at her home in Sussex. During his second visit she accepted him, and on 29 Nov. 1897, they were married in Kensington, and set off immediately for Egypt. On arrival, Hilda was entranced by the colours, sights and sounds of Egypt, and was not put off in any way by the rigours of travel nor by the spartan conditions of the camp they set up together in some mud-huts at Denderah. Straight away, she started marking and drawing finds, cataloguing objects, and helping Petrie in the field with surveying and planning. She thought nothing of twenty mile tramps in the desert on market-days, searching for rock-tombs and prehistoric sites; both would take their paint-boxes and sketch desert scenery and sunsets for relaxation. By the end of that first season she had learnt some colloquial Arabic and had become a skilled copier of Hieroglyphic inscriptions. Thenceforth for the remainder of his career until his death in Jerusalem in 1942 she was at Flinders's side throughout all his field-work, except during her confinements with their two children, John and Ann, and helped and supported him in every way, illustrating his publications, accompanying him on lecture tours, and fund-raising for the British School of Archaeology in Egypt, which he founded to finance his work. Never can a field archaeologist have had so ideal a wife.

Over his whole career Petrie worked at sixty-two sites in Egypt, certain of them for several seasons, and five in Palestine. In all he published over one hundred books, and in all approximately a thousand books, papers, articles, reports and reviews. It is not the purpose of this preface to give any account of these, as this has already been magnificently achieved by Margaret Drower in her fine and authoritative biography, *Flinders Petrie: A Life in Archaeology* (Gollancz, London; 1985). The present book is a companion volume to that work, with a different aim and emphasis. In it, Margaret Drower has selected passages from the vast archive of Flinders's and Hilda's correspondence from Egypt to their family, friends and supporters at home, in order to give a picture of their life in their archaeological camps, mostly on the fringes of the Egyptian desert. How they managed in the midst of their strenuous digs to find so much time and energy for correspondence is a mystery; Margaret Drower informs me that Flinders Petrie's letters for the season 1881/2 alone (preserved in the archive at the Petrie Museum at the University College) contain approximately 500,000 words! These must for the most part have been written at nights or before sunrise, and one feels perfectly certain that no archaeologists working abroad since their time have ever managed a comparable flow of correspondence. They are, however, remarkable letters. Although they contain many details concerning the excavations and Petrie's administrative problems, which form no part of this book, they also contain many beautiful descriptive passages concerning the scenery of the Nile valley and the deserts, the villages and their people, their own simple and spartan camp life with their faithful servants and workers, and all the dramatic incidents, absurd, comic and pathetic, of their daily life and intercourse. Both were sensitive and informed observers, with strong poetic and artistic traits in their natures, and both were interested, not just in archaeology, but the whole panoply of the natural environment and man's sojourn within it. This sensitivity was, however, wholly unsentimental and unselfconscious, and their correspondence gives, in a way which an account of their doings and achievements cannot, an affecting picture of two very fine and exceptional people and the ever-deepening bond between them.

Margaret Drower is herself a distinguished scholar in the fields of Ancient Near Eastern History and Egyptology. She is the daughter of Sir Edwin Drower, a high official in the British Administration of Iraq after the First

World War, and of Lady Drower, the eminent Mandaean scholar and co-author of the only existing dictionary of the Mandaean language. She was brought up partly in Iraq, where she became fascinated with the Near and Middle East. She studied for her degree in Ancient History and Egyptology at University College London in the early 1930s, and attended some of Petrie's lectures, conceiving a lifelong reverence for him and admiration for his work. She worked with Oliver Myers on the Egypt Exploration Society excavations at Armant, and in 1937 was appointed a lecturer in Ancient History at University College. Over the next 42 years (excepting the period of World War II, when she served in the Near East) she taught the ancient history of Egypt and the Near East from the earliest times down to Alexander the Great to a wide variety of students from many London University colleges and institutes. Her courses formed the focal point for historians, archaeologists and philologists, and the breadth of her knowledge, her critical approach, her endless patience and unquenchable enthusiasm were crucial to the training of many distinguished Egyptologists and Near Eastern scholars. Despite her exacting teaching commitments, she wrote important chapters for the second edition of the Cambridge Ancient History and contributed to several general works on Egypt and Nubia. She also found time, in addition to her private travels, to accompany many tours of her beloved Egypt, of the Mediterranean and the Near East, on which she was a most popular lecturer. She has, moreover, played an invaluable part in the running of the Egypt Exploration Society, serving as a Committee member (1938–72), as Honorary Secretary (1957–78) throughout the campaign to rescue the monuments of Nubia, as Chairman (1978–82), when she guided the Society through its centenary, and subsequently as Vice-President. She is a Fellow of the Society of Antiquaries, and an MBE. On her retirement in 1979, she was honoured with a Fellowship of University College, and became an Honorary Research Fellow in both the History and Egyptology Departments of UCL; since 1997 she has held the title of Honorary Visiting Professor in the Institute of Archaeology, University College.

Even before her retirement, she had started to read and transcribe the Petrie correspondence in preparation for her Biography, with the active support of her friend and former fellow-student, Ann Petrie, Flinders and Hilda's daughter, who found much new material among the family papers. Over the years between 1979–85, she studied the whole archive, and has become the undisputed world expert on the subject of the Petries' lives and work. Moreover, she is also probably now the sole surviving person to have known both the Petries personally. These various qualifications make her the ideal person to have selected and edited this volume of extracts from their correspondence, a task she has performed with fine critical discrimination and personal sensitivity. The result is a vivid picture of the life of these two extraordinary people, bound to each other by a rare unity of spirit, imagination and intellect. Beyond this, it depicts aspects of Egypt different from those portrayed even by most of the famous travel-writers. Here before our eyes are the dreary mud-flats of the Delta, relieved only by the teeming, noisy life of the sparse villages; the wide, empty flats, dunes, hills and wadis of the western desert, littered with camel bones and palaeolithic flints, but, for a few precious days in spring, carpeted with gay, sweet-smelling flowers; the uproar and exciting smells of the local *sûq* on market days; the excitements of discovery and the anxieties of pay-days; the prying eyes and furtive manner of local antique dealers; the braying donkeys and foetid canals; the call of the *muezzin* at dawn and dusk; and everywhere the fatalistic patience of the long-suffering, gay, humorous, passionate but intensely loyal Egyptian peasantry. For those with a love not only of far-off, wild and exotic places but of the comedy and pathos of the human scene, accurately yet imaginatively observed, this book will be an intense and memorable experience.

H. S. Smith

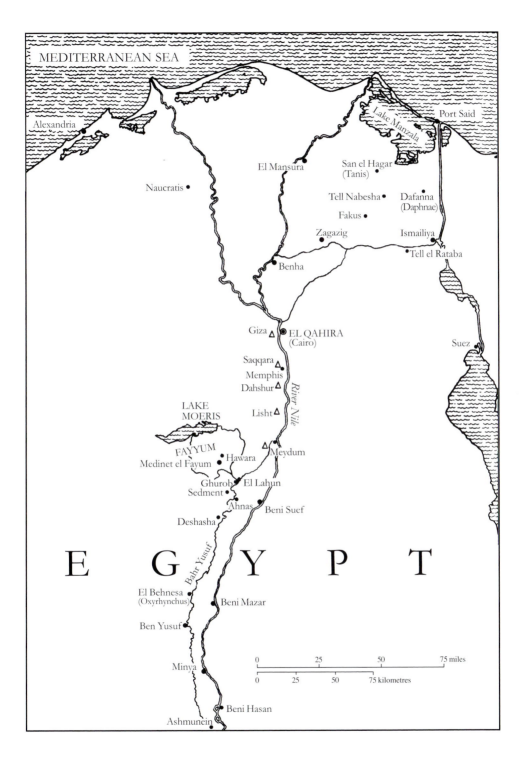

MEDITERRANEAN SEA

Alexandria

Lake Manzala

Port Said

El Mansura

San el Hagar
(Tanis)

Naucratis

Tell Nabesha

Dafanna
(Daphnae)

Fakus

Zagazig

Ismailiya

Benha

Tell el Rataba

Giza

EL QAHIRA
(Cairo)

Suez

Saqqara

Memphis

Dahshur

River Nile

LAKE
MOERIS

Lisht

FAYYUM

Meydum

Medinet el Fayum

Hawara

Ghurob

El Lahun

Sedment

Ahnas

Beni Suef

Deshasha

E   G   Y   P   T

El Behnesa
(Oxyrhynchus)

Beni Mazar

Ben Yusuf

Bahr Yusuf

0		25		50		75 miles
0	25		50		75 kilometres	

Minya

Beni Hasan

Ashmunein

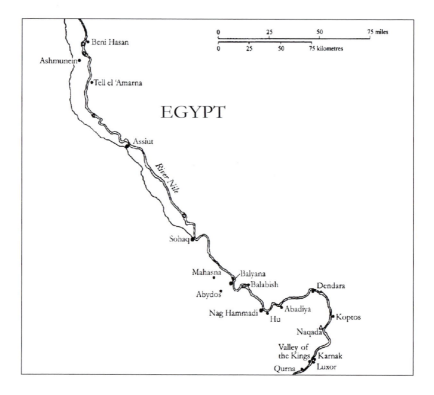

EGYPT

Beni Hasan
Ashmunein
Tell el 'Amarna
Assiut
River Nile
Sohag
Mahasna
Balyana
Balabish
Abydos
Dendara
Nag Hammadi
Abadiya
Hu
Koptos
Naqada
Valley of
the Kings
Karnak
Qurna
Luxor

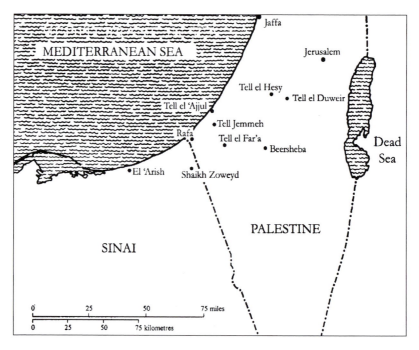

Jaffa
MEDITERRANEAN SEA
Jerusalem
Tell el Hesy
Tell el Duweir
Tell el 'Ajjul
Tell Jemmeh
Rafa
Tell el Far'a
Beersheba
El 'Arish
Shaikh Zoweyd
Dead
Sea
SINAI
PALESTINE

A Digger's Life

In 1884 Flinders Petrie began digging at the ancient city of Tanis (San el Hagar, Biblical Zoan), the most northerly city in the eastern Delta. The article that he wrote whilst working at Tanis provides a good insight into what life was like on one of his digs; how he chose a suitable site, selected his workers, found or constructed a place to live and of the logistics and practicalities of dig life. From reading this extract it is difficult to believe that, although this was not his first experience of Egypt, it was his very first dig.

From The English Illustrated Magazine *1885–6, p. 440ff.*

In digging for history the results are ever varying, no two sites are alike, no two days yield similar objects, no two discoveries are the same. Every day there is a new light on the past, a new clue to the work, unlooked for interests turn up, and in no matter is it truer that it is the unexpected that happens.

... The other day the question was put "But how do you begin on an ancient city? Do you dig into the side or the top?" My reply was "First find your city." Having found your city, find your labourers and then whether you begin at the side or at the top, or anywhere else, is no matter, provided you begin with some definite clue to what there may be, and with some clear purpose in view for each step of the work.

The first business then is to get scent of a lucky site, or as many of such as can be found, either by cross-questioning native dealers in antiquities, or by miscellaneous travelling, map in hand. By a good site I mean one in which there is a fair presumption of finding something that will rewrite whole pages of history for us, or alter all our ancient atlases; a place from which we may perhaps take a fresh departure in our history of art, and learn more of the literature or work of some age than was ever suspected before. Our site may perhaps be a low dusty mound in the midst of luxurious corn- and bean-fields, or steep hills of ruins in the salt wilderness, with marshes all around, or a slight swell in the billows of desert island, with houses and tombs and images half rising out of it.

Wherever we may settle the first business is to get quarters to live in, and to gain the confidence of the people. There are no cheerful notices of

'Apartments to Let', there are no hotel touts to greet you; if you are in a rocky place you may be tolerably certain to get an ancient tomb-chamber or quarry excavated in some cliff-face, and no better lodgings are to be had anywhere for solidity and equable temperature; the minor advantages may be a question of taste, such as the gratis supply of ancient bones or mummy-cloth in the dust and sand of your floor. But if no such accommodation can be had you may perhaps find a room or two in some bearable Europeanised accommodation (Arab huts are unbearable) or else live in a tent, or build a house out of mud and stones and ancient sculpture and Roman bricks and anything else that can be had. Each of these dwellings has its advantages, but the tomb is the best. There will be all sorts of strange tales floating about, as to your object and your personality. You may be put down as the forerunner of a whole regiment of soldiers that are supposed to be coming, or a government surveyor for the land-tax; your money may be said to be all false, someone will swear that you are a Greek if you speak Arabic at all rapidly, and everyone will be on the lookout – the sheikh of the village to the smallest child – to find out what can be got out of you. The sooner therefore you show your hand, and declare your intentions, the better; and if you can get a dozen people to work within a week you have made a good beginning.

Trenches, pits and holes of all shapes and sizes have now to be made, with only one uniform rule – wherever you begin, go to the bottom. A house at Zoan[1] took a man a week to clear it out, and just at the last in a corner of the cellar he found a rough red pot with a stone on top of it. In the pot were necklaces of silver and precious stones, and a ring of gold. Another house at Zoan that had blazed in the pillage of a civil war was cleared, and after dozens of tons of earth had been carried out and but little was found in it, there were some flakes of tinder, and we were upon baskets full of burnt manuscripts, priceless treasures, the religious and literary remains, the accounts and calendar and memoranda of an old Romano-Egyptian lawyer, whose own statue was found a little lower down, in the bottom of the cellar. Of the successive temples of Apollo at Naucratis only trifling chips were left from the plunderings of stone-seekers, but going to the bottom of the ground the old rubbish pit of the temple was found with pieces of hundreds of bowls and vases dedicated to the great god of the Milesians – pieces so old that they were buried out of sight long before the Father of History trod the streets of that city.

The regular way of digging in Egypt – whether it be for the foundation of a Cairene house, for making a canal, or for finding antiquities – is for a man to chop up the ground with a sort of adze, next to scrape the broken-up earth into a plaited palm-leaf bucket with the blade of an adze, and then deliver it to

---

[1] i.e. Tanis.

a small boy to carry away on his head or back. Hence all the excavators are grouped in independent units, each consisting of a man and his boys; there may be only one boy if the earth is left close to where it was dug, or there may be four or five boys or girls to one man, if it is to be carried to any great distance. A great part of the art of excavating consists in grouping these children properly; if anything of intrinsic value is likely to be found, then cross the party, by taking a man of one place and children of another, so that they will not agree to conceal things. If many trifling articles are found, put on a sharp boy who has shown his skill by picking up things before; a really bright fellow will bring in a dozen times as much as a dull one in the course of the day. In all cases the children have to be proportioned to the distances and the class of the work; and this is but one branch of what really requires more attention than anything else – the adjustment and arrangement of the work. Glancing at a group of workers it might seem that labour may be economised by some little distribution or order of the work, but on watching them it will be seen that labour may be economised by some little change in the distribution or order of the work, making a man cut away this patch before that, making a fresh path here, or joining some cuttings there, throwing the waste heap a little to one side or the other, changing the children from hole to hole, or a host of other little points. Often a man will neatly contrive such an order of work as looks very fair... but by which he is really doing about two-thirds of his proper allowance. A favourite plan is to cut a hole so deep that the man cannot lift the basket to the boy's head outside the hole, hence each boy waits till the other returns from emptying his basket, in order to be helped up with his own, and thus the man and the boys all do about half their proper work. The cure is to make them cut steps down into the hole, so that each boy can go down and have his basket helped up by the man. Another dodge is a cutting where half a dozen children are engaged is for them all to wait until their baskets are all filled, and then go up together singing, and meanwhile the men stand idle below because there are no baskets; then the children all come down and carry their baskets down with them. Thus they all do half their work, and they are not best pleased when the singing is stopped, each boy or girl is made to go up the moment the basket is filled, and each is ordered to throw down the basket when empty, so that it may be filled ready for them by the time they have got down to the bottom of the hole again. In short it is necessary to try to imagine some more efficient arrangement of labour before ever being satisfied with what you see going on before your eyes; and the density of the mechanical sense in the Arab mind is such that they will blindly continue any arrangement once begun, though it may afterwards be wasting half of their work to continue it; to adapt their plans to the circumstances is not dreamt of in their philosophy.

Having settled a good site, and arranged everything in working order, the usual course of a day is much as follows. In the winter we begin an hour after sunrise, to somewhat avoid the thick fogs and raw reeking-wet air; but in the summer at sunrise, with a longer halt at midday. Turning off my blankets about 5 a.m. and slipping into as much clothing as the country requires, I go out with my own overseers or *reises*; they never belong to the place we work in, but are brought with me from a distance, so that their feelings may go more with me than with the people. Out we march, and pick up many of our ragged regiment along the roadside waiting for us, others are ready in their holes, and the rule is that everyone must be in and ready to begin when I come on the ground. Then name-taking begins, and going round with a wage-book in hand, every worker has the day of the month entered against his name. Generally some of the hundred or hundred and fifty are absent, and the question goes round, "Where is Ali Basha," or Fatmeh um Ibrahim, or Mohammed Dakrori, as the case may be. "Not here today, but here is his brother, only just for one day." Now his brother may be anybody, a man's brethren are as universal as the Mohammedan address "oh, my brother," which is applicable to any of the faithful. If the proper man is an old hand and a good one, his brother is taken, if not objectionable; but if I want to get rid of him, no brother of his will do. I turn to the tail which always follows me – new hands waiting to be taken on. There stand, anxiously watching me, some dozen or two of men, and a host of children, down to little mites who are almost lost beneath the basket they bear. I look at each, each looks at me. Then, pitching on the best of them by his face, I call him out, and he springs down into the work, delighted to get on the books. It is worse than useless to take anyone on recommendation, or in fact to listen at all to any person's opinion of anyone else... the faces of these people are far the best guide; out of hundreds of workers I never had to dismiss but one that I liked when picking him out; and that one was an excellent fellow, barring an assault on a most irritating small boy, for which he had to go.

Having then gone the rounds, directed them all, booked all the names, and started such fresh work as may be needed, after three or four hours I turn back to the house. Then bath and breakfast set me up for the day. A petroleum stove is invaluable... with an oil stove, and a store of biscuits and tinned food, one is independent of the country, and cooking is reduced to manageable proportions; some fresh vegetables, tomatoes, cucumbers, etc. and fruit are all that need to be marketed for, and eggs are to be had from almost any of the villagers. While at breakfast often a maiden or two from the huts below my house would come up with a batch of eggs in a fold of her dress, and stand and chatter and laugh at the door; then perhaps one would put her head in and turn and whisper to another in wonder at the strange

ways and properties of the *khawaga*, or foreigner, which were always a source
of amusement. Sometimes they indulged in two visits a day, coming up to ask
if I wanted any eggs first, and then coming to bring them; and the smallest
joke was cheerfully received. If one of my *reises* came by they would scuttle
off at once, for they are accustomed to but scant courtesy from their own
people. This however was on the west of the Delta, at Naukratis, near the
modern Teh el Barud; the women on that side of the country have far less of
the Mohammedan customs, and are never veiled unless they go to the large
towns. They are thus unlike the Cairenes, or the people of the eastern side of
the Delta, where even the little girls of ten years old are put into face veils.
Most wondrously cumbersome their wealth is as thus displayed; one girl who
brought up the water to my house at Zoan (about forty miles SW of Port
Said), wore three gold coins, nearly thirty large silver coins, and a quantity of
chains, beads, etc., all across her face, stitched on to the black veil which
reached up to her eyes. The unveiled ladies of the west are quite as much
patterns of propriety as their veiled sisters on the east, I believe, but they are
happily free from the most oppressive custom. Perhaps we should look to
some influence from the days of Greek colonisation there to account for the
difference.

Eggs bought, and breakfast done, I go out again to look over all my men,
or to work with them in any part where special attention is wanted; and then
at noon, or earlier, going to some point from which they can all hear, I sound
a blast on a large whistle; from all sides goes up a shout, baskets are tossed
up, and away scamper the children to their dinners; some go home, others
form groups with the men, and the lettuce and onions and thin dried Arab
bread is brought out, and many an invitation I have to join them as I go
about. Generally there is some work to do in putting away antiquities in the
house, so I go back to attend to that. The noon rest is not very fixed in its
beginning, but they are always allowed a definite amount; an hour in winter
and three hours in the long hot summer days, when they begin at sunrise and
finish at sunset. The whistle sounds again, and everyone is expected to fall in
directly and go on with the work. Once at Zoan they became more and more
lazy and dilatory, and tried to put off their return as long as they could; this
was cured entirely and for ever by going down to them one day when they did
not come up at the whistle, and saying that as they had not come it showed
they did not want work, and so there would be none that afternoon, except
for a few who were already up. I never had a man late again.

The afternoon is spent in watching the men in different parts, and often
working with them if necessary. To keep up a proper activity in the work it is
needful to hold the dread of dismissal before them continually. If a man is
caught standing still he is noted, and after any further laziness is informed

some morning that his services are no longer required. But if he is caught
sitting down it is all up with him; he knows he is found out, and works extra
hard all the rest of the day, but next morning he is paid off. Naturally they try
to show their best side when I am about, and hence some care is required to
get at the truth. By examining the ground around the work, lines of approach
can generally be found, by which it is possible to come near the men under
cover; and when coming up, a quiet look without showing more than the top
of your head is advisable. They thus learn that the chances are that you will
see them before they see you, and a sudden dismissal of any lazy man, when
they imagine they have not been watched has a most healthy effect. They
show some ingenuity in keeping up appearances; sometimes the children are
set to carry empty baskets to and from while the men do nothing; but even
from a distance this may be detected by there not being any little cloud of
dust which always rises when emptying a basket; a telescope soon clears up
this device, and they suddenly all find themselves dismissed on the spot.

Besides the detective business over one's own men, there were sometimes
sharp steeplechases after Arab dealers. They know that their coming to the
work is morally indefensible, and they have an indefinite dread of being
identified or caught. As however by law nothing whatever could be done to
them, the object is not to catch them, but only to act on their feelings so as to
make them flee before you. The way is to walk straight at any suspicious
character, openly and ostentatiously; he moves off; you follow; he quickens;
you quicken; he doubles; you cross to cut him off; then he fairly bolts; and
off you go, with perhaps a furlong between, across the fields, jumping canals,
doubling, hiding behind bushes, and so forth; if he once gains a village it is
useless to look for him in the houses, so the way is to keep him out in the
open for as much time as you can spare for the game; two to four miles is a
fair run. This exercise is valuable both morally and physically; the rascals are
always laughed at by my diggers for running away. ...

Far more serious matters however, have to be attended to personally; if a
find is expected at any point the work must be continually watched, and if
there is a dunce at the hole he is shifted away, and a picked man put on, with
special directions. If papyri are possibly to be found the anxiety is great, and
the first little flake of tinder is the sign for stopping the men at once and
taking up the work myself. Tinder, I say, because there is no chance in Lower
Egypt of buried papyri being preserved from rotting unless they have the
good luck to have been carbonised in a conflagration. Then going down into
the hole the earth must all be scraped away tenderly with a pocket knife,
checking at once if there is the horrible silky rustle of scraping a papyrus; at
last the earth is all picked away grain by grain, and there lies a mass of rolls of
tinder, here and there burnt to white ash and the difficulty is to undermine

them so as to get them out without their dropping to pieces, for the smallest amount of earth lying on them when they are lifted will break them by its weight. Yet such may be their importance that no labour is too much to give in order to save whatever remains of them. Perhaps a whole lump all matted together can be removed *en bloc*, and carried up to my house for separation of the individual documents; then each wrapped in soft paper, and packed in small tin boxes, they will make the journey to England safely enough. After that the still more tender work begins of peeling leaf from leaf of the crushed rolls, which are generally cracked into separate slips; these slips mounted between sheets of glass then await the attention of some one who can *see* them – for all the writing is merely dull black ink, on no less dull black tinder – and someone who can *read* them. ...

Another sort of work that must be attended to is making plans and surveys; a map is the backbone of a research in any place, and no reasonable labour on it is wasted. It is well to have a rough plan as soon as possible, to guide the work, and to mark down on it any particular sites. But all this takes time, and it is almost impossible to do any continuous work of this kind while the men are on one's hands. Copying long inscriptions is also a tedious affair; but a cheerful tediousness, considering the value of the results. Besides this it is always requisite to keep an eye forward, and to have some piece of work ready planned, to be taken up whenever a man is at liberty. It needs some imagination to invent fresh work continually, which shall have some fair reason for its performance, and some useful connection with what is going on already. All the facts yet known have to be remembered; as far as possible, a sort of scheme of the site must be kept floating in the mind, and crystallising day by day as fresh facts turn up; everything that is likely to be found, from analogy with other places, or historical information, should be imagined as fitting in with the fixed data already found; and as many possible combinations have to be considered as in a four-move chess problem, which *may* have no solution.

When sunset comes near, it is time to go round, to all the workings where things are likely to have been found, and take in the spoils. One man hands up, perhaps, a perfect red jar, and some little scraps of figures, and I book in, say, threepence to Sidahmed Abdun; for owing to the scarcity of small change, and the quantity I should need, all the small payments are worked on paper, and settled when they have accumulated. Then at another hole there will be a small bronze figure and a few nails, and fivepence goes down to Mohammed Dafani. Then a boy brings a handful of scraps: one by one I look them over, and perhaps only a couple are worth having, so Mohammed Hassan Dahabiyeh gets a halfpenny to his name. So the selection goes on until sunset. Then the whistle sounds again, and up spring more than a hundred workers from the ground, and cover the plain where a minute before scarcely a sign of life was to be seen. The work over, then comes the saturnalia of the day: a shouting, merry crew of men, and girls, and boys all speed homeward as fast as they can. I lead off at a brisk rate, and away we all go together; a man begins to race me in walking, and we spin along at well over five miles an hour until he makes a spring to keep up, and then he is laughed down for running.

On we sweep to the crazy old bridge, everyone tried to seize the inside of the curve round the canal, to be first on the planks; and some one way, some another, they file off in the orange twilight to their huts. Many, however, come on to my house; the girls bearing the baskets on their heads full of pottery and small antiquities, and many a child with some scrap, for which he or she hopes to realise the value of a chop of sugar-cane. I stand in my doorway and take in one thing after another until all the clear space on my floor is littered over with rows and heaps of fragments. When the last boy is settled with, they go off chattering, and I am left to pottery, dinner, and my own reflections. There is, however, a quantity of evening work to do, beside my cooking. The finds have to be sorted over, selected and marked, and the rubbish cleared out; plans have to be plotted; and a journal to be written up. Then at last it is well if I get under the blankets eight hours before I must turn out again; for eight hours is none too much, after sixteen hours nearly all on foot. Such is a digger's daily life.

But Arabs will not work without money, any more than any other men; and I shirk daily payments – the paytime is Saturday afternoon. This is a great saving of time; one of the best-known explorers occupies more than an hour every evening of his work in paying his men, but by booking names daily, which is done during the morning inspections, and in itself does not take a quarter of the time of paying, the accounts can be settled weekly. On Saturday afternoon then, while the men are at work in their holes, they are paid off; the great advantages of paying while they are at work being that no time is wasted by ninety-nine men waiting while the hundredth is paid.

At one hole I owe a man fifteen piastres (three shillings) for five day's wages, and one-and-a-half piastres for the things he has found; now it is impossible to get enough piastres in this country to pay everybody; if you did you would be in a ceaseless strife over the false and the worn coins; so sixteen-and-a-half piastres I have to pay with one and a half parisis (worth nine-and-a-half piastres each), half a franc (two piastres), and one-and-three-quarter-piastres in copper, which is worth one-seventh of the silver. Almost anything will pass, and the bulk of the currency is made up of Spanish dollars, Maria Theresa dollars, francs, lire, leis, drachmas, shillings, florins, parises (struck by the Egyptian government and repudiated), and finally the silver piastres (struck by the Egyptian government and decried by them), Turkish gold and piastres, copper piastres (also struck by the Egyptian government and repudiated), and finally the silver piastres, which are the government money of account, but which are so often forged and so largely worn that they are the most troublesome of all to do business with. Each of the above variety of coinage has two or more rates of exchange, the town rate and the country rate, and particular coins are in favour in particular places. Hence it is not so easy to pay your way in Egypt, even if you have the sinews of excavating in your money bag.

Besides all the digging work there are the happy days of prospecting when you cast aside dull care, load up your donkey, and tramp off across the countryside day after day. This is a most delightful life, in a perfect climate where there is no rain to be feared, and no cold winds to be dreaded, for such is Egypt in the spring; one donkey easily carries a small tent, about seven feet by eight, a roll of blankets, a petroleum stove, a canvas saddle-bag with a store of provisions in it, and often a small boy on top of all to drive the beast, looking at a little distance exactly as if he and the donkey were all trussed up together, ready for roasting, with the two tent poles sticking out crosswise from the mass. Then with a trusty Arab, whom you know, you can tramp over the hard mud roads, along the canals with the fragrant *sont* trees[1] overhanging the path, through the bean and clover fields and over the dusty plains. Mound after mound is seen on the dead-flat horizon, and visited. Sometimes nothing promising may appear, at other times some strange and unexpected find, and continually you see heaps of ruins of the town of former days, which seem only to need you to put the spade in to turn up almost anything you can dream of. No wonder that a people living in such a country have their heads full of treasure and jinns,[2] a country where continually peasants find what is equivalent to several years' wages, and where you often hear of some man having been enriched by finding a donkey-load of gold.

One amusing, but fatiguing way of travelling is to put up for the night at the village sheikh's. If you have the luck to light on a rich man you will probably have to sit up on the dais in the gateway, and hear some cases finished off in the dusk, for your host is magistrate of his village. At one end squats the clerk, reading over by a flickering lantern light the report of all the cases which he has drawn up, the sheikh putting in a correction now and then, which sometimes leads to a long discussion. ... At last, after almost going to sleep hearing the interminable drone of the old clerk and the buzz of

---

[1] *acacia nilotica.*
[2] A powerful being in Muslim mythology.

the busy-bodies, there is a welcome break up and some prospect of dinner, for it would be a mortal offence to set about cooking your own provisions if you go to a big man's house for shelter, and though you may have been on foot since sunrise, you must sit up in hunger and patience for a couple of hours of darkness before any food can be had. You may be served with a table all to yourself, in French fashion – according to their ideas – if in an over-civilised place, or you may be asked to sit at the round table where sits the sheikh or bey himself, his sons, his clerks and bailiffs, yourself, and your donkey boy, all around, each tearing off a leg or a wing of a fowl, and grabbing handfuls of rice from the great dish to stuff in his mouth. Perhaps the backgammon board will come out afterwards, and a few games fill another hour before you turn in for the night. All this is wearisome after a long days work, and the strain of having to talk and understand Arabic for hours, and make up conversation that shall be both interesting and intelligible, is not restful. On the whole it is better to stick to your own tent and stove, and your independence; pitch where you like, feed when you like and have a long night's rest after your fifteen or twenty miles' walk. Towards sunset you pick out a clean piece of ground near some village or town, and then with your man in a few minutes the tent is up, and everything inside; get a pan of water, light the stove, and go for a stroll while it is boiling up; if stopping near a Bedawi settlement you will be asked to dinner, and if you decline probably a big tray of fowls and rice and bread will be brought down in the dark, with perhaps some son of the sheikh come to dine with you. A few tins of jam make an excellent return for this. I have known a young Arab quietly save up the spoonful of raspberry jam to which I helped him; when asked why, he said it was for the harem. So if you give a supply it is pretty certain to go through the tenthold, and thus put your name in good favour all round. One of the best forms of *bakhshish*[1] in return for considerable help or services from well-to-do people is silver plate, and it is well to have some silver spoons (forks are useless to people who use their fingers) and a silver cup or two, if you expect to be thrown much on the assistance of sheikhs. The rule of the country is that when money cannot be given, some present of about equal or rather greater value is to be made, and your character will not stand very well if you behave unreasonably in this respect. But for small matters a most kindly spirit may be found among the country people. I have known a man insist on my riding his donkey across two miles of marsh, while he plowtered through on foot, and at the end stoutly refused to take anything, even for his children, baring his wrist and showing the cross as his reason for dealing thus with a fellow Christian. He was a Copt. ...

---

[1] Tip or gratuity.

The country people or fellahin are a cheerful and kind-hearted race in general, compounded in varying proportions from a Coptic and Bedawi ancestry, according to whether the Egyptians in each place were driven out or forced into Mohammedanism at the conquest by 'Amr in the seventh century. In some parts of Upper Egypt the people are nearly pure Egyptian, many large villages of Copts also remaining among them, while in the Delta, Copts are scarce, and the people have probably as much Arab as Coptic blood in them. The one way to the fellah's respect is absolute firmness, and the one way to his goodwill is a good joke; but bright as he may be so long as he is under, he is intolerable if he gets the upper hand. An Arab or a Turk can bear being in authority, but there is no worse tyrant over his fellow countrymen, and no more avaricious leech than a fellah sheikh.

Egypt is not at a standstill at present; it is moving faster, for better or worse, than it ever moved before. And this is true of its antiquities as well as of other things; the ancient cities are being in the present day dug away and their earth spread on the ground as fertiliser and this is going on at such a rate that some have almost entirely disappeared already, and fields of corn have taken their place, others are diminished to half the size they were a generation or two back, and are still diminishing every day. And the time does not seem very far distant when scarcely a site of a city will be able to be identified. Certainly Egypt will have exhausted its antiquity fields before England exhausts its coalfields. And up the Nile tombs are opened every year, and fewer left to be discovered. In one sense we are only just beginning to explore Egypt, and the treasure seems to us inexhaustible, but that is only because of the puny scale of our attack from the scientific side; in another, and terribly true sense Egypt is exhausting itself, the natives are ceaselessly digging, and unless we look to it pretty quickly the history of the country will have perished before our eyes, by the destructive activity of its inhabitants. Never before has that land of monuments been so fiercely worked upon, daily and hourly the spoils of ages past are ransacked, and if of marketable value are carried off; but whether preserved or not is a small matter compared with the entire loss of their connection and history which always results in this way. If we are not to incur the curse of posterity for our Vandalism and inertness, we must be up and doing in the right way.

1880–1884
From Surveyor to Excavator

Flinders Petrie's first visit to Egypt began late in 1880, when he was twenty-seven years old. His aim was to obtain accurate measurements of the pyramids of Giza, currently the subject of considerable interest aroused by a book written by the Astronomer Royal for Scotland, Charles Piazzi Smyth. In 1865 Smyth had gone to Egypt to measure the Great Pyramid. Based on a hypothetical unit of measurement which he named the pyramid inch, he had propounded the theory that the pyramid of Cheops had been built under divine inspiration, and foretold world-shaking events in the past and future history of the world. Petrie would have liked to believe this but felt that further corroboration was necessary. An experienced surveyor, he decided to test the accuracy of Smyth's survey and so test the credibility of the British Israelites who depended on Smyth's calculations. His letters from Giza during two winters were addressed to his parents and one or two close friends; they were posted once a week in the central Post Office in Cairo, where he collected his mail from home. His father, who had intended to follow him, never came.

20 December 1880

After café, to the station, saw all my boxes lying there safely, then posted journal, and then to Consulate. Saw Mr Raph Borg (an Italian I presume) who was Secy. and is now Vice Consul. Told him what I wanted and he said that I had better put it in writing, so I went back to my room (within ¼ mile) and wrote off a formal application for a letter ordering the Sheikh of the Pyramid dostrice to grant me all due protection, either from the Prefect of Police whom Borg suggested or other authorities. Borg was very polite and was just going to the Prefect, Dr James Grant, an English doctor practising in Cairo who was to prove a valuable friend, so there was no delay. Then I went off to the Citadel, as told by Mr Borg, to see Genl. Stone: an Arab officer on guard spoke only Arabic, and he tucked up the name of the Kasr en Nil barrack in such a long and rapid sentence that I could not catch it; I pulled out the map and he showed much attention to my wants, but remarkably little intelligence, he could not even read the French names. So I had to name them but at last hit the Kasr en Nil, which is at the extreme end of the city. By this time it was too late to get there in time before the noonday closing, so pushing through a crowd of donkey boys who had collected expecting a job, I stretched off at 5 miles an hour, leaving them behind; a plan which always amuses the bystanders, who laugh at their disappointment. I tried some sugar cane which is just now in season and is laid out in heaps all along the roadside by street sellers, but I found it sickening and could get through but little. Then I strolled through the Sukkariyeh and other bazaars to the Muski, and after a stroll up and down it, turned into the restaurant for dinner. Then down to my room and was just on the point of going out to Genl. Stone, when my hostess knocked at the door and there stood Ali Gabri with a card from Dr Grant, saying that if I would come with him to the Dr's we would settle matters. So I started off and chatted to Ali on the way; he speaks very fair English and though no beauty he has a very pleasant and trustworthy face, looking calm, simple, decided and straightforward, a man whom I would trust without a recommendation and considering the excellent character given him by C. P. S., Weyman Dixon, Mr Gill and Dr Grant, I feel every confidence in him.

At Dr Grant's I waited some time as they have various domestic troubles on hand: an old housekeeper who managed all for 5 years just left and also a table servant, and their kitchen stove was under repairs. I had a talk to Mrs G. who was most kind and pleasant and gave me sundry hints on diet and health here; bye and bye the Dr had settled about their stove, and came in to settle matters. I had written out all that I thought necessary to settle, and Dr G. took my paper and talked over each point with Ali Gabri in Arabic, Ali saying that regular Bakhsheesh to the Shekh was quite unnecessary, only giving when any special service was required. Having settled it all, and engaged Ali at £1 per week from that time forward, (he saying that he did it for the love of Mr Smyth and Mr Gill and not for the sake of money) we then left. They much wanted me to stay to tea, but I wanted to *get on*; Mrs G. also invited me to come over for Christmas Day to them and stay there over Sunday but I said I could not think of intruding on their party then, she very kindly pressed it, and also asked me to drop in whenever I came over to church on Sundays, saying that Mr and Mrs Gill always did so. They said that Dr G. would consider me under his charge in all ways, both in affairs and in health. Altogether I could not have been more kindly and almost affectionately received by them if I had had the strongest claims upon them, instead of being a total stranger, and I thanked them heartily for it all.

Then I went with Ali to the station, he engaged two carts on the way and we then and there loaded them under my direction, so as to have the instrument boxes arranged secure from falls. As an extra charge would have been made for leaving them till tomorrow, I by Ali's suggestion had them taken out to the house of the owner of the carts; and Ali sleeps there tonight.

I went round with him to see the place. I had no hesitation in settling thus off-hand, without *making* delays (of which there are plenty in this life, ready and inevitable) as Dr Grant, who knows all the people there and the native character, thought it quite suitable to go at once. Then I went back to my hotel and ordered coffee and eggs to be ready when Ali should come in, as he did in a short time. I looked over his testimonials, which he was anxious I should see. They speak of him in even higher terms than I had heard before; C. P. S., Dixon, Watson and Gill and another traveller who took him up the Nile, all agree in his great intelligence, scrupulous honesty and protection of his travellers from any imposition and his gentlemanlyness and companionability. From my talk with him this evening over coffee, I can only say that his manners are those of a perfect nature's gentleman, and one feels that the same delicacy and politeness is due to him that one would use to any gentleman.

I gave him 5 fr. as a starting baksh(ish); we settled that I should join him about 6 tomorrow, and see the things off, then overtake them by donkey and get an hour or so to look over the tombs before they get there. He suggests my taking Wayman Dixon's tomb, of which he has the key and which is all ready and putting the boxes in one adjoining as W. D.'s is too small. I made the old Frenchwoman have a hearty laugh with me over my patchwork of French and Arabic; knowing as much or more of the latter than of the former for everyday life, they come out in layers of a few words each, it is intelligible at all events. Literary and scientific and even newspaper French is worth nothing for details of living, so I am very glad to supplement it.

21 December 1880

Flinders woke early, had breakfast and paid his landlady's bill; Ali arrived with the carts, which they loaded and sent off; two donkeys were hired,

... and we jallacked off. I soon found that the principle was to put plenty of weight on the stirrups, get a good grip with the thighs, with the toes turned out, and sit upright; thus I got on pretty well, but when the beast trotted hard, my inside was churned most unmercifully, a gallop was really easier. Over 10 miles of this was pretty well for my first experience of donkey back. I chatted to Ali a good part of the way. We reached the pyramid about 10; a lovely morning with delicate mare's tail sky, and the pyramids, one side warm with sunshine, the other grey blue with slight haze. I then looked over all the tombs available, the Arab village has been moved since C. P. Smythe was here, and his tomb is no longer to be had. Weyman Dixon's is however all ready to go into, Ali having the key, and door and two windows perfect. So I decided to take that, at least for the first, but it is small, and there is a beauty just below it, two large ones side by side with a hole in the wall, thus only two openings to secure, and a huge room perhaps 30ft long. W. D.'s is really three, side by side with the walls broken away; about 14, 18 and 10ft long and 6–8ft wide each. The fine pair below would want a huge quantity of sand, bones, mummy wrappers etc. cleared out, as I should think there is an average of 3ft deep in it, perhaps 4; so I rather think I shall stick to W. D.'s at least as long as I am alone here. I went for a little run over this (E) side of the pyramid ground, many pesterers old and young being in chase of me; but by doing just what they did not expect, and making sharp bolts over ground not usually crossed, I gave them a long run before one of them caught me up, and then I was polite but quite indifferent to all the objects he wanted me to see, and stuck to the trial passages and other things which were quite out of the usual line.

Then back to the W. D. tomb, which had been cleared out and freshly sanded; the carts now in sight, and I sat and had a talk with Ali. By about 12½ the boxes began to be unloaded, Ali attending below, and I placing them as they came up; all but one (including the big box of the square), were carried by a single man each with a cord round the forehead, up about 100ft. rise of steep, sandy slope, some lighter ones the children did; the very long box was carried by four men together. Ali settled all the payments to the natives, giving nothing to the helpers belonging here, as reckoning to pay them in along with any other jobs they may do. He is most careful about money and refers everything over a few pence to me, though I gave him *carte blanche* to do as he reckoned proper. He only paid 5 fr. each for the carts (11 miles) and 1 fr. to each of the two men and did the two donkeys for 5½ fr. I then unpacked stove and food first which entailed doing sundry other things so that by 2 I was ready for feeding (chocolate, herrings and aerated)! having only had light café at 7½. I went on all the afternoon straightening, Ali going off to his house and mosque for a couple of hours. I then made my bedstead out of 1 inch board and rigged up the hammock cloth stretched over the two sides thus as I did not like the swinging motion; the legs raise the top 2ft from the ground. It seems very comfortable and strong enough. Then after supper on ship biscuit eggs and chocolate, during which Ali's son and negro servant came in and I gave them a taste of the biscuit, the hardness of which amused them (all with the view of shewing them that I had not luxuries and expensive things) Ali bid me good night leaving his negro to sleep inside the tomb door as a night guard, and I now hear the fellow fast asleep breathing most curiously hard and quick (32 per minute) about double my rate. I then rigged together the two owl red curtains with pins, and stretched a string to hang them from, the negro most attentively helping so as to divide off my bed tomb and by the time all was finished it was about 9½. Then I hitched up my bed sideways (and a very nice easy chair it makes) one side to the shoulders and the other under the knees) and wrote up this.

I settled with Ali all that he had paid, and agreed to do so every night; there is just as much ventilation as I wish for around the loose fit of my window frame, of course there is no glass. I saw Smyne[1] who shewed me his testimonials, but he is of no authority here, and only hovers about to deal in antiquities, both genuine and largely otherwise. Now at nearly 11 I really must give some rest to my eyelids, which are heavy.

22 December 1880

Lay awake for some time and at 6½ was woke up by Ali's slave calling on the 'khawaga' to get up (sounded 'khhaghha') and on looking out from my curtain his negro face gave a broadly smiling salute; he belongs to the tribes who slash their faces, and has three orthodox furrows in each cheek. I instructed him to bring me some water for the bath, which he presently did. I then after dressing, the water boiling up meanwhile, had breakfast; though not hungry here, still I get through a quantity when I begin, and the symptoms of a full meal never come. I then unpacked a little more, and began overhauling my defences; the shutters were the most shaky, so all the morning I was remaking them, with doubling the wood and putting a bar etc. to fasten them securely, also strengthening the boards beneath the shutters. This lasted until after dinner and when done I set about shelving, and put up 5 shelves of 5ft 10ins. each, with room for a sixth; then I put all the tools and things I had loose about in order, and had supper, after which I put my bed frame together again (in about 5 minutes) having taken it to pieces and put it outside for the sake of moving things; then after moving various boxes and altering arrangements I went to be, where I now write this lying on my back, being too tired and stiff to sit up. The negro and a nephew ? of Ali's sleep together in the next tomb, with only a thin rock between, so I can knock them up if necessary. This is the permanent arrangement.

After only a short time working in Giza Petrie writes of his horror at the destruction and general disregard of Egyptian heritage by local Arabs and those in authority.

10 January 1881

The savage indifference of the Arabs, who have even stripped the alabaster off the granite temple since Mariette[2] uncovered it and who are not at all watched here, is only superseded by a most barbaric sort of regard for the monuments by those in power. Nothing seems to be done with any uniform and regular plan, work is begun and left unfinished; no regard is paid to future requirements of exploration and no civilized or labour saving re-

---

[1] Ismain (Ismail).
[2] Auguste Mariette Pascha, Director of the Egyptian Department of Antiquities.

appliances are used, nothing but what the natives have; all the sand being carried in small baskets on the heads of children. The very rough and rudely cut rock tomb interiors which had puzzled me, were it seems all lined with fine carved stone, which has all been ripped out for building and for lime burning, even in the last few years and by the time the mischief is done, then an order comes from the police (from Mariette) that no one is to touch the place in question and so it is perhaps left a mass of chips and fragments. It is sickening to see the rate at which everything is being destroyed and the little regard paid to preservation; if allotments all over the hill were made to the different European Govmt. museums, with free leave to clear and take all they liked and power to preserve it here, something more satisfactory might be done. Anything would be better than leaving things to be destroyed wholesale; better spoil half in preserving the other half than leave the whole to be smashed.

13 January 1881

Off with Ali and the two loft ladders to the entrance, put the ladders together and then thoroughly examined and measured all the details of the two pairs of sloping stones over the entrance. ... Several parties of travellers came; some Egyptian, two of whom brought a wife each and most amusing it was to see the little creatures, sprawling and slipping about and laughing at their tumbles, evidently enjoying their outing immensely; they were gallantly helped by their husbands, a youth bearing a bright red handkerchief bundle and a bunch of big bright green lettuces swung together over his back making his way into the passage after them. The youth and the luncheon accompaniments however backed out again very soon, one of the gentlemen turned back at Al Maamoun's hole, but the plucky little Fatimahs were bunched and hauled all through the passages and came out as lively as possible, after their lords had returned to fresh air puffing and wiping. I saw all the parties very plainly from my ladder just 20ft or so over the entrance.

Two old Greek priests, a young and old Greek and a Frenchman made another party. To see the priests (much like Mr Benest) with enormous flowing beards and wide hats and long black gowns, careering along the plain on frisky donkeys was good; the young Greek pompously bestrode a camel, rather absurd for such a little journey.

14 January 1881

Awoke at 12½ a.m. by someone calling me, and found Dr Grant had driven over for a night of measurement etc. I tumbled up as quickly as I could and found the Dr outside. So he called up Mohammed and the boy, M went off for Ali. I got out the ladders for the G. Gallery and after putting things together, we went off, Ali and M. joining us soon. We got the 10ft ladders in easily, and the sides of the 140 inch ladder, which I screwed together inside while Dr G. looked at the peculiarities of the well mouth and made notes. Then he said we had better take the worst first, and go down the well, to shew me the peculiarities of the grotto and to see if the way into the entrance passage was blocked. So we let the rope ladders down, and though the holes in the sides are quite sufficient and the best for the feet, yet the ladder was found very good to hold by, especially in bad places. In the grotto which is a hollow in the loose conglomerate which there occurs, and which through the well has been walled around, we stopped and Dr G. shewed me the place he supposes might lead to a passage; I set to work and scraped up the sand and stones as far as I could, but when I had once got it all as steep as the angle of rest in all available space, nothing more could be done; I excavated a great deal with my feet, being unable to reach it otherwise; then I wriggled my feet in as far as I could, about 2½ft and felt it all round with them; it was a hollow apparently leading down westwards and all full of pebbles and sand. Ali tells me this afternoon that it is a loop line into the subterranean, and that Howard Vyse[1] cleared it, this I doubt. The Dr had meanwhile gone farther down and found the passage blocked at 1170 inches below the grotto; this by C. P. S. plan is close to bottom, but H. Vyse's measures would make it about 40ft short, I cannot reconcile these. I did not know the Dr had gone down, so I went on with my hole as far as I could and then saw that Ali, who had come down to the grotto, was just winding in string from the Dr below; I set off down. All this was done in thick dust, so that a double face veil was soon white over the mouth and Ali's moustache was as if floured. The lower passage was if anything worse and I could not *see* the candle even till within 50ft or so. When I got down I was horrified to find the Dr in a state of collapse, moaning and breathing hard and quick, hardly able to speak. I instantly set off up again, after he had called my attention to one or two points and which he would not leave unnoticed; he followed me very slowly and I was fearfully anxious to think what I could do with a stout man fainting at the foot of 170ft of passage, or rather pipe, partly vertical, all steep, and impossible to pass from its narrowness, all full of dust haze and mostly hopeless for a person to move in except by their own exertion. About half way up to the grotto, he wished for liquid, so I bolted up and got his bag from Ali, and took it to him; he had an orange, and then got up to the bit of vertical shaft below the grotto; here he waited a long time, clinging to the ladder with his head over his arms; at last we encouraged him and hauled him partly up into the grotto; here stretched out he very slowly got through a

---

[1] Who investigated at Giza in 1835.

sandwich and some tea that he had and after a long rest, during which his questions shewed how far his external senses were upset, he at last mustered strength for the mainly vertical pull up into the Grand Gallery. I followed close behind him pushing and lifting whenever I could, but the prospect of about 15 stone, half fainting, scrambling just over your head, in a place where the holding is poor at best, made me quake to think of his possibly slipping. Once up in the Grand Gallery he stretched out on coat and bag and had a long rest. Of course all other work was out of the question for him and for me too as I had a headache with the dust, close air and awful worry. So I tried to persuade him to be carried out at once, but he preferred to wait. I then stowed away the ladders in the Queen's Chamber to avoid both the trouble of getting them out (and the 14 must be all unscrewed) and also the risk of damage to the steel straps in dragging about. So I thought best to leave them in the least frequented place. Then I bolted off to the tomb to get some hot stuff ready; boiled up some soup, and then put some water on to heat, put out biscuits etc. and blankets for a seat and then back to pyramid carrying a cup half full of hot soup. I was thankful to find the Dr walking out by the kiosk where his carriage was waiting so I gave him the soup and then persuaded him to come down to the tomb and refresh. After more soup and coffee and a wash (which he was not up to even when he first came in) he slowly walked back to the carriage. I saw him settled in all safe and his own coachman and servant on the box and bid him goodbye just as the dawn was coming up. I then put things a little straight at him and went to bed about 6½. I got five hours sleep. ...

16 January 1881

... After a quiet read and a light dinner, I went off for a walk in the desert; going about 2½ miles hence over the low rolling hills of sand and stone, due west, in which direction my nearest neighbours are 350 miles off in the oasis of Ammon. Ali reports that about 5 miles off in that direction there is a hill full of tombs, which he pointed out to me the other day. A few footprints in the sand here and there are all the traces of life to be seen, not even a jackal shewed himself and the plants are few and far between, perhaps a tuft of something at every furlong or so, with here and there a clump of half a dozen wiry or succulent herbs. The wind was blowing from S.W. across the pure uninhabited desert for 300 and 400 miles, beyond which no one knows anything about it and 'entirely unexplored regions' are entered.

18 January 1881

Two travellers who came in, in a breathless state, all streaming from the heat and exertion, were astonished on my saying that I staid there 6 hours a day;

they said they should be dead in an hour. They are as a whole rather amusing, not enough to be troublesome and all too hot and uncomfortable to wish to stay for talk or mischief. Ali tells of one active man who came over two or three years ago and went up the 1st, 2nd and 3rd pyramids, all without help; pelting Ali when he went too high on the 2nd, which is difficult in *any* way.

22 January 1881

After putting up last journals ready for post, went with Ali to [pyramid]. He found a man going to Cairo, to whom I gave letters and order for any letters for me. Then into [pyramid] about 11. Went into King's chamber; hung a plumb bob in each corner from the ceiling (finding my waxed holders very useful) and took offsets of top and bottom of every course of each end of each wall, thus plumbing it most thoroughly. Then with steel tape measured a distance of plumb bobs on floor, they being all close to 50 inch marks (i.e. 200, 400 and 450 owing to plumblines being 4 or 5 inches out) so that minor lengths were all readable with ivory scale. Though I could not go along N. side owing to big hole in floor and stone in the way, yet I took both diagonals and so obtain it as well as the angles, only losing a check. This occupied till 6 and though I took in biscuits I did not stop for anything, as having plumb lines fixed I could not risk travellers disturbing them (especially one over doorway) so worked quickly ahead. Only two travellers came and were a hindrance but no trouble and the only other delay was an ugly tumble into a big hole quarried by Howard Vyse in the floor, which gave me a headache and some bruises, including one on my jaw which bled slowly for some hours, the best thing it could do, but rather sharp considering it was through whiskers. This made climbing ladders and stooping my head on the floor doing the tape measures rather unpleasant, but I had too much work spoilt if not finished off tonight to make me stop for a trifle. Then out again and home. Had supper (tomatoes again) and then worked out the measures clearly, calculating the plan of the plumb lines.

28 January 1881

Off by 10½ to Cairo, a fine morning with high misty clouds which prevented it from being too hot. To the post first and got letters and papers; then to Dr Grant. ... I must say Dr G's is the place to meet agreeable and intellectual people. I was very glad to receive a letter from home and hear that thanks had been sent to him for his kindness. ...

Then took donkey again to Genl. Stone's and found that he was out riding; so straight home, getting in about dark. The worst bit is that beside the road to the pyramids (this end of which is useless from disrepair) there runs a sort of arm of Nile water, which shallows to naught at the hill here and this crossing is a stretch of deep black mud in every state from liquid to hard; to sit a shaky sort of donkey while he picks his way over this in the dark is not desirable.

Every line I write is so much lost time from useful work to be done here; as I want so much sleep, that the whole of the dark is not too long for that and supper etc. I am much disappointed at finding that my wants in food and rest are quite as great as in England; I had hoped to be able to go with little of either.

7 February 1881

A typical day. Off by 7.45 with Ali to station on hill top W. of pyramids, placing signals on the way there. Then began observing, but the wind was so high that three times I had to leave off and take a run of ¼ to ½ mile end back to replace signals blown over; also it kept the theod. in a shiver, so that I had to steady telescope and micros by hand in order to see anything and it was dull and cloudy so that I had not enough light on the distant ones; to add to which a gust constantly came driving sand into one's eyes and making one screw them up for a minute before anything could be seen again. However, having no sun I was free from tremor of the air and expansion of instrument. I pegged away at the work and on reduction find it better than on previous days, only 1.0" mean error of one obsn. after allowing for a shift of 4.5" in azimuth[1] at one point. Then had biscuits and dates about 2½ and then moved over to another station on a small by [...], Ali had vanished for some time (as I after found taken up by a traveller who knew him) so I had to go to and fro moving things; the theodolite of 36lbs was a lug to carry ⅓ mile and then up a slope of rubbish. Hence I took azimuths to 5 stations, the wind gone down then and then just finished by sunset, packed up and then went round and collected signals, getting in by 6½. After supper reduced all observations and then wrote this and to bed about 11.00.

9 February 1881

Off with instruments to station on 3rd temple; found 2 of my 3 signals left out had blown down and the third I had to alter; so leaving them out only saved collecting last night. After putting up all signals, set up theod. and then took azimuth till sunset, then rough altitudes and packed up; took in several signals, but left 5 out as a trial. The risk is of Bedouin finding them when out feeding their camels in the neighbourhood. Then home to supper. I was rather dubious what to have, so Ali took the idea that I had nothing suitable

---

[1] The angular distance from a north or south point of the horizon to the intersection with the horizon of a vertical circle passing through a given celestial object.

Flinders Petrie at Giza

and after saying goodnight, sent up very kindly a basin of stewed rice and milk and sugar. I began on it but soon had to stop and *drain* off the sea of butter swimming in it; after that it was very bearable. Then reducing ob. but all the dogs around made such an incessant row that I could hardly get on and had a headache; also was listening to catch a mouse in a biscuit tin as I had done twice before; at last it went in, but the box tipped and I tried to grab it by hand, but it got off, hope this fright will scare it off. Finished by 10½ and so to bed.

10 February 1881

A very windy day with sand haze, so I did not attempt surveying; went up to the N. face and hunted over the diggings; two good pieces I had marked are gone; I marked some more in hopes of possibly preserving them. ... I measured the angles of the pieces lying about for fear they should disappear and also approximately to angle of stones *in situ*, in case they should in any way be covered again. ...

Then I went and took angles of slope of nearly all the good tombs of a quantity of 2nd [pyramid] casing fallen and found one block *in situ* within 20ft of a soclet giving a fine fixing of the true plane. Then measured angles of 3rd casing both fallen and *in situ*. By this time it was dark so back to supper. After which not having much writing of obsns. to do, wrote to Mrs B.[1] To bed abt. 11½. A roar of wind sounded not long ago, so fierce that I went to the door and saw in the cloudy moonlight whirl of white dust and sand from earth to sky travelling across the plain, about 500 feet across. The sound was astonishing and I should think the trees of the avenue must have suffered. It is strange how much noise the wind makes on the steps of the pyramid; quite a howl when a blast comes past.

11 February 1881

A very windy day, worse than before; the fierce gusts that almost blow one over, charged with small shot of sand are very nasty. ... The evening was beautiful, crimson clouds in the east, rosy in zenith and on one side a smoky mass of that filmy, misty, translucent cloudiness which the sun half shines through.

11 February 1881
Gizeh Tombs

My dear Spurrell,[2]
I have long had your name down for a letter, but really time flies so fearfully here that I do not get through half I wish for. I think you have seen some of my accounts sent home, so I need not tell you of my general deeds and surroundings. I am paying special attention to the methods of workmanship here, and trying as far as possible to get into the minds of the old people; for that is the only way to realise what they intended, and how they looked at things. The entrance to the third pyramid is one of the most curious things I have seen, a perfect picture of *how they did it*. The granite casing which went about half way up (limestone casing above that) has never been finished off; the blocks are duly squared and polished down on the sides and back where they met, but in front they are left anyhow, thus at a slight drafted line shewing how far they were to be cut and polished down in situ; then along the front edge three big bosses or handles to lift the stone by projecting 6 or 8 inches and on some stones a boss half way up the face. I have found traces of such bosses dressed and polished off on granite stones inside the Great Pyramid, and am told they exist in full in some of the remote parts. I picked up one big boss in a rubbish hole, just as it had been knocked off by a blow beneath it, preparatory to dressing the stone down. I also found a line drafted diagonally across one of the biggest granite blocks of

---

[1] A neighbour.

[2] Flaxman Spurrell became a great friend of Petrie's, helping him unpack and catalogue his finds back in England at the end of each season. Flinders wrote many letters to Spurrell and encouraged him to come out to Egypt – he never did.

the pyramid, shewing how they word a true plane, when beyond the scope of the surface plates that they used. Many of the granite stones have a line drafted down about ¼ inch wide all along their edges, *ground* and polished quite smooth, evidently to give the workmen a true boundary to reduce the plane face to. The beautiful straightness of the joints and their microscopic closeness, both in granite and limestone, is something overwhelming, when one looks at the size of the blocks and the vast amount of them.

I have planned out and made a good beginning, in a large survey of geodetic accuracy, to extend round all the Gizeh pyramids and to shew us their real errors of construction. Few people will sympathise with such a work, but I feel it is shameful not to even *know* the accuracy of the finest work of ancient times; to attain to it is something beyond the zeal of modern architects, but at least we ought to be able to *measure* more accurately than they *worked*.

Mr Loftie[1] was at the Hotel du Nil, but after what you said I did not try to see him, though I might easily have done so. When one gets on as well as one possibly can, which is what I am happy to say I am doing now, it is rather dangerous to try anything or anybody fresh, complications so easily pile up.

I heard of your fearful account of the storm, and indeed am happy to be in a tomb here; the delights of an invariable temperature, never beyond 60° to 68° for two months, makes such a home far preferable to any Grand Hotel. Life here is really comfortable, without any of the encumbrances of regular hours, bells, collars and cuffs, blocking, tablecloths, or many other of the unnecessaries of civilisation. My Arab who has charge of me and mine, comes up from the village every morning, goes out carrying all my baggage for the days' work; generally absents himself for an unconscionably long time under the plea of devotional necessities (which includes dinner and seeing friends etc. I suspect) and then lugs back my theodolite or whatever I may have; has a talk while I get supper and then in an hour or two sends up his negro slave to sleep in the next tent as guard. I find a paraffin stove most useful and boil my kettle and eggs, stew tomatoes or rice and heat my tinned soup, very readily and far easier and cheaper than with a charcoal fire, which is the only thing used here.

13 February 1881

After breakfast and reading I strolled out, picking up sundry odds and ends in my way; went round to the 3rd [pyramid] and observed what I had before suspected, that the highest remains of the granite casing on each face (the stump backs of one or two blocks) is at exactly the same course on all sides which very strongly suggests that that is the highest course to which it extended. Then round home, picking some of the desert hyacinths on the way; they are light clove-brown and though without smell when picked, I observed a faint hyacinth odour on looking at them in the evening. I am

---

[1] A clergyman who frequently wintered in Egypt and was a keen collector of antiquities.

gradually making up a collection of desert plants. ... back to supper. Ali came in and had a long chat. The shekh has made a man clear out all the rest of NE socket; just as well, for I did not order it, only told him I should want it bye and bye and it shews they wish to help and get some stray cash. Ali explained the regulations of the community. Any traveller paying the regular fee to the shekh (or anything the shekh may get from me publicly) the money is divided, ¼ to the shekhs and the rest equally among *all* the Arabs. Then, if by pestering, the guides can get extra baksheesh, *that* is divided among the guides 'family'; not family of relationship, but family of guides, they forming brotherhoods of about 4 each, who equally divide the surplus spoils which any of them get. And a social regulation is that the guides to a party must be taken out of different 'families', or comradeships, so that extra bakhsheesh may not fall too much into one party's hands. This is all far more complex and communistic than I had imagined and I rather think hardly any Frank knows of it; I know the Grants, who know more than most people here, are quite in the dark about it.

20 February 1881

The donkey did not come till 8.40 and I immediately started, but without Muhammed, who however picked me up after half a mile or so.

While going in today I passed one group of camels of which the last two were lively and began waltzing about in the road, at last pitching off two men who were on one of them. They came down all of a lump and a yellow fluid poured out after a thud which accompanied their fall; rolling and tumbling up they got on their legs and disclosed that one of them had had a big jar full of fluid honey, wrapped up all along with him in his overall which now he held up dripping with the sticky mess, while the jar lay smashed in the road. The peaked conical hoods are a striking feature of the dress; I saw the hugest of them today over the head of a hideous old Arab with a pair of big round blue goggles on, there was room inside the coal-scuttle-of-a-hood for voluminous whitest wraps all about his head. The two things no amount of civilization ever beats out of a Turk or Egyptian are wrapping the head up and doubling up the legs. A most European looking man will suddenly tuck up a foot, as if there was no comfort in life without doubling the joints and vigorous, even ferocious faces will be seen wrapped round with a striped silk handkerchief, like the tamest of invalid old coddles in England, while all the rest of the dress may be suited for the Strand or Pall Mall. ...

I got into town just in time to go to post before going to church; I got to the American Mission before the close of the Arabic service by Mr Lansing and saw a good-sized native congregation; duly separated men and women by a red curtain down the middle of the room. An innocent Scotchman and his wife asked, on coming in for the English service, if they must sit apart, but the curtain being withdrawn, settled their doubts.

25 February 1881

Too windy to survey, so I set off for Cairo and having a cold I wanted to walk it off. Ali had not appeared while I was getting up, so I could not tell him where I was gone, as he cannot read even a word of Arabic; in fact he does not know it from English when he sees it. I got over the Nile bridge just as it was going to be opened for two hours 1–3 as usual; the sight of the rush to get over at the last was most amusing. When open there is a large ferry boat, for which of course passengers must pay.

27 February 1881

Temp. nearly down, being 99° in morn at 10½. I staid quiet in bed till 2.0 when Ali came round. Then I turned up, wrote a line to Mr Loftie postponing Abu Roash till Thursday and to Dr Grant telling him that nothing was really the matter, so as not to trouble about me if he heard I was 'ill'. Then had some tomatoes and mock turtle and to bed about 4½. Temp. then down to 98.9, which is only normal for that time of day. Did not get any sleep till 11 or 12 and then broken by 1st trap down, big rat, killed and reset. 2nd Mouse about trap for long, though bait must be eaten, got up to see. 3rd Fleas. 4th Mouse let trap down without going in, got up, reset it. 5th Mouse in, got up, killed him, re-set trap. 6th Fleas. 7th Dog set up a protracted conversational barking (just by my door) with sundry neighbours in adjacent villages; went out and pelted him off. 8th Woke in heavy perspiration, had to change night shirt and take off sheet. If this is *not* the way to get over a fever-cold, I cannot help it. Slept on till about 10 next morn.

6 March 1881

Had a long sleep, for somehow I never seem to get enough here and however long a night I may have, I could always sleep all day beside. After an afternoon breakfast and some reading, I strolled out about 2½. Several fresh excavations are begun, the authorities being encouraged by the loot of a tomb lately here; all in the usual style. A group of small children carrying a few pounds of earth each and dropping it in the first convenient hole which may very likely required to be cleared out next. It is sickening to see the wretched way even the authorities work in and the incompetence to form any regular scheme of work or to shew the least foresight or superiority to the style of the most ignorant Arabs. I copied a scrap of inscription which they had turned up, on a block which the degraded brick builders had used for a door step; the pillar with inscription had vanished apparently, so it is well I secured a copy immediately.

7 March 1881

There was an unusual swarm of travellers today, about 40 Ali said, and we promised an old man a piastre,[1] 2½d to guard a signal in their way; he actually did not grumble when paid and asked for more, but then he did not belong to a village Ali explained. Looked at various diggings going on; Maspero is having one of the most ancient wells cleared out, of which things will be of early 4th Dyn. I shall much like to measure the tomb chamber when they reach it. Some more of the Roman brick builders' stolen stonework turned up, which I must watch for inscriptions. I gave a boy 10 paras (copper) = 10d. for shewing me an inscription, so I am sure to be told of any others. Another digging is coming close to the side of a tomb well, which really seems to be sunk through the late Roman nitrous earth and brick; if so it must shew some tomb wells to be made at a very late date; I watch it carefully, as a few hours, when it is reached, will probably see it all pulled to pieces and carried off. ...

Unfortunately a horse died on Saturday night and the utterly wasteful Arabs instead of burying it, or even skinning it, carried it out and left it all for the dogs. So they are most riotous, quarrelsome and noisy, all last night and tonight, barking continuously; if this was constant I should have to move my quarters, but I can just bear the row in ordinary. ...

28 March 1881

Got up at 5½, had a scrap of rice and coffee and then packed donkey and off with Ali and Abu Saud driving at 6¼. Had a look at Gill's base which he measured for the Govt. survey. The Arabs have torn out the terminal I saw and taken up or broken most of the intermediate stones and Dr Grant told me it has never been used. Then looked at site of Roman village, full of pot. Then saw the fossil shell hill, but did not carry anything from these sites. Then walked on to Abusir pyramids. Saw there a site of brick buildings being dug for earth; they had turned up fragments of early tombs, which had been used by brick builders two good pieces of figure sculpture, some among them carrying standards; I copied the hieroglyphics and also of another bit I saw many flint hammers etc. as at Gizeh.

Then on and looked at the Sakkara tomb of Ti; the outer court of it, inside being locked up. Then on to Mariette's house, a ground floor building, with large covered terrace on N. side. The caretaker or reis[2] said I could not have a room, or even sleep on the terrace, though Baedecker mentions both. So I put my things *pro-tem* in the corner of the terrace, put some water in my kettle,

---

[1] A small coin found in several Middle Eastern countries.
[2] Also the name for the foreman of a dig.

boiled up (as it is filthy muddy here) and had some chocolate, cold rice and biscuit. Then about noon went off leaving Ali with the things and looked where Mr Loftie told me for the newly opened pyramids but could not find any opened there; there must have been some mistake between Brugsch[1] and him. Then went down the hill edge, and into sundry tombs, some of which I measured; others were so rough, fallen in, built up with mud walls to support the roof, full of dust and broken, that I left them. I had a nap in one, for the long walk in the sun after getting up early had made me sleepy. Then had a look over the late (Roman) village and up to the Step Pyramid; had a look at it and went up it easily, though Baedeker says its ascent is "not without danger and on no account without the help of the Bedouin". It is far safer than going along the face of the Great Pyramid. The sun was just setting and the view is interesting, though nothing like so striking as that from the great [pyramid]. I then came down and looked at the make of it; it has evidently been built in coats, each step covering over that which rises about it. Ali came up and said that the man was not settled and would not let me have any part of the house or sleep in a convenient neighbouring tomb. So I went up to house and found the reis very civil, but he said he had had orders not to let people use even the terrace, but from the sequel I doubt it. After much talk in which the reis impressed on us with the most appalling gestures the dangers of sleeping not locked up safe and insisted that we ought to go down to the village (probably to some friend of his who would charge handsomely) Ali and I agreed to take the tomb near, so we carried the things in, but the reis professed to be shocked (all this is fudge, as Baedeker writes of sleeping out as a natural thing there) and offered to let us use the tomb of Ti, one of the show places, but soon changed and said we might have a room; this probably resulted from his seeing that we were going to take care of ourselves and all backshish[2] slipping away from him. So we moved back and into a room where I soon settled in, had supper, wrote this and to bed about 9.

29 March 1881

The reis not only stopped himself, (sleeping on one wooden sofa, Ali on another and myself on a third) but had up two men to sleep on the terrace all in blessed anticipation of backshish. I got up about 8, had breakfast (no washing facilities here) having a run out to see the pyramid that has been opened by the step pyramid, while the kettle boiled. Found it had been still further destroyed by throwing down a lot more of it to cover the entrance again, so jealous is Brugsch of any information. Then off with Ali and looked

---

[1] Émile Brugsch was Mariette's assistant at the Boulaq Museum.
[2] A tip or gratuity.

at another pyramid lately opened. ... Then as it was a hot day and rather close and moist (a thick fog this morning) I left Ali in shade of mastaba, as I did not expect to want much and went off light, without coat and only 3 of the thin measures, a bit of candle in pocket and a few matches. Went two miles over the desert to the big pyramid of Dahshur. This is the largest next to the two of Gizeh and is better work than any about here. ... the entrance is about halfway up it, so I clambered up and went in. The passage leads to huge chamber with 11 overlappings, much like Grand Gallery; then having measured this, I went into the next chamber; here, while measuring, I heard the stones knocking about at one end and as I was unaware of the number and nature of the beasts and had nothing but thin measuring rods and no one within two miles, I beat a retreat without investigating the cause; it is probably a jackal's lair but *might* be hyena or runaway slave. Owls inhabit the place and were much disturbed by my candle.

31 March 1881
Up about 8 after a rather restless night on my table, which was rather too hard for comfort. Went off, after just a drink of water, to copy inscrips etc., had another look at Step Pyramid. ... Then down to tombs, copied all the continuous passages in one tomb, which has evidently never been done before, as it is all plastered over with mud, just as left by some Arab family. A great deal more might be copied by cleaning and washing. ... then up to house again to go to Apis tomb and Ti tomb when open for other visitors; found two Englishmen just leaving Apis for Ti, so hooked on to them and they seemed glad of such explanations as I could give, for though I had never seen it before, one gets an eye for such things and takes in with practice the meaning of a group more readily than at first. Then went off to Apis tomb; found door ajar, so went in; they are huge galleries cut in the rock, of which my one candle scarcely shewed both sides, while at intervals they branch, or have great recesses or chambers, in which the enormous black granite sarcophagi of the bulls. ... after seeing part of it Ali came in and I looked at some more, but it is not a favourable place to measure for many reasons and I wanted to get back this afternoon. So I left and back to house, had breakfast about 12 and Ali hunted for a donkey but could not get one; meanwhile, not to lose time, I set off, leaving Ali to settle with the reis, as I hate the perpetual squabbles over every piastre, which are necessary here unless one showers silver and gold too, enough to fill all mouths. ... The reis was squabblesome on receiving 10/- for 3 days, besides 2fr. for one man and brought up all the men he had chosen to send up there to sleep, asking which of them all was to have the money, a favourite figure of action with him. He would not let Ali have his donkey unless he had £1, so hiring two men they carried the things

down to some camels; there getting a camel coming this way the things were taken about half way; Ali branched off to see about them and all I know is that they have come in by detachments. ... I left Ali at what seemed like a Roman station, two parallel walls about 550ft apart. ... I pushed on but was very *pumped* with the deep sand walking; having been on low rations lately while at Sakkara (4 biscuits and chocolate etc. *per diem*) I was gaspy and oppressed with it, being very thirsty as well. I went up to sundry shadoofs, but the water was all too thick of black mud to be bearable, so I had some very bitter tomatoes from the remnants of a patch left wild and got home at 6½, done up. ... If this heat is going to continue right on, I should pack up soon, but I expect it will go over in a day or two and be about 70 or 80, quite comfortable. One cannot do much in active work with air over blood heat, let alone the risk of sun stroke if one does go into sunshine.

6 April 1881

The worst of the hot weather is that it drives all the fleas and flies into the cooler tombs, hence troubles in all hours of the 24. Fleas abound in the sand of the ground, in pottery heaps or in tombs they readily entertain you, but when they all retire into the cooler recesses, one has to slaughter by the dozen. Of flies I counted 70 in a biscuit tin lid and 30 on *one* side of a bowl, while at breakfast. It was again too hot for outside work, so I set about measuring the tombs all round mine. The true air temperature in the shade, briskly waving a thermometer about was 100° which went down to 98° when the thermom. was laid on a rock ledge. ... Ali says that only a day or two occasionally is as hot as this in the summer. ... I counted 240 flies on edge of sheet hanging over side of bed this morning. I go to Cairo *early* tomorrow.

14 May 1881

Antiquities began flowing in again. Ali brought a batch for which a man wanted 60 francs, but I only wanted a few things. ... The main thing I had was a fine head of Osiris in bronze, knocked off a statue anciently. Then I went on packing and got all the pottery packed. Then in the evening Omar brought in some little stone things, of which I also took a few. For everything in the way of antiquities I have run up £6.8s (for 16 scarabs, 28 bronzes, 21 stone and 18 glazed trinkets = 83 articles, besides 16 coins and big shrine of Ptah) so I must not go much farther, but I am sure to get the cost from any collector in England, or turn a penny by selling at a sale, as I remember being horrified at the prices for which a collection sold a few years ago.

20 May 1881

Put some old gutta percha soles to boil up while I had my bath and working the bits up into a mass, I gave them a final boil and wrapping the saucepan in an old cloth went off to the granite temple. There I got a tolerable cast of the most decisive of the tube drill holes in the door socket, but could not make the gutta p. squeeze into the narrow circular groove all round; still it shews it clearly. Being an upside down hole, plaster will not do at all; perhaps beeswax might do it well. The Arab employed by the Museum here as a general superintendent met my going down with the saucepan; I exchanged 'neharak saida' (good day) and he went to Ali who I had seen near, and asked him what I could be doing? Was I going to cook? So Ali, delighted to throw him off the scent, assured him I was going to do cooking in the temple. As I came out I met him again, evidently waiting for me; he said something, I forget what, so as I had my hands full I bid him look in the saucepan; lifting the lid with great curiosity he saw a tin pot floating in a lot of dirty warm water, so clapping it on again with a laugh he left me, probably convinced of the insanity of the strange khawaga by this time.

22 May 1881
Not up very early; after breakfast reading etc. I had a talk with Ali and considering and arranging several matters which I must do before I go. I hope now that I shall get off tomorrow even. or Tuesday morn., but I leave undone a lot of things I wanted to get through; however, I suppose I shall feel always that there is plenty more to be done whenever I go and I hopefully look on this leaving as only a temporary run home for a few months. We must if possible be *out* again by middle of October, so as to get the fruit season and have all the best cool time for work.

In October 1881 Flinders returned to Egypt having spent the summer months back in England. He landed again in Alexandria on October 13th and, while waiting in Cairo for his baggage to arrive by freight train, he paid a couple of visits to the Giza pyramids, where he was cordially welcomed by Ali Gabri; but on going to the Great Pyramid he was horrified to find an American putting an advertisement for a quack medicine across the entrance.

... of course it was disgusting, but the place is so mauled with modern graffiti that I really did not care much; and he was impervious to any hints, nothing short of a row would have stopped him. ... About 4, as I was thinking of going, the two Americans Moore and Watson turned up. With go-ahead energy they had done Sakkareh in the morning, ridden to Gizeh and then done all up to the Pyramid. I shewed them the sprawling advertisement, at which they boiled over, and instantly put a couple of franks each into my hand, with an urgent request that I would see to its being cleared off; and wished to leave more even. They said that all the most beautiful places along the American railways had been disfigured with the same words.

13 October 1881

We landed about 3.); and as most of the passengers went off the quay, I took the boat and rowed across the harbour, the men carrying up my luggage; this avoided the bustle, and was cheaper than a carriage from the quay, which is a long way out of town. ... I went straight to the Hotel des Messageries, washed up, and then off to Moss to enquire about baggage. It will not arrive for about a week, and then cannot be in Cairo for a few days. Then to the Consulate, asking them to forward passport to Cairo. Posted last journal. To station for train times, then a stroll out towards Ramleh. Returned about 6, feeling very lazy. Sewing on buttons and c. Dinner at 7½, at which I laid in a sound meal; and then to bed.

14 October 1881

After a slight breakfast off by train 8.0 to Cairo. Got a basket of figs, about a dozen or more for 2½d. ... Got to Cairo by 2½. Walked to hotel, where old Madame seemed as pleased to see me as the waiters at Alexandria (Mem. practical inference that bakhshish was sufficient last time I saw them, therefore repeat the dose in proportion). Had a wash after the outrageous dust of the train. Then to Dr. Grant, as I should catch him during his *at home* hours. ...

I had a talk with the Dr. about various matters. ... The Dr. had seen Ali (by sending on a letter to him) the day after he arrived; had been to Maspero and found it best not to do *anything* till I came. ... After looking at his list of visits, the Dr. then drove me down with him to Maspero's boat anchored off Bulak Museum. There I had an interview with M. He is an honest-looking man, and appeared genuinely inclined to help me, besides expressing himself very friendly to the project. To save delay and trouble he proposed instead of getting a formal governmental firman for me, to put me nominally in his employment, as working under his own license; this he had done for other English last season, and I could not see any objection to it, as in any case I must submit to him and put all finds at his disposal. This then merely needs his written permission, and a direct application from me to him, to be formally passed on as showing to the Ministers what he had granted. This firman from him he promised that I should receive on Monday, on applying at his office. I am also bound to take into pay at 2s. per day one of his own men for the work; of course as a check on what I do. After various talk with the Dr. on antiquities, we bid him goodbye.

On the Sunday (October 16th) Petrie was accosted by a group of Egyptian soldiers whilst out walking near the tombs of Caliph. This letter records the events as they unfolded. At the subsequent hearing the soldiers denied the accusation of robbery and, since one vital witness disappeared and another withdrew his testimony, the case was abandoned.

Letter from F.P. to Raph. Borg Esq.
H.B.M. Vice-Consul, Cairo
Hotel d'Europe
16 October 1881

Sir,

This afternoon I walked on the Abbasiyeh road for some distance, and then turned across the plain and entered the track leading through the tombs of the Khalifs, intending to return to Cairo by the Rue Neuve. I passed a little way to the East of the waterworks, and continued the way past two stations of soldiers who saw me, and one called "Neharak said"[1] which I returned. Then about 6 o'clock in clear daylight I approached another and smaller group of three soldiers standing outside a stone hut or tomb, which is close to the tomb of Solaimân (judging by the map); I observed that they were talking about me, and when about 30 yards off, one of them (whom I will call A) approached me; the others (B and C) following. He said something to me in Arabic, which I did not understand; I asked in Arabic for the road to Cairo, pointing to the city. After a few more words he took me by the wrist, and led me to the hut. To this action, and all the following, I gave enough resistance to show my dislike, but did not resist with any violence, not wishing to have injury added to insult. There after a few more words A made me sit down on a stone near the door. They then all questioned me; A. and B. impatiently, but C. always checked them, and took pains to explain what they said. They particularly referred to a carriage, which I had seen by the mosque of Barkûk; and, as I understood, inquired if I came by it, or by donkey; I replied that I had come on foot, which they seemed to disbelieve. They then asked me apparently to give them 4 francs to let me go to the carriage, then for 3 francs, then for 2 francs. They several times asked if I had money for them, which I refused; they also asked for tobacco, cigars, etc., and if I had cognac, C. smelling my breath to see if I took spirits; finding that I did not, they ceased asking. During this examination, B. went into the hut and brought out a musket with fixed bayonet, shaking it at me in a threatening way. A. then turned out my coattail pockets, examining each article and asking about it, C. in each case restoring the things which A. wished to keep. I found my handkerchief was gone, and asked for it; A. refused it, C. persuaded him to give it up. By this time we had all risen, and A. gradually let me draw it out of his hands. C. then patted my back and pointed me away, so I went on towards the Rue Neuve.

---

[1] i.e. Good Day.

A. immediately followed me and took my wrist again, when I asked him to go to the consulate and told him I knew the Consul (meaning Mr. Borg). At this he paused and looked at me; C. came up and made him let go again. Finding that I could not get clear of them, I turned and went towards the carriage standing near the mosque of Barkûk, the soldiers following; a respectable Copt came up to them, when they called to me that he was a Christian, I looked round and he affirmed it; but I went on to the carriage, running at last as it began to move. On reaching it I found in it a Greek gentleman, who afterwards kindly gave me his name, Nicolas Brakalis, living in the Rosetti Garden. The soldiers and Copt joined me, and they all began talking to M. Brakalis; A. catching sight of my trousers pockets as I stood upright, tried to put his hand into one, which I resisted; he insisted, so I pushed forward to the carriage door and called the attention of M. Brakalis to what A. was doing; and he saw him searching in my pocket. In that pocket I had £29.0.0 in English gold in a small leather bag drawn at the mouth with a black braid; and over this my purse with rather over two pounds in it. A. fumbled in my pocket for a long time, nearly half a minute; and I could not imagine what he was doing, as I knew there was no difficulty in taking the purse out. He drew out his hand partly closed on the purse, which he had turned upside down in my pocket; I took the purse out of his hand immediately and he did not much resist; his hand closed, and dropped down; he demanded to see what I had in the purse, and turning to B. and C. remarked triumphantly that I *had* money. I put the purse back in my pocket and immediately found that the bag of gold was gone. I instantly said to M. Brakalis and A. had taken £15 (not wishing to over-estimate the amount, of which I was uncertain at the moment); The soldiers clamoured and I demanded that A. should go in the carriage to the Zabtiyeh; this he refused, and tried to drag me from the carriage to which I clung, M. Brakalis expostulating with him. A. then reluctantly let me enter the carriage, still dragging at me. The Copt had also entered the carriage. After a minute or two of this confusion, on my again repeating the charge of robbery (which I had mentioned already) A. then fiercely denied it, took off his blue cloak and threw it at me, and offered his purse to the Copt to see, and challenged us to search him; but he had had plenty of opportunity to pass the bag to B. or C.; and in the temper they were in, I judged it impracticable to make any efficient search of their persons. The driver was then ordered to go on by M. Brakalis, and B. clung to the carriage and got partly in, while he talked with heat to M. Brakalis, A. and C. dropping behind. At last B. left us after about 100 yards, and the carriage drove on unmolested. We drove down the Abbasiyeh road, the Copt dropping off when near the end of it, bidding goodbye to M. Brakalis. Finally we stopped in the Place de la Bourse, where M. Brakalis gave me his name, and I parted from him.
W. M. Flinders Petrie

The soldier A. was a rather mild and pleasant looking man with brown eyes, tall and powerful.

Postscript (attached to the draft of the above)

The examination of the witnesses in the affair of the recent robbery by Egyptian soldiers at Cairo took place on the 24th Oct.; Mr Petrie put in his evidence, as stated to the Vice-Consul in writing; the soldiers' defence is that they were afraid Mr. Petrie was going to blow up the powder magazines and therefore searched his pockets. M. Brakalis then unhappily could not in the least remember seeing the assault, though it was committed under his eyes only a week before. Two officers were present during the examination; one of them made such remarks at first, that the consular interpreter had to forcibly remind him that he [was] there to listen, not to judge the case. He then contented himself with often hissing the soldiers, when he considered they were giving unsafe answers; and he then repeatedly stopped answers in the examination, where they [were] liable to be contradictory. The case will now come before the native tribunal after Beiram.

(A Persian has been so much injured by some soldiers, that two European doctors were called to his consulate to examine his state).

19 October 1881

Up early and packed my things, out for carriage and off by 8¾ for Bulak. Found that the young official I had seen was to go to the pyramids with me; this was better, as he spoke French. The museum official tried to frighten me about sleeping in a tomb apart from the village, and recommended a house he knew in the village, as I suppose wishing to get me quite under the eye of a man who would report my doings; as we walked to the village he again expressed his hope that I would go to this house, as there was a bed with a fine canopy and a beautiful mirror etc. I replied I only wanted bread and dates and water, and the rest was of no consequence; a speech which went down well with the Arabs, who said I was an "ibn el beled" (son of the country). He much wanted me to stay for coffee at this house, but I walked down with him, and then went off to my tomb, having much to do. I took everything out, large and small, and dusted it, had all old sand taken out, walls brushed, fresh sand brought in and then replaced the boxes. This occupied about 7 hrs. and only just got straight by dark. The Museum man came, after his coffee in the village, to look at my tomb, and wish me goodbye; he was amused with it, and expressed surprise at my venturing or liking to live in such a place. As we drove up he saw me saying goodbye to an Arab, and asked if I *knew* him, to which I replied that all the Arabs here were my friends, and I knew them all more or less. Got settled in and had some dinner by 7, as I had only had some coffee and a few biscuits since morning. Ali sent me up a plate of vermicelli. The rats have made havoc in my trunk, thrown many things off the shelves, bitten card boxes to pieces in search of the contents, finished two packets of tapioca etc. and the moths have got into the few biscuits I left, so they are all magotty. I gave Ali £1 for taking care of the place, which he was much pleased with and would hardly take.

20 October 1881

Up at 6, straightening things, and by 8 at pyramids, where they had begun work. Ali had got six on the work, a man to dig and a chain of five to pass the baskets up the passage, among whom were Abu Soud, Mohammed the negro, and little Mohammed; so it is almost a family affair. They worked very fairly; and Mohamed was all alive, doing more than his share and whistling and joking all day, even until sunset, finishing with a jackal race when he came out. I searched for the edge of the pavement in front of the entrance, but could not find anything clear; also for the pavement between the entrance and the north-west corner, but though I went four or five inches below its level in two places, it was not there, so I cannot recover the alignment in that part. Then I went inside and watched work; a big limestone was smashed up before dinner and taken out in bits; but a bigger granite weighing about a ton I did not wish to smash as it had two worked faces and a drill hole which looked ancient, so I had it cleared around, and then finding there was easy room over it and two breaks in the side wall just below it, I jammed a piece of board across the passage and wedged the stone up from it, so it cannot slide. They got to the end of the rubbish so that one can see over it, and I expect a few hours more will clear the passage, unless there is a heap at the bottom. The chain was rather too weak, so I joined in the afternoon; and this made the museum man ashamed and he took a share, so we got on well. But to work at eighty degrees in a narrow passage, in a chain with three negroes and five Arabs in various stage of undress down to only a waistcloth, and with the air so thick of dust as to shew shadows, is not pleasant to one's nose and lungs; chucking the empty baskets down sent out clouds of fine dust.

At the end of March 1882, Flinders was offered an opportunity he could not refuse: to see something of the Fayum and the desert beyond. Cope Whitehouse, an American who held eccentric views about the pyramids and Lake Moeris in ancient times, offered to take Flinders and a young artist, Tristram Ellis, who had been helping him at the pyramids, on a surveying trip to the Fayum and beyond.

30 March 1882

After packing up and arranging things, went off at 10 for Bulak station; got there about 12 after a hot walk, donkey carrying things; waited till 1 for train. I could not find the ticket office at first, but after enquiring I went round to the outside of the building and there under two high windows, I saw a clamouring crowd hanging onto the iron bars, thrusting their money in and demanding tickets of an easy-going official, who had a face like the moon for roundness and extinct volcanoes, which would have rejoiced an anti-vaccinator. Our crawling train went on at a leisurely pace, averaging, with stoppages, about 13 miles an hour. ... At last I got to Medinet el Fayoum by 6½; went to Mason Bey's house, as Mr Whitehouse had told me and Mr B. himself opened the door. I had a short talk with him and a first course of soup, while waiting for the train, the starting of which for Abu Kasah (pronounced Abuksah) is quite uncertain. At last at 7¾ supposing it nearly off, as it professes to go at 7½, I went out to the train and got into the carriage; here I waited till 8¼ before the train left, reading some pamphlets on Nile management that Mr B. lent me. At 9½ we got into Abu Kasah (where Whitehouse had appointed to meet me) and here I got out and enquiring for *Khawagas*, was told there was one with a beard, staying at the sugar factory; so shouldering my baggage I went off to him, as I had no doubt it was Ellis. When I got to the house (an empty one belonging to the factory) I was shewn in by the servant who went with me and opening the door, I saw Ellis in bed under a mosquito net and hailed him "So there you are, Ellis" but up looked quite a *different* face and a gentleman informed me that he was not Mr Ellis and knew nothing of him. So with apologies I backed out and not being able to hear of any other Khawagas I went back to the train and the officials, finding that I had made up my mind to sleep in the carriage, left me in peace. So unrolling my blankets and finishing off some few biscuits I had with me, I prepared for the night. Just before turning in, I saw some camels passing and wondering at the station people working as late as that, I looked out and there I saw Ellis and Whitehouse passing with their baggage. So dropping out, I joined them and we ended by settling in the next room to Colonel Monier, whom I had so unceremoniously looked in on before. After a bit of cold fowl, we went to bed, I turning in at 11½, the others much later. They had been round the N. of the Birket Karun and come over in a boat, reached shores at 5 o'clock and then taken 5 hours to get camels and come about 5 miles from the beach.

31 March 1882

We all turned up before sunrise and got the train at 6½ for Medinet. We went to a Greek restaurant for breakfast, for which I was quite ready, as I had scarcely anything since last breakfast in tomb. I went off to Biahmu, stopping at the mounds of Kom Fares just N. of Medinet, to examine them. I did not see anything that could be put to Greek date. I found the hind quarters of a large lion in grey granite and the die of a column in red granite which I photographed. Here came on a fearful khamseen,[1] which blew directly over the immense mounds of fine dusty rubbish of the old town; it swept along in such a cloud that I often could not see the road I walked on and to see the palms at a furlong off was as much as could be done. It looked like the Essex marshes on a foggy day, but instead of mist, sand; instead of 40°, 90°; instead of a calm, a raging wind. Unhappily it was exactly behind the mounds, being a S. wind and I requiring to go N., so that I could not avoid being in the very worst of it. I pegged on to Biahmu, asking my way and by the time I reached the so-called pyramids, the storm had moderated. I examined the two pyramids and took several photographs. From all I saw it looks to me as if they were seats for enormous statues. I then returned to Medinet by 7, had dinner, a good wash and to bed by 9½. It is curious how common nose rings are in the Faium; one family of four little girls had each a ring, 3 silver and one gold.

1 April 1882

Ellis went off back to Cairo. Whitehouse went down to the Mudiriyeh for an official letter to take on the journey and I went down and returned with him. While we walked back, the rain began and continued in heavy showers all day, so that we could not start. I had a sleep in the morning and in the afternoon we went between the showers to see the Copts that W. had known here before. The schoolmasters were away as Easter holidays had begun and the bishop or abuna was at his siesta, so we had a talk to several of the boys and some priests. They brought us in large cups full of dark pink liquid, which was presented with a towel held under the cup. Now, was this rose water for washing the fingers and the towel for drying on? or was it to be imbibed? Puzzled, so asked W. to begin; he politely refused; more at sea than before – until they held it close to my face and then I made up my mind that it was to be drunk; luckily I did not begin by dipping my fingers in it. It was sickly sweet and aromatic with rose water and I had to sip slowly and often; the sight of a towel, not over clean, just under one's nose, not tending to increase one's internal stability. Then coffee came in, which was a relief. I was much astonished at the education of the boys; there are 150 or so in the school, of which 70 are in the 1st and 2nd classes which are taught English and French; the 3 boys we saw, about 12 to 14 years old spoke English excellently; clear, distinct, good pronounciation and seldom a wrong word. They were extremely polite and friendly and pressed us to come to service tomorrow, which they assured us was very beautiful, every one bringing palms (being Palm Sunday). After W. had made many enquiries about places, we went off, a R.C. Copt

---

[1] A hot, dusty wind.

pressing us to go and see his church, so we went and saw the three Franciscans here. ... After a talk we went down and saw their tawdry church, which looked miserable after the Oriental-Byzantine quaint ugly plainness of the Coptic. Then we went to the Mosque of Kait Bey, now half ruined and saw the fine bronze covered doors and ancient capitals within. It is placed partly over a bridge crossing the Bahr Youssef which runs out in front of the Mosque from under it. The mud was fearful and we could hardly get along the slippery streets; I saw two natives fall. Then after dinner, the rain came again in a deluge, thunder and lightening incessant and everyone declared such a storm was not remembered in the Fayum; the rain came through the flat roof of the restaurant and completely swamped the floor; cushions, rugs etc. were all bundled up on the billiard table and some of the people took boots off and went home barefoot. ... One of the most comic sights of today was a Coptic priest trying on my pith hat, which was almost on to his shoulders and then in exchange he offered me a trial of his turban which much amused the rest of the party.

The rain was so heavy that it stopped the railway, by washing down earth over it, so that a train was stopped up and the engine displaced.

2 April 1882

At 2½ in the morning I was woken up by a Greek being shewn into my room and appropriating the second bed which Ellis had before. After breakfast W and I went to the Coptic church; we slid about on the mud anyhow and getting to the gates of the Coptic quarter found a lake in front of it, which was running into a hole some men had dug, while they spread the dry earth over the mud. At last we got in and found a considerable number there, all with branches or pieces of palm, which they were busy plaiting into ornamental crosses during the service, chatting and laughing all the time. Three collectors went threading and pushing their way through the throng, two with flat dishes of woven palm fibre and one with a brass pan. A few piastres lay in each dish and as the collector came up, a man would begin examining the half and quarter piastre, and finally selecting the two good ones would drop his whole piastre, thus giving ¼; so the plate circulated, the time occupied by the examination of the change by the congregation being enormous. Towards the end of the service, everyone began waving about the branches of palm holding them as high as they could; it was a strange sight, the half dark church, with light coming in from an open court joining it and all the air full of rustling branches of palms waved about by the excited congregation. The singing was very curious, the men and boys antiphonally, in strange meandering pointless quaverings, not unlike the character of the old Saxon church music. After the waving of the palms, the service was considered over and a comfortable looking old priest who had on his head a white cloth with pink and blue embroidery of Byzantine style, came to the door of the little chancel (which is screened off with a solid screen with two windows) and seemed to enjoy sprinkling the people; then our two little Coptic friends led us off, leaving the deacon reading as hard as he could at a lectern, to whom no one seemed to pay any attention. After service I wandered out over Kom Fares again, picking up a quantity of varied marble mosaic from some destroyed pavement. After lunch W. and I walked out over the sloppy fields of mud to the obelisk of Ebgig of Amenemha the III 12th dynasty, the only old Egyptian thing besides the labyrinth in the Fayum.

Petrie's Book "The Pyramids and Temples of Gizeh" was published in 1883 and won him much acclaim. But he was determined to return to Egypt. During his work on the pyramid survey, he had begun to collect and study small antiquities brought to him by dealers and picked up in the ruins. He concluded that by observing 'the varieties of glazes and fashions' it should be possible to fix the age of any object 'within a few reigns'; pottery in particular, which was usually discarded as rubbish by excavators, should be recorded as an indication of the probable date of the building in which it was found. In October 1883 he was appointed by the newly-formed Egypt Exploration Fund to excavate at Tanis, a great site in the Delta. On October 27th 1883 he wrote to the secretary, Miss Amelia Edwards, "the prospect of excavating in Egypt is a most fascinating one to me and I hope the results may justify my careful noting and comparison of small details, as in more wholesale and off-hand clearances".[1] There was no road, Tanis would have to be reached by water.

26 November 1883
Hotel du Nil Cairo

This morning I went to Cook's to hear about boats, and to try and settle what terms should be offered to the owner of the dahabiyeh.[2] No other boat can be got much cheaper. To Borg on one or two points. Then to Dr G's,[3] and overhauled all my boxes there. Three of the boxes do not seem to have had anything taken out. In fact I do not miss anything whatever. The photos and plates, papers etc. are as I left them. The moths have flourished on the ship biscuits and in the various old clothes used for packing, but strangely have left my great coat almost untouched. Opening and sorting all the things and packing what I wanted for this winter took all the morning from 11 to 1.

---

[1] Petrie's letters this year are all addressed to his mother; she passed them on to Amelia Edwards.

[2] Nile houseboat.

[3] Dr Grant.

After lunch looked over scarabs etc. with the Doctor. Then went to a friend of his who owns some dahabiyehs to enquire about rates; he says that £10 or £12 is quite fair at present for a small one.

In evening to Dr Lansing who has been to San[1] twice; he speaks very well of the people there. He told me of a point of great importance, that two rows of circular bases of pillars (which I know in the Map) are very large, 8ft. diam., of granite, and were *cut up* by Ramesses II for his temple, as there is a piece at R.'s temple uncut, and a column in transit between the temples. This then is the temple of the XIIth dynasty, and probably the old statues come from here originally.

2 December 1883
On the Philites

At last I have got fairly off, with all on board, within 9 days of landing in Egypt, which is not a very bad start after all, though the delays were wearisome. I found that I could not get a smaller boat than this, which has 4 cabins beside 2 sitting rooms (all small), but this is said to be only half the size of Naville's[2] boat last year. Quite unexpectedly I found that Prof. and Mrs Sheldon Amos[3] were wanting to take a change, and his legal engagements left him free just at present; so I offered to take them on for a week or two, they returning whenever they wished by rail. It was an opportunity to make use of the extra accommodation of the boat which would otherwise be wasted, and to secure pleasant acquaintance for a short time at starting. The Prof. is invalidish rather, a quiet, thinking, rather satirical man and Mrs Amos is an utterly unconventional, active, sensible woman, with her own opinions and ideas on most subjects, a great manager and accustomed to roughing it. She is strong on social and educational subjects, siding with Octavia Hill and Dr Barnardo.

Getting in the stock of bread delayed us a good deal, or rather was made the excuse for delays; after spending a day waiting for it, partly at Bulak, and partly down at Shubra, 3 miles below, I thought they were shamming, so as the old reis had gone 'to look for the felucca with the bread' which was to follow us to Shubra, and as he did not come back, I started for Bulak, taking one man with me and making him run trotting all the way by walking fast. At Bulak I found the bread waiting in the boat, but no reis; I said that did not matter as he might follow us on foot, but I let the man run to fetch him; in a

---

[1] i.e. Tanis.

[2] M. Edouard Naville, a Swiss Egyptologist.

[3] Maurice Sheldon Amos was a lawyer, at that time judge in the Court of Appeal in Cairo. He and his wife were keen advocates of the education and emancipation of women.

few minutes the old sinner came running down as fast as he could, and scuffled over the other boats to the felucca at a great rate; the other men came in sharp and we were off at once, and rowed very fairly down to Shubra and got on board. Then the metal ticket of the boat was wanted to show the tonnage in passing the bridge, and as soon as it was inspected I pocketed it and said that perhaps the reis would not be there when he was wanted again. This turned the laugh against him and as some of his previous remarks as to where we were going were inopportune and I had told him to "shut up" in the briefest way (oskut), I think the old fellow felt shorn of his dignity somewhat. We got through the bridge and then had to wait at the rail bridge ½ mile further on. This was only open at 8 a.m. and there was no chance of getting it open that afternoon, so we waited in patience. As trains passed every ½ hour or hour, and as the rails had to be all unbolted (32 units and screws to undo) it was very reasonable not to undo it. This morning they opened extra early and let us through by 7½ and by 9 we were up opposite Heliopolis. Here we spent the day wandering about over the ruins of the walls around the obelisk and walking over to a village near where there were a few stones. I went over to Gizeh one day and saw all my old friends there, Ali, Abu Saud, Muhammed, and dozens whose names I do not know. I got a prize at Gizeh, which I hope to see safe in the British Museum, the upper part of a finely wrought figure in alabaster which I take from the style to represent a Carian mercenary about 600 BC; it is more Greek than anything else. It comes from near Kafr Dowar and I hope that I may recover the rest of it and parts of other figures found with it; it was about 8 inches high when perfect.

I post this at Shibin, while at Tell el Yahudieh.

December 6 1883
On the canal, Belbeis

I have to confess that I have been shabby in the matter of writing lately, and my only excuse must be that I have hardly been able to find time for what I have done in that way. When, beside running about all day, one has two clever people living with one always ready to talk, it is not easy to find time for more writing than is a matter of business. I am now all alone, as Prof. Amos was not well and needed to return to Cairo for advice. Mrs Amos is however so longing to see Tell el Maskhuta and San that she said, "If Sheldon is not well enough to come while you are there, I will try to bring down one of the children to come and see you." As she is old enough to be my mother, don't be shocked. We had delightful talks on board, for Prof. Amos works a little at hieroglyphs; so after a meal, before washing up, out would come dictionaries, lists of kings etc. and we would be thick in the discussion of a dynasty when conscience would whisper, "That tapioca pan will be hardening if you do not wash it soon." So four or five days passed in a fascinating jumble of history, antiquities, cooking, ancient towns and subjects social and educational, all coming one over the other as if Herodotus ruled our life.

Now I must give some notion of the sort of surroundings that I am in. The boat is far too roomy for one alone and it seems a shame to be going about in this way when there are so many people who would delight in such a trip. First after the sailor's deck comes the door of the long poop, covering more than half the vessel. On either hand inside is a small cabin, one for the donkey-boy, the other used for cooking. Then comes a saloon, 11ft wide by 8½ long; then a passage, with my cabin on one side and a cabin I use for photographing, stores etc. on the other; then a disused tiny bathroom (the foot of the bath goes under my bed place) and then a stern cabin 11ft by 11 in extreme, which the Amos' had. Ibrahim, the donkey-boy, suggested that I should feel very lonely at having all this space to myself and on my telling him of my tomb at the Pyramids, he asked if I was not afraid there. The whole crew here is nine in number; the old reis, Ismayn Hassanen, has been very proper since I fetched him away so abruptly from the delights of Bulak; he is a small thin old fellow with a short white beard. Ibrahim, the donkey-boy, is I suppose nearer thirty than twenty and seems a good fellow; he is very active when he does move and trudges away at over 4 miles an hour with me, of his own choice, making any other Arabs with us run to keep up; this physical activity of his makes him willing to go about and do things. His English is not grand and anything outside the regular track of business taxes my Arabic and his intelligence to a great amount. Of the crew, three are blacks; Ahmed Ise, a broadfaced, jolly fellow with some intelligence, Mahmud, whose natural ugliness is heightened by smallpox, and Hassan, whom I called the baboon at first sight; I took him out with others antika hunting, and the poor baboon only found about a quarter of what the others did, and looked very monkey-like while hunting and when being laughed at afterwards. Then there is Hassanen who is half black and has but one eye. Then a young Arab Abd el Halim who is fairly intelligent; a boy of about 15 called Khallel, who is also a useful fellow, observant and careful and lastly the best of the lot, the little cook-boy Abd el Halim the lesser, only about 10 or 11; this little sprig is always all alive, ready to trot with me for miles carrying baggage and found more than any one else when out grubbing at Tell el Yahudiyeh. He is not more courageous than the Arabs in general, for yesterday I having trotted Ibrahim and Mahammed about 10 miles to Shibin and then to the boat at El Menair, I left them on board and took out little Abd el Halim up into the desert to prospect; though there were only two lots of people in view for miles and neither coming our way, yet the urchin was incessantly looking round in every way and said most innocently (in Arabic) "I'm very much afraid." This continual fear of the Arabs is really ludicrous. When we were out at Heliopolis, I left Mr and Mrs Amos when about two miles from the boat, in order to get in sooner and put the kettle on as it was just dark. We had Ibrahim and two of the crew with us, so that there was a good party; but as I came on I saw a light bobbing about and found that it was the old reis with the ship's lantern and four men came out to look for us. He spoke to me as if I had murdered all the party and when I assured him that they were coming on behind he went on in a grief-full manner, but sent one man back with me to the boat. ...

Since writing the foregoing I have had a walk in the Wady Tumilat, and a walk that I do not long to repeat. At first we got on pretty well, though the ground was rather soft and moist. Then at Tell Nuir we were told that the water was out and we must go round. But, while looking about for the road, up came a very reasonable man with a donkey which he offered me to get across with to Tell el Kebir. I gladly mounted, and found it a capital beast; it knew the road well, and all the little dodges for getting over each bad place seemed quite familiar to it. When at last we reached a hamlet whence the road was fair onwards, I got off, and offered some piastres to the owner who had ploutered on foot through all the mess. But he would not hear of my giving anything, but uncovered his wrist and showed me a tattooed cross, thus I found that he was a Copt. He would not even take anything for his children, but seemed really to have a soul above bakhshish. I asked him if there were many Copts there; he said there were only five or six. After parting from him with many thanks I went on into Tell el Kebir; there are no ancient remains at the *Tells* here, they are only little outcrops of desert in the mudland. As Ibrahim had a thorn in his foot since Shibin, which was bad now, I told him to wait there for the dahabiyeh while I went on to some reputed remains in the desert to the south with the boy Khallil. We got round Tell el Kebir very well, and then the troubles began: the country is merely a great marsh, rather salt, growing scanty, woody grass, on which goats and buffaloes feed. There have been in some past times regular embankments on which one could walk, but these are so often broken away that they are useless. At last I had to wade continually through the marsh, which stunk abominably, and it was a rotation of deep mud over the ankles, filthy-looking red water, and salt-dust ground full of thorn bushes which pricked one's bare feet unmercifully. On the whole the deep mud was the pleasantest walking. After all this we reached the desert and went on for more than a mile over the sand, looking for this reputed site of stones, but I could not find it, and after a considerable circuit we tried a fresh way back again which looked more promising at a distance. But this was worse than before, the water was nearly up to my knees and mosquitos airily alighted on my legs when I reached dry ground. At last we reached Tell es Sugheir or the 'small tell', and here heard that the place we were in search of was farther to the west and thus I had been misled by the direction which a shepherd boy pointed out to me. Here we found a fine dry path to Tell el Kebir, and rejoiced in it until suddenly close to the end it ran down into deep mud. We waded again and I went down so deep that I lost my balance in trying to pull my feet up, and over I went sideways. I saved myself by sticking in the hand in which I carried my shoes and then by the camera stand and Khallil, I got on end again and hauled myself out. My shoes I lost out of hand, but grabbed one and then began raking with my hand in the mud about a foot deep for the other and pulled it out at last. We had a great washing up at some water that looked quite clean by contrast, it was only muddy and neither green nor red. At last we got in to the dahabiyeh by sunset; I found the canal order awaiting me, and the letter No. 5 with enclosures which many thanks. People here do not look on the Soudan affair as anything closer and more personal than you do in England; it is said to be very sad etc. etc. but as to making any difference as to what is actually done *here* no one thinks of it. Perhaps there might be some hesitation about going beyond the Second Cataract, and some people might object to Nubia, but no one makes any alteration in their doings here in the least. ...

11 December 1883
Kassassin
Yesterday I went all over the hill of Tell el Kebir, for as being the highest point of the country around it was the best place to examine the desert form in search of any chance of tombs. But though I carefully looked over the desert north of this with a telescope, I could see nothing but low, gentle, sweeps of pebble-covered ground; there is no trace of any rock face in which tombs could be cut. Indeed from the nature of the ground such could scarcely be expected. The nearest rock is about 5 to 10 miles south of the Wady in the Arabian Desert; all north of that is sand and flints over which lies the mud of the Wady Tumilat and the Delta. The cuttings of the trenches[1] show that to five or six feet deep the ground is all sand with small pebbles; though strange to say about one to two feet below the present surface is a band of large flints, like those of the surface, showing a period of wind action before the present top was deposited. The outworks of Arabi's camp extend far into the desert, five or six miles I should guess, and such a quantity of new mounds and ridges quite mask any ancient heaps that there might have been there. I

---

[1] The battle of Tell el Kebir, in which British troops under Sir Garnet Wolseley had defeated the army of Arabi Pasha, had been fought on September 13th 1882, barely fourteen months before.

was struck by the very little degradation of the earthworks since they were thrown up 16 months ago; the edges of the ditches still stand quite sharp, slightly overhanging just as the earth fell in the digging and in very few parts did the bank and ditch appear worn down by the rush of the attack. Most of the traces of the action 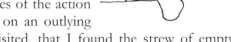 have disappeared, and it was only on an outlying part, which had not been much visited, that I found the strew of empty cartridges where each man had lain behind the bank.

The quantity of stores left lying about partly buried is astonishing; in one place are some hundredweights of shells, some unexploded, others uncharged; also some canister shot and a quantity of balls, about a cwt. of lead all in one place; there are also packets of charged cartridges, and a strew of gun fuses. All these things were just put under the surface, and are being dug up again piecemeal by Bedouin and Arabs. It is illegal to take them and if a Bedawi is caught at it, he is 'put in the police', as they say. This, of course, delays the distribution of the things, but they are sure to be taken sooner or later.

The English cemetery is being very nicely got in order, with white marble monuments and plantations of shrubs. There is a pleasant Arab as Bridge keeper, who is learning English by dictionary and phrase-book, but he has a fair pronunciation.

16 December 1883
Ismailia

I went to visit Tell el Ritabeh, where there is nothing much on the surface, but a promise of results by digging. On my return to my great surprise I found Prof. and Mrs Amos back again; they had trained to Ismailia, and not finding me there had taken a boat back along the Canal until they met me. They had been out 30 hours or so, sleeping at a railway station. ...

We had great excitement on going through the bridge at Nefisheh. As we came up the bridge was partly open, so we went straight on to go through. The keeper did not open it wider, and so just as we got up to it, the boat swerved and caught the mast against it. Over tilted the mast, creaking awfully, and we expected to see it fall and smash up our cabins, but it did not go over altogether. Then the keeper was so indignant and vociferous that he never saw the stern mast coming on, and that caught also but not so seriously. Then he had not warned the reis to lower the lateen yard, so that caught the telegraph and broke one wire and twisted the others: we also splintered the wood of the bridge. The troubles arose from the keeper not opening the bridge properly (it is a turntable bridge) and not warning the reis and our having too strong a wind to carry us through well, though we had no sail up. We stopped as soon as through to haul up the mast upright again and stuff in wedges, big and small, cracked and whole, to hold it up (N.B. it only fitted in a loose hole with a lot of various wedges to begin with); and after attending to the rigging, I made them push on to Ismailia. There we found that we had sprung two leaks, by the wrenching of the mast; and after bailing dry at night there was over a foot of water in the morning, that is to say, up to within 6 inches of the floors. We got a man to come and attend to it and he caulked up the cracks and we have been dry since then. The old reis is responsible for whatever happens, as he is sent in charge by the owner, and has the sole direction of the boat and men.

I have met here (by means of the French Consul and an Arab doctor) with an excellent Bedawi who knows all the country well, and walks splendidly. I did 17 miles with him over the desert, going over 4 miles an hour on the good ground; but much of it was heavy sand. ...

Early in 1884 Petrie embarked on an expedition to investigate the site of San el-Hagar, ancient Tanis, the most northerly city on the eastern side of the Delta. His letters to his mother tell of his arduous journey by boat to the site and describe setting up camp.

28 January 1884
Cairo
[Letter to Mrs Petrie, Bromley, Kent]

Unhappily, I have nothing to tell this week beyond the mere fact of getting better. My cold has proved obstinate, and after stopping indoors for some days without clearing it off, Dr Davis said I must take to bed. So I have laid up for nearly three days and Mrs Amos has been looking after me with hot slops and messes in the kindliest fashion. I have now got over the congestion and general muddle in my chest and head and barring a little scraping and clearing up I am pretty well right and hope to be off in two or three days. The weather also is improving, but it has been wretched. High cold winds in Cairo; heavy rains in the Delta, Tanta almost impassable; *snow* on the Gebel Ataka at Suez at midday; and at Alexandria three days storm, thermometer at 36°, five ships lying in the offing unable to get into harbour and those in harbour unable to discharge cargo. ...

Chinese Gordon has come and gone; and much I regretted not being able to see him. The Sultan of Darfur (said to be a lad of 18 or 19) he takes with him; they went by special train and the Sultan asked three days to collect his household; Gordon was indignant; then might he take his wives? Yes. So at 10 o'clock at night when they started he appeared with *42* black women. Whether they were all shot into the train seems dubious. ...

My time, here in Cairo, has not been wasted, the various times that I have been here, if only for the advantage of knowing the various heads of police, public works etc. and so being able to appeal at once about anything that may arise.

On Feb. 4th we moved down the baggage to the boat, from the station at Fakus. The boatman had professedly been cleaning the boat; and perhaps it was as clean as a fish boat could be, well-scrubbed and cleared out; but of course the smell was irremoveable. At first it seemed impossible to stop in it, but it is astonishing what one can become accustomed to. There was also a Greek going to the boat, and some Arabs, beside the boatman and his brother (two quiet, respectable old men) and their families. At first we continually ran aground, but the canal deepened further on, and even a little tracking was possible; but in general we went with the stream and a little poling. In some places the current winds so much, in the broad expanse of about 50 feet of the whole canal, that the boat had to be turned across the canal Z-fashion to get along at all. There was a little cabin or rather roof at one end of the boat, about 6 feet long and when it was too windy and cold in the evening to lie or squat on the top of it (N.B. it was arched ⌂) I turned in below on my boxes, with the Greek, and had supper. We started at 11 a.m., but though the distance is but 21 miles by water, it was about midnight before we reached San. I had gone to bed, undressing and settling in between my blankets; and after the boat had stopped, and the tramp of the polers was over, and after a long conversation between the boatmen and their friends, I had some sleep. Next morning before sunrise I was off ashore to see the position of things, and to settle where my house should be. The mounds are not, I think higher than those of Bubastis were, before they were cut away so much: but the outskirts of the site are very extensive. The great temple has no mounds over it, nor indeed within the high enclosure walls, but it was buried under about 10 feet of stuff, partly washed in from the walls, and partly composed of limestone chips, which show how much has been destroyed. The temple itself has been cleared down to the level of its base by Mariette, but whether he has reached the boundaries of it or no is not certain. Most probably a good deal remains to be found beyond the limits of his clearance; and there may be earlier things below the level of Ramesses II.

I soon saw that there was but one really suitable place for a house, on the enclosure wall by the entrance to the temple area; this commands the temple and also the village outside. And there were walls of a RomanoGreek house to be traced there which would give an excellent foundation. The mounds in general are fearfully loose for building on, and their unsuitableness was exaggerated by the recent rains, which made them boggy in places. Then the shekh's sons and other Arabs came up to see what was going on, and who we were: so going back to the village I interviewed the official of the fisheries and the shekh. The personal letter of permission was read over and considered satisfactory, and I gave them an outline of what I wanted. The old shekh is not a very prepossessing specimen, but the fisheries official seems a pleasant good-natured sort of man. ...

Then the boxes were unloaded, arranged on a clear spot by the village, and the tent pitched over them; so thus I have the boxes as a floor, all accessible and raising me well off the ground. After this and having some breakfast, we went up to clear the ground for the house, having first to make out the plan of the old walls and then fit the rooms on them. ...

Next day we got several men and boys and cleared up the walls of the old house and settled the lines for building on. Then they made some mud mortar down in a hollow by the great pylon; the upper part of a gigantic statue of Ramessu II lying in the midst of the big puddle, and serving as a steadying point to the men as they trampled up the black batter. Next they hunted for stones, bricks and anything that would do to build with; for yesterday I had tried all the old brick houses and not found any bricks sound enough to bear being taken out and re-used, so I am short of building material and had sundry negotiations going on during the day for Arab crude bricks. The rain came on today in showers and at night a gale sprang up which seemed certain to carry off the tent; and after that a drench for hours. Ali I have sleeping in the tent with me, as he has a cold; and Muhammed and Mursi had made themselves as happy as they could with my boards. Next day the ground was all so sopped that it was quite hopeless to work and so no men were taken on, and everything is at a standstill. Between the showers I cut up the wood into the lengths that I should want, and tacked it roughly together into a shelter for the men. I am glad to say that I keep well, but if this weather goes on I must go into a room in the village, though I dread the dirt and smells of it. ...

The old reis is a fine figure, with a commanding voice; always with a large black wrapper over his head and falling down round him; wearing a pair of huge black goggles, which with a nose and a grey beard are all that I have seen between the edges of his overall wrap; he is always, sitting, or standing, or walking, carries a long stick bolt upright, ready to smite the wicked. The people were scared at seeing him come up to inspect, as they remembered his former doings under Mariette, but Ali assured them that he would not be allowed to go on in that way now. One man that was refractory about carrying a big stone from work for my house, he gave a fearful whack to the other night, and Ali had to come in as moderator. It is very well to have such a man here, he will serve as a ferocious sheepdog, who would bite if he dared; the Arabs will appreciate mild treatment all the more, and I can let him exercise himself if occasion requires. He cannot do harm so long as engagement, dismissals and the money-bag are all in my hands, and any one can complain to me at once. I mainly want him for the sake of knowing exactly where things were found, and what ground has been worked; and he may easily double my results in this way. ...

On Monday many more workers came up, and though I took on 52, several went away disappointed. A quantity of girls came up finding their working was not objected to; two of them were quite grand young ladies for this village, with face veils ornamented with gold and silver coins (one had four gold and 25 large silver pieces); and it seems strange to pay anyone with such a lot of bullion on them 5d. a day for work at carrying platters and bowls of mud. We began a large trench up to the most accessible point of the temple boundary wall, as I want to see the ground level there; and also did some other trenches, finding one piece of inscribed statue. The builder came from a neighbouring village, and he got up the walls of my first room about two feet. It is queer after English prices to pay 15d. a thousand for bricks; but then they are small, and of such mere crude mud and straw that they could not be carried for two or three days after the rain for fear they should drop to pieces. A wall looks as if of straw outside, here; the rain washes about an inch of mud off the face of the bricks and then the straw protects the rest inside.

10 March 1884
Zoan

For the first time since I came up to this room, I had a heavy storm this afternoon (23rd): first came drippings through between the boards, and finally there was hardly a dry spot to stand in; the rain then began to run down the wall inside, and gutterings of mud came dropping down the earthy wall, while the splashing drops made a paste with all the dust that the past windy days have accumulated on everything. My bed I kept dry with the American-cloth wrapper of the blankets: at least when I say bed, I mean the heap of blankets on a deal box on which I have slept for the last three weeks. I cannot fit up my canvas sacking bed until I get another room built, and Ali's[1] room has to be finished first, and the builder has deserted us. So, the floor is the only air-tight part of this room; the two mud brick walls that have no professed openings, ventilate freely between the bricks for lack of proper spreading of the mud; a third wall is nearly all door, with gaps, above, beneath and all around; the fourth wall has two small windows, and a large doorway (to lead into the room that is to be), and these are merely loosely filled with piled bricks; as to the roof, it is airy, the spaces between the warped boards lighting the room with a curious diffused mild light by day, and showing the stars by night. The rain was so heavy that the men could not do anything, and a hundred human beings were all tucked away so safely in trenches, pits and under stones, that not one could I see from my doorway which commands the whole temple. At last, in a lull, Ali straddled down in the mud, and gave word that they had better all go home and have their week's pay tomorrow. So there was a rush. Afterwards by sunset when the storm was over, about ⅔rds came up to be paid. Now paying money may seem simple enough when you have it to pay, but it isn't. Firstly, I cannot get enough change here, and have to persuade the workers to group themselves so that I can give a dollar, half a napoleon or sovereign, or even a whole sovereign. Most of them I have to pay with Parisi's; and these coins have no fixed value, but as they are all genuine they are much preferred to piastres. In the taxes, a Parisi is only worth 8½ piastres, in Cairo it passes for 9, here for 9½ and at Salahieh for 10. These coins so curiously uncertain in value were all struck in Paris for the

---

[1] Ali Suefi, still *reis* in charge of the workmen.

Egn. govt. and profess to be 10 piastres; but of course there was some trickery or jobbery about the business, and their value is anything you please according to the locality. One of the greatest blessings to daily business in this country would be a reformed coinage. When you come to deal with ¼ parisis, worth $19/_8$th of a piastre, the odd value must be evened by means of copper currency worth $1/_7$th of its nominal value; there is a mess of accounts to be squared at every payment! ...

12 March 1884

There was a *fantasia* here the other night, and they thought to honour Ali by sending him up the head of a big fish cooked; but Ali did not relish the compliment at all, and it took all reis Muhammed's explanation that the head of a fish here was an honour equivalent to the head of a sheep elsewhere, to pacify his feelings. I think that he has had rather a surfeit of fish, for tonight I offered the water I had boiled some fish in for cooking their rice (a thing he had greedily looked after, and reproached me for throwing away, at first) but his answer was "No, thank you." "What, Ali, don't you want it?"; "No, sir, don't want any more with these fish." "Didn't you like that fish's head? Wasn't it good?" I asked. "No, I didn't eat any, I've had 'nuff fish."

One trouble in my new quarters is the fleas; they must have been brought in in the clean sand for the floor, I think. People in England speak of *a* flea with bated breath (like Beau Brummell's pea) and have the same respect for the singular number as when they speak of having *an* egg. Here one never reckons about less than half a dozen of either article; they are not dealt in retail. Last night I was up three times, and slaughtered about two dozen of my depletors. ...

Today a man brought in some antikas from the neighbourhood, a tell[1] a few miles off. There was nothing of interest, only some plain funeral scarabs and little lapis lazuli figures, about XXXth Dynasty; as however I want to encourage the dealers about here to bring things in, and want to open relations with them, I bought them seeing that he was well content with about half of the Cairo value or a quarter of the English rate. A little bronze carving was turned up yesterday here of the Greek bull's head type, very prettily executed, as good as gold-work. I have finished working on a lot of early Roman houses on the N. of the temple, as they were not productive; I only got poor pottery from them, though mostly in good preservation. We are now cleaning up the immense mass of granite blocks of the temple; my intention which I hope to carry out is to see every side of every block here, copy every piece of inscription, photograph everything worth having, and make a plan showing

---

[1] Ancient mound.

the place of every inscribed block. I began with the stele of Taharka and the XIIIth dyn. inscription which are the most important, and now I am doing the Ramesside stelae, and shall then go on to mere blocks of walling. Meanwhile five men and ten boys are grubbing out the earth between the blocks so far as is safe all over the place, ready for me to work on. ...

15 March 1884

Those who have not heard it, could hardly realise how largely direct personal abuse is employed by an Arab taskmaster, and to what little effect. Khalifa, who is the most energetic driver that I have, has given the tone to the working, which is copied by Muhammed and Mursi; all day the trenches echo to the shouts of "Ya ibn el kelb! Ishtaghal, Istaghal, ya bint! Hawafi, ya shekh, Hawafi! Ent ze hamir! ("Oh, son of a dog! Work, work, oh daughter! Gooday, oh shekh, good day! You are like donkeys!" This *hawafi* is new to me; Ali says it is "goodday" but he cannot explain the particular value of such a remark, and it seems to be equal to "I've got my eye on you"). To all which the reply contentedly, and even cheerfully, is "Hader, ya sidi hader." ("Ready, oh my lord, ready"). What a realization this is of the old words in the tomb of Ti[1] to the workmen: "You are like apes," and their reply: "Your order is executed, the work is well done." Old reis Muhammed sits squat in a heap, wrapped in his black robe, at the top of a cutting, with his rod of correction held duly vertical in front of his nose, and scolds – and scolds – and scolds. He longs to lay about him with that rod, and asked Ali if he might not castigate a man whose strength lies rather in his tongue than in his arms; the reply was that I would attend to the case by a change of work. When a man is lazy there are two good places for him; one, the top man in a trench, as his standing room is cut away by those below, and work he must if he intends to stop there; the other place is between the middle and lowest man to hand up the baskets they fill to the surface, which is pretty hard work and has to be kept in time with the others.

Whensoever I wish to administer a good scolding I bring up Ali to the spot, and inform him of the heads of offence, and he then pours out a torrent – not of abuse necessarily – but of authoritative grumble, I cannot call it anything else; and the way in which he rolls out sentence after sentence in a gruesome voice of rebuke makes me shy of turning the tap on unless it is really wanted. Often a mere remark of mine, that such a thing has not been done as I intended, gives him the text for a long injunction. Arabs when they have a grievance talk exactly like their dogs; first loud, then fading off; then another and another burst, again and again, slighter and slighter, until at last

---

[1] At Saqqara.

there is a sort of inarticulate murmuring growl, ending in the human species in a grunt, which means "There, I've told you my mind; you're a pig; and if you don't take it quietly I'll give you another dose." Ali has a greater talent in this line than anyone I ever heard; Mursi's capabilities lie rather in sending long-range shouts after errant boys or girls in the distance.

We have now cleared up the pylon considerably, taking out the earth from between the fallen blocks, and on Saturday I let down one of the big blocks weighing about 8 tons into a better position to show its sculpture; first a bed was cut where it was to lie, with a bank of earth to prevent its rolling too far; and then, after undermining it as far as was safe from below, a little loosening of the earth above sent it rolling over to its new place. It is an exciting thing to see such a mass bowling about like a brick-bat, and to know that you can't stop it when it is once off. ...

Now I must try to give some idea of my house. In the first place as you approach from a distance it looks the same from all points of view, somewhat thus... and I may as well say at once that it has no pre-tension to architectural beauty. (Here the paper blew over on to the paraffin tin, hence these marks.) The materials are charmingly antique, and in fact I live in the remains of past ages actually and metaphorically. Only one room is built with modern mud-bricks; the rest are mainly of broken limestone, limestone probably brought here by Ramesses II, pillaged from his buildings by Si-amen and others, carried off by people of Greek and Roman times for their doorsteps and floors, and finally reduced to portable blocks for my walls, which in turn may very likely be burnt for lime after I have gone. The burnt bricks which are lying in piles in my courtyard wherever they can be useful, and weigh down my roof, beside being used in the walls, are all of late Roman period; we found a beautiful supply of them in the mounds, where there was a thick wall all laid with mud, so that the bricks could be taken out as if from a modern stack. Even the very mortar of the walls is derived from the sandy ground of the temple, and the mud washed down off [...] wall. The plan is thus: *[see page 54]* and I may safely claim several advantages in such a form of house. In the first place you cannot lose your way. Who does not know the misery in a strange house of not knowing the doors, and fearing to open the wrong one? Here, on the contrary, you only have to go ahead until you reach what you want in either the European or Arab quarter. The dining hall, or sitting room, as I have modestly called it above, might perhaps be stigmatised by cynics as kitchen, scullery and bathroom all in one. The first thing you see on entering is a telescope lying on a couple of nails over the windows, ready drawn out; with this I continually watch how things are going on down in the workings while I am up at breakfast. I only now wish for a telescopic voice to

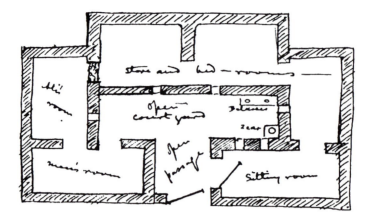

Plan of Petrie's dig house at Tanis.

hit the offenders. Along the walls are sundry boxes, and piles of biscuit tins, and behind the door on a box is the paraffin stove. My easy chair is a box which contained tins of paraffin, and here again I claim an advantage over stereotyped civilisation; whoever had a chair which they could vary to three different heights according as they may want to sit up in dignity, to put a platter on their knees, or to work on the floor? Yet all these benefits I have by just turning my seat over. ...

The next room I intend for my bedroom and for photografic and other matters, but at present I sleep in the end room. Why people ever encumbered themselves with bedsteads I cannot see; and the worst of it is that things act and re-act, and because the first step in a career of luxury was taken – that of sleeping on sacking – so now there are waterbeds and airbeds, and soon folks will not be able to bear the contact of anything but will need to be shot into space for their repose, timing it so as to hit the earth again in the morning ready for business. All this is merely a matter of habit, and after a month of reposing on a deal box I fear that I shall become quite sybaritical now that I enjoy the softness of a sand floor on which to lay my pile of blankets.

Another point in which modern civilization seems to have gone strangely astray is the absurd and needless use of egg cups. Why on earth (or anywhere else, for that matter) should people open an egg at the end; I am neither a big-endian nor a little-endian I am thankful to say; no, I follow the golden mean, and break my eggs in the middle; thus their metacentre is far above their centre of gravity – to use a naval definition – or in other words they won't upset, and the encumbrance of employing special supports is happily avoided.

By the form of my house it will be seen that I have no windows in the outer wall, and but one door; thus there is but one attackable point, and I have two windows which command that point. The doorway between Ali's room and the last store room is only blocked up slightly with stores and mud, so that if more room is wanted for the men I can contract, block the next doorway, and leave them another room. The rooms are all about 6ft. wide and 8 to 12ft long; height 6 to 7ft. I have provided for being able to take in two friends if it should be necessary, only one will have to sleep among the pots in the store room. Rain – rain – rain. ...

31 March 1884

What strikes me very strongly, in seeing the dealings of Arabs with one another, is the absence of the practical idea of justice. They may be just towards equals, much as dogs of equal strength will respect each other's rights of scavenging, simply from past experience that a row in such conditions does not pay. But the idea of the rights of an inferior seems nowhere. I see this very much in the treatment of the workers here, by Ali and the others. Ali is a favourable specimen of an Arab, he can see the faults of his countrymen, and has had his ideas expanded by intimacy with English; moreover, he is a really honourably-minded man to begin with. Yet no sooner does a man complain than Ali rates at him, and tells him to be quiet and work; and if a boy has a grievance, the reply generally is simply to threaten him without stopping to understand the case. With the others, the manner is still more overbearing. I have continually to check their settlement of some objection, and go into the matter myself; of course nine times in ten the dispute is either false or absurd, but putting the tenth to rights makes it worth while. To give a case in family life. There is a poor girl here – an orphan – who has not quite all her wits about her; she was rather a nuisance, as she never stopped at the same work, but went shifting round exchanging with others, and was always getting into a row and going off in hysterical sulks. However, considering the circumstances, I tried generally to find some place that would do for poor Bedawieh; though she managed to squabble with old men and young, with girls and with boys. She began work in a garment that was somewhat scanty and well worn, and it went on from bad to worse, shorter and more full of splits. At last when it came to the point of an appreciable portion of time being occupied all day long in keeping it together by hand, I thought it time to interfere, and (through Ali) made the munificent offer of an old pair of trousers. (N.B. They came out as packing 3 years ago and the moths have lived in them since). Then the tale came to the surface; though an orphan, the aunt with whom she lived was well off, and her cousins were among the best-dressed girls in the place. Her wages, which were plenty for all her wants, were absorbed by the said aunt, and she was left to grub on as well as she could. Ali turned the occasion to good account, with his ready eye to saving money, by declaring that if the said aunt did not reform the arrangement, Bedawieh should be paid in clothes and not in cash. That stirred the stingy aunt; that afternoon Bedawieh came back in an old dress of her cousins (Mem: put on over the rags) and next day she came out resplendent in a new snowy-white garment, from under the edges of which drooped down tails of the old blue rag. She looks quite happy over it; and there is a report – which Ali does not know the truth of – that she is to be married next week.

There seems a great amount of illness here among the children; continually a boy or girl disappears from work, and when I enquire about them I hear that they are ill. This is not merely an excuse, as other are accounted for as being away or otherwise employed. I should think as far as I can remember that about 1 per cent disappear every week, so that they must average an illness every two years. The fresh children that appear from time to time from the village are, I presume, those who have recovered.

12 April 1884
San el Hagar

[Letter to Reginald Poole, Honorary Secretary of the Egypt Exploration Fund]
Dear Mr Poole,

In sending the accompanying journal I must also write to you about a sad business. There was an accident here on Tuesday; the side of a cutting which was supposed to be quite sound, suddenly gave way; the slip buried two boys, one of whom was recovered uninjured, but the other one was found to be dead. I cannot tell you all the misery this has been to me, it has undone me altogether, I have not the heart to do anything, and only the necessity of seeing that the work suffered as little as possible has kept me going on. I cannot write about it. I have not mentioned the whole affair in the journal, as so many persons see that and I thought that you might not wish it talked about at present.

Of course there has been a proper official enquiry; a party of soldiers and an officer came over with a doctor; evidence was duly taken; and the report is "Death by the act of God". The only points which they requested should be attended to in future being the employment of larger boys (my standard is however much above that of the Museum works), and the registration of the village as well as the name of workers from a distance. This last request is in consequence of the people pleading that the boy is an unknown stranger, in order to avoid the extortion of the soldiery in the future. I am practically certain that the boy was from San, but as I have no direct evidence as to that, of course I let them take their own course. When two men were killed in Mariette's works here, the soldiers came over every month or two to extort money, on the plea of finding evidence, for *six years* afterwards I am told. Of course the family will come forward as soon as the official business is over, and I shall give them some compensation *myself*; but as all the people here recognise it as a complete accident which no one in the least expected, it is a matter of gift and not of legal right. The earth which fell was old settled soil, apparently as good and hard as hundreds of yards of similar cutting; no one in the least expected any failure there as there has not been the least yielding of similar stuff. After having taken all reasonable precautions, and always done the most risky things myself rather than risk one of the men, I feel it very hardly.

Now as a matter of business I must say how far this will affect future work. In the first place the people bear no ill-will on the matter; and beyond the excitement of the family at the time no one has cast the onus on me or on the work; on the contrary several of the people in the kindest way insisted on leading me away after the boys were taken out for fear of any abuse from the family.

Of course there has been a scare owing to the soldiers coming; but then I have now 82 at work, the majority of those from the village, and the strangers will probably come in in a few days.

I am hoping to go round the neighbourhood next week for three or four days; but if the south wind lasts it will be too hot. Today it is 95° in the shade on the N. wall at 9a.m. and now at 11 it is 98°. I find that the depth of artificial soil in the N.W. corner of the area is greater than I thought; and as I do not wish to ask the people to go on with deep cuttings at present (that in which the accident happened was only 8ft deep) I purpose clearing out a large room in the N.W. and making a very wide pit in that, as the brick wall prevents any crumbling or yielding. This week I have had them all on surface work, clearing houses.

Believe me,
very sincerely yours,
W. M. Flinders Petrie

[Postscript to letter dated 8 May 1884]

P.S. Private

I do not think that the accident has made any serious difference to the working; the falling off in numbers being due to the harvest and not to any fear. The boy that recovered came back to work only 6 days afterwards, and has been here ever since.

I have just seen a curious sight. It is 31 days since the accident (reckoned probably a month) and the mother, and another woman, came up here and sprinkled water all round the front of the house and burnt two little heaps of rice straw. I asked Ali what that was for; and he said "That's for his shaitan not come up." I asked if they did so in other places as at Gizeh. He said no, but that if anyone was killed at Gizeh, they drove nails into the ground at the place, and washed some lentils, put salt in the water and put the liquid over where the blood had been shed, throwing the lentils away. These men went over other parts of the mound round here, and sprinkled water and burnt straw similarly. They did nothing at the site of the accident, and therefore I rather think that the idea is that of protection to the living than satisfaction to the dead. ...

May 1884

The course of life here is now generally thus. Up at 5, round to see after all the men till 8. Bath and breakfast. Then dust and stow pots, or copy inscriptions in temple, or other work till 11½. Men whistled off; receive tribute of all that is found, do some writing, and have an hour's nap. All go to work again by 2½, and I go round for 2 or 3 hours in aft. to look after the work, and then go on with my own personal work till 7, when all are whistled off for the night. Then I get back to house, receive things, and attend to matters in general. Pot boils by 8, and I have supper, and write up this, and to bed about 9½. Thus I have dropped into two meals a day as I always do when alone, barring a few fancy biscuits, or so, at noon. Both meals are on much the same pattern; some bread and meat or fish, (steamed dry-bread), a few cucumbers if I can get them, some bread and jam, and a cup of strong black coffee thick with sugar. On this I am better – with a cleaner tongue – than in England; I have not run down at all, I think, after four months of it. Now to bed; it's over 9½. Very good weather; half cloudy, fair breeze and thermom. 80° to 90°. I feel under 80° rather chilly now. ...

[Letter to Mrs Petrie, Bromley, Kent, sent 7th June 1884]

I have kept a man on digging out a house on the ridge on which mine is built; it seemed of no importance, and I was just going to give it up, but told him to clear it out down to the bottom of the cellar, much against his inclination. Tonight he came in bringing a lump of silver chain, over a pound weight, with a gold ring (double snake-head pattern) and a lot of fine stone beads, evidently some ladies' finery stowed away down in the cellar in troublous times. I believe the house is Ptolemaic; and if so the snakehead pattern rings are earlier than the recent great Damanhour find of such, which was Byzantine. I dusted up the lump of chain and weighed it in the spring balance roughly, naming to the finder an approximation of its being worth about £3; I must get balances from the village and weigh accurately. Of course I deduct ¼ for chlorination and dirt. I fear it will not clean up, it is so far chlorinated. Ali, even, is grieved at my want of proper business-like ways in promising the full value of the silver: "Give him half", was his advice; the idea being that it is a good opportunity for me to make a *coup*, regardless of consequences. I am rather astonished at the man trusting my giving him full value, and producing the find at all; I think it arises from my giving full value for the gold eyes etc. found with the mummies lately; and one man so paid was working on the above house – just for half a day as it happened. Of course to give anything less than full value would just wreck the hope of receiving future finds, and spoil all the education that I have been giving them. It is really an excellent opportunity to encourage them. ...

I have at last put down a proper drain to the courtyard, so that another storm may run off without damage. First I had to find drain pipes. They are "after the antique". A row of damaged amphorae crowded up my yard; so picking out all that were not exhibitable, I cut of the bottom of each, trimmed off the handles, or remains of them, and then thrust the head of the one in the mouth of the other, so ⌒⌒⌒ or else put them head to tail and thus a dozen ⌒⌒⌒ amphorae made a fair row of drain p i p e s . ⌒⌒⌒ And then I had the pleasure of laying them, mining under two walls and cutting across one room; but it seemed a delightful home-like occupation, something quite touching, enough to reconcile any Englishman to living here. ...

Another cool day (19 June?); north wind under 90° all day, and rooms down to 80° at night. I nearly finished the survey of the temple; the avenue and pylon to come. At last I finished off completely all the survey; and wound up matters, delivered over the house to the old shekh's protection, giving him £2 for the guards (which he declared at once to be but £1 to the others in order that he might bag £1 for himself), and at last left San at about 4½ on Monday (23 June) morning, having sent on my two boxes of antikas the day before by a camel. I walked about 8 miles to Gezirat M'naydi; and then rode on into Fakus, getting there by 11; which left time for breakfast etc. before the train started at 12¼. ...

We reached Cairo by about 5, and leaving Ali and the others to load up the baggage on a cart, I went off to the Amoses to get two small boxes of antikas which I had left there. I saw Mrs Amos on the balcony looking down, and she said that she was expecting me to appear from the various reports that she had heard. She insisted on my stopping with them for a few days instead of going on to Dr Davies directly as I had intended. So when the cart came up for my two boxes, I unloaded my personalities and then went on with all the antikas to Bulak. Saw M Maspero, who was most friendly, and left the boxes in a room to be looked over. It seems so strange to get back to civilization; first I got my hair cut, which had gone its own way for five months and hung out like the brim of a flop hat all round my head; Mrs A. said that I looked like Robinson Crusoe, and her daughter confided to her that I looked like a bear. Then I wear socks once more, and a black coat, and don't have to cook my meals, and sleep on a spring mattress, and don't need to brush the sand off my feet before I get into bed. All so strange. And in the evening we turned into the Esbehiyieh Gardens, and there was a crush and babble of Europeanism, and a vigorous band of the Highlanders blaring away, and lots of lamps. So strange. Next morning I woke with the conviction that my men were making an abominable row about the house and even down as far as the temple; it was Cairo street din. ...

In the winter of 1884 Petrie worked once again for the Egypt Exploration Fund, this time with an assistant, young Frank Griffith. Together they excavated the Delta site which Petrie had suspected must be the city of Naucratis; the abundance of Greek pottery and a Greek inscription confirmed this.

1886–1892
In the Field

After many disagreements with the Committee, Petrie finally resigned from the Egypt Exploration Fund at the end of 1885. That winter he returned to Egypt and, with Frank Griffith, hired a small sailing boat in which they travelled up the Nile from Cairo to Aswan, examining sites along the river. They began the excavation of two temples at Tell Nabesha in the eastern Delta; in February Petrie decided to leave Griffith alone in charge of this excavation and move to another promising site, Tell Defenneh in the eastern desert near the Sinai border. This was easily identified as the site of Daphnae, mentioned by Herodotus, the Tahpanhes of the Bible, and known to the Arabs as Qasr bint al Yehudi 'the castle of the Jew's daughter'; it had been a place of refuge for Jews who had fled from Nebuchadnezzar after the capture of Jerusalem.

22 March 1886
At Nebesheh we have developed still further the site of the old temple of Ramessu in the middle of the temenos; finding the retaining wall of the foundation along the S. side and on the E. as well as having a fair idea of where to go on the W. and N. I think Griffith ought to be able to get at the corner deposits (if they still remain) in a day or two more. Unluckily, he has got a bad place on his foot; and so, instead of cutting a hole in one of the many pairs of damaged and rat-eaten boots he possesses, he went barefoot for a long time: standing on damp ground at sunset has given him a sore throat. Hence I was loath to leave him and go to Defenneh; however he had Mursi and Medani and promised if he were any worse, to go up to Cairo; and as a number of men were waiting to start with me, I went off. Everyone has been asking for weeks past, when I was going to Defenneh, and whether I would take them, and all the population seemed determined to go over. I steadily refused to have any but a few good ones I selected as I knew I should be sure to be swamped otherwise. At last we went off, a long string of men, and girls, and boys, about 40 in all, straggling along in groups for a length of ¼ mile and two camels with my baggage bringing up the rear. We had gone but a few miles before the sky turned slatey-black, only relieved by columns and clouds of yellow sand borne along by the advancing gale. There was a general rush, most of the people getting to a village ahead, while I and a few

others made for a sakieh,[1] under the wall of which we sat. The tempest lasted 1¾ hours, with much thunder! but at last we got over the ground again. Another storm passed just in front of us in the afternoon. These storms soaked the ground; and so long as it was sand we were glad; but when we came to patches of salt dusty earth the mud was fearful. The camels had to go a long round, and we only just got to Defenneh before sunset. It is quiet in the desert, no cultivation or trees within many miles, all sand and salt ground, and unhappily saltish water. I do not know how we shall go on, but I fear the best water here is rather too salty to live on. We have pitched by the side of a canal among some high mounds of dust and sand covered with tamarisks, the people cutting recesses in the sides of the mounds and heaping branches across them to make shelters. It is a picturesque spot, and the orange glow of the big fires they make below these bushy hillocks light it finely. ...

A great advantage of this camping far from habitations is, that we have no loafers about, no dogs, no cats, no rats, no flies and no one to carry off stones and to be kept in check. I am not happy as to my feet; my boots have gone to pieces, baring one good pair left to go home in; and the Arab boots I got at Mansura pinched my toes horribly for a week until I cut slits for the ends to come out. Then the sand here is always inside one's boots, and going to Rome on peas is nothing to it, the grains are as big as small shot, and roll about, above and under one's feet all over, grating the skin all day long. Then wading a canal, I cut the sole of my foot on a hard twig, and though only skin deep it developed into an awkward crack, by the constant working about and salt dust. And on all this, I have to do 12 to 15 miles a day. ...

I have written to Cairo for 5 dozen St Palmier;[2] and I have found rather fresher water here, which is just drinkable, only it makes one's tongue sore and lips dry. ...

For working in any desolate place in future, I think it would be well worth while to begin by work[ing] in a settled place near it and then move on, as I have done. If I had come here direct from Cairo, I might have waited weeks to pick up stray people and should not have known who they were, or had any hold on them. As it is, I start here at once with 40, who know and trust me and shall have shortly many more and thus we make a considerable settlement, who all hold together and with whom there is no bother about payments or work.

This place makes a strange sort of *fantasia* to live in; here on one side of my tent, is a group *doing* the der-wishes, all in the dark, howling and groaning in set phrases, *ya há-ah-há, ya há-ah-há* as it sounds (probably *ya-allahu*), repeated

---

[1] Water-wheel.
[2] Mineral Water.

hoarsely hundreds of times, quicker and quicker, until they break down, one by one, the combined noise sounding most like a great engine puffing hoarsely, with the voice of a snarling dog for its sound:[1] on the other side, a party of the girls are wildly singing shreds of songs half in unison chorus, clapping hands; play, the boys are playing games, slapping each other a counted number of times; around are the clumps of tamarisk bushes, with the gleam of the old canal on the one hand, and the mounds of Tahpanhes on the other, seen in dark starlight, with the glimpse of a fire here and there, under the bushes. And not another soul within 10 miles of us, nothing but sand, and tamarisks, and marsh and water and desolation. But I like it better than the more civilized places; one lives with the people more; and the ever-fresh desert air and living in a tent, doubles one's contentment and peace of mind at once. Neither Gardner nor Griffith would appreciate it, I fear, they neither of them like having to do with the people, and would prefer an immense excavating machine to do their work. To me all the bye play and jokes and songs and will and ways give a colour and an interest to life here, which one will never reach in staid, schoolboarded England. Fine *nebbut* play, like old English quarter-staff, goes on here whenever the men feel fresh; fencing and foiling each other, with long staves, most gracefully, while another generally plays the double pipes.

Our colony progresses, and in less than a week we number 85 workers, and I have turned back about 30 and so dissuaded probably many more from coming over. It is now a case of every bush has its bird, pretty nearly; some have made an approach to huts, with walls of earth left between their holes, and branches over the top, others have made a sort of tent of branches, 7 some have only a sort of scooped-out lair, much such as a dog will scrape out to lie in. ...

19 April 1886

I have generally been writing in a hurry and have not done justice to the weather we have had. For the first fortnight it was hot, and sudden gales arose; one day I had to proclaim half a day's work: all around was a brown air of sand and nothing visible beyond a hundred yards. The tent shook horribly and I hung on to the tentpole in the gusts. ... Now it is pleasant again; of course hot in the midday, but not oppressive. ... long may it last so! The canal is a great resource in hot days. It is just deep enough, all over, to sit on the bottom with one's nose out and a quarter of an hour spent rolling and splashing about makes the hot winds seem bearable afterwards. ...

---

[1] A good description of a *zikr*, a religious exercise performed from time to time in the villages at dusk, by men only, see also p. 153-4.

Up to 1 May 1886
Tell Defenneh

I have now been to the most out of the way corner of the Delta, I think; Defenneh is tolerably "out of humanity's reach", as I have found in getting money etc. from Cairo, but 9 miles due N. of Defenneh lies Tell esh Sherig. ... I first crossed our canal and then sundry more stretches of water on the way; on the whole I had better have left my trousers behind when I started, as I had to carry them in general. But the wading was the pleasantest part of it: the other ground being (1) dust so hot, that one could not stand still on it, but had to scrape a hole to the cool ground, if stopping for a couple of seconds; or (2) ground strewn with crystals of sulphate of lime, which threatened to cut one's feet, and which did stick in through the skin occasionally in spite of all care. (N.B. It is impossible to wear boots when one's feet are continually crusted with mud two or three inches deep); or (3) hot black mud, which could not be crossed for more than a few yards, any length of it would necessarily have stopped me altogether. Or (4) best of all, mud and water two or three inches deep, with a crust of white salt on the top which kept it fairly cool. At last, I reached Tell esh Sherig, a low mound about $^1/_3$ mile long, and half as wide, and 20 or 30ft. high: a mass of dust, with pottery and brick scattered over its surface, so far as one could see it. Around, either water or salt flats, almost as far as one could see, with scattered desert bushes on the landward horizon. I think it beats every place I have seen for desolation; the immense stretch of water on the N. and E. is so bare of visible islets that I could just see the white gleam of the Port Said buildings 20 miles off, across it. The mound is all late Roman and Cufic;[1] on the surface, and I picked up coloured glass. ... this is interesting, as shewing how late this district was inhabited, and therefore cultivated. ...

Back at Defenneh

I am gradually getting through the soaking of the Greek vases, doing two large basinsful every day, in three waters; and so the heap of unwashed outside is shrinking. I have to keep watch somewhat on the quantity of pottery etc. lying outside and this, and a general sense of being one's own policeman in this country and this place particularly, produces an excellent watchman condition, so that the slightest noise wakes me at once. Hence the last few nights have been much marred by some mice that have appeared out here; every time one rattles a scrap of pottery or rustles a paper, I wake up, much to my disgust; and the frame of mind, with regard to the mice in particular, is not conducive to sleeping again. I tried to scare them by all

---

[1] An early Arabic script.

means, including shooting (I can't do much of that safely, what with tinned store and pottery in here) but in vain – so now I have had to put down arsenic in hopes of getting some peace. ... To save being bothered for empty tins and bottles, I now let them scramble for them. No sooner does the cry of a bottle to be had goes out, than out rush about a dozen or twenty lads and boys and dance expectantly; up goes the bottle or tin and they all rush together, one moment it is all heads up, and the next it is all heels out, as they fall in a general heap, of which nothing but struggling legs can be seen; at last out comes a dishevelled boy from the bottom of the pile, hugging his prize. I gave a scramble for girls alone; but a little wretch of a boy rushed in and snatched the tin; he did not take much by that however, and he had five big girls on the top of him at once and finally came out distracted looking. Once a small boy thought he had caught the tin between his legs and so did four others, who fell on him at once, but it had *gone through* and was caught by a solitary urchin behind. *The Diversions of Daphnae.* ...

1 June 1886

At last I can sit down quietly in Alexandria for a morning, without anything else to do but writing. The last week at Defenneh, 17–22 May, was a scramble to pack up in time: each day I turned out about 5.30, went over to the camp where my men were tiering all the surface over and took names down. Then back and worked away at box making, repairing and packing till 11 or 12, all in full sun. Then stopped for breakfast (or whatever you like to call it), took in what my men had found, up to noon, had a nap, sent the men off again about 2½, then a bathe, and then packing again till dark. Muhd[1] worked capitally, and did nearly all the rougher packing; his feelings were not so acute as mine about risks of damage, and so he packed straight ahead and was always asking for more boxes and more pottery. I had 24 petroleum boxes from Port Said, but they were the wretched Russian boxes, very badly made, very dirty and much damaged, in so much that I had to practically re-make each box and many of them were knocked to pieces to mend others. At last, I had to stop for sheer lack of wood nails and time and leave heaps of pottery behind, most of it complete amphorae and dishes, broken, but all there. I sent off three camel loads one day, three more the next, and expect to wind up with some on the next day after, leaving on the fourth morning. But the second day to my horror the camels came back with the news that the train was altered, and left the third morning. So I finished packing that night in all haste, ending by ¼ to 12. Then lay down and got a doze in an interval when the mice permitted, and then up again at ¼ past 2, packed the tent by

---

[1] Muhammed.

moonlight, loaded the camel, searched the ground to see that nothing was left, heaved over several good things I could not carry into the bushes along the canal, and left all packed by 3½. ... The canal looked lovely in the dawn, the high clumps of reeds rising straight up for 10ft. out of the water, the birds all shrieking and twittering in the tops and the clear reflection of the amber dawn in the cool still water. It made me realise the truth of the Old Kingdom paintings of the fowling scenes; I had always thought the blank wall of reeds straight up behind a boat was a highly conventional way of merely shewing that the boat was among reeds, as *we* always show reed clumps graduating down with shorter ones on the outside. But here were clumps with a blank flat side of straight vertical reeds exactly like the backgrounds of the sculptures, rising to well over a boatman's head. One seemed to expect to see a papyrus punt come round a corner with some Api or Teta standing on it and a few little Ptah-hoteps and Neferts squatting around him. ...

His hasty departure had been unnecessary: on reaching the railway station at Salihiya he found there had been a change in the regulations: no "antikas" could be conveyed without an order from the Museum. It took five days to get his, and Griffith's, boxes to Cairo; in the Museum the Director of Antiquities, M. Maspero, made a generous division of the finds from Nebesheh and Defenneh, most of which were destined for the British Museum in London.

In 1887, with Miss Amelia Edwards' help, Petrie found two financial backers, wealthy businessmen who intended to present to museums in England whatever finds the Egyptian authorities would permit him to take. He chose Fayum as his sites and obtained a permit for Illahun and Hawara. His excavations were rewarded by some of his most spectacular discoveries: he entered the brick pyramid of Hawara, excavated a remarkable necropolis of crocodiles, found a number of Graeco-Roman mummy portraits, and excavated a whole town of the Middle Kingdom, built for the builders of the pyramids. Extracts from his letters and journals reveal the excitement of his discoveries.

1–7 January 1888
Medinet el Fayum

I went into Medinet on Sunday, and saw Mr. Hewat, inspector of irrigation. He is most friendly, and willing to help in my work any way that is available. He wanted to stop and dine, but as I had a touch of fever on I declined, and am going in to see him next Sunday. He walked out with me as far as my tent, as it was time to close his office. ...

Monday no one came to work, as it was paying off day at Medinet for a lot of canal work. So I went over and prospected at Biahmu in the afternoon. ... Tuesday we got well to work, the number running up on following days to 25, 52, 72 and about 80, which is quite as many as I want. I am now discharging for laziness freely, there are so many applicants for work.

I got the people into tolerable order during this week; they all agree to take wages once a week now, and I have scared them by sundry sharp dismissals for lazyness, so that they work fairly well when they do not know they are being watched. The place is so covered with house ruins that one cannot get up under cover pretty close to any part of the work, so as to see what is going on.

The museum inspector here is a very civil lad, who does not look over 16 or 17, but, may be 22 or 3 perhaps. He has been about two or three times, and really does not get in the way or make himself troublesome. His professions are of course everything that is amiable and his practice fairly tallies, so far. The museum guards here are rather glum at not getting any pay for themselves or families anyhow out of the job, but remain civil; and a negro came buzzing about one day in grand new yellow slippers, to see if I wanted a reis. As work goes, Muhammed does all the main lot at the pylon; and I circulate and watch the outliers, and keep them pot boiling all round. M.'s little nephew, Omar, an infant who was never three miles from his village before, plays watchdog at the tent. He can run alone, and speak plain, after his fashion, but I cannot say much more. He has wits, however. I requested that he and his garments might be washed. Doubtless he has sometime or other fallen in the water, and his present shirt by its length cannot be the first he ever had. But on such matters I am obliged to rely on the indirect evidence of these presumptions.

22 December 1888
Hawara

My dear Griffith,

Thanks for your letters and notes on inscriptions. I am glad to hear of your taking a run over to Paris, but do not squatter away all your holiday over these Siut matters. Remember it does not much matter when you bring the inscrps out, as you have so much better material than anyone else has that no one can forestall you. So let them fill your leisure, but do not sacrifice holidays to anything that can be done in your evenings. Unluckily you cannot like *en Nabi*[1] go to Paradise and back in one night, nor even to the paradise of Americans – good ones.

I have at last got masons to work in the pyramid, but it is fearfully slow work; at this rate it will be 6 or 8 weeks before we

---

[1] i.e. the prophet Muhammed

are through the roof. I find from levelling that the water must be up to the top of the wall or nearly so. A pleasing prospect for reading inscriptions.

I got three large perfect Greek deeds of about 5th cent. A.D., over 100 feet run of writing in them, in brilliant state. They were rolled up, with splints of reed, and put in a big jar, in cloths.

I am clearing out one of the crocodile sepulchres. They were like the Apis tombs at Memphis but we are now 30 ft. down on the sloping floor and have not yet got as far along as the roof. The place has  never been opened, and I hope to find a croc. in all his glory, sarcophagus and all. The way down is over 6 and a half ft. wide.

At Tell Gurob we find little things, rings etc. of Khuenaten to Ramessu II; nothing beyond those limits; and only <u>one</u> building of houses, never rebuilt, or renewed. Excellent for dated objects therefore. Illahun pyramid waits till I go there; and when that will be I do not know, if these croc. sepulchres turn out good

I have always seen that the *reises* had no respect for Naville or his party; and strange to say they always seem to prefer the memory of my work, when they had less of their own way. I am now without any reis, Muhammad being over at Illahun always, and I get on quite well without him. I shall not engage any fresh reis if I should give him up, but be my own reis in future.

13–19 January 1889

About an hour before sunset the fellow from that rich amulet tomb (from which we have about 600 amulets already) came to me, radiant, saying he had some large figures. So off I went with him, taking my flannel nightgown to work in as usual, I think I mentioned that in a recess on the north of the large chamber I observed that at the back of it was masonry and not rock; and I thought it probable that there was something behind it. They had accordingly dislodged one large stone, and were in the act of moving another when they found some ushabti in a hollow cut in the stone. When I went in I found about a dozen of the very finest quality of large green ushabti of a man, Horuta, of exquisite work, the faces elaborated to show the dimples and muscles, and the details of the pick and hoe and basket all standing out in high relief; the material hard pottery merging into stone ware glazed throughout; long inscriptions beautifully incised all around, and the figures inches high and some more brilliant ones of 10 inches. They are just of the finest class I have ever seen. I thought at first that this dozen was all, as usually there are only two or three as fine as things in any interment; but they said there were yet more, so raising the stone further from the hole I felt in and looked, and could see rows of heads yet; I pulled some out, but could see that I could not get them all from such a position. So I set about shifting the large stone which lay over the recess, and having got it aside could get at the hollow. I then looked in and saw. ... row after row of these ushabti, all stacked in order with their faces inward toward whatever tomb may be inside (to the N.) slightly leaning back one on the other. By this time it was after sunset, and so I ordered down a lot of the people's baskets and *went on clearing...* Maurice[1] came down to see, and was astounded. The lucky fellow of the tomb, looked into the hole, and then dashed back and danced round and round in the water, snapping his fingers and yelling with delight. And I went on clearing. I stretched in and raked them out row after row, filling basket after basket. And I went on clearing. At last twelve baskets were filled by the time I stretched in to the end of the recess, and when I stacked them in my tent the tally was 203!!! I gave that most lucky party of four in that tomb the glorious baksheesh of £10; and though it may sound absurd to some folks, it must be remembered that I should say they are worth in London 10 times as much, or more even. I have never seen a finer class than these, and only two or three miraculous-looking specimens in Bulak exceed their quality. The glaze is rather browned on some of them where they were exposed to air and damp, but it is as bright a green as ever where they were covered with mortar. There was about five inches of sand in the recess, on which they stood. But these are only the advance guard of what is to come behind all that masonry. What amulets! What gorgeousness! may we look for. ...

Next morning, I gazed on the great stack of ushabtis in my tent, as a sort of solidified phantasy; they are about the biggest, the finest, and the greatest pile that I have ever seen of such.

3–16 February 1889

While the men with a long train of boys finished clearing out the pyramid passages, I was packing up and preparing to move; but the measuring of the pyramid took over two days. ...

At last we had a boat down the canal from here and moved all our things down the canal from here to this inspection house. This belongs to Mr Hewat's department, and is at his sole disposal, so we occupy it as our castle. It is looked after by two very respectable civil fellows who keep the register of the canal inflow here and are generally responsible. They will readily do anything we may want, and we have our little attendant ("the cherub") who keeps the house and washes up and is useful all round. ... At the back of the house is a wide stretch of water, and about 500 yards off across that is the village of Hawara Eglon. It is a lovely outlook, with palms and trees fringing

---

[1] Mrs Amos' son, aged 18, who came to help Petrie for a short time.

the water and sea beneath the grove of young palms which shade all the back of the house down to the water. Indeed it would be hard to invent anything pleasanter in position. So here we are well established for as long as we care to stop. As Mr Hewat only occasionally uses the place for a day, and as we can put him up more comfortably than if we were not here, there can be no hesitation in making the best use of the premises. I am digging tombs at Illahun, and clearing away at the pyramid. ... At Tell Gurob I have not begun more work yet, only just holding the place with two men. ... There is a large site of a tower out N. of the temple of the pyramid, but it seems to be all of XXX dy. and Ptolemaic times. ... A lot more mummy cases have been found, some with bead networks over the mummy. One case I found apparently almost crushed under fallen pieces of rock, but as on peeping in at a broken bit of the lid – I saw the inner carved case with a painted face in good state, we cleared it carefully. On getting the lid boards off the inner coffin was found to be much rotted, so I began to break away the lower part so as to remove the head and shoulders alone. I soon saw some beads shewing at the feet, so as I wished to note the pattern of the network for re-threading it I cleared it delicately. Next I found on the legs a band of hieroglyphs *executed in beadwork*, and then spied the corner of a pectoral showing. Now all these beads simply lay on the mummy, the pectoral being completely rotted, and it was utterly impossible to move them or the mummy without shifting them all and losing the pattern. I thought over it, and then laying some boards over the beadwork, and turning the men out of the tomb, I went off to the house for my petroleum stove and pot of beeswax. It was blowing a high cold wind full of sand which did not improve the walk to and fro. On returning I lit the stove down in the tomb, melted the wax, lifted and blew off the dust and stones which had fallen through on to the beads, and then with the wax almost chilled (so that it should not run in too deep down in the bandages) I laid it on by spoonfuls over the beads. So soon as it was firm, but yet just plastic, I lifted it gently, and all the beads came up on it in one sheet, every one perfectly in place fixed on the layer of wax; the under side shewed the pattern better even than the upper, and no wax had run through under the beads, owing to my using it only just melted. The result is as perfect as it could be. Thus I secured the band of hieroglyphs, the four genii, and a glorious pectoral of a scarab and wings all in bright beads, 14 inches wide and 5 high. This is probably the finest piece of beadwork known; certainly far larger than any in Brit. Mus. and above all I know now how to secure beads. Blessed be beeswax. ...

[date unknown]

At Illahun. ... another place that we are clearing is the cut rock base of a very large mastaba. The rock is dressed out to receive the stone about 6ft. high, but all the superstructure is gone, and only broken blocks remain of the masonry. This is doubtless of XII dynasty, and I must find the tomb well of it. One of the two men there nearly did for himself; he carelessly cut under a block until it fell and pinned him, jamming him tight and scraping his neck and leg. He lay helpless; and the other man, instead of loosening the stuff under him, and getting him out, ran off to the village (½hr. off) for men. About 30 men came, and then fearing he must be killed many ran away again, for fear they should be called as witnesses. Some wanted to break the stone up on the top of the man; at last, after two hours, the poor wretch was released. He looked rather shaky, and had his leg tied up, when I saw him two days later, but was beginning work again. I gave him a compassionate allowance of a shilling, for which I was heartily blessed, but protested that it was no affair of mine if he chose to squash himself.

1 March 1889
Illahun

My dear Griffith,

Thanks for your letter and remarks. No doubt you find delays in what you have to do, everyone does; and the people who get things <u>done</u> are those who draw the fine line between delays that are worth stopping for and delays that are not. The boldness of sacrificing a part for the benefit of the whole is a very necessary one. So far your delays have seemed worth while; but be ready to drop some point of perfection that may make much more delay.

Coffins continue to flow in. ... I much wish to settle the ages of these, and so I send you a few details for you to ruminate over.

[description of coffins, with hieroglyphic texts]

I do not give any particular of finds, because I hope that you will see the journals from Mrs. Amos. I think I have a town of XII dyn., as well as one of XVIII, now in my hands. ...

The Hawara book is all done and I send back proofs of print by this post.

16 April 1889
Medinet el Fayyum, Illahun

To Francis Griffith,

I cannot yet make up my mind about returning. You will see from the journals that I have a splendid prize in hand to work. Not only a town of the XIXth (which is done practically) but the workmen's town of Usertesen II, with ranks of chambers one after the other. ... And as this place pays in finds, as well as in its extreme historic value for dated small objects, I cannot say when I shall drop it. The alphabetic marks half developed from hieratic (?) are intensely interesting, and will utterly recast all our theories on the alphabet giving two stages of alphabets well dated, and in very different degree of development. The public won't care much as there is nothing pretty to show, but these marks will be the test for much brawling in the Greek world for the next few years I expect.

And there are papyri, of which here is a rough list [*list of seven, with comments on the hieratic*]. Now I rather imagine that these are more than all the XII dynasty papyri yet known; is there any of this age except the Prisse? The style of these hands is like that, and two lots were tied up and sealed with early scarabs, scrolls and sam-lotus patterns. I say nothing about these papyri in Egypt at present, and I hope to get them all to England in a lump with my Greek ones. Pieces of Plato and of tragedies seem trifles compared with these. I have unfolded them all without any damage by wrapping in a cloth, wetted and well wrung out, for a few hours.

We have had excellent weather this season on the whole; not over 6 or 8 hot days in all, and not one howling hot sandy day. The two sandy days, which were very pea-soupy, were both cool winds, with a breeze at 55° blowing through the rooms, to cool them down, I always open all the doors and windows when the wind is cool and so keep the place pleasant. The work is so far off now – about 3 miles – that I breakfast about 8.30, putting away all that has been found yesterday before that; and go off by 9 or so. Then measure up the early work 10–12.30, rest in a rock tomb for a couple of hours heat, and then go round again till we leave off. It is all metre work, and I do not want a reis in the least. Most of my men are old hands of last year, who come over here.

During the winter of 1889 work continued at Gurob, Kahun and Illahun and Petrie's findings are summarised in his journal for January 1890.

18–19 January 1890

Having now returned from my round in the Fayum, I will state the results. We started from Gharak (extreme S. of Fayum) going past Gurob, and up the desert; from the top of the ridge there is a splendid wide view about twenty miles each way. It seems certain that there never was any canal higher up than the present, and hence no greater extent of land can have been irrigated than what lies below that canal. After a smart shower we reached the inspection house of Gharak, a little E. of the village, just at the weir where the canal branches into the Gharak basin. Hewat has built a number of these houses about the country, looking like so many little Methodist chapels. They are divided into two rooms inside, with an outhouse for each wing. Their usual colour is a faded festive pink, which has one advantage that it is quite unmistakable.

The main object in coming here was to

see the ruins of *Talit* where the inscription of Ptolemais was found last year. The stone Hewat gave to me, and will come in this season's things. The puzzle about Ptolemais was that Ptolemy's Geography puts it in the south of the Fayum, but calls it a *port*. I had suggested that it might be so-called as the terminus of the ship canal, where goods were shipped. Here I found that the town lies just by the side of the end of the present canal, where it is divide into small irrigating streams The ancient canal must have been just on that line, as there is a sudden fall into the Gharak basin. The conditions all point to this being the end of the old navigable canal, and therefore exactly answering to the Ptolemais Hormos of the Geography. Moreover it was the most important town in the district and the centre of a great corn trade, as there are innumerable millstones of enormous size all over the town: this again shows it to have been a business emporium, and probably a place for shipping grain. About 1½ miles to the S.W., on a commanding hill in the desert, stood a Roman fort to secure the place from Arab raids; the nearest horizon from the fort being to the South, 5 or 6 miles. So far all this exactly, hangs together, and we may well consider Ptolemais as fixed by the Geography and the circumstances, as well as by the name being found here. I also found two or three other settlements all of Roman age.

After returning from Gharak, Mr. Hughes-Hughes[1] was not inclined to go to Tamieh, as he was waiting for business letters, so I went alone. I started north, and went first across the way and on up to a white heap on the top of the desert hills, due E. of Medum. Here I found the remains of a great mastaba of rough stone, about 25 ft. high yet standing. Some one (probably Maspero) has cut into the N. side of it, down to below the foundation, right into the middle, but without reaching any chamber. The stuff cut out is so piled up on the N. side, that it will be very troublesome to open it properly by clearing the ground around to search for the entrance. As it is up about 200 feet of rugged hills, it will be awkward to work there if I take it.

I am much struck at finding that the very tops of all these highest hills here are formed of gravel and washed stuff, shewing that they must have been overtopped originally by higher hills to the East which have been since entirely denuded away. At present the hills rise up to a sharp ridge, so sharp that one may sit with one leg dangling in the Fayum and the other in the Nile valley; and the slopes are so steep that a stone once loosened goes rolling away for a hundred feet or more below you. This is the natural effect of rain wash on a hill-ridge of gravel.

Hence I went down into Fayum again, and seeing a rather regularly built hut, among all the scattered Arab tents and booths which skirt the desert

---

1 W. O. Hughes-Hughes, a trainee; he did not accompany Petrie for long.

here, I proposed to camp by it. To my surprise the very outermost inhabitant of the Fayum proved to be a Scotchman, one Hugh Main. So here I pitched. He is a well educated man, quite a gentleman, and wears an Egyptian decoration, but here he lives in a mud hut without furniture, stores, bedding, or visible means of cooking, intent on reclaiming some 500 acres of land, and planting his potatoes, barley, peas, carrots, etc. with all his heart. He apologised for not taking me in, but I assured him that I had everything I wanted, and was quite independent. So our establishments were separate. Next morning I wanted to go up to see the cemetery whence the painted portraits were obtained, which went to Germany; but Mr. Main would not let me go alone, as there was a party of thieves somewhere in the desert it was believed, who had just been robbing and murdering at Beni Suef; he was also uneasy about the hyaenas, as he had seen a man attacked by one lately. So we went together, he with a breechloader and revolver and an Arab, and I with my revolver. We met one party who were rather suspicious, but who left us alone after some crossquestioning which we hardly saw the drift of. I went over the cemetery which seems nearly worked out, and which belonged to a very large Roman town here. It is astonishing how all this side of the Fayum the ground which has been cultivated is sprinkled with chips of pottery. I then bid goodbye to Mr. Main, and went off on my own resources, along the desert to the north, tracking two Roman towns and making a wide circuit round to Tamieh (N.E. corner of Fayum). Of course I kept a good lookout with the telescope on everyone that came within sight for miles around, so as not to be caught napping. At Tamieh I found the inspection house locked up, the guard having gone to Medineh that day; so I had to pitch tent again, my man and cherub having arrived there by the direct road while I went round the desert.

Next day I went off to see Kom Wezim, a great town N.W. of Temieh in the desert. It was an important trade centre, as I saw four huge stone weights in different places about it. One perfect one I measured, and make it out 473 lbs; it is marked W on the side. Here two men came about, but were less obtrusive when they saw my revolver; I edged round so that should never get behind me, and after many questionings they made off. I then went further west but did not see any sign of another town I had heard of in that direction, so decided on going a long way to the east to pick up some tombs which I had seen the day before in the distance. I saw a large hyaena, which seemed more afraid of me than I was of it, and tried to lie down so as to sham a shadow of a rock; but seeing I watched it made off a little. The desert is here most curiously covered with domes of limestone produced by the weathering of  the rock.

I kept a good look out but saw nothing suspicious except a man who rode up just to look over a hill in the distance and then retreated again. I next found another large Roman town, and beyond that the tombs which I sought. They proved to be very rough chambers in the rock face, but had contained some mummied bodies. This was a long round of 25 miles almost all in the desert.

Next day, we came back from Tamieh to Lahun; a heavy shower in the morning made the ground so slippery that we could hardly get along, and a misdirection led us into a mesh of canals. Furious sandstorms and a tearing cold wind followed, and I was very glad to get in, a little after sunset. Altogether I have done over 40 miles in the past eight days, including one day's rest. ...

The previous July (1889) Petrie had been approached by the committee of the Palestine Exploration Fund to spend a few weeks at the end of his season in Egypt excavating a site in the Holy Land. He had agreed to do this and in April 1890, having been briefed by the authorities in Jerusalem, he walked extensively about the hill country of Judaea choosing a suitable site; he decided to tackle the huge mound of Tell el Hesy, which he tentatively identified with the ancient city of Lachish.

27 May – 1 June 1890
Tell el Hesy, Palestine

... A grand riddance has been the harvesting here, leaving the ground clear to get about. Hitherto I have had to go about 5 times the direct distance round the crops to get at the work, up and down hill too. I tried buying the crop on the tell and the path to it, by offering fully the value of the grain when reaped and threshed, five weeks before it was got in, and the fool of an Arab thought to get more and would not take it. Then about a week before the harvest he came round to my terms, but too late, for I did not then want the ground or path, and I had bought fodder all the time for the donkey and did not want the crop for feeding. He was paid out for his troublesomeness, for the Arabs who come constantly to stare at the work trampled his crops mercilessly. He comes for eye- lotion in the meekest way now; and he has learned some lessons by this time; among others, that what is said will be done; and instead of futile rows, such as we daily had at first, he is now quite content with my assurance that I will level the crop ground again before I leave. So soon as the reapers were over the ground, within a few hours I had the men sinking pits all about the crop land to test the depth of the earth. I find that the ground close to the tell is just like that all over the enclosure: only a few feet of man-made soil with Amorite pottery, and a little later stuff, and then native clay. This town had no suburb, but was strictly limited to its walls.

A question of manners. Query, when a man greets you in a narrow path by drawing his sword, flourishing it about, and seizing you by the arm, what should you do? I had no precedents, and tickled him under the chin; a light, and sufficiently deprecatory way of meeting such advances, as I presume. ...

2 June 1890
Tell el Hesy

> To Miss Kate Bradbury,
> Riverevale, Ashton-under-Lyne.

Dear Miss Bradbury,[1]
Though I have not written to you this season yet, [about] our business it has not been at all "out of sight out of mind". For, truth to tell, I never pass a day without preparing breakfast; and I seldom do that without making tea, and I never make tea but in large quantities; and an ocean of tea always brings to my mind the propensities of Miss K.B. of Riverevale. So you will see the train of cause and effect, "the connection of which with the plot one sees" as Calverley puts it. Now the making of tea in "my establishment-" is on this wise. I am the blessed possessor of an enamelled iron pot, of this most business-like shape holding 2 or 3 quarts. I cast half a handful of tea into a saucepan and pour a quart of boiling water on it; after a few minutes I decant it into my pot, and float in it a pail of cold water to cool. Then, at intervals, do you suppose I fiddle about with cups? No, no, not so, I raise that pot to my lips and with that brown sea before my eyes, I drink, and drink, and drink. How trumpery any number of cups seems – even Johnson's four and twenty – compared with the satisfaction of taking a pull out of a quart right away. The most refreshing drinks I ever have are when sometimes I deliberately, and unutterably thirsty, sit down, take a bucket in my hands, plant my elbows on my knees, and then – gazing into the depths of clear water before me – gradually absorb it. Appearances count for a great deal in this life, and I can hardly believe that a little thirsty Cairene can enjoy a suck out of the brass mouthpieces at street corners without seeing any refreshment, unless he has the power of imagination enough to realize the whole waterworks reservoir as supplying it.
    And so you are already inquiring for more laundry work. There is plenty for you; thirteen boxes, entirely packed with cloths around the pottery; and coffins, etc., so there is quite as much as last year's, if not more. These are all woollen, and many nearly or quite perfect garments in good state. There are some good pieces of colours among them: saints, flowers, and bags worked in patches of colour all over. There are however two conditions I have to make: that you will present a true and complete account of your expenses, and that

---

[1] Miss Bradbury was a friend and companion to Amelia Edwards; she had been busy cleaning and mounting textiles found by Petrie.

you will utilise at least a third of them for presents to your friends in America and elsewhere. I hope to be in England by the end of this month, and to get all my boxes turned out by the end of July. So you will probably see the stuffs about the middle of July, if you really are so charitable as to take another batch in hand.

I was very sorry to hear of Mr. Bradbury's relapse of influenza; I too capped my third bout of it with a dinner party, out in the open night, and had a bad chest in consequence. It is a most pernicious complaint.

You have had a fearful worry with our poor Amelia's arm;[1] it was a terrible misfortune altogether, and you will have found that it is no light matter to act as philosophogogue to a lecturing Ph.D.

I have constant illustrations of Ps. lxxxviii,13 before me at this season: the thistles dry up, break off short, and the whole round bunches go bowling around the country for miles before the wind; a curious way of distributing seeds for the plant itself to perambulate. It is strange to hear also Ps. lxix.25 as the commonest swear in the country, every hour of the day, "*Iharab beitu*" "May his house be ruined"; it is applied to flies, to potsherds, to people, to stray stones, and anything and everything which is disagreeable, even a father to his daughter, as readily as an Egyptian father will affectionately call his son "the son of a dog" as an endearment! Truly the misuses of language are a strange study.

And now I expect that I shall probably not have an opportunity of posting this until the mail which brings me to England.

Yes, I can.

Yours very sincerely,

W. M. Flinders Petrie

In June, after a few weeks of excavation in which he meticulously recorded the pottery of each level of occupation on the mound (establishing his reputation as the father of Palestinian archaeology), he decided to pack up and return home, on the way exploring the hill country of Judaea for other possible sites.

June 1890

I am reckoning on one of my village guards with the baggage to Jaffa, and taking the other with me as a companion, leaving my man to go with my camel man. But all my plans dissolved mercilessly. First one guard, and then the other, said they must go off to harvesting. Then the Arab guard did not stay by day, and when my man went off (as he was fond of doing) I was left entirely alone to look after three tents some way apart, and to do my packing. Not a man could I get out of all my workers to come and fill in the holes in the crop land, everybody went to harvest. Then the difficulty came to get

---

[1] Miss Bradbury had accompanied Amelia Edwards on a lecture tour of the United States where she had fallen and broken her arm.

anyone responsible to send with the baggage to Jaffa. At last I agreed to send 30 miles to Jimzu for the first camel I had. But no one would go; so I had to send one of my Arab guards. When the camel man came he was alone, for no one would come with the second camel. So he had to be sent with the baggage to Jaffa, in which was a large sum in gold, surplus funds, which I thought that the best way to get back safely; I put it in the bottom of a tin box full of photographic plates, the weight of which would prevent thieves suspecting anything below them, and of course no-one had a notion about it. Then my Arab guards refused to go with me to the next village eastwards – Dawaimeh – as they had a feud there and dare not shew themselves. So I had to give up my zig-zag exploring, and stick by the camel with my man Muh[ammad] only. In fact not a single one of the villagers or of the Arabs could I get to go a mile with me, one because of harvest, the others because of their squabbles. And they do squabble. The other day I saw dozens of shekhs all riding past to go and see the Pasha at Gaza. They fell out by the way, and at a village – Beit Hanum – two were killed.

We slowly wound our way up from 300 to 900 feet into the hills; ... On the way I was astonished at the hills being covered with an emerald crop of young durra (maize) which grows here without any rain in dryish ground. The Dawaimah folk are a decent lot, but their water supply is tea ready made; when poured out in a thin stream from a bottle it is dark brown, strong tea colour. The guards were most troublesome however about talking at night, they had talked all their lives, and the pernicious habit clung to them I only got stray dozes, until about 3 in despair I rolled up some blankets and walked off down the valley, and found a cave where I settled; there was a hole at the end suggestive of jackals or wolves, but I got some sleep there. I was not astir until the sun was high, and so lost my time for looking over the ruins about there. I went to Mejdeleh again, and looked at the tombs there. After some time we reached Deir el Asl, and a huge well Bir el Asl, now all but dry. I went up the hill to look about it, but – as might be expected from the name – it is all Roman. Muhd and the guide stayed by the well, and some of the men harvesting from Dure were inquisitive as to my baggage. We went on up the hill a rugged trace of a path, where the camel and donkey could hardly get footing. At the top the guide said he would go no further, as he had objected at first to going all the way, and Muhd tried to persuade him to come on, yet strange to say he did not clamour for his pay. We went a little further on the top of the hills, the camel straggling on in advance, I next, and Muhd riding the donkey behind. Suddenly I saw a man, with his face tied across up to the eyes, pass from one bush to another over the road, and I guessed mischief. Then two, three, and at last four shewed themselves, all with faces tied across. They seized the camel and threatened to fire, I also threatened, being about 30 yards behind, and two of them tried to close behind me, but I backed up a slope to one side, revolver in hand. I then reckoned that there was nothing worth much on the camel, but as I had 8 or 10 pounds in my pocket, I had better get rid of it. Meanwhile Muh-d had run back to fetch up the guide (whom he found quietly sitting down) and it was no use for me to tackle four, as there was a pistol and four swords among them, and stones all about handy and continually doing duty. So I backed away toward cover, and when Muhd and the guide appeared they and the camel load completely occupied the four men, and I dropped my purse and bag of change into two bushes; leaving by accident, rather fortunately, a roll of ¼ mejidis in my pocket, about 8d or 10d worth. I knew that we could not lose anything much, and there was nothing worth the risk of bloodshed on either side.

The men were fellahin and not Arabs, and not at all bent on stripping us but only on some small loot. They did not attempt to search all the baggage, but grabbed out a new suit and a couple of flannel shirts from my portmanteau, and got hold of a waist coat of Muh-d which had about 30/- of his, and unluckily about 50/- which the camel man had entrusted to him for safety, and which I did not know of. My revolver was the main attraction, and all four made a rush for me; as the money was safe I took it quietly, and let them know that it was quite needless to grab me by the throat. They were immensely disgusted that I had hardly any money, (the ¼ mejidis were enough for a show) and they turned my pockets inside out, felt me all over, and searched for a money belt but in vain. The elder man particularly returned to me my note-book, measure and handkerchief.

Altogether I think the business was conducted quite as pleasantly as such affairs ever are. They then made off down the road we had come, to Deir al Ash. I had some difficulty in making Muhammad collect his mind to the needful business of roping up the camel again, tying the cut ropes etc. I sat down to make notes of what was gone, by where my money lay, so that if the robbers were watching to see if I picked up anything they should not detect it. Then I pocketed it, and we went on. I had forgotten to take off my watch, and one of the robbers was much disposed to have it, but I immediately reminded him that it was numbered, and that decided them to leave it. The whole affair was much of a scuffle and there was not time to be too precise in one's arrangements. Happily all my notebooks and papers are safe. We soon found our guide man gone on ahead. What share had he in it? He could not have conspired at Dawaimeh as he was only picked up suddenly at Muh-d's choice at the last moment. He cannot have conspired at Deir el Ash, as he was with Muh-d all the time. But I think he saw the men go off before us at Deir el Ash, and suspected mischief, and hence his reluctance to go on. That he went on afterwards with us all the way, looks on the one hand as if he was not really anxious to return, on the other hand as if he had no thought of being charged with complicity. On the whole I should not accuse him. The thieves were almost certainly not from Dawaimeh, as I had there said to everyone that I was going by a different road to that which the guide took.

We reached Dhaheriyah about an hour before sunset, owing to delays, and pitched it an high N. wind. The cold wind after being heated in the valleys gave me a sore throat. Really the result of the robber's grip, as I had it for weeks after. I wrote a full account and inventory of stolen goods to the acting consul W. H. Khayat, a Syrian, at Jerusalem, Mr. Moore being gone to England.

Since visiting the site with Frank Griffith in 1864, Petrie had always wanted to excavate at Tell el Amarna, the site of the ancient Akhenaten, where important discoveries had already been made. In 1890, with a team of men drawn from his workforce in the Fayum, he had excavated the pyramid and tombs of Meydum; now he intended to take the best of his team with him to Amarna, on the east bank of the Nile.

13–21 November 1891

Having determined to leave Cairo and trust to my contract following, I went first to the Fayum, left baggage at station, left money in care of my friend the Coptic postmaster and after lunch at the Greek inn, I walked over the 13 miles to Illahun. There I went to my old quarters and soon had dozens of my old hands around me, some twenty or thirty were in the room most of the evening. I explained my movements, and had plenty of volunteers to go. Some of the best men were occupied, as I expected; but I easily got four men and boy who were with me to the last in the Medum work, and all of whom I thoroughly like. I was astonished at the eagerness shown. One man who had an easy post as guard at 30/- a month was longing to desert his work and come for £1 to £2 a month according to the hardness of his work. So on the average he would be harder worked, and away from home for months, and yet it was only his brothers' dissuasion which kept him from deserting his business. Another lad who was rampant to come would hardly let go of my hand, was only lately married; his bride declared she would go home to her father if he left and so *his* father insisted on him staying, to avoid such a family scandal.

Having at last settled my men I told them that I should give 1 piastre a day more than each before, raising 3p. to 4 for men and 2p. to 3 for boy, in consideration of their having to buy all their food instead of having to fetch it from home, for I thought this only fair to them; the whole extra is only 1s. a day. I then walked back next day to Medinet, the men going direct to Wasta on foot. I trained to Wasta and joined them; went to Hewat's house but he was still away. So I slept in the store room, and next morn packed up what I had left there and moved it into the station, a couple of miles; and thence took train with my 5 Lahunis up to Derut. ... I went to the Greek locanda, which is far below the Fayum one in accommodation, but good enough for me. ... Next morning we had the heavy matter of moving down all my baggage to the canal, which proved to be about ½ mile from the station. My five Lahunis behaved excellently: the lot of 18cwt. was just as much as they could physically manage, the lads staggering along with rigid faces under the heavy boxes. But they never flinched once, nor hinted at having any extra help I encouraged them up to it, and then gave a judicious dole of 1/- after it was over, to buy some little native luxuries after their kind. I have one fellow of about 25, tall, one-eyed and split-nosed, a worthy fellow who has distinguished himself by never once grumbling at his work, though it was some of the hardest at Meydum. I value Muhd. Mansur in spite of appearance. Then there is Musid, a cheerful affectionate lad about 17, who has I think been drilled out of a little laziness he had. Ali Suefi is one of the meekest, most conscientiously obliging lads I ever knew; he was not thought smart enough by Hewat, to whom I recommended him; but he kept him as long as there was work for him. I was very glad to get him again, as he is the most devoted fellow. A strapping lad of about 20 is Abdallah, who has the advantage of reading and writing (as Misid also a little); and he has a good sturdy way of doing his business. With him is Hussain, his brother about 14; a most winning, lively little fellow, full of jokes and fun, whose laugh alone is worth his 7½d. a day. Such are my special five, whom I thought worth bringing all the way with me; more willing or kindly fellows no man could find. ...

Having all my baggage on the boat and my shopping done, we left Derut and tacked downstream against the north wind to Haji Kande. We reached it about 1 hour before sunset. I ran off ashore to look for a good place to settle in, while the men unloaded the boat. Various natives followed with many suggestions, to all of which I listened. Of course there was the usual wish to stick one in the middle of the village and the usual desire to ordain all one's business. But I found an excellent place just where I wanted it, N.E. of the village, so that the strong S.W. storms would be broken, and not swamp one with dust. A long straight boundary wall running N. and S. with clear open desert and ruins outside of it was just the place. Of course nearly everybody wanted me to do something different; but I found a curiously effective way of settling objections, by taking one aside and in a very slow and low voice imperatively stating that I must do as I intended because of so and so. They are so accustomed to loudness and declamation that the strangeness of it reduces them amazingly. I had the satisfaction after all the to and fro of hearing that "all his words are good"; which was more than might be expected as I had done exactly as I thought best without heeding anyone.

In the hour we had I got up everything, with a couple of natives to help (for which they never claimed anything, so I shall give them a trifle some day) and by dark I had pitched my tent and made a hut of boxes and boards for the men, and got everything in under cover.

Next morning I was rather spoilt, for what with dogs and guards I had very little sleep. I sent a polite message to the owner of the worst dog close by, giving a triple choice: either tie up the beast in the house all night to quiet him, or produce his carcass, for which I would give 2/-, or let him go on in which case I should shoot him next night. There were stifled howls and smothered barks next evening; and the beast was successfully repressed. ...

My men went into the mud business with a zest, Misid stamped about in a huge pudding of mud and sand mortar, little Hussein plastered with glee and the others brought up basins of mud and handed me bricks. By night I had built a large room 8 × 11½ feet inside, and 7½ high, built against our big wall. This roofed with boards laid and covered with maize stalks to keep the sun off will be a good habitation for me; then I am putting a similar room next to it for storage and visitors, and a rather lesser room for my men beyond. Thus I shall be well set up for staying on into the heat of the spring. ... Having established myself I sent to the post and was glad to find my contract come. I then set my Lahunis and the guards here to begin a bit of house digging while I walked over the place, and entered on my heritage.

It is an overwhelming site to deal with. Imagine setting about the ruins of Brighton, for that is about the size of the town: and then you can realise how one man must feel with such a huge lump of work. After a few hours I concluded that I should not attempt to make a continuous plan of the whole place. ... This place would need a lifetime of work to exhaust it properly. ... I went all over the place with a copy of Lepsius' plan, identifying the buildings and examining them. The palace of Khuenaten I have fixed for certain I think. ... to thoroughly exhaust this site will probably cost £200 or £300; but it is the most promising place for (1) pieces of the finest carving and glazed work of that age (2) valuable things hidden or lost (3) any historical objects such as papyri or clay tablets. ... I am delighted to see some Mykenae pottery turn up here; as the history of this place is so brief (under 50 years) we shall have things well dated. ...

6–13 December 1891

My repose here is not yet assured. I got the two dogs tied up at night who barked close by; but then others came from the other side of the village to make up for the silence. They kept me awake about three hours one night, so I made the best of the matter, and announced next morning that not having slept at night I must do so during the day and hence there would be no work that day: and I slept most of the day up in the quiet of the ruins to make up for it. Now the forty people whose pockets were thus affected by this "lockout" were all indignant with the dogs and next night dogs were chased and hunted away diligently, and if a stray dog is found about in the evening he is ignominiously taken to his owner to be tied up. I have also drilled the guards into not talking loud enough to be heard round the corner, and my own 5 men who sleep next to me never make a sound, so on the whole I have secured amazing quiet for the side of a village camping ground. ...

The shekh here is troublesome. He told his people to secrete anything valuable and bring it to him, and he would pay them better than I do. This was so outrageous that as soon as I heard it I wrote a letter to Corbett on the matter, and sent it by a man who went for some bread next morning. The shekh, suspecting it concerned him, followed and took my letter and destroyed it; and the messenger returned saying that he had lost the letter in the river. In the middle of all this, the shekh comes in his pushing way and demands why I am so annoyed with him! So I told him plainly. And when he heard that I knew the end of the letter and would write again, he came very differently begging interminably that I would not write (assuming all the time that the said letter was about him and not to his credit at all, which proved the case completely); but I told him that I had many friends and should write to whoever I chose. Next morning I sent by one of my own men a letter to Corbett, adding the fate of the last; and asking him to get some official to write a little note of instructions to the Shekh for his soul's health. He is a fellow of unlimited effrontery and requires to be firmly taken down. I have told them that if I have anything going wrong in the work here I shall dismiss everyone and go and live at the other village and employ their rivals. ...

There is plenty to do here with eyewater etc. and one of my men bruised both his hands, and so produced those horrid gatherings in the flesh which belong to this land. I had one once in my thumb. They come without any breaking of the skin and last for a week or so, discharging and very sore. I had brought his over quickly by syringing out the place, a day after it is opened, with bichloride mercury.

13–19 December 1891
At last a young English engineer came over from Major Brown to see about the pavement. The instructions from Cairo were to take temporary measures for its preservation till Grebaut[1] acted. But, very sensibly, he said that as it

---

[1] Director-general of the Antiquities Service.

was not a large affair it was best to do it at once, rather than let it spin out. So he agreed to put up the room over it and settled the details with me and then gave orders and a plan to a native engineer, who is to see to doing it. I am to give an eye to it and to do the final clearing out of the place and try fixing the colours by sprinkling with very thin tapioca water, as I expect I must experiment on bits of it to begin with. ...[1]

The engineer is here, the house over the pavement is begun, with 50 or 60 boys and men ravaging all over the place to get stone and brick from the ruins. I have my own way with them, but have to keep a constant look out to avoid mischief. We found an ancient well in the palace, close by where the water is wanted for building, so they cleared it and use it now.

I hear from Corbett that Johnson Pasha will send my shekh a good wigging and teach him manners. ...

I began clearing some chambers on the side of the road opposite to the palace, which I thought were only storerooms. But I found all the dadoes finely painted with lotus groups, and above that in one room the bottom of a scene remaining, of Khuenaten and the queen seated on low stools face to face, on a richly embroidered carpet and attendants between them; only the feet and knees of the large figures and the lower half of the others remain; but by the queen's side, in the foreground, is an exquisite group of two of the infant princesses one half reclining, the other seated squatting, on rich cushions, one talking and holding the chin of the other: they are about 6 inches high, painted so closely like good Indian miniatures that I was startled. The condition is perfect, except a crack and a bruise, the colour quite fresh. This is *not to be published*. To preserve such a treasure was the question. After measuring, examining the condition and thickness of the plaster and searching for cracks and weak places, I determined how much I could safely remove in one piece. All the usual methods of pasting over the face etc. are quite out of question with this delicate distemper colouring. I very gingerly took away the wall from the back of the plaster, having first cut nearly through where I intended to part the face. Brick by brick I loosened the wall, taking the greatest care not to punch the plaster off in shifting each brick, as corners tend to push forward in turning it. At last, the sheet of mud plaster was left standing on edge in the air scarcely holding to anything: a box lid of larger size was then set against the face, sheets of paper dropped in between and then firmly clasping together the plaster with one hand and the lid with the other, I lifted the painting clean away on the lid, a matter requiring much care

---

[1] One of Petrie's first discoveries at Amarna was a large hall with a pavement painted with naturalistic scenes of calves gambolling in a garden. About twenty years later the pavement was destroyed by a villager, since visitors from Nile steamers had to pass through his field in order to see it.

as the slab of mud is heavy as well as delicate. Lashed down in the lid with tight string and pads of paper, it travelled safely on a man's head to my hut. And now I have it on my conscience to decide what I can do with it. Any wet backing is very risky, for fear of bringing away the paint by damp. Wax backing would be good, but it must be melted in some way, and might run through to the face and spoil it all; and in contracting by cooling the waxed back might tear off the uncoated face. On the whole I see nothing better than a gridiron of wooden slats; the back to be scraped down that this may lie as close as may be and then bed it on with as thin a layer of mud as may be. With a protective edging, and lashing over to keep the plaster tight against the back in travelling, I hope this may do. To deal with a cake of mud, much pierced by white ants, 30×16 inches and not 1 inch thick, and to prevent any chance of its breaking up and yet not to be able to use any fluid backing – wet or melted – is a troublesome matter. Any trouble is worth while for what is the finest Egyptian painting that I have yet seen. ...

The fresco is safely transferred to the wooden grids and bedded in fresh mud plaster to support the back. It seems none the worse for the transfer, and the little princesses are intact. I long to see them safe in South Kensington.[1]

Many visitors stopped to see the pavement on their journey up the Nile by boat.

I was surprised at the general delight and interest taken in the pavement, and the gratitude for attention and explanation that I could give.

Dr Anderson the zoologist has been staying here with me for a couple of days to overhaul the collections of reptiles that I have been making for him. He is working up the subject for the Brit. Mus.: a very pleasant and clever Scotsman with wide knowledge, having travelled much in the East and head of Calcutta museum for years. He, and all the dahabiya parties with whom we dined different nights, have left me a shoal of invitations to look them up in London. If *I have time*, well and good.

6–12 March 1892

There is little to describe this week, for we have had a "lock-out". Someone stole my two hammers, which were lying in my hut and so to emphasize the fact and perhaps get them back, I stopped all the work. Evidently none of my workmen were implicated, so I kept them out of work for three days (besides a Sunday between) without their being able to find the hammers. However the loss of work will make them all careful about things disappearing.

---

[1] Brought safely home, it is now one of the treasures of the Ashmolean Museum in Oxford.

I went with Carter[1] for another long desert walk, working up one valley and down another. Those valleys are cut out of the whole depth of 300ft. or so at the mouths, and gradually shallow up in the 6 or 8 miles length, with a few falls, towards the upper parts, until one comes out in a slight hollow in the top plateau of the desert. Once on the height one sees around for many miles, over a nearly level ground cut up by valleys, and with distant hills and points sticking up 5 to 10 miles distant. Probably no European has walked in and out of these valleys before, but I am planning them all and shall have a fair outline of this region. The valleys are very hard walking, in the lower parts deep sand on rough stones, in the upper frequently masses of boulders. To *pace* over such ground seems at first hopeless for getting any distances. But I am surprised to find how close the results come out by different lines, checking one another. There does not seem to be more than 1 error in the positions, after long distances of many miles pacing and compass bearings, though one way is up a valley, and the other down. ...

26 March 1892

The excavations are now mainly closed for Ramadan, though several of the men prefer to eat and work in spite of the customary feast. The main interest of the last few weeks has been the wide-spread patch of pottery and rubbish on the desert. This has provided a large quantity of fine Greek fragments and I have over 100 distinctive pieces of form or pattern, beside many times more of plain lined fragments. This collection will be invaluable for future reference and I have copied most of the good pieces in colour, to guard against loss or detention at Ghizeh. ...

My days are occupied largely with putting in the wooden gangways for visitors in the pavement house. The work cannot possibly be trusted to Arab carpenters, so I have to do it all myself. I have been five days and expect to be many more at it. I shall then have some weeks' work to do in coping before I leave; and there is all the packing to do as well.

28 March – 3 April 1892

The waste-heaps which I am clearing almost certainly were the rubbish ground of the palace. They contain so much brilliant stuff, Aegean pottery and things with royal names. I have now about a hundred pieces of Aegean ware with distinctive patterns, besides mere circles and many pounds weight of other pieces. As these are so very important for dating Greek pottery in various other places in Greece, Palestine and Italy, I have made sketches of

---

[1] Howard Carter, new to Egypt that winter, had been sent to Petrie by Mr Amherst, his patron, to learn something about archaeological method.

all the patterned pieces so as to secure them against entire loss. These drawings can go to the Athens school, when the originals are safe in Brit. Mus.

11–16 April 1892

The rubbish heaps of the palace are now finished; and the houses which I was working proving fruitless, no more will be done to them. So beyond a few trifles outstanding no more excavating will now be done.

I have been all the week copying the pavement on $1/10$ in outline; and though I have gone on as quickly as I could with accuracy, I find that barely a third of the large room is done in five days. At least 8 days more is needed for that, beside the coloured full-size copy of parts of it. ... Meanwhile Ali is busy all day plastering up the broken edges of the floor and with some supervision has done it very fairly, so that I need not give my time to that affair. ...

I found two roads running up the east cliffs and joining on the top into a rod going due east into the desert. This looks much as if it led to Khuenaten's alabaster quarry and I must examine it. Also a straight road which runs to the north cliff leads up a path there, across the top and down another road to a limestone quarry.

Two days later Carter and I went off to track the road. I soon saw that it could never have been used for moving stones, as it often runs over steep slants from side to side. We went tracking it, getting fainter and slighter until in place of regular lines of stones there were only two or three blocks far apart as marks. At last after crossing many valleys it failed altogether and we returned having done 27 miles in all. As there are several patrol roads here I think this must be done, to enable guards to go along the eastern desert and look into the various valleys without any fear of losing themselves. Carter found a nest of the great vulture (which spreads 9 feet across) in a little thorn bush out 10 miles in the desert. The bird flew up and C. secured an egg of monstrous size.

1893–1897
Edwards Professor of Egyptology

While Flinders Petrie was at Tell el Amarna, news came of the death of Miss Amelia Edwards, his friend and patron. By the terms of her will, she left a sum sufficient to found a Chair of Egyptology in University College London. She had let it be known that she wished Petrie to be the first Edwards Professor. Duly appointed, Petrie planned a syllabus for his students: he would lecture to them during the first term, go to Egypt for a winter's digging, and return to the College in late spring in time for the summer term. During his absence Frank Griffith would hold classes in hieroglyphics. Petrie proposed to take with him a student assistant whom he would train in the techniques of excavation; for this purpose he appealed for funds. The Egyptian Research Account set up as a result was to provide him with an assistant in the field for many years to come. The first recipient of this studentship was James Quibell, a recent graduate from Oxford. Together the two men went out to Egypt in the autumn of 1893. After a few days in Cairo Quibell was sent to the Fayum to pick up Petrie's best workmen, including Ali es Suefi, collect the stores Petrie had left at Hagg Qandil, and join him at Coptos or Quft (Qift) a town some 25 kilometres north of Luxor, a promising site which had already been probed by Maspero. Below the ruins of the temple there they found sculptures of an older building and some archaic sculptures, including two huge figures of the fertility god Min which are now housed in the Ashmolean Museum, Oxford. They were joined in January by Bernard Grenfell, a young papyrologist; for him too this was an introduction to archaeology.

Setting up camp, Coptos

I had enquired in Cairo and was assured that Cook's agent at Girgeh would stop the post boat for us at Koft. He however said he could not possibly do it without orders. So I telegraphed, and got his orders. We had the post boat run up along side, and got off with all our baggage at Koft about 3p.m. But so long were the delays about camels that the party and baggage did not come up the two miles to the village till dark. I had gone on in advance, and selected ground to settle on: and when we got the camels up we stuck candles all over the place and unpacked by candlelight. I have pitched by a piece of the old city wall which is nearly 30ft high and on the north of it so that no sun can come on any part of our huts till late in the spring. There is also a good corner by a projection bastion, so that no-one can approach us on two sides anyhow. It has taken 3 or 4 days to clear the ground, put up huts and arrange matters, and we now have as good a place as we could possibly get, well open to north entirely shaded, with open court in front to store stones, and with men's room isolated a little in front so that we do not hear them. My old lads and boys have done very well all through, and the cook will succeed – perhaps – probably – we may hope. We are closely watched all day long by an old Coptic dealer and his son, whom we must explode on by the time we find who *they* push forward for work, so as to find out their men. I have made out a preliminary plan of the town and shall begin on the temple at once.

8–22 December 1893

We have had much trouble from dealers and loafers and spies about in our work; as a public road runs through the temple site, we cannot keep people out entirely, and there are frequent rows. At first a Copt dealer and his son (the "old beast" and the "little beast") were constant watchers, but we huffled them out of the way. Then dealers came riding in and prying about. One who had been poking his nose into half the holes produced to me a hideous forgery with an air of conferring a favour, when I went up to him and asked him what he was about. I shied the stone into a pit. He produced a figure and I did the same with that and told him to clear out at once, which he did without a word. He then consulted with his man, and went to go round the mounds to get his beloved forgeries. But I baffled him; and after a long talk with some people he sent in a man to try and get at the forgeries; but I fended him off, so that he dare not come in. So they went off; but plucked up courage to come in soon after and demand the property. I refused. "But he paid money for them" said the man. "That's a lie like the stones" said I. "He really did." "Then he is a fool." "But he must have them." "What business had he here." "Oh! he lost his way from the road."!!!. Considering that the road is very clear, and he was riding all over my work up and down, I replied that that was another lie like the stones: and finally they had to go. Next day the "little beast" here had got the forged tablet (evidently not knowing its source) and brought it up to try and sell it to me. So I have confiscated it a second time.

Both Q[uibell] and I have had regular tussles with men who would not move off; quickly seconded by our own men, who mauled the loafers considerably each time. Altogether we have educated the spy party into fleeing at once whenever they see us coming in the distance; and the old beast and little beast dare not shew face in the region of excavations.

I went up to Luxor for a day, and happily found Wallis[1] going up on the boat. So we went together over the dealers. I got several nice things... *[list of purchases]*. ...

The boat to return only gets to Koos (variously spelt Gus, Qous, Kous, Gous, Goos, Gouss etc. etc.) by 8½ p.m. and no donkey man will come over so late. So I slept on board, and settled to get off at Ballas next morning as that is four miles (but not on the west bank) whereas the station of Kous is 9 miles from here. So in pitch dark at 5½ a.m. I was shuffled into a boat off the steamer. As there is no landing stage there, a sailor carried me on shore and deposited me on the dry land. But no officials, postmen or guards could be found, so the letters for Ballas (which were all unpaid) could not be left, but were taken back to the steamer. I wandered up in the dark, but could not find any living thing for some time. At last I saw a flame, and went over to some fellahin, sitting over a few thorn sticks blazing on the ground and guarding their durra[2] harvest. I sat with them till it was light enough to see to walk about and then walked up and down to keep warm. After more than an hour I found an old boat, with planks being repaired and in the hulk was a man with half an eye and a minute boy. These were the deputies of the guard of the post, and had twenty letters waiting to go off. But as the sailors had landed me ¼ mile from the right place their shouting had not woken him. Such is the post in Egypt. I got over by the ferry at last and up to my quarters by 8 a.m.

After spending some hours in turning over the Triad on its back and raising it about a foot by rocking up, we sent for some boatmen to see about moving it out. They came and broke some ropes over it; then got chains on and drew it about 3 or 4 ft. up the slope. Then we had a palaver over terms, and they accepted my offer of £2 to get it out of the work about 100 feet away, with 6/- a day extra if it takes over 2 days. It will need 20 men, so it will not pay them to delay at this rate. So I hope to see it moving off and leaving our work clear to proceed, as it is very much in the way at present. (Rather zigzag writing as I am lying in bed resting on my elbow).

The boatmen came up in force and succeeded in getting the Triad up the slope out of the hole and dragging it out of the Temple area. It was then left by the roadside, ready to go on to the river. ... The Egyptian boy delights in an insult, whenever he can indulge in it *quite* safely. We had not left the Triad half an hour before a boy had carefully spit into the eyes of each of the figures!

Next a great granite headdress of a colossus of Ramessu was found, near

---

[1] Henry Wallis, the artist.
[2] Maize.

the Triad. I hope we shall not find the statue, for it would weigh 10 tons or so.

Then Mr Wallis came over for a couple of days, and immediately we had visitors' luck, which always comes with friends. A complete stele of Ramesses III on a boulder of red granite, about 3 × 2 ½ft. very thick, weight about a ton. ... Then in a hole against the south wall of the temple area I saw a long block of limestone, lying deep down in some sand bed of foundations. I thought it was a piece of a clustered pillar. At last when it was cleared I found some carving and on turning it I saw it to be the legs of a statue of Khem (or Min as I should now write); and to my delight it was the primitive statue of the temple, perhaps the oldest statue in Egypt. This may see "a long pull and a strong pull and a pull all together" on the belief of my friends, but here are reasons. (1) It was the great statue of the temple at some time, and not a mere private object, as it must have been 15 or 16 feet high: the legs alone, from the fork to the ankles, are about 6 feet. (2) It is of soft limestone; whereas in any late age, or any historic age almost, the great statue would be of granite or hard stone. This seems to belong to the time when hard stone was not yet used, like the temple of Sneferu. (3) The work is extremely rough and plain, just a rounded mass, with a slight groove on each side this section, and rude indication of knees. It could hardly be referred to any of the known ages of Egyptian art. (4) The attitude is not that sanctioned by regular use, no back pillar and one hand being at the side: differing therefore from all known figures of Khem, although there is enough of it to prove it to be of him. The hand at the side is very rude and elementary and pierced through to tie things on to the statue. (5) And on the surface on one side are several low relief carvings, most like the prehistoric rock figures of the white cliffs. ... The whole thing seems to have been a rude block only roughly shaped almost like a Greek island-figure and then occasionally decorated with stray carvings. From all these considerations I believe that I saw before me one of the primitive idols of Egypt, which may date from the days of the first settlement of the dynastic people. May we soon find the remainder of it.[1]

Next day we found the head of Khem; a round-topped lump, with big ears and whiskers but no face. Only a flattish smooth surface where face should be. All of it is very rudely fashioned on a shapeless lump; and I guess that finding no sufficient depth of stone in the top of the primitive monolith we carve a face, they flattened it and stuck one on, carved out of wood.

We found more of the Antef temple (I write awkwardly as I skinned my thumb tip with a stone). ... As a wide piece of that ground was in the hands of

---

[1] The head was not found. The figure is now in the Ashmolean Museum, Oxford.

a single pair of men, I thought I would give some of the chances to my best lad Ali who had had no success hitherto. So I set him to grub out the sand bed of a pit of which we had already turned all the paving and carried off the Antef slabs. In an hour or two his boy came saying that they had pottery. So I went and found a foundation deposit begun; Ali shewed me the place of the two or three pieces he had moved; he had kept the rest undisturbed for me. So I grubbed it out. Results: *[A list of objects in stone, bronze and pottery comprising a foundation deposit of Tuthmosis III, and more from a different deposit uncovered by Ali].* ... And here darkness stopped me; so we banked up the place, and patrolled at intervals with revolver till the moon set, to see that no-one poached about it. I could not persuade the fellows to go and sleep there. ... After all we settled to guard the deposit; so Q[uibell] and Ali went and slept in tent beside it. There were two men in the region about there when we went to pitch at 10.30 which was very suspicious! Probably we were only just in time! Next day I was all day sitting in the hole 3 ft. across, getting beads, scarabs, etc. out of the still wet mud and it still goes down, how far we don't know.

The workmen trained by Petrie during the 1893 season in Quft were employed by him in subsequent years elsewhere in Egypt and later in Palestine; experience turned them into a highly professional body of excavators. The site of Petrie's excavations the following winter (1894–5) was Nagada, a few miles from Quft. With Quibell and from time to time other helpers, he excavated a large cemetery area; finding hundreds of graves containing pottery and other objects quite different from those with which he was familiar. What he found puzzled him; he thought that he had found the burials of a "new race" of foreign invaders. His letter to Karl Pearson, his colleague at University College, shows his excitement. Petrie later came to realise that these were not the graves of foreigners, but of Egyptians of the Pre-Dynastic Age.

1 February 1895
Nagada, Upper Egypt

[Letter from Petrie to Professor Karl Pearson, Professor of Applied Mathematics, University College London] [1]

My dear Sir,

As I corresponded with you before about the skeleton business I now send you an outline of what is going forward, which please pass on to all whom it may concern. When I began here I stacked skulls and bones on a broad shelf in my bedroom, with a pleasingly perfect mummy lying below. Soon I had to

---

[1] UCL Pearson Papers 815.

stack them in boxes to await packing. Then they overflowed and formed a heap, which encroached on our courtyard until, I could hardly get into my room. Now the heap is extending daily and threatening to cut off the entrance to our visitors' room. The skulls were laid on shelves across the end of the court, but have now filled all the ornamental openings of the brick wall. And still every day more come in.

We have cleared over 400 graves, and from them have over 100 good skulls and probably a large part of each of 200 skeletons. Many graves had been anciently plundered and the bones broken up.

Every grave has the contents sketched in position; every bone is marked with the number given to the grave (except fingers and ribs and toes which go in marked bags); every object and every pot is kept (except the very commonest potter and also marked).

So when I return this summer I hope to supply to you this summer about 200 skulls, and 400 skeletons, more or less. The bones I propose to have classified all of one kind together; so that all the femurs – for instance – will go in a row, each numbered. Thus peculiarities will be more easily seen, and the measuring can be more quickly done. Nearly the whole of this material is of one age and of one race. It belongs to a most unexpected people: a cannibal race occupying Egypt about 3000 B.C. There has not been any suspicion of them hitherto, and their pottery has been attributed to the Egyptians. But they were quite distinct; and not a single object in their cemetery is in the least like any Egyptian product. The full study of them will therefore be a matter of great ethnographic interest. The skulls are very fine, with small hook noses, and strong brows.

I hope that when the boxes arrive in May or June some energetic medical or art students will be encouraged to help in all the sorting and classifying of the bones, so that they can be measured this summer. There are interesting diseases: hunchbacks, chalky patches in bones, lateral curved spine, diseased spine patched with added growth joining 6 vertebrae, etc. But I have only seen one fracture, an arm.

You could not have a better lot of material for homogeneousness and age: and I think it deserves to be worked up into a classical memoir in anthropology. All the bodies are decapitated, and the skulls misplaced. In one tomb – a grand one – the human bones were broken and scooped out for marrow, and gnawed by teeth. But in general the cannibalism appears to be only ceremonial. I suspect the people were Libyans.

Yours sincerely,

W. M. Flinders Petrie

In 1896–1897 Petrie was to focus his attention on the mounds at Behnesa on the desert edge, twelve miles west of the town of Beni Mazar. This site was known as Oxyrhynchus by the Greeks and was to produce hundreds of papyri which kept Bernard Grenfell and Arthur Hunt busy both then and for years to come. In the meantime, Petrie explored the surrounding area, finally opting to dig an Old Kingdom cemetery at Deshasha.

17–26 November 1896
Beni Mazar

Left London, had a baddish crossing and needed plenty of balancing to keep aright; slept in Paris, and through to Marseille as usual. ...

Here one begins to live again, for it was mere existance (sic) in the last few weeks of English weather. The rich thymy air from the hills, the deep blue sky and bluer sea, the warm slopes around the chateau crowded with flowers in fullest bloom, the luscious scent of heliotrope and maze of humming bees, all give one a double vitality, and make more hideous than ever the memory of Sheffield and Newcastle. There is no decent life north of the Alps; and why mankind ever went off the Mediterranean seems a dire wonder. The trees are still half yellow, loath to unclothe; and the glittering dark ilex full of red berries looked perfect against the blue sky. I can't believe the wisdom, and even doubt the sanity of folks who will stay in chilly fogs, enduring in terror of something worse, when the full life of the senses in every sight and scent awaits them only a single day from London. (Specially intended for my East Anglian reader).[1] ...

Our voyage so far has been delightful. The smoothest seas and bluest skies were ours down to Sicily. I saw for the first time the whole breadth of the island clear, without a break from side to side of the clear horizon. And, above all the wild dark tumult of the Sicilian hills – rough like a sea in storm, and black with cloud – there rose high-shouldered snowy Etna glistening in the morning sun. Never have I seen it from this northern side across the island before. Clouds hung over the straits, and the end of Italy looked strangely forbidding; above, brilliant sky; then glittering white cloud, under which a murky darkness covered the land, whose shore came out into full sunshine, while the sheen of the white cloud on the sea in front filled the eye.

At Alexandria we were first off the boat – *we* being Mr Geere[2] and myself, and up to the station. I went and settled about forwarding baggage with Moss, and then off to Tantah. Here we got out to hunt for a site of mounds marked on the French map of 1801. After a false start, owing to an error in

---

[1] Spurrell, whom he had repeatedly urged to come abroad.
[2] H. V. Geere was Petrie's new student.

the name of a place, we got on the track. The large site of mounds by Shoneh has been nearly all dug down.

26 November – 1 December 1896
Cairo

Frazer came in and had a long talk before returning to his survey work in the Delta. He tells me that a roll of early Greek poetry, Bakkhilides, found at Eshmunein has been bought by the Germans for £300. Next day I found Sayce[1] much put out by the news, as he had hoped to get it to England. I went to one dealer and found a pile of things just brought down from the south by two dealers whom I know there. So they picked out all I feared for; and I went off to their native inn, and saw the rest of their stock and took more, some twenty vases, etc. including a very fine palette of wood with 8 places for colours, several remaining filled; also some very sweet beads, and the greater part of a cylinder of (Ne user Re'). Corbett[2] came and had a long talk in the evening. A telegram from Quibell at Luxor said that Ali Suefi was coming down by the Sunday train to Beni Mazar; so my plan of going up on Monday morn will do well. It will be a great pleasure to have him about me again; for I feel as if all must go well with such a faithful, quiet, unselfish right-hand to help. As far as character goes he is really more to me than almost any of my own race. Few men, I believe, have worked harder for me or trusted me more. Perhaps none are sorrier at parting, or gladder when we meet again. A curious link in life; but a very real one; as character is at the bottom of it Kipling's "East and West" is the only expression of such a link that I know in black and white. ...

I called in on Sayce at his boat on my way back. Justice Scott came in while I was there, and was very cordial as he always is. Sayce tells me just what I see and hear all round, that matters are going worse and worse. There is no check on pillaging and places are being destroyed in every direction. The police and magistracy will not act, and the guards of the department are mostly corrupt. It is a horrible lookout, all due to accursed politics. All we can do is to save from the wreck as much as possible while we can. All agree that Behnesa is less worked out than any other region, and think that I have a fine field. Even the grand mastabas of the IV dyn. at the pyramids are being cut up and brought in by Arabs to sell in Cairo.

I have done a good deal of dealer-hunting not yet noted. Certainly I must have seen about two thousand papyri, and searched them all for literary

---

[1] Petrie had met Professor Sayce in Oxford. He had accompanied Petrie on his trip up the Nile in 1882 and became a life-long friend.
[2] Eustace Corbett, a friend of the Lofties, had frequently visited Petrie at Giza.

pieces. Nearly all are accounts, but I have a few scraps of literature, and eight complete letters in Greek. ... But the thing of all others is an ebony statuette of a young Nubian girl about 12 years old, driving before her an ape which bears a dish on his head. This is one of the supreme pieces of carving of the early XVIIIth dynasty, finer than the boys at Liverpool, or the girl at Turin. The modelling is superb, full and muscular without losing anything in dryness or hardness; the suppleness – the grace – the movement of it, with the back foot half raised, and the sweetness of the expression, are beyond any of the carvings that I remember. The structure is exquisitely true, and yet almost hidden by the firm plump flesh, so that it is only by searching that the full beauty of it is seen. Not a single detail is scamped, the underside of the chin is perfect and the back and shoulders are perhaps the finest part of all. The owner merely thought it a fine figure, without seeing how far it exceeded all others: if he had known more about it I should have had to pay three figures I expect; as it was, he only asked a small fortune. Certainly I have never found, nor seen on sale, anything to equal it; and I doubt if any of the finest carvings that I know can come up to it in all points. It is a perfect joy to look at the silhouette of it in any direction, for its elasticity and expression.[1]

The next day, 30 Nov. we left at 8.0 for Beni Mazar, Wiedemann[2] and his wife going together with us to Bedrashen, for a couple of days at Sakkara. They will come and stay at the work near the end of the time.

At Beni Mazar I found Ali waiting and all our baggage ready, from Luxor, Alex and Cairo. So we got camels for it, and then I went on quickly on donkey to see over Behnesa before the baggage should come: I took with me Mahmud, Ali's younger brother, whom I had as a small boy years ago. He is a good, observant, sweet-mannered lad, much like what Ali used to be; rather more lively, and with less of that strength of righteousness about him of his elder brother. I am very sorry to find that though Ali is so saving he has not the power of keeping money. Out of the fortune that he got last year from the work, about £25, but little is left. His family sponged on him for pound after pound, not for necessity but simply to get it out of him into stuff they could keep. After three months he went away south with what he has left; but even then he took not only his wife and baby, but a destitute little girl – a cousin – and his younger brother. I fear that he is too kind-hearted to hold his own. As he has an elder brother in good business there is no reason for him to be sponged on thus.

I went over the immense mounds of Behnesa, about a mile long and ½

---

[1] It is now in the Petrie Museum of Egyptian Archaeology in University College, London.

[2] Karl Wiedemann, Professor of Egyptology in Bonn.

mile wide. All I saw was late Roman, excellent for Grenfell[1] but not for me. But there must be a fine cemetery here somewhere. I finally fixed on a piece of spare ground, by the canal, and surrounded with young palm groves, to make our camp. No camels came, and I met a police sergeant waiting about. He proved to be a very tidy fellow, and we had a long talk. He was over, exactly like myself, to look for a settling place, as a police house is to be made here. This is excellent for us, as on this west side of the canal the place is very open to Arab raids, and most of the villagers have decamped and live on the east side to be safer. I have settled that if we are attacked we shall all leave the goods, and let them take what they like. They could not do more than a few pounds of damage, as our goods are quite useless to Arabs; and a single broken limb would be greater damage. All my money is safely buried.

Still, as no baggage came, I sat waiting on the bank, but at sunset we – myself and the two policemen – had the most pressing invitation from a dumb man to come over and stay with him on the east side. I had sent Mahmud to search for bread, so would not leave till he turned up. At last he came, breadless, and so we all went over the canal. The dumb man was younger brother of a rich shekh who is building a very grand house. He received us most cordially: coffee, a long talk, and dinner followed. We had the regular big tray, a large dish of rice and a couple of disjointed fowls, plates of spinach soup and piles of bread. He had spoons, so we did not need the graceful dexterity of sweeping up mouthfuls of rice in a pinch of flap-bread, and we each excavated our hole in the rice round the edge of the dish. Then Geere and I had a room with mattresses and rugs. But the cattle and dogs outside kept me much awake. Next morning after a dish of hot bread and milk we went off. The baggage had come up the night before about two hours after sunset. We went to see the village jeweller who makes nose rings for the Bedawi women of the desert. He had "a statue with a golden girdle" which proved to be a little Roman glass figure, with a twist of gold wire around it to hang it to a necklace. He also had a few Roman gems: the only one of value convex amethyst with rather a good figure: worth perhaps a pound or two in Europe, but here thought much more of, as all gems are.

We pitched tents, stowed all our baggage, opened all the old stores and took out what is most wanted; and planned out our house, which will be of 10 rooms if I find enough to keep me here, that is for (1) sitting, (2,3) Geere and self, (4,5) Hunt and Grenfell, (6,7) visitors, (8,9) Ali and men, (10) cook. Late in the day we had a light rain for some hours, but all was under cover by then.

---

[1] Bernard Grenfell, the papyrologist, who with A. S. Hunt excavated and published many papyri from Behnesa (Oxyrhynchus).

2–9 December 1896

When I first came here I looked out for bricks and enquired the price, saw two good stacks of about 18,000 and thought we should get on. But it seems that the village is being slowly shifted over from the west to the east of the canal, and there is evidently a good deal of prosperity here, and everyone is intending to build or rebuild. So it comes about that no bricks are to be had. The first day Ali went and hunted the prosperous side, but no one would sell bricks. The second day he hunted this side, but no one would sell. The third day he engaged a man to come and make bricks, but the man returned the earnest money instead of coming. So I settled that my own men must do it, and I started making a brick mould, but found the saw was ground out by cutting up cartouche bricks last year. So our building began by sharpening the saw to cut the board, to make the mould, to mould the bricks, to build the huts; which is beginning rather far back in the story.

I cannot begin to excavate yet, awaiting the official permission. It is of course only for careful work that any such permission is needed: for plundering and destruction any native may do what he likes and no one hinders him. So after getting our tents in order and marking out our intended ten-roomed house (don't be alarmed at the grandeur of it, the cost will be about £2 or £3) I began a survey by fixing the positions of a line of minarets and other landmarks exactly, so that we can plan everything by them. I then struck out to the north and west to explore and found far-stretching mounds of Roman buildings, and many small isolated mounds which seem to be either separate villages (as at Amarna) or tombs. They are very promising to examine. Then we struck back into the desert at sunset, and found buildings running about two miles back, one large one with Corinthian capitals lying about. We had a posse of village boys running by us, all very good friends and not annoying, and I tried to see how far they would go after sunset, as that is always a dread to the fellah. All dropped off but two, who stuck to us till nearly dark, when we turned and came back at a 6-mile trot, which is one of the best paces for covering sandy ground, with a short shuffling step. Next morning we went off southward exploring, and found on a slight ridge, two miles back, a line of flints, perhaps tombs. It was a splendid fresh morning, and I did much of the way barefoot on the sand. Then we turned to reach the canal, and had a long stretch of mud soft, and mud hard, ditches and sloughs, to wade. This ground is pasturage for half settled Arabs, and those we came across were most pleasant and friendly. All the people about here are unspoiled, and many are as good as one could meet with, while none are troublesome or offensive.

Our dumb friend came over to see us and we had a long conversation. He is a very sharp fellow, and sees the meaning of anything that is shewn to him very quickly. He gave a long and moving account of our dangers on this side and how the Beduin with masked faces would attack us, take every scrap of clothing and leave us wounded. I replied that they might take what they liked, there was hardly anything of use to them. So he expatiated on the wounds, and gave a comic description of the visit of enquiry by a pompous official who would count up everything. He urged me to always carry a revolver in a belt; but unluckily for me my revolver has disappeared in the division of baggage up at Luxor by Quibell. He pressed me much to go over and dine with them, and I vaguely told him I would in a few days. He enquired about my large Arabic vocabulary, and took in at once that it was for Arabic and English. He travels about the country, knows Cairo, and the Zoological Garden there. I see that the people here talk to him very freely about business by signs, and he certainly gets on remarkably well without language.

Our brick difficulties seem slowly bettering. After engaging three men, who each failed to come, we have got now two who do 1000 a day, and I hope to begin some building in a day or two more.

On returning after my morning's surveying I found my dumb friend here, and after lunch he went round the ruins to shew me what he knew. The mass of stonework which has served the town as a quarry for years past has passages and chambers in it, and from other people I hear of 3 statues having been found in it. They were smashed up, and made into coffee mills. It looks to me as if it might have been a catacomb for the sacred fish, a tomb for any one prince would not have been so large. Then he shewed me the city wall, at the end where it was scarcely visible, and went some way along it, till I told him that I knew it and had planned it the day before. Then he told me that quantities of papyri were found there, and began grubbing; in a couple of minutes he turned up a piece of Greek accounts 2nd Cent. A.D. But so soon as we got on the Arab part of the mounds – though I had not yet noticed the difference – he observed that there were not any papyri there, that was all no good, all of Muslim age. But the whole of the Roman part not capped with Arab contained writings. He is also very anxious that I should beware of untrustworthy men about the place. Altogether we get on as well with signs as with speech.

Having planned all that I can do here before digging, and not yet (7th Dec) having my permission (which was supposed to be granted on the 1st), I went off to see the hills back in the desert, and to search for tombs. On the higher ground, gently sloping up from the town for four miles, there seems to be a great cemetery. Some mounds must be tombs, thousands of hollows may be tombs, and there certainly has been a great deal of salt digging which leaves the ground all in holes. So how much there is to be found I dare not yet say.

Our friendly shekh, who took us in the first night, came over and insisted on our going to dinner with him. We had much the same dinner as before but rather fuller, including a quarter of lamb, which was duly pulled to pieces by the party; for a few spoons are all the appliances which they use here.

At last the bricks were dry enough to run up my first room, but they needed very careful handling or they broke across; for a pat of mud is not a tough thing until it is very dry indeed. The men turn out 1500 a day now, and so I hope to see a room done every two or three days. A tent 6½ft. square, containing seven boxes, 2 bags, bedding and miscellaneous books etc. is rather a small dining room for three people it has been lately. We have got guards regularly here now for the night. So I hope that I shall hear no more about the dismal terrors of our palm groves, the shadows of which are full of thieves to the native imagination. There is certainly no place for miles around so pleasant as ours; a piece of open field on the canal edge, the water being about 20 feet below now, and palms on three sides of it. The younger plantations fill the ground entirely, as their branches still spring from ground level; the older trees form a fair shade, in which we sit during the day and have lunch, the stems being tall enough to carry the heads out of our reach. A little of this may be imagined from the next page. And yet I await for this ridiculous permission to excavate, while I watch camels carrying off tons of stone from the important building of the place at which I may not yet turn a basketful of earth. I hope that I may get the document by the messenger who takes this in to post.

The only letter received from any of my friends, as yet, is from Dr Walker.

9–19 December 1896
Brugsch still plays his game. On the 6th he wrote saying that my permit was signed (that was really done on the 1st) and asking for my address; the enquiry was rightly addressed. Across that I wrote enquiring for the permit, and of course giving my address, as I had already given it to him at the Museum. Nothing came, so on the 10th I sent saying that I had now been ten days here watching the destruction of the main building of the place, without being able to stop it or to turn a single basketful of earth. But yet no answer on the 11th.

Ali reported that he had seen some bricks at double price. So I sent for them, as ours take so long to dry. But the reply was that they would not be sold for five times the price. Ali then offered all round, half as many bricks more, to be delivered as soon as finished, if any one would let us have stock at once. But all in vain. Meanwhile I ran up a room for myself from the still soft bricks, with the result that the bonders cracked, two corners gape, and the bricks have yielded so much that I expect one or other wall to topple over. However, I have a passable room now, 12ft × 7½, which is a great improvement on the tents. All the ground in front of our premises is covered with bricks laid out to dry, about 10,000 made, and 4,000 more have to be done. We shall hardly get rooms up before Grenfell and Hunt come to work, and our visitors come to stay.

I went over for a long walk to the north, mainly to see a village called Kom el Hassal, but there was no Kom there now. Zigzagging about the fields and canals is tedious work; Ali and I were on the tramp over rough ground for some hours, but did not get many miles away after all. I have now searched for six miles round here in each direction; but the desert cemetery is the only place of importance.

In the impossibility of doing anything more here until I get the permit, I am reduced to sitting out on the mounds with brush in hand. Here is Behnesa from the south over the rubbish mounds, with a curious minaret the top of which is supported on wooden poles, so that at a little distance it seems to be hung in the air over the lower part.

All the town of Behnesa is in a tumbledown state; not a new house has been built for years – at least none of any importance, as people prefer to live in Sandafah on the inland site of the canal. The fine old mosques are all falling to pieces, and seem as if a year or two must bring them down. The scattered tombs with domes and minarets, in the desert outside the town, are half down, and the less pious inhabitants attack them for stone and brick. The minaret above has been nearly half cut away and while I was looking at it a man began hacking at the hollow to see if he could bring it all over. In the town Ali found out an old public bath of fine building, probably XVIth cent much filled up with rubbish, but still having a brilliant inlaid pavement of coloured marbles in the hall. It is very instructive as shewing how buildings have been anciently buried in heaps of ruin. I see here the present formation of a Tell or Kom of ruins before me. Away to the north stretches a mile of mounds, beyond which is the desert, the green strip of bushes fringing the cultivated land, and in the distance the white limestone cliffs, as attempted above. While I was sitting by the canal bank near sunset I heard that our boy Mahmud was returning from post (he has been 22 miles every day looking for that permit), and with him a man in coat and trousers. This proved to be a miserable little worm of an Effendi[1] sent down to spy on us, at 4s a day from us, as I learned when I read the agreement, which came by post. As De Morgan promised me both last year and this that I should not have an Effendi down here, I have at once signed the agreement under protest and written to both Brugsch and De M. about it. Of course it is a game of B.'s to plague us. To De M. I have said that keeping us here for a fortnight idle is equal to £30

---

[1] Townsman.

loss on the expenses of the year, and so I hope he will not impose a charge of £25 more. Also the agreement is for Behnesa only, without saying anything about the *voisinage*, which was to include, the whole region. I have asked De M. about this, as otherwise I may easily find that cannot turn a stone outside of this place without waiting weeks for a permission. All this petty annoyance is just like what has been the rule in that office ever since I knew it.

So on Monday morning I began to enlist men, having been over the market the day before to look for suitable fellows. I began work on the isolated small mounds outside of the town. Later on I tried some of the rubbish heaps. On Tuesday night Grenfell came, and stayed Wednesday looking over the place. The result of three day's work has been to show that the isolated mounds are small villas perched on platforms of brick, and that they are IInd–IIIrd cent. A.D. The great stone building I have not yet tackled; but the flakes of the statues smashed up there shew that they were Roman by the quality of the marble, and the style of finish. And immediately outside of the enclosure wall are heaps of pottery and pieces of papyri of the late IVth cent. A.D. The enclosure wall is of good stone well dressed, but small blocks. My impression is that it is a great church and monastery of Helena's like the great buildings at Sohag. It cannot be earlier, nor yet much later. The rubbish mounds on the edge of the town contain pieces of papyri, and some nearly complete letters of the IInd–IIIrd cent. A.D. The strangest

place is a space about 40ft square with rows of shallow pans made all over it with mud brick cemented over. The pans are 4ft across and 6ins deep. Those in one row are a foot apart, and the space between the rows  is as deep as the bottoms of the pans. The use of this is as yet unexplained. The cement is too slight to hold water, as there is only mud brick below. They cannot be holes for bases of columns, as there is no sign of removing any stone from them. There are 6 or 7 rows of 6 or 7 pans each.

Having got together a very good gang of 40, beside my four here, and got their confidence for weekly payment etc. I then announced that every one must bring a water bottle, and we should all go into the desert to hunt tombs. No one objected, and most of them were anxious to go, although it means 8 miles walk daily.

Ali has started an oven, for baking the wide papery sheets of bread which they eat here. The section is thus... the fuel being burnt in the lower half, and the hot air and flame passing off over the floor of the upper part. When in full blast a rush of hot air and flame comes out of the uppermouth over the bread. A large pan of paste is made; a small girl picks out a handful and throws it on a circular fan of palm slips about 18 ins across, held by an older girl; she then tosses the lump on the fan until it spreads to 9 or 10 ins across, and then gives it to Mrs Ali who sits crosslegged in front of the furnace. She tosses this flap until it spreads to 15 or 16 ins, slips the fan into the oven, and with a jerk whips the fan back leaving the flap of bread in the oven, by the side of one other that is finishing. In about a minute it is baked. A long iron is used to stoke the fire below, and to rake out the flaps as they are done. Altogether stoking, tossing, and raking out flaps is pretty hard work for the baker, who sits facing the blaze the whole time for hours without rising. I mention this because it is very seldom that the women's work of the fellahin can be seen.

We have now tried for three days about the desert for the cemetery. About four miles out on a ridge are some pits, with two or three rough chambers about 3ft high at the bottom of each. But without any trace of bones or burials, and only a few jars of Coptic or Arab pottery. They may be tombs cleared out to serve as shelters in the Christian or Muslim troubles, or possibly originally cut for such a purpose. The mounds which looked so much like graves are all natural. The ground is largely composed of gypsum and flints; and where a great pocket of extra-sized flints was naturally swept together in deposition, they have formed pockets of flint as the sulphate of lime has been removed by denudation. We cleared also large patches of 30 or 40 square yards of ground to search for tombs in the most likely places; but, so far, all beyond a few rude pits are a patch of Roman graves about a mile behind the town. I hope that I may find more; if not, I shall soon leave here exploring up and down the country.

Please forward to... *[list]*. A second letter from Dr Walker is all that I have to acknowledge from my journal friends.

"The fruit of a fig tree is not perfected at once and in a single hour" saith Epictetus. No more is an excavation; and so I console myself.

21–27 December 1896

Having tested the outlying parts I concentrated the men on the Roman cemetery that I had reached. We opened about 20 graves, mostly poor, or else plundered. In one were the pieces of a painted limestone statuette of the deceased, about 2 feet high. As all this proved only Roman, and Grenfell and Hunt had come and settled in, I then handed it all over to them, and prepared to go exploring for a site.

The hospitable shekh here came to ask for some broken limestone to burn for lime to plaster his house. So I said that if they picked out a heap of it they might take it, but no quarrying in the ruins could be done. Two days after I see camels laden with stone down to the river as before. And on going up to the church I find eight men digging up stone as before, and quarrying tools lying about. I ordered them out altogether and told them that though they might have taken scraps, yet as they would quarry the walls there was an end of it. Of course they talked profusely but did not go. So I pounced into the hole, caught up the two crowbars about 30lbs each, gave one to Geere and marched off. Then the old sinner of a quarryman followed and began all sorts of usual lies and promises. Three times during the day he brought up village worthies to play compurgator, ending with the shekh. But all to no purpose. I laid down that as he refused to go at first, and had then made a false excuse to get in again for lime-stuff, and again refused to go, there was nothing for it but that his crowbars would remain with me so long as we are here. Of course endless promises were made, but they count for nothing. I have got the crowbars, and he can't do much without them. Taking a solid pledge for conduct is the only way to get a tight hold on an Egyptian.

I then went off for five days camping out with Ali, to search the country between here and Minieh. I first noticed a large space of old quarrying in the nummulitic limestone along the desert edge. We saw two town mounds (Roman) and went along the desert edge until by sunset we reached a large place, with a square enclosure, probably an early monastery. It was all Roman. There I struck into the cultivation, and some Arab settlers told us that our donkey with baggage was awaiting us in the village close by. So I pitched on a bit of spare ground, ¼ mile from the village on one hand, and ¼ mile from the Arabs on the other. Both parties protested that we could and should not do so. But I sat out their protests, and assured them that I should not go to either party, as I would not be near the dogs. So I slept in peace. All along this W. side of the country 3 to 6 miles in width is swallowed up by Arab squatters, who run up *durra* straw fences round their tents, and so make settlements which last for years. All the Egyptians are much afraid of them; and they have a flavour of wildness in their outfit, as every man carries a revolver and a blunderbuss. The first is fully loaded ready, as I saw on looking over some of them. Robberies are usual here. The next morn we left these ruins of Tenideh, passed several cemeteries of Roman age, and some graves where beads shewed the pits to be of XXIInd dynasty. It is almost impossible to know where you are when on the desert, as a high line of sand dunes cuts off all view of the villages of the plain.

At last near sunset we struck on to the dunes to get into the cultivated land, and reach water for the night. In place of one or two dunes there are several parallel ridges of sand, each 40 or 50ft high, and between them are lakes, which dry off at once into wide green meadows of short grass. This gives most delicious barefoot walking: the cool moist ground, and grateful soft tufts of young grass, being perfect to the foot. The next morning was even better when it was covered with a sheen of dew. When the sensation and perception of the foot is lost in a hard boot, half the pleasure of walking is gone.

That night I struck up to a town mound of Roman age, which is covered with the tents and shelters of Arabs, who have dug it to pieces in the last 30 or 40 years. It has the common name of Kom el Ahmar, "the red mound", and is just east of Mahdiyeh on the map. There I pitched a little apart, where I should not hear so much of the dogs. First we had a fine old shekh with grey beard and a splendid silver-plated blunderbuss. He of course objected that we must go to the house or tent of someone, and was with difficulty appeased. Then came a suave middle-aged shekh of the guard, who blustered furiously at our being there, and swore by everything that we should go to his house. He also was talked down. Lastly came a jolly old shekh, with as thorough a "make-myself-at-home" manner as any Yorkshireman. He bundled into my little tent, filled half of it as he settled down, and was positive that I must move; but of course to no effect. He was a fine, vigorous old hand, with a cock-eye, a slit nose and a cheery patronising way about him. Next morning, after seeing some wretched pieces of late Roman carving, we left the tent pitched, and went off for a day out and back, to the south. After going for a little – about 5 miles – we found two Arabs following, who had been sent out to protect us. They shewed us cemeteries, and I found at last where those painted plaster heads come from, which have been sold during the last 2 or 3 years as being from the Oasis or from Meir. The pieces were lying about, and the guards told me that they had found them coloured, as those we know. Coming back from our furthest, which was 1 or 2 miles south of Minieh, I found rows of parallel dunes, and at one point I saw four long blue lakes lying between the yellow sands, one beyond the other; while on the other side were two more. Each lake is about half a mile wide and two or three miles long; they make a scene utterly unlike anything else in Egypt, and I expect that hardly anyone has an idea of them. No tourists ever go there, and probably no officials; from the cultivated land it seems as if the rolling sand hills were the interminable desert, and there is no sign of the lakes between. So far as the map goes it is absurdly wrong, and has no relation to the actual form of the ground. This region, so far from the Nile, beyond a band of swamp, and apparently all desert, is outside of even the tax collectors' ken. The scattered Arabs who live by pasturing their flocks in the meadows are a friendly race, and we had no trouble with them. The girls wear four or five bangles, large enough for the arm, put through the ear; not by the lobe, but through the shell of the ear, which becomes a mere band of flesh to hold up the jangling gauds.

Our usual day's routine was that Ali began pot-boiling before sunrise, when the boiled water for the day was done, and coffee made, we had breakfast. Then packed up, loaded our baggage donkey, and sent him on with his owner to our next station. Ali and I then rode our donkeys or walked all day along the desert, lunching on some bread and a tin of food, and reaching our station by sunset. Tent was then pitched; shekhs, guards etc. all talked over; Ali cooked a pot of lentil soup and boiled more water; we had dinner, and an hour's talk after it before lying down for the night. To have "domestic providence" (as I called him last year) always at your elbow, ready for sketches, donkeys, cooking and everything else, and withal one of the pleasantest of friends to be about with, is the luxury of travelling. I have heard more of his ways in these five days, and respect him even more than before.

The next day we sent on our baggage 14 miles north, and went with guides to see a pit tomb out in the desert, which was described as 2 hours to the west. After going about six miles to the *south* west, at last I was shewn a ridge about 5 miles further and told that the pit was there. So I had to give it up, and found ourselves 18 or 20 miles from our night's rest near noon, with donkeys fagged out far back in the desert. The only resource was one's own muscles: so I went off a long stretch of about 12 miles without a break straight across desert, much of it heavy sand, with sun full on our backs, and no wind except a faint hot south air. Getting down to a meadow we had lunch, twenty minutes on one's back, and then on. Donkeys were no use, the sand was so heavy, so it had to be all walking to near the end. I have not had such a pull for some time past: some 17 miles at full speed, on mostly very heavy ground, and a hot close day. However it suited me as well as ever; and I was not very tired, and quite fit next morning.

We visited three more Roman towns on our way back to Behnesa, where we got in about the middle of the afternoon. Now, after two days' refitting, we go off on a nine days' round northward; so no journal need be expected for a fortnight after this.

Grenfell has been getting plenty of Roman tombs, but nearly all plundered, and nothing important as yet. ...

I was very sorry to leave Behnesa; the place was one of the pleasantest I had ever been in. The palm groves round the house, the splendour of our establishment of 9 mud brick rooms, all made me ready to lament like the Moorish lament on leaving Valencia. Here at Er Riga we are absolutely bare without a tree near, no minarets to look at, but only some fields and sand dunes. Yet it is quiet, clean ground and good water and our row of six huts is quite good enough for the time we are likely to be here. The peace of life consists in learning not to trouble about what is not essential.

So soon now as I can get de Morgan's orders I shall begin work. At least I have done a good stroke already in a full survey of the sites along 90 miles of country which was scarcely at all known as yet. My address will now be *Bibeh Upper Egypt*. Of course letters to Beni Mazar will be sent on, as the Egyptian post is very good at this.

Little Yusuf comes in and squats in my doorway just for society, now that Ali is away. I beg my friends' pardon if I give too large a dose of Arab affairs; but it is very seldom that one can see so far into their minds; and nothing is more fascinating to me than getting inside the thoughts of another race of men.

11 January 1897

For three days I have been writing letters, journal, report etc.; all the stuff which everyone seems to expect, but which very few seem to think worth acknowledging. A journal is something like presentation copies of a book, a sort of spontaneous product of nature, sufficiently impersonal for anyone to thank Providence and pass by on the other side.

I went over to see a reputed Kom,[1] which I found had existed, but was long since all dug down and built over with a village. Meanwhile I was waiting for permission.

Suddenly a man said "there they are"; I caught up the telescope, and saw Ali and the man whom he had taken as witness and – another figure – the penitent Fatma, following behind. Ali went prepared to pay anything in reason, to be quit of her; but was talked over by an inspector of police, two chief Shekhs and the Qadi. The Inspector told him that a new regulation decrees that ladies who flee to their ancestral home may be brought back by a posse of police; I rather suspect it was a pious fiction of his to sooth Ali. Fatma protests that she only went in dire fear of her brother giving her a drubbing, a fiction also I rather think, as she went to him herself. Perhaps as effective a cure as any in the case is that (as Ali reports) her reprobate family are near starving and filthily dirty. A condition of things that extracted a dollar from A., which was really the bait that brought the man over here. However it all came about, matters seem re-settled; and above all we have the strict injunction of the police and shekhs to seize the brother or any of the family that come around, bind them and send them under escort to the mudiriyeh. How some English folks would bless the law that allowed them to handcuff an unfortunate and impecunious brother-in-law, and hand him over to the High Sheriff in the county town. I must confess that – from the Muslim point of view – I was a trifle sorry to see her turn up again, since she can't be trusted. However as she is the breadmaker, and my prospective cook as well, I suppose prudence must rejoice.

---

[1] Ancient mound.

At last I got a reply from de Morgan saying that he had telegraphed to me (I never got anything) and also to the Inspector in the Fayum, that I might work here, and has written to Ghizeh so as to avoid any hitch. When I want to go to Ahnas I am to give him a week's notice and he will order that also. So tomorrow I must go recruiting for good fellows in the villages, as I do not want to have too many Arabs of our hamlet, for they will not be tough like the fellah. I noted a good strain of lads in the next village. The real name of this hamlet is Er Righa. ...

I have for the last few weeks taken to half native dress and only wish that I had done so long ago out here. I expect I shall find the return to trousers rather miserable after the comfort of the wide calico bags that I now wear, which are far better for walking and riding and the only dress in which one can sit comfortably cross legged. Socks of course I never wear here; and a pair of scarlet leather slippers finish off my dress below. I stick to the black jacket above, as being much more convenient than flowing robes.

As I came back from the first day's work I met Miss Oldroyd and her nephew strolling out. They had not waited for the boat, as time was getting short, but trained to Beni Suef and slept there and then came on here next day, so as to divide the long amount of road. We had not yet got our roof on, but luckily the straw had come, so we could put it up.

19–25 January 1897

... We had a south wind which broke in a furious sandstorm. One could hardly stand against the wind, which hid the country in a cloud of sand. It wiped off half of the straw covering of our roof, which had to be replaced by little Yusuf on the top.

Another curious burial, not mutilated, but in a large coffin cut out of a single trunk of a tree, 84 × 23 × 20 deep. The old lady in it was very powerfully built; had broken her right thigh just over the knee when a child, so that it was 2 ins short and walked therefore with a stout stick which lay beneath her; and was very demonstrative, wagging her head so much that the pivot vertebra is greatly worn away. I am keeping all the skeletons of early date, and marking all the bones, so that we shall really get a firm knowledge of the details of the early Libyo-Egyptian. This solid coffin was in good state and I have brought it away.

Miss Oldroyd and young Borwick left after a week's stay here, which they seem to have enjoyed, in spite of our having no cook. On consideration Mrs Ali seemed so much under the wicked brother's influence that I could not be satisfied at leaving all our premises at his mercy if he came over again, as we are all out all day long on the hills. So I sent up to Grenfell for a Behnesa boy who would cook and guard here. He sent one – whom I thought desirable –

but the urchin was utterly despondent, declared he could never cook, and was so fearfully mournful that I sent him back. I have now got another who seems to take to his work fairly well, and is very attentive. We want someone, for I have to sit watching the pot boiling for breakfast while I mark skeletons, and divide my attention between vertebrae and eggs, ribs and coffee. Alas! the new boy suddenly turned off and the guard here came forward saying that the boy would not stop here, to which the boy assented. I told him that he must stay for a day or two, and went off to the work. Geere and Ali tried to keep him by all persuasion possible, but he bolted and was not seen again. Such a repeated affair shews that there is someone here making mischief. I have been talking over all possible causes for such a scheming and Geere and I can only imagine four possibilities, of which three will be settled by the removal of Fatma from this place. So next week's work begins by setting Geere to work at the Roman town about 3 miles north of this, with Ali to support him and of course Fatma packed off there as well. Then I have asked Grenfell to send me down a stout man to do guard (day) and cooking here and then I shall see whether I have thus crushed this affair, whatever may be the cause. The night guard here is in the working of it; both boys were tractable until he saw them; he acted as spokesman for getting the second boy away; and he has told a futile tale of excuse for him since. So we have our diplomatic amusements here.

An interesting reburial was found, of about XVIII dyn. in an old IV dyn. tomb, the first tenant of which was pushed on one side. The new comer was not mutilated in any way, but lay at length. At his head two large jars one on either side, and between them two small painted Cypriote jars. At his right side lay a cubit measure, of 13 inch foot found before at Kahun, *not* the Egyptian cubit, long or short. A four stringed lute had been broken across and lay half on either side of the body. While on each side was a throwstick. ... All the wood was much rotted, so that it could not be lifted, except in short lengths of two or three inches. I first measured the cubit, then packed all the pieces of wood in a tin box, filled with sand to keep them from drying and splitting in the outer air. At night I opened it and took them out, much reduced to bits under an inch long and then dipped every scrap in melted wax. Now they are all safe and can be mounted up on tablets in England complete. ...

Then I have found the long façade of a great tomb; plundered, but – I hope – containing sculptures, as the forepart has remains of figures and hieroglyphs. The whole front must be over 50 feet wide, if it is symmetrical. ...

26 January – 1 February 1897

Perhaps my friends hardly understand what sort of work this is every day. I spend as much time as I can copying the sculptures, but every hour or two a boy comes to say that a well is opened. I then go over to one of the half dozen groups of men who are tomb digging. There I find a pit open, anything between 10 and 40 ft deep. I see if there is enough clear for me to get into the chamber: hand the rope ladder down; strip, for it is far too hot to wear anything but light Arab drawers down in the deep holes; and then swing down the rope ladder. At the bottom light a candle and begin to crawl full length into the hole. Inside I find a small chamber, only 3 or 4 ft high, in which I spend half an hour or an hour, clearing sand away, planning out the skeleton to see if it is complete or mutilated, noting the position of everything, sending basketsful of bones and woodwork up to the top and streaming all the time with the exertion and cramped position in the heat. When all is done I come up, dress and go back to my copying, where I get a few more sheets done before the next well's ready. Some of course are shorter, but others – such as the great find of statues – take several hours.

It is all well worth while. For no one has ever yet recorded fully any cemetery of the pyramid age; and all that I am doing is the only information that we possess about such burials. All that has been hitherto done has been more plundering to get show specimens.

I find that I must make yet another experiment in the cook line. I totally distrusted this man as soon as I saw him; but hoped, against all experience, that my prepossession was wrong. First my jam had a flavour of sardines, shewing in what order his finger had sampled the tins. Next a few breadcrumbs, with which I adorned the jam in the next tin, have disappeared, along with a good lump of jam. And yesterday morning he was drunk with *hashish*, and began spooning ground coffee into a cup of water far from boiling and afterwards put out a lot of tea, quite beside himself. I was wondering what to do, when there turned up a couple of old Fayum hands of mine, two of the best from the work 5 to 8 years ago. One of them is not overstrong, and I think I shall make him a cook. Tomorrow I clear out the present fool. ...

A very interesting lot was turned up in a tomb well, just as we stopped for the night. A pan of the IV–Vth dyn. shews the age and with it were four mallets of heavy wood, and eight *wooden* chisels, much knocked over shewing what they used for cutting pits in the hard gravel here. ...

Grenfell is having grand times with Greek papyri, both Biblical and literary. So there will be plenty of glory for the Fund this year between papyri and *ka* statues. ...

16–23 February 1897

We are having an unusually cold winter here. For over six weeks I have never been too warm; and most of the time the high, tearing cold winds have made me keep to my thickest coat. Today I even had to wear a cloak, for a gale at 50° chills one down.

The Keneh dealer came over here on his way down to Cairo, as I had given him notice where I was. I got a batch of things from him, including some New Race things: a perfect flint bracelet, two bright bowls of white line on red, a few pots and a lot of ivory combs broken. ...

I am doing as much copying as I can all day long. Each morning I work on the coffins and painted woodwork here at the huts. For if they are good they are very likely to be taken at the Museum and perhaps never seen again. If in bad state the paint is very likely to be lost in travelling, owing to flaking of the plaster. So the only thing to do is to make full size coloured facsimiles of everything. Then all the afternoons I am copying up at the tombs, in the intervals of running after the diggers and their pits. If only I had someone who could copy here, I should have done in half the time. Geere is slow at it and makes such puddings of feet and such uncanny limbs, that it takes me as long to correct his drawing as to do it all myself. ...

Another untouched burial was found in a single block dugout coffin. The body was slightly pitched and so firmly dried, skin and all, that I brought it down unshifted, stuck tight in the coffin, with the head rest under the head. The interest of this was in the great quantity of clothing laid over the body. All of it very brown and powdery; but by great care I managed to separate each article, took them all to the rock tomb near by and spent an afternoon unfolding them and measuring and noting all the details of the making. With a few pieces of the stuff and fringes as patterns, it will be easy to reproduce exactly the dress in detail. The main article is a loose long smock with very tight sleeves, exactly like the modern *galabieh* except in the neck cutting. It was open back and front for a foot down and the edges of  the slit tied together with 3 pairs of strings in front, and the same at back.[1] It never rains but it pours. Another tomb with clothing buried in sand and gravel and in good condition. One of the smocks perfect and so white and fresh that I folded it up and put it by as if it were clothes just come from the wash. I expect to be in London about 25 March.

---

[1] See Deshasheh 1897 (E.E.F. Memoir 15) ch. VII and pl. XXXV for further description and discussion.

23 February – 2 March 1897

I heard that the tomb-guard had been levying on the boys' wages from the work. So I made enquiries quietly of the boys and found that two had had a piastre each (half a day's wage) screwed out of them on the pretext that they came from the next village. So I payed this pillage back and when pay day came round I gave the guard 12 instead of 14 piastres, and remarked that as he had one piastre from Abu'l 'Elah and one from Aweys that made up his money. Of course he shouted "No, No", but I walked away and heard no more of it. He explained affairs to my men by saying that the boys had been repaying a loan that he had made to them long before!! This guard is a typical Bedawi. Capable of more prolonged indolence than seems possible; never doing anything that can be avoided, fond of watching others work and of reproving their laziness. In short he is a thoroughgoing loafer. ...

Ali has been keeping Ramadan like all the rest, with the expected result that his stomach has broken down the third time this season. After a fortnight of it, I had to insist on his having "medicine" as I called it, because he was ill. This medicine being a decent midday meal with me.

I am writing this on the bottom of a basin put on my legs, as I sit cross-legged in a tent at Ahnas. I had done most of what was needed at Deshasheh, and as I was anxious to see if there was anything within immediate reach at Ahnas and had only a fortnight of the season left, I determined to push on, try Ahnas and if important – go to and fro leaving Ali to look to it in my absence. ... At present it is still blowing cold gales at 50°; such a thing as I never knew at the end of February. My old worker, Mekowi, who is back from his soldiering, has just lost his son, a boy of four or five and is evidently cut up by that. Having heard from England a report that Kitchener was disliked for his severity, I asked Mekowi about it; but he says that "Kitten" – as he is abbreviated – is all right with the good soldiers, but very hard with the careless or dirty. Certainly his service has done Mekowi good, and he would do well as a chief workman in any place; he is orderly, respectful and clear-headed, and knows how to give directions and manage other men. I have left him in charge of my room at night while away, and fully trust him.

I have now had a look over the temple site here. What is exposed is clearly only the front portico and part of the peristyle hall. Hence the heart of the temple must be far behind that. ... *[diagrams and description of ruins]*. The clearing already done by Naville[1] does not go beyond the Ramesside pavement, and there ought to be a good deal below that, while $2/3$ or more of the site is still deep in house ruins, according to the indications I have just noticed.

---

[1] M. Edouard Naville, a Swiss Egyptologist.

Of course I cannot in just the tail of a season do anything at finishing this. All I propose to do is to test for the temenos wall, to find its limits and to sink in the exposed part already excavated to settle how deep the foundations go and whether they include inscribed stones. A week on this will shew how much remains to be done another year. ...

The foundations here, in one place where we dug right through them, yielded four fragments of earlier work. So there is doubtless much to be got there. At Koptos all the early stuff was in the building of the heart of the temple, and not out by the entrance; and so probably it would prove here. ...

I go back to Deshasheh today and leave this place for a future season, having settled what there is to be done.

2–9 March 1897

Drawing coffins and finishing off the copying of the outside of Shedu's tomb is the business in hand, while I arrange and look after Geere's packing. ... The Keneh dealers came down again with a good cargo, and I took most of it. Twenty stone dishes and jars – alabaster, basalt etc. of early times *[list of purchases]*.

Ali's sister came over with their mother on the way to a town a little beyond where she is to be married. She is much like A., with all his refinement of expression. I gave her a blessing in words and in cash as she went off; and was glad I had done so, as just after I had to play a different part. The bad brother turned up again, in spite of all the solemn threats that had been dealt out to him officially before. This I could not stand. So I ordered A. and my soldier Mekowi to arrest him, but they were very half-hearted. A. in fact had slunk into the dining room and had left him in possession of the field. So I seized his defieh wrap and stick worth a pound or two; and told them to take him to the Shekh.

But they began mere bland expostulations on the way. So I followed up, and had a long time of talk to and fro at the Shekh's. Of course everyone said "Oh let him go, and *next* time then shoot him when he comes etc. etc." The usual style of weakness and tall talk. I ordered the guard and men to take him in to Beba to the police. But after the guard had made a great fuss with him he turned to me and said "Now give him his donkey and he will never come again." My only reply to all this was that this was the talk of the *last* time; and we must do much more now, there was no time for mere words. Evidently none of them reckoned on finding a will in the place. My soldier was worth anything. He stood sentry guard at once; bound the man's arms when I told him and we then set out, two villagers in front, the soldier and prisoner, and myself riding the man's donkey in the rear. I went about 8 or 9 miles, and then handed the affair over to the soldier to finish at Beba, as it was getting late. Here arose a delicate question. If I gave absolute orders to police the man, there was strong likelihood that they would not be obeyed. I should then have spoilt my soldier, by making him both lie and disobey, as there would be the greatest temptation to let the man go. So I began by telling the soldier that I knew they would want to let him go and if they did so I should be annoyed, but that would be the end of it. If however they did their duty properly and brought me a written reply from the police on the matter, I should give the soldier three days' pay. Thus I should avoid spoiling my valuable man over a small matter. This openness answered. They came back late that night, with the police answer; and left the man in custody to be handed over to his own village as a disturber of the peace. How much the police will do I care not. There was a tolerable donkey and some good clothes as the man's visible assets and these give good scope for blackmailing. What happens we need not enquire.

All this breaks up matters. Geere refuses to have Ali and Fatma here after I leave, as he cannot boss the business in case of trouble. So they must go to Behnesa. And if I work anywhere in this region again A. will have to choose between F. and the work and I told him so. Fatma has tried to bolt again on hearing that the brother was cleared off. But as she took the little girl A. followed and brought her back. So it is evident that she prefers the rascally half-brother who has just been two years in prison, to the virtuous – though somewhat faddy and exacting – youth who should be her all. Alas! for perversity. I told A. plainly that he was very weak in the business, and must be more of a man. He must get more fire and grit about him, or he will have a bad time in life. On our way up to the tombs in the afternoon he had made up his mind to be quit of Fatma finally and should send her off next morning; and in the evening he told me that she had torn her garments and was much distraught at the notion. Thinking that his position was rather embarrassing in his hut (a servant staying out a month's notice is nothing to it) I said that if he was annoyed he might like to come and stay in the sitting room. "No, I am not annoyed, what should I be annoyed about?"

Another sentence throws some light on his mind. "I had better pay £6 or £8 for another wife than break my word to you, after I promised that there should be no more rows." "They are all liars, and if they are going to tell lies like that I had better have done with them." It really seems as if one friendship were pitted against another; and the worse must go to the wall.

This is all dreadfully unarchaeological. But there is nothing going on but copying and packing; and as some folks seem to be interested in this study of human nature I give this continuation of it. It is scarcely ever that a fellah's mind can be known so intimately, so it is well to understand it and see the total absence of motives which are the strongest in other races. ...

Next morning we had an awful hour or two getting Fatma off. She was ill and could not go – and was altogether obstreperous. Whenever things came to a deadlock they came to me; but as far as possible I kept out of the business. So far as I could understand and observe, there was not a trace of personal feeling in the case: it was mechanical declamation against an unpleasant situation. Ali complicated matters by trying (illegally) to keep the child.

My soldier came up excellently and volunteered – as we could not get anyone from here – to be one of the two to go and take Fatma back. He pulled Ali round about the child, and got the party fairly off. I told him I had not asked him because I thought he would not like to have to do with the matter; but his reply was "What am I here for, but to do what you want?" So I thanked him, and hoped that I have seen the last of this unwholesome business.

I must do Ali the justice to say that he was wheedled into having Fatma by his mother, contrary to all his inclinations, as he declared he would sooner have the blackest negress. So he cannot be expected to have much feeling in the matter, considering her behaviour. The whole thing seems a hideous travesty. Meanwhile the bad brother is haunting the villages near, and got a Shekh to send in a guard with a peremptory demand for his wrap "by order of the police." I asked to see the order of the police, which was not forthcoming and I hear that the said shekh is fit to kick himself at his bluff having failed. We had Ali in to dinner, as all the other men were away, and he enjoyed himself. …

There is a gale blowing, so that we can scarcely keep a lamp alight in the room. It has been raging now for 24 hours; but is not so cold as winds before, only about 65°. Yet it is not pleasant in a country where everything is done out of doors and where no light comes into rooms except by the doorways, which face the wind. Here is nearly the middle of March and we have not had a single hot day yet, only two or three pleasantly warm.

I have done over 80 negatives of things here, all passable and some very good. So I shall have plenty for lecture use. … There will be about 1000 square feet of pencil-drawn sheets of tomb copies to be joined up and inked in for lithographing. There will hardly be another journal to go round, as I shall be back in London almost as soon as the next journal would arrive.

2 March 1897
Henassieh (or Ahnas)

Dear Miss Urlin,[1]

I was measuring in the temple here, when the postbag unexpectedly came over. I shuffled over all the envelopes for your hand, as I always do, and then sat down to read your letter forgetting all else. So many thanks to you for all its news, and for the drawings. I am delighted to see how you grasp the hieroglyphs, so that no Egyptian would be ashamed of them. Most people think that if a sign is roughly made it may be copied anyhow; and the result looks hopelessly un-Egyptian. As for the scrolls that is only a question of time and practice. I always find each year when I begin to drawn scarabs again, that I am out of practice and make hideous pothooks at first. I know personally every one of those you send. And the best of all your news is that you will be willing to turn to such things again this spring. I have a large piece of work coming back with me, the inking in of all the drawings of the tombs of Shedu and Anta. I think that it will be exactly in your line, remembering your success in those tracings. I must get it forward as soon as I can, as I want to work up lantern slides from the drawings, especially the war of the Sati and Egyptians.

I can quite understand how the time flees by in the hideous winter time with its chilly short hours, and shut windows, and cold hands, and dull light. I am very sorry, and not surprised to hear of frequent colds and headaches in such a life. The living here in the open air day and night is worth anything. Not even the through draught which I enjoy all the summer comes up to this. The last three days I have left my brick hut at Deshasheh, and am living in a little tent under a clump of palms here at Henassieh, just to prospect the temple site and see how much remains to be done. Naville made many great holes all over the wide space of the town ruins, and so found the temple; but then he abandoned it after clearing just the parties, because only the foundations of the rest were left and he never searched for them under the floor level. There is plenty to be done here for one season. And when will it be? and who will do it? All that we shall see.

How transient everything seems by the side of the Egyptian things. I often think looking at scarabs how I am just a little episode in their history. They are almost imperishable, and ten thousand years hence they may be the joy of some collector of that day.

This season has not been a bad one, though not so sensational as the New Race or the Israel tablet. We have got a good view of the Old Kingdom, and for making a show the statues are a fine return. The real value is in the details of the burials and the small things, but the statues fill the eye.

I have got my steamer date, and leave Alexandria 19 March. So I hope to be at the College 26–30 March and after running out for lecturing, expect to be there from 5th April onwards. Don't waste one visit there to put that key on the table; bring it after I am back.

Yours ever,
W. M. Flinders Petrie

---

[1] Later Mrs Hilda Petrie.

1897–1901
With Hilda in Egypt

When Flinders Petrie returned to London in the spring of 1897, he had made up his mind to propose to Hilda Urlin, the girl to whom his letters had been addressed from Egypt during the previous winter. After some hesitation, she accepted him. On Monday November 29th, in their travelling clothes, they were married in Kensington at eight o'clock in the morning, and leaving their guests at the wedding breakfast, took a taxi to Victoria to catch the boat train for Dover. After a stormy voyage, Hilda at last glimpsed the harbour at Alexandria: her lifelong adventure had begun.

29 November – 12 December 1897

We left Victoria at 11, and hoped that the wind might have abated, as it looked tolerable at Dover. So, rather than lose a day which I wanted at the Louvre we risked the crossing. But the sea was much worse in mid-Channel, and at Calais it broke over the pier so badly that we actually had to turn tail and go back to Dover. There was no mail to France for 24 hours, a thing that has not happened for years past. It was an awful four hours, very cold and rough, and I almost fell asleep with fatigue as I stood. H. also was bad for the first time at sea. By dark we found ourselves back at Dover and by 6 got some food again, having had nothing since a glass of milk at 10½. Next day, though it was still rough, the wind had gone round to the south, and Calais was practicable. But I was badly shaken by three such channel crossings. At Paris I was able to dispense with my fur coat, and left that and another to be sent back to England. The usual route to Marseille by the day express, and the usual visit to the Museum there filled our time till we got off on the 2nd Dec. from Marseille. The voyage proved a rough one on the whole. Past Sardinia and down to Stromboli was good enough, but then we went into a gale through which we toiled for 36 hours at half speed. ... the last 30 hours to Alexandria were very good and smooth.

At Cairo I have been going over the dealers and getting some nice things, but nothing astonishing.

The main affair here is about the permit. Loret[1] wants to screw me into

---

[1] Victor Loret, the newly appointed Director of the Antiquities Service.

new and disadvantageous – almost ruinous – terms. So I went and saw Sir John Scott (chief justice, as to legal aspect) and Sir Wm. Garstin who is president of the Committee which Loret had persuaded to pass the new terms. Garstin sees the absurdity of them and will summon a fresh committee and alter them at once if he can do so. Nothing could be more cordial and friendly than he was. ... Mace is building my rooms at Dendera. ...

Loret is already out of touch and disliked by everyone – Museum people, officials, and natives. Brugsch said to an Arab that De Morgan was a small devil but Loret is 20 devils, and this has gone the round of the natives.

I hope we may get up to work in a week or so; but one can never anticipate what official delays may be. Certainly Loret will not relish after trying to thrust an agreement down my throat, being obliged to rescind it by superior powers. I shall probably gain his respectful hatred in place of his officious arrogance. ...

11–21 December 1897
[Several days spent in visiting dealers, and sightseeing around Cairo].

On her first visit to Egypt Hilda Petrie wrote a number of letters to her family and made entries in Flinders' journals.

5 December 1897
[H.P. writes]

All the next day, nothing but pitching, rolling, tossing, in a strong gale, and a lashed-up sea. We kept to our bunks for 36 hours airlessly. F. ate nothing, and I reeled off and got food whenever there was any, but never got up till the storm was spent.

6 December 1897
[H.P. writes]

Fine weather at last again. It was delicious to sit up on deck again, and to make up for lost air and sleep. One or two nameless small islands appeared only.

7 December 1897
[H.P. writes]

But now at last we are sighting the African coast, and Pompey's Pillar is the first thing we can see. We land at Alexandria in another hour (Wednesday) and oh! the landing! We took up our stand, with our bags, close to the square hole one emerges from, and then waited, and the whole Arabian Nights poured in upon us, pell-mell, in every wild richness of oriental dress – porters tumbling in for baggage. We got through the Customs and drove straight to the station, but it was already too late for the aftn. train, so we got back to a hotel, and waited to reach Cairo till today. Part of Alexandria looks French, and the streets are a strange medly of French, Greek and Italian faces, dresses and inscriptions, with a rich glowing admixture of Eastern life. The Oriental street crowds were a magnificent sight, so rich and varied in their details, so brilliant. And then we pottered about the native quarter until dark, and lived in the Arabian Nights – the colour and glow and richness of it are inexpressible. I never could have imagined so much brilliancy, or such picturesqueness of attitude, and movement and drapery, and expression of life in all ways, in those glowing, jostling oriental groups. I shall never forget the narrow Arab alleys of tiny shops full of gorgeous stuffs, and scarlet slippers and red and orange dates and pomegranates and pottery and the gorgeous natives at their work, or squatting idly everywhere in picturesque confusion, old men chanting their wares, looking like prophets, women in black, veiled – then towering up above them a white minaret, and over all the Egyptian sky.

8 December 1897, Morning
Alexandria to Cairo

[H.P. writes]

We are travelling up the country now, 9–12 o'clock, and seeing such wonderful things all the way! I never thought Egypt could be so Egyptian, or everything so rich and strange; it is a delicious medley of Biblical and Arabian Nights pictures. The very station was good to wait in, and then our way lay through all the ancient ruins of Alexandria, these being cut through the débris of the old city, and strewn with granite columns! and we saw remains of cisterns and courses of Roman bricks.

Ever since, there have been great wide picturesque marshy flats, full of colour, green with cultivation, and grey with sedge-covered waters and here and there are brown mounds, which are the sites of Roman towns, and all along there are modern native villages, a curious conglomeration of brown mud huts and domes, huddled into a heap and strewn with straw. Besides acacia, there are huge thick-stemmed trees of tamarisk; and the most wonderful things are the great tall graceful feathery date-palms, with brilliant clusters of dates hanging from them in richest profusion, wherever the palms are not already stripped. The country life is deliciously interesting to watch, all along the way – the brown men in their turbans and draperies along the straight mud paths, the women in black, with water pots on their heads, the cattle and donkeys and buffaloes ploughing, and the great loaded camels swinging along, are so fascinating.

(We are just crossing the Rosetta arm of the Nile.)

One sees cotton on many stages, growing in the fields, and the cotton-waste after it is gathered in, and then in sacks slung on the camels, and lastly in trucks-full along the line ready packed for England. There are hedges of prickly pear, and in the canals the lotus grows, all along. F. saw some flowers just now.

It is getting sunny and dusty as we go further south, and everything keeps getting more oriental and more fascinating every minute. The crowds of orientals at every wayside station are so picturesque, and the types of dresses so various. Even the boys with water jars are delightful, chanting in mysterious Arabic Water, O thirsty ones! water the excellent!

11 December 1897

[H.P. writes]

The first day in Cairo was rich in the excitement of pottering about from dealer to dealer, and seeing shopful after shopful of curiosities, from which F. picked out with rapidity but thoroughness all the scarabs, statuettes and other anticas he wanted; looking over everything takes several days, and it is a glorious feast. We had no sooner arrived than a number of wondrous prophets in trailing draperies flocked round us in a dignified group, and showed piles of small anticas. They and F. bowed and salaam-ed and invoked blessings on each other – conversations are long and animated, and interesting to listen to. We wandered thro' the native bazaars in the evg.

[F.P. continues]

Another day we went out to Old Cairo by electric tram, which is a great convenience for getting about. Three long lines intersect in the middle of Cairo and lead out to six outskirts. H. was delighted at picking out of the mound a spoon and various pieces of patterned clothing, belonging to about XIIth cent A.D. Late enough, but yet a first taste of the joy of grubbing for antikas on one's own account. ...

At last I got a letter from Garstin on the 14th saying that Loret agreed to set aside the new clause about their taking all royal objects. So next morning I went down to the Museum, saw Loret,[1] who took his defeat with easy assurance and from whom I got the agreement duly signed before noon. We are saddled with an inspector at 4s a day, but I put in a word for having a very decent capable reis whom we had at Thebes, and whom I saw in the Museum only doing attendant duty; so I hope we shall get him. The great question of the division of things remains now where it was before Loret's new move,

---

[1] Victor Loret was Director-general of the Antiquities Service from 1897 to 1899.

the Museum to have anything up to half; but no jot to take more – no matter how important – unless they pay the expenses of the work. As this means that they must pay double the proportionate cost if they want to take the second half it is very unlikely that they will ever care to put this piece of the law into force.

The Petries, with Norman de Garis Davies,[1] started by train the next morning for Upper Egypt. The journey by train took 13 hours; at Nag Hammadi the line came to an end and they were forced to spend the night there so, as Hilda said,

We stumbled off in the dark to an untidy village on the river bank, and were left there to make the best of a Greek wineshop for our night's lodging. Our room was a rough semi-stable in a mud courtyard – a mud room with palm stick bedsteads and no furniture. We prowled round the village by dark and again at sunrise, reckoned that donkey could scarcely do the 30 miles next day, and that camel was unsatisfactory, but that boat might do it. So F. hired a queer old dirty cargo boat at sunrise and after some coffee, we disembarked and tried to tack away southward with a slight breeze. ...

21 December 1897

[F.P. writes]

Next morning (16th) we were off from Cairo by 8 a.m. and got to the terminus of the rail late in the evening, where we got some primitive mud-floor cabins at a Greek shop for ourselves and Mr Davies who joined us in Cairo. He is a friend of Mrs Griffiths returning from Australia, who volunteered to stay in Egypt and help in the work this winter. So he is going up to Dendera with us. Mace[2] is there already and has built our huts, and got Ali[3] up ready. Another worker is expected out, MacIver[4] from Oxford, next month. ...

Next morning after debating the various advantages of boat, donkeys and camels for getting to Dendera, we concluded that boat would be far less fatigue and a fine north wind all the previous day gave us good hopes. So I went down and struck a bargain for a boat to Dendera and we set off by 8 a.m. A little wind at first helped us along, but it dropped to almost nothing at Kasr es Syad, and we merely crawled on after that. As sundown came on it

---

[1] Davies was a friend of Mrs Griffiths returning from Australia. He was an accomplished copyist who was to contribute many volumes to the record of Egyptian tombs.

[2] Arthur C. Mace, a young Oxford graduate, later to make his mark in Egyptology.

[3] Ali es Suefi.

[4] David Randall MacIver.

was evident that we should not reach Dendera, nor even Dishneh halfway, and to avoid the chill there was nothing for it but to crawl in under the half-deck. So before dark Davies, Hilda and myself all arranged ourselves in the small space with what spare clothes and few blankets we had, and there we made the best of it for twelve hours, anchored in mid-Nile. The deck was only four inches above my nose as I lay down, and each had to crawl in end on as there was no room to turn. At last dawn came, and we got our boatman on, poling and towing, for there was no wind. By 2 we were about 10 miles from Dendera, and saw we should not be in before dark. So leaving Davies in charge of the stuff Hilda and I set out to walk, and got to the huts by dark. We needed all the twilight to find them, for Quibell had placed them in a hollow of the desert ¼ mile from the cultivation. And by some strange oversight he ordered them to be built facing SW, the worst quarter for heat and duststorms. I wanted them to be N. or E.

We found Mace in good condition, all the rooms built and our stores and things all ready. So next day we spent in fitting up shelves and unpacking and after that I started a lot of my old Koptos men on clearances just behind the house, which seem to be ibis pits, and we may get some nice things and should in any case clear them. But the main interest will be in the tombs which from their shape and style seem to me to be very early. These I hope to begin upon in a few days' time.

Davies did not get up here till 2 in the morning, guided by a party of my men whom I sent down to meet the boat.

22 December 1897

[H.P. writes]

The last two days at Cairo were full of interest; it would take several quires to describe all the things that filled our time, and the delicious visits to native houses to see dealers' wares, and our excursions to the Gebel Ahmar, upon which we clambered about and got splendid views of the Delta and pyramids, and to the tombs of the Caliphs, and the great high Citadel of Cairo, and then our long day at the Pyramids.

The Pyramids are even mightier and more interesting than I expected. We looked at the Great Pyramid narrowly and carefully, getting as much idea as possible of its details and proportions and its marvellous jointing, and then from farther afield realised its gigantic size, and then explored some of the early tombs around it, and the mastabas, and saw Sneferu's name on one of them, and then went on to the second pyramid, and explored the great temple of Khafra connected with it. ... We pottered down into the Pyramid village, and had tea with a native and saw a number of antikas, and then up the desert again and managed to escape the crowd of Arabs, and thoroughly investigate both the very top and the very inner core of the pyramid of Men-ka-Ra. Without the usual tedious help I got to the top, leaping from ledge to ledge, at the south-west angle. From the top one gets a glorious view of enormous extent. The clamber is of no exertion (with skirt off). We lit candles took off half our clothing, and crawled down 2 passages into the middle sarcophagus chamber of Menkara. The changes of light and colour, and disposal of shadows on the pyramids during all that day were a continuous interest and joy.

F.P. has related our becalming, and this ended in our spending two days and a night on that little open boat, with a ledge scarcely big enough for the 3 of us to tuck ourselves away on, when the night grew cold. Fortunately F. had laid in a stock of bread, and 30 little fritters, and some tins of beans and jam, just before we started. These just lasted out from the Friday sunrise when we started till Sunday morning dark when Davies emerged from the Merkab[1] safe at Dendera at last! Fortunately also F. bought 4 blankets at the last moment, so we got thro' the night warmly. ... The boating in that queer old Nile boat with a large 3-cornered sail, and 4 very picturesque much-draperied boatmen, who talked and sang and crooned by day and quarrelled in the night, and towed and poled by turns when the wind sank, was a curious experience, and our chief needs were supplied by a single knife of F's (which cut up all our food by turns, and cleaned me down when once I got buried in soft mud a foot or more!) and an old tin mug which leaked, but served for drinking Nile from, and equally for washing purposes!

All along the way grows the tall graceful Egyptian maize, the 'durra', which the Blessed work among, in the Elysian fields, and then at the industry along the banks is a 3-fold water-raising to different levels by means of a shedouf, a swinging pole heavily weighted, with wicker or leather baskets to empty water above.

It was all a most delightful adventure, and everything hugely picturesque and strange!

Last of all we left the river edge of cultivation and struck across near a great quadrangle of white domes which is apparently a great tomb, looking in the sunset all marvellous in an unearthly glory of opaline and amethystine glow. I shall never forget this first approach of Denderah. The place itself only seems to consist of a great brown mud mound of a ruined town out of which the square temple stands, on the edge of the cultivation; then lies a vast extent of stony sandy desert in all directions. We are ½ mile on to this, with desert all round us therefore, which swells here and there into little mounds of Roman remains, and early tombs. How early not yet known, but there is

---

[1] Boat.

every prospect of very primitive remains. Here and there on the outer edge
are flat Bedawi tents encamped, but we are far into the Gebel, remote from
even the Bedawin, looking across flats of warm desert, which form the
horizon towards sunset, opposite our doorways, but which are edged by a
great cliff-face of mountains 1400 ft or so, both south and north-west, the
which are wondrously purple just before dark, and lighted up gloriously at
dawn. ...

F. has an army of Quftis, old Koptos skilled hands, such fine men and
lads, whose mere dress is an inexhaustible pleasure to my eyes – their drapery
folds are so picturesque! and these are digging parallel trenches into the
mound here, and after 2 days such work, are penetrating the parallel brick
tunnels of apparently an ibis cemetery. Several Roman pots turn up, sealed
and filled with bran-bags, and garlands even, and herbs, and some Roman
division walls have emerged, and many ibis-bones and a few other remains.
We potter among the clearings and F. is continually measuring up the work,
to reckon the cubic metres, and to allow the men to turn over the stuff as
they excavate, instead of carrying it outside. Just now I was called into a brick
tunnel, in case a record was necessary, and Flinders began clearing a patch
carefully, for some glass had turned up – it turns out to be about 100
smashed-up thirds of cylinders, in brilliant blue and red and bluish-green
glass, such as was never found before, and F. believes them to be the broken
legs of furniture such as incased metal, probably the furniture of some ibis-
temple near the cemetery. It is a unique find. All these fragments have to be
washed now, and pieced together. The colour of them is wonderfully rich
and deep, and they will be a valuable part of the year's results: such a set has
never come to light before.

At various parts of the day we potter about the desert: it is much diversified
by mounds and early tombs. One day we find a wooden sphinx, another a
fragment of a carnelian bead – in hollows, the surface is strewn by mummy
fragments and human skulls and bones. The great hills across our courtyard
wall are really several miles away: tomorrow we shall get a 15 mile tramp
along their base to hunt for rock tombs, as it is Kena market-day and the
work will be stopped. The desert is certainly the most glorious place: and our
row of mud huts, the most curious little long brown burrow, 6ft. high, and
invisible until one tumbles upon it. It is of rough mud sun-dried bricks with
no doors or windows but doorways hung with green grass mats, through
which there is always enough sunlight. One has only a bed and basin, and a
straw mat, and a couple of old boxes to place things on. The first day was
occupied in contriving the furnishing of the huts out of planks, namely a
wooden shelf for each, hung from the roof boards by string, and a great
rough table for the dining hut. F. has also made me a rough door to use as a

barricade at night, and I have made myself a very primitive cupboard out of an old store box. The meals make up in their plentifulness for all lack of ceremony, and even of what one considers necessaries at home. All the things of domestic usage at home which one considers quite indispensable, one suddenly finds to be entirely unnecessary here, and life is simplified a hundredfold.

The sunrises are beautiful, and especially the sunsets, the sky is marvellously clear always and the zodiacal light far outshines the milky way. One sees the sky through one's roofboards and doorways always. And in the daytime there is no indoors for us. The desert is so sandy that one cannot wear stockings, but one gets over the ground well, and can cover long distances without noticing it. It is cold, morning and evening, and often windy – then the sun between 10 and 3 is very hot; so that after 3 hours or so of morning, one sheds one's coat at 10, and goes into a shady hat covered over with a handkerchief to protect head and neck.

Yesty. at the hottest F. and I explored the cool shades of the great Temple of Denderah, a huge Ptolemaic building with 2 great halls of HatHor-headed columns, and we investigated staircases and side-chapels with candles and F. found unsuspected entrances to new crypts. We also climbed all its roofs, until lately the site of an Arab town, and penetrated the side temples of Horus. It is a splendid open free life, this life without the ordinary necessaries in so many ways, but rich in sensations of the splendour of the East, width of desert, glow of sky and mountain, and unfolding interest of excavation going daily forward.

An even greater excitement than the mound of innumerable tunnels on whose edge we dwell – productive of so much, daily, in the way of bones, pottery, mummies, glass, bronze libation-vases, ivories and other things of interest, is the Old Kingdom mastaba[1] now in course of excavation about ¼ mile off, across by the desert edge, and facing the Temple mound of Denderah. The first day two inscribed stones turned up, as given in detail by F. The second day came the news of a larger monument having been found: we hurried off and looking down into one of the corner chambers of the mastaba saw a great false door in situ, standing built into a brick wall – in a westward position as false doors usually are, though here the rest of the tomb faces north, as here the lie of the land is sideways, so to speak, and the Nile runs westward, from Keneh all along our district. F. superintended the heaving round of this heavy stone false-door, a slab of about ½ ton's weight, and the men dragged it up a slope of sand and rubbish, out of the funeral chamber, by means of ropes and tent-poles, and then twenty men or so

---

[1] A tomb with bench-like superstructure.

dragged it right across the undulating stone desert, all the way to our huts, round the tunnel-mounds, tugging with all their might, and shouting in monotonous sing-song, with a somewhat Gregorian tone about it, the invocations "salli aleh" – pray upon it – all the way along, for perhaps a quarter of an hour, heaving as they came, in slow procession behind us, with their dirge-like refrain filling the air – it was an interesting sight to see those Egyptians, some much draperied, and others bare-limbed – all of them picturesque – and the great stone behind them smoothing itself out a broad level path as it ground along – and then the width of warm desert on all sides, and the great parallel cliffs of all the neighbouring mountainous region catching and reflecting the last sun glories of the day, make such a glorious framing to all the day's achievements, every day in this glorious Sa-id, the blessed land.

The days pass very fully and richly. Somehow one keeps no calendar. One can never remember what day it is – the Sundays here are Thursdays, so that is confusing to begin with! Then as to the month, it is always August! September set in for two days lately, and F. says we must expect it for 6 weeks to come, and that is to be our only winter. Today however August returned in full force and I have been almost too hot, lounging at my hut-door all the aftn. in dressing-gown and white umbrella! Yet at supper time one is suddenly reminded it is actually New Year's Day! I have lost all realisation of fog, or rain, or English festivities even. Everything is so totally different here: one only just remembered it was Christmas Day, one of these hot sunny days of exciting excavations, and of course remembered folks at home particularly, but I can scarcely realise it can be winter anywhere!

Time passes so rapidly here, and I find I spend all my time in doing nothing but taking in fresh impressions, and going over the new ground again and again, to make sure it isn't only an Arabian-nights' story, and the week-ends slip away, with no journal written, and I find I cannot write any somehow, or set myself to any washing or needlework as I meant! After this, I hope to keep some record to send home however, instead of leaving every day (an outline of whose incidents would in reality cover 6 or 8 of these sheets I feel!) untouched, as I have hitherto contrived neglectfully to do. There has been no empty day yet.

It is just a fortnight since we came: the long courtyard into which all our huts open, is filling daily with finds of the rougher and larger sorts – great amphorae, bronze fragments of inscribed pottery, 18th dyn. glaze soaking in basins, slabs, stelas, lintels, with Old K. sculptures and hieroglyphics on them, mummy wrappings, vases, embalmed hawks etc.

Then F.'s large hut, our sitting room, is getting filled up with the more delicate glazes, and bones, and glass and ivory, besides being a storehouse of boxes and tools, and tins and apparatus of various sorts. All personal property lives on plank shelves round the walls. I seem to have innumerable neat instruments and cases, and tins of things. Clock, aneroid, remedies, writing things, strong shoes and flannel shirts are all that I have need of much at present. All other things remain packed away, and seem de trop: so much of one's clothing is totally unused!

No one is to be seen up here. The 3 men and I have had the whole Desert to ourselves: tourists do not stray beyond Dendera itself – once on a steamboat day, we spied them as specks on the temple roof. The Marquis of N-hampton came and looked up F. one day, with his little girl and governess, and doctor, in white helmets, on donkeys, and found us grubbing up ivories and ibis-bones in a tunnel, and Mr Wallis[1] turned up another day, but only for 5 minutes, missed F. but I shewed him the glaze and bronzes.

I haven't been down about Denderah, or crossed to Keneh (we walked here from 10 miles distance) one never needs to leave the work. F. has taken me all about the great Ptolemaic temple twice. One very hot mid-day we spent in the cool, mysterious darkness of its passages and side-chapels, hunting for entrances to further crypts. ...

In a journal entry for the end of 1897 Petrie adds,
As I find that Hilda does the general account of things with more freshness than I do, I shall in future describe the discoveries more fully and leave the rest to the better hand.

2 January 1898
Denderah

[H.P. writes]

I have had an entire fortnight now, of the exciting excavations, and the mud-hut life, in the Desert, and I begin to wish now that I had put down the details of it more fully. But it has all been so fresh and strange and absorbing, there has literally been no moment to give to more pious duties hitherto, and so it has been more convenient to wait until the new year to turn over a new leaf.

Thursdays are our holidays here: Keneh market day, and consequently our Sunday; and freedom from the Work once a week, gives us our only chance of getting up on the high Gebel (1500 ft above us here) and far away into the interior, where we can look back across striding edges into the Nile Valley, and across to the other great Gebel beyond it, all of which runs east to west.

---

[1] Henry Wallis, Joint Secretary of the Committee for the Preservation of the Monuments of Ancient Egypt established in 1888.

Our last such holiday was the day after the find of P. Mena's falsedoor and its triumphal procession across the desert, and we have had several days' quietude, and cessation from any such excitement, until today in the further of the two mastabas, when a large fresco with cartouches of Pepy I and II, is beginning to turn up, in apparently the chamber of offerings of someone named Adu, and groups of servants carrying things, depicted. We hope that, another day, behind this frescoed room, the Ka-chambers will be found, with coloured statues, who knows? Meanwhile the work progresses fast daily, and the entrance to this mastaba turns out to be by means of an arched tunnel running down as into a pyramid, from a staircase by the outer door. This 6th dyn. brick arching is the oldest yet known.

3 January 1898

[H.P. writes]

We are 3 or 4 miles, here, from the foothills of the Gebel plateau, and the first week we were here, our first holiday, we made an excursion to them. We took tins and bread in a saddle-bag and a bottle of water, an aneroid, and sticks, and I left skirt and all encumbrances behind, and we crossed the plain, visiting mounds along it, covered with rings of stone and tombs, probably early stairway tombs. F. estimated there were 60–80 within close reach. We spent all the middle of the day resting – or asleep – in the shelter of a flat cave, ½ cemented probably in Roman times; it was so lovely being away at large, on the low desert, grey and yellow, and bare, and undulating, with nothing on it but an endless quantity of crystalline fragments, felsites, porphyries, granites and then tracks to be observed in the sand, footprints of small birds, of great stalking cranes, and of camels, and mice, and jerboas, and donkeys, and the wrigglings of snakes, with incessant jackal-tracks making scientific contours in all directions.

The last holiday, our only other at present, was much more wonderful: a really good tramp, equal to 21 miles, and carrying us not only across the plain, but up the flanks of the hills sideways, and along a saw-like edge or crest which juts out from the cliff-line of the plateau, and up high on to the plateau itself, 1500 ft. above; one ascends by steep staircases of jutting limestone, and along a precipitous ridge, and so on to flat terraces of brown Neolithic flints, where we picked up a few flint implements, and saw even the bare workshop (with its surrounding chips and flakes) of Neolithic man! Thence we climbed on, and at about 1200 ft. reached far older levels, with beaches of blackish orange flints far more compressed and settled looking, and here we picked up a good dozen of Palaeolithic flint implements. The ground was strewn with flakes, and cores, and chips, and implements in various stages. From this level we looked down precipitously into steep valleys on both sides of us: I can't describe the rich complexity of the scenery or the structure and appearance of it all, but I never saw a more impressive sight. Here the hills are far more diversified F. says than in other parts of Egypt. It is no mere cliff line separating two dead levels; it is real diversified mountain scenery of a high order, and the great panorama outspread below is a marvel of beauty, and strangely far-reaching. The opposite plateau close by was 15 miles away, the cliff ends of it 30 and 40 miles, looking quite close! One sees 50 and nearly 100 miles in some directions without any sensation of indistinctness or even of distance! It is all yellowish desert or plateau, or differences of light make these and especially the cliff faces, golden or pink or orange: the skies are indescribable, of course. I never knew what sky could be, before. The loveliest thing perhaps from the high desert, is the fresh bluish green line of Nile cultivation, a strip between the two greyish yellow masses of flat stony undulating sand, and steep cliffs and high far-reaching plateau.

Miss Oldroyd and her nephew joined the encampment a few days ago; she chiefly sews and cooks, the youth is sometimes about the work. Everyone sits about in the sun mostly, so one doesn't see much of them. The last two days however I have done rather the same, as I have been resting after a day's fever. Strange natives come about the mounds now and then asking for work; F. takes on a few local ones if good. Many look so ruffianly or incapable, they need nothing but a negative, but they often squat about for days in a listless oriental way, and don't seem to take it, and then F. gets rid of them by main force. His language increases in definiteness and vigour, and finally he runs for them, and chases them all down the desert, prodding with his stick, and one old nigger he fairly butted at, and deprived of his turban, which lies rolled up now in a corner at home, adding to the picturesque confusion of his hut. The nigger stalked over to reclaim it next day, but was told that if he came any more, his skull cap would be taken from him also!

Three suspicious characters with baskets and touriahs (hoes) were seen squatting near the mastabas the other day, waiting for sundown to come and rifle them apparently, so F. arranged for some of the men to sleep down there, and when we all left at sunset, Mr Mace remained judiciously hidden to see if they began a raid – however everything blew over, and all remains intact. We have constant trouble from dealers, spies and persistent natives, but hangers-on are always cleared out of the place as speedily as possible.

Fresh inscribed steles keep turning up daily from the mastabas, and as they have many chambers in them, and deep wells, we hope to find some good things as the digging progresses. ... We have spent all of each afternoon lately upon them. The three mounds are a mass of rooms, passages, and wells; they have entrance staircases and Adu's has that fine sloping tunnel. The fresco is very indistinct, but F. has made out most of the inscriptions. Adu is dark red, on a grey ground, and stands up in a papyrus bark with a spearhook across him in his hands; his wife sits at his feet, Beba, and his children and servants surround him. ... We take paints with us each day, and F. sometimes sketches down less common hieroglyphs; we come back just at sunset, and each night, the whole north, i.e. the great Temple, its earthen mounds it is sunk within, the cliffs behind the river, the Desert foreground, all are suffused in a ruddy orange glow that is marvellous – the mountains east, and N. west are rosy pink, with blueness of shadow, the southward range, at whose foot we live, becoming a delicate amethystine, gradually deepening, and fading, as heliotrope, the north west is pinkish and all indescribable colours, sometimes rather hazy and delicate, the West is impossible to describe – the crimson, and blue, and golden green, and the sometimes furnace heat of it – the sunsets are very different from night to night.

5 January 1898

[H.P. writes]

It is pay-night, and in sun and wind, everyone is sitting about, this last afternoon of the week, wrapped up in brown canvas overalls, and with white head-shawls. It is almost too windy and dusty to write here; swirls of sand keep blowing past. F. is measuring up, and going thro' the accounts with each of the men. A fresh stele of Adu has just turned up, covered with hieroglyphics – we are all on Adu's mastaba as I write. The brown temple mound just opposite it, begins to grow warm in colour now, and gets gradually more glowing, till its climax of orange splendour fades away just before sunset. ...

F. and I have been doing a little indoors sketching these few mornings lately. I spent nearly all the morning sitting under the courtyard wall, numbering the bones of skeletons. Each skeleton wants a separate number, and each bone requires to be marked in a certain part of it: they were chiefly rib-bones, skulls and collar-bones.

The tall sails on the Nile are flapping hard round the bend near Kena today. Everything is so clear and glittering; it is glorious.

A party of American tourists on donkeys assailed us this morning, taken in tow by a Cambridge man and a dragoman, and wanting to see the work. But they found the mounds too rough for their donkeys and left it in peace.

We have two guards, armed and draperied, squatting at our courtyard entrance, who keep us in the protection of the village. They have only shot a stray dog at present, and no alarms beset us.

It is almost impossible to believe that the hills before me – brilliant pink with cobalt shadows – whose thousands of diversified lines I catch at every careless glance, are indeed 15 miles away: they look no more than three miles distant. The palm trees banded along the green strip of cultivation, every branch and stem of which I see, are two miles distant! The range of cliffs ending, towards sunset, not so very far away are in reality 30 miles off.

It is a fearful waste of time sticking inside one's hut from week's end to week's end. Every one else is off at the Works dabbling in coins and jewels, and new excitements every day. Meanwhile the courtyard is getting impassable, so I hear: it is crammed with innumerable great tablets and steles and cornices, and piled the length of its walls with skulls and bones, and crowded with pots. I haven't anything much to say, this week.

9–16 January 1898

[F.P. writes]

This is a triste journal, without any accompaniment, for Hilda has been in bed for a week with a feverish attack, beginning with a bad cold in throat and neck, and going on with continued high temperature, varying 2° to 4° up. It began from getting sundry chills, owing to not realising how easy it is to get cold here. The dry air and general out-dooriness leads newcomers generally to do things they would not think of in England at 40° or 50°. There seems nothing the matter now, but the tempr. will not go down, so she has to stay in bed and drink lemonade all day and be dreary, and very patient. It is very hard and tantalising to be tied up thus; and a great blow to me and to all the work that is waiting to be done in sorting and packing. Miss Oldroyd has been very kind, and done much small cookery etc., but of course most of the feeding and straightening up is my business. Mace is luckily working excellently on the excavations and Davies is also useful, so I can rub on. ...

Mace is doing very well: he spends nearly all day grubbing out XII dyn. burials very carefully and preserving all the minute beads. Davies has lately been useful in looking after the Ptolemaic burials and amulets. This place can absorb any amount of work. The cemetery is about ¾ mile × ½ mile wide, all a dense mass of mastabas, pits, graves walls and holes of all ages. It is less plundered than any place I have yet worked in. Fully half the burials are untouched.

10–17 January 1898

This is another triste journal, as Hilda has been in bed the whole time, with some amount of fever. It is different to anything I have seen before and Miss Oldroyd is also puzzled. The conditions are in most ways as good here as possible, out in the desert air, perfectly fresh, and with any quantity of St Galmier water to drink, for H. has had nothing else while ill. Our ordinary water supply is also very good. So I do not see that any external circumstances can be in fault, but rather this illness – which is nothing at all dangerous, though very wearying – is the payment for a deal of over-tiring and chills that have gone before. I have been always playing moderator, fearing that too many risks were being run. ...

Loret came to Dendera, and sent up for me. I found him in the temple, which he and Mme. Loret and her brother and Legrain all went over in a touristical fashion. I pointed out our work about ¼ mile off, but L. did not seem in the least inclined to look at it, or to take any interest particular in what was found. They spent about 1½ hours over the temples – just like green tourists – and never wished to see anything else. I was only too glad to be saved having to trot them over things; but imagine a director of antiquities never caring to see a lot of excavations and antiquities just found, when he is within ½ mile of the mall, and spends a morning about the place!!!! I was astounded. ...

Adu I is finished and all the stone chamber taken out. I got Loret to agree to take that at the Museum. So that ought to choke them a bit and will cost us £60 or £80 less than if I brought it to England.

Today 29th we began on the great east mastabas, two or three important ones, which I suspect are IV dynasty. I am very glad to say that Hilda has at last picked up and got rid of the fever. I telegraphed at length (100 words) to Dr Sandwith at Cairo, but he could not clear up matters. Then we had the luck to find a pleasant Dr Richmond, travelling on a post boat and got him to the huts. He examined and said the mischief was congestion of the liver, owing to bad chills. H. was already turning better that day, and after medication she has entirely got rid of both the high fever and the malarial fever. The first day I got her up she was much wrapped up to sit in a chair in my room, but the sight of a revolver worked wonders, and when it came to shooting off went the shawls with "One can't shoot straight with all these fiddle-faddles." She can now walk a little about the near work, and only needs feeding up to be all right. After three weeks in bed on washy diet, it take some time to get strong again. Miss Oldroyd has been very kind and stayed here to help in cooking and nursing. ...

29 January – 5 February 1898

At last Hilda is up and about again, after a weary three weeks. A few days have set her up well and she is going about the work almost as before, but better in some ways for the long rest. She has taken enthusiastically to plan-drawing and is plotting off the plans of the mastabas to a scale of 1/1000, from which they will be photographed down for publishing. The general survey of the place I am doing on 1/2000, which will have to be reduced to 1/4000 for a plate. It will be a great help to me to have the plotting off my hands and I hope she will do the measuring soon as well.

5–16 February 1898

We expected to have had some difficulty about getting men to work in Ramadan. The pay day before the fast began I enquired of several men if they would fast or work and they all replied that they would work I heard one good old worker saying to the guard here, "Ramadan yegi fil gebel? La, la, m'darabnish heneh" (Shall Ramadan come into the desert? No, no, it shall not smite me here). ...

We have been turning over our house a bit. We get up about 6 and breakfast before sunrise. Out by 6½ at sunrise to survey etc. and go over men till 11. Then heavy lunch, rest and light reflection and we go out till 6 and lastly dine at 7. This gets us out early to work, and leaves all the hottest hours for indoor matters.

6 February 1898

[H.P. writes]

The hot weather began yesterday, that is to say, September has turned into August; and though I suppose it is very mild compared with what it will be in two or three weeks, one has arrived at going out without a coat, and with a handkerchief hanging round one's hat, and the desert is too hot to touch, and one's feet begin to burn in one's shoes: it is ordinary English summer weather, and thermom. about 70° in one's hut, at warmest.

I have been on the tramp for about a week now, being wholly recovered, and F. and I go out, all round the works morning 10–1, and afternoon 3–5, and he investigates pits and mastabas and tombs, and measures up the men's work, talking Arabic hard all the while and by this time I get in detail all the sense of what he says, generally, and in the pauses I enquire the meaning of unknown words and write them down; so I am collecting a useful vocabulary, and find that I know over 300 words by this time. The more interesting feature of the work is the detailed measuring up of mastabas for plan-drawing: and I am promoted to writing in the numbers of inches in the rough sketch, while F. measures, and also to making out the plans at home to scale of 1:100 and, as interesting as anything, the triangulation and use of sextant, and surveying and planning in general, and it is fascinating.

The face of the entire desert is altered during the month that I was stowed away in the huts! When I took to my bed after the New Year, there was the great extent of tunnel-mounds, long since worked-out, near the huts, and ½ mile of undisturbed Gebel between these and the three great princes' mastabas (Mena, Adu I and II). But now that I get about again at the end of January, I find more than ½ mile square of desert all raked up into mounds and pit-holes in a confusing jumble of every variety of tomb, and ranging in date all through (dyn) VI–VII, XI, XII, XVIII, XIX, Persian and Ptolemaic.

I lose my way at every turn among them. The first day I was out among the works again, we had a grand day of grubbing blue cylindrical beads off mummies from the top of the sandstone sarcophagi, and F. crawled right inside, and grubbed in airless heat, with a small lamp, and secured the inside occupants' amulets. The tombs are in a hollowed-out cavern, reached by a steep flight of steps. It was so dim and mysterious, and so like something in the Arabian Nights; and 4 picturesque Arabs – Oh! their draperies and colours! disposed themselves round us, all the time, full of pious exclamations.

An intrusive native doctor has just arrived on a donkey, desirous of seeing inquisitively all we have to shew: however he is not allowed to be shown anything as he may be a dealer in disguise, and dealers are not allowed to shew their noses here. They come occasionally, however, and various loafers come, and squat down all day idly in Arab attitudes about the place, they look like prophets in the distance with long sticks, and imposing draperies, but near at hand, they look suspicious characters and one feels dubious as to their intentions. Flinders spots them from afar, and generally at ¼ mile distance, begins suddenly to run very fast, in the sort of way that would overtake anybody or anything, and then there is a general fleeing of loafers, and the works are left in peace. Or he walks towards them, and then begins to run most alarmingly when near; it is terrifying to the loafer, and most amusing to the onlooker. Sometimes these chases extend right down to the cultivation, far distant!

8 a.m. (sitting on a mastaba out in the desert)

I may as well describe a picturesque incident in our domestic house-keeping which occurred yesterday, in which the buying of a turkey seemed a delightful and romantic thing of the Arabian Nights, and strangely contrasted with your dull resorting to a poulterers along pavements, in fog or rain, elegantly clothed, and feeling stultified with advertisements and all the other atrocities of civilisation. F. and I were at large in the desert measuring up mastabas, when a small white donkey approached us with measured paces, and thereon a large old prophet, very picturesque and very lean and scraggy, whose long brown feet almost touched the ground; by his side came a little girl, as brown and as necklaced and earringed as they all are, and in front of him the old man held a muktaf, a green rush basket, and the basket held a large and intelligent-looking turkey: so F. and the prophet conversed, and the turkey changed owners, and he went on to deliver it up to Ali, and we sat down ¼ mile distant, and looked at porphyries lying about the desert, till Ali had shouted to us the right number of piastres F. was to give. Ali is a great bargainer and is very proud of his successes in marketing. 3 or 4 turkeys wander up and down the courtyard here all day, and the evening's dinner investigates one's hut in a placid but inquisitive manner: and sometimes the turkeys quarrel, and pursue each other up and down the loads of pots and piles of bones, and then the cook boy Mohamed, and Yusuf have to separate them, and one is popped on to the wall, and another on to our greenery-covered board roof, and the third into an empty hut. Mohamed is a sweet youth, with wondrous manners, all salaams and salutations, and is becoming a good servant, quick and bright. ...

We have alternate mornings of photographing and mastaba-surveying now. A number more of named mastabas are daily coming to light and our large cemetery, just behind the temple of Denderah, is the oldest, and here we are beginning to come upon a series of IVth dyn. mastabas: there are two imposing ones, and several of a lesser order. Here one gets more than elsewhere the idea of

Hilda descending a tomb-shaft by rope-ladder, perhaps at Denderah 1897–8.

what these buildings must have been, for instead of low walls only remaining, of mud brick, some height of wall has been exposed, and in the finest IVth dynasty one, the great stone slabs remained in situ, the facing of the walls, and these recesses of the false door were covered with outlining in red and black for sculpture still not begun, except in the door itself. ...

The workmen are an intelligent set of fellows whom F. has trained in work at various places in various years, so most of them work well, and understand how to look for their walls and pits. They work in couples – man and boy – or in groups of 4. At present they are all engaged on mastabas, as the tunnels were worked out months ago. They sleep in the tunnels, so they are all within ¾ mile of their work, and are close to the huts. They all begin to sally forth about 8 a.m. in their long brown overalls, like bees from a hive, from the great tunnel-mound every morning, and get down to their respective pits with their green rush baskets like carpenters' baskets, and their short-handled hoes; one works at the bottom of the hole, shovelling sand and stones into the basket with the broad edge of the tool, and the other, the boy, carries the basket to and fro, on his shoulder, and throws the stuff down in heaps outside, on the nearest spot where they will not want to dig. In deep excavations, 10 or 20 or 30ft. two boys haul the basket up by ropes. They sing weird monotonous tunes, somewhat like Gregorians, very frequently, but oftener quite unlike anything I have ever heard. They are dressed in picturesque garments of white or blue or brown – which I now notice come in that sequence, and the variations mean varying degrees of dress and undress. The white shirt is loose-sleeved, and shaped round the shoulders and arms by means of a white or red string crossed over the back: on this is hung little square red leather packets or books, sentences of Koran therein considered as a sort of talisman, with a sundry bead or two sometimes added. The blue garment is likewise flowing and picturesque – sometime a bright blue, the brown outer one is of very coarse canvas. The red slippers are taken off and laid aside for work.

15 February 1898

[H.P. writes]

The day before yesterday when we were down by the Roman houses under the temple walls, the northern boundary of our cemetery, we saw quite a procession of people on donkeys – old men in long robes – women in black – children in brightly coloured draperies, astride in twos – all wending their way to the north-west corner of our ground, where a small modern cemetery stands. Such a collection of folks were there already, groups of Arabs, and some twenty donkeys turned loose to wander also among the tombstones. A crowd of women sat in rows on the ground round an open grave, swinging their arms backwards and forwards, and swaying to and from with a rhythmical movement of the body, and moaned and half-sang in the monotonous minor way that only an Egyptian can; their lamentations rose to prolonged howls now and then, and sometimes in a sustained soprano shriek, and were very weird. It was all strangely picturesque and Oriental, and dismal, and the little unenclosed group of whitewashed tombstones, with the isolated mourners and straying beasts, looked so desolate in its expanse of open desert. There are little collections of graves at frequent intervals along the desert edge. We came upon large-spread ones, in our exploration to How, also, at which place I watched a long funeral procession across the cultivation up on to the desert, and was much impressed by their long slow deeply-sung dirges, somewhat Gregorian-sounding.

During the feast of Bairam, Flinders, Hilda and Ali undertook a five-day trip following the edge of cultivated land to the west ending at Hu (also Hiw or How). The proliferation of finds there convinced Flinders that he should return the following year to investigate further.

21 February 1898

[H.P. writes]

We got off early, quite successfully, and our appearance was most impressive. We had three good white donkeys with great red leather embroidered saddles, who trotted well, and even broke into long cantering: one day they carried us 20 miles, and as all the ground is full of dips and rises and covered with large stones, it is difficult riding. Then a huge brown camel stalked behind us with a huge bolster on each side of him, namely our four large blankets each, containing our night things and water bottles and roped around each, with a green grass mat, then the two sacks of food piled above, and the two tents roped up, and hanging from one side a tin lantern with coloured glass let into it (inside this, we kept a tin of condensed milk, looking like a relic in a reliquary, by day, and my hairpins by night – it was our safest repository!) and hanging on the other side of the camel (making him look somewhat like a Kens-vestry dust-cart!) was a tin pail, full of saucepans. Arabs in short blue garments and white turbans, bare-legged, ran behind in the procession – donkey-man and camel-driver. F. and I were dressed alike in baggy white native garments (I rode astride) and coats cover flannel shirts, he in cap, and I in felt hat with puggery.[1] Ali had on a long tight aesthetic greeny-blue cassock with a pink striped vest, a brown skull-cap, and huge yellow slippers. He is a splendid young fellow – a host in himself: he manages everything quietly and thoroughly, and is master of every sort of work: he cooked and carried for us, contrived all neatly, got information from everyone in each village, showed infinite tact in everything, and hunted indefatigably for flints whenever we were feeding or resting. The donkeys flew at the sound of his voice! He is very observant over sites, and often scoured off across the plain sideways to see if mounds were Roman or what.

Those details may enable you to picture the expedition: F. seems to be giving our route and the results of our search too fully for me to add more.

The first day, cool and pleasant, we had a delightful ride along the middle of the desert, to Marashdeh, 12 m. We had walked along much of its cultivation-edge, and meant to ride home under the hillrange, so all the ground got covered. The village looked like a mediaeval fortified one almost, in the distance, as it is chiefly composed of great square pigeon-towers, whose pots along the top make them look battlemented. We encamped on a raised dike by a dry canal ½ mile short of the cluster of towers, under a row of huge tamarisk trees, 40 ft. high, with thick red trunks, and long boughs; it was a public road, and many folks, and donkeys and camels passed. Our own

---

[1] Veil hanging behind.

lay down round us, patriarcally by our tent doors, but were driven into the village for night. Opposite us was a deserted looking farm building chiefly consisting of a saggieh,[1] near which we must pitch, for our drinking-water. It is always a picturesque sight – the couple of oxen driven round by a small brown boy perched in a green basket, upon the great rough wooden saggieh-wheel, which interlocks, as in a cog-wheel, and there is another at right-angles, so that one sees a great number of long round pots circulating and splashing their water from a deep well below into a shallow trough on the surface, whence it runs by a narrow channel and waters the cultivation all around: they are generally on the edge of the desert, and one always gets one's water from a saggieh.

The shadoof is the other means of raising water: it is the long pole, heavily weighted by a lump of mud at one end, and worked by a man who dips his basket and raises it thus about ten feet and empties it into the next above; there are generally three such together, at intervals along the banks of canals and Nile. The men sing the strange monotonous crooning dirge, minor, with little twists, which is the only song they have: and the saggieh-wheel creaks in a sad but pleasing manner, and can be heard for miles – it is rather a fascinating sound.

Two draperied guards with big old guns saw to our night safety always. We had two capital nights, 21st and 24th at Marashdeh, quiet and peaceful, but the intervening nights at Shekh-Ali were much disturbed by all the village dogs barking all night, and talkative guards near us and a braying donkey. F. made sallies at them, but we couldn't get much quiet.

The tenting was great fun: the tents we easily pitched in the sand, always under trees and near water. The tent poles were forgotten, but one donkey went back for them ½ way and returned before sunset. The tents are full length for lying down in, but narrower than their length, and by the time the blankets are spread, the field is more than occupied, and ends have to be tucked in! There was a piled-up rim of tins, bottles etc. all along our heads and uncommonly little room for anything! One's clothes have to be tucked into the blankets, that no hand from outside might steal anything. Ablutions it seems customary to perform in the starlight on these occasions, and there is certainly no room within.

We had a nice walk all round Marashdeh, and out across the desert a mile to Roman remains, the first evening. After sunset, on our return, we found Ali cooking a pot of lentil soup for us, with a fire of durra straw on the canal bank under our tamarisks: we ate our meals on our beds, out of the same plate very often. The stores lasted well. We brought six tins and some aerated

---

[1] Water-wheel.

water back, so could have faced another day or two if necessary: but the bread was very bricky the last two days and had to be soaked in water a little. We had a tin of meat, and peas, and jam, also loaves and oranges, and a water-tin in a saddlebag, always with us, for our lunch far up in the Gebel, and meanwhile the main baggage made its way majestically along the edge of the country to our camping-village; the saddlebag generally came back full of flint implements.

Our first day was mainly along alternate XVIII dyn. and Roman remains: we sighted mounds our lumps, or patches of flint, miles off across the desert and rode straight for them, and then dismounted, and F. and Ali investigated, poked with sticks, and looked for scraps of pottery to indicate the date. Every undulating roll of desert, every rise, was surrounded by splendid scenery; the long pink cliffs on both sides the Nile, slowly unfolded their detail to us, as we rode along day by day. Every way has its distinctive feature – the dry water channels are lined with tufts of vegetation, spiny and spiky bunches of greenery, very refreshing to the eye, and some of the flowers are so pretty. And there are occasionally great masses of cactus, or castor-oil plant, or a large succulent shrub with bulging seed-vessels, very tropical-looking: and in the cultivation, or in the villages, date-palms and dom-palms, and the sort which is an acacia, and the nebbek[1] whose leaf is like dogwood and the growth somewhat like birch, drooping and graceful.

We pitched our tent the middle night of the expedition under a row of nebbeks near a deserted farm building and beside a large patch of sugar-cane. The desert rose above us in this village, and there was the modern cemetery near by. The cemeteries are very interesting: they spread away over desolate desert quite unenclosed: there are numbers of them along the desert edge (4 within sight of the Denderah tunnels). All the tombs are white plaster ones, very dazzling, roughly made and the upright part is bunchy and irregular in shape. Some are very gaily painted with the representation of coloured mats of openwork embroidery, crude red and green, and on the end of the gravestone of the women's graves, rarely depicted mirror, comb, and scissors, very childishly done! Ali says this custom of painting only dates from a year back. The smallest graves are sometimes very bright and quaint. There are generally half a dozen large white scattered domes of shekhs among the ordinary graves – landmarks for miles.

F. has described our interesting hunt along New Race graves for fragments to decide the date, at Semaineh and onwards, and how a large part of the great Beiram concourse of people pursued us; several hundred followed us, and the day grew hot and at last we settled down in a shady nook by the

---

[1] The nebbek, or lebbakh *(albizzia lebbek)*.

cultivation to look at New Race pots. F. bought some and the stragglers who still remained round us were 90 when I came to count them! New Race and XVIIIth seem to alternate here for miles and once we came upon some unopened mastabas, and a good patch of IVth. From here, while we lunched and tramped, the donkeys went on to Shekh Ali without us, by mistake, and we had a hot walk after them, and I got a neuralgic headache, but got over it next morning, to start as usual on a long ride of exploration. The sight of Kefaltieh, a large village or rather small town, levelled ruthlessly to within a yard of the ground, was very strange: it was all of brown mud, and the corn-bin towers tilted in all directions looked so curious: the desolation of it all reminded one of so many passages in the Prophets. From a rubbish-mound in its midst, one quite saw what the gradations of respectability and prosperity in its buildings had been: the handsome architectural quarter of the village looked very different to the tumbled mud hut quarter. More XVIIIth and Roman, towards How. We started just after sunrise, and reached How itself by about 10; and have put up for the day under the temple walls in the shade – a hot day. We explored the temple ruins, and F. tramped over some monotonous cemetery, and we looked at green cultivation, and How itself on the river, a town with minarets: we went back along the steep tomb-covered edge of the cultivation, and found that Shekh Ali had been at work cutting down the very nebbek trees under which our tent was pitched! Our tent that night was full of small beetles, and other like creatures: I turned out all that I could find, but F. seemed on such good terms with all the beetles he came across, that I gradually grew more reconciled to them. 50 villagers squatted round our camping ground while we pitched, and 40 I counted watching us breathlessly when we started on a walk. I suppose we really did seem very strange to them; if they took me for a typical Inglizi I certainly looked anything but that. Many of course have never seen an English woman before, we were entirely out of the beaten track; and some of the Gebel which we explored, the hills 10 miles in, have never had Europeans about them, F. says. They seem entirely unknown, and are still unmapped.

24–25 February 1898

[H.P. writes]

Our return journey was far inland, up among them.[1] We rode 8 miles up into them, so as to explore their spurs for tombs of VIth dynasty, and then got all-day rides across bays from spur to spur, so as to have 10 miles of desert on either side of us; for the undulations of the hills here, in forward spurs and backward bays cover a 10 miles' width of winding.

---

[1] The Gebel hills.

A tramp up an old desert road to a Roman pottery rubbish heap, and a great bay to cross, riding.

Up to the same point again, and an all-day exploration of all the valleys of the great spur thereabouts, with the result that we found a curious hermit's cell of perhaps III century, scooped in a fissure of the limestone, 300 ft up, with an elaborate zigzag path leading up, much Roman brick outside and the cell and outside cliff-face covered with Coptic graffiti. We got home an hour after sunset, at a gallop.

26 February 1898

[H.P. writes]

F. and I and Ali have just returned from a most delightful 5 days' riding tour, in and out of this wide strip of desert, sometimes along the cultivation and oftener up under the cliffs of the high Gebel – a 70 miles or so of exploration extending to How. We intended starting on the 20th and over-night we had two tents, and our blankets and night things, packed and a sack of bread and oranges, and a great sack of tins of meat and jam; and we were ready at sunrise the next morning to start, but the donkeys never turned up till 10–11 and were then found inefficient for rough fast-riding. Meanwhile F. and I had started on, and we tramped some miles along the edge of the cultivation, enjoying the scenery and picking up flint implements, and expecting to be overtaken by our beasts and baggage. A messenger overtook us at a near point with information that we could have 2 donkeys and a camel, but the creatures were not forthcoming, and after sitting an hour or two on a high mound, eyeing the desert-track for them, and watching the peaky sails along the Nile, and resting, we were starved into a return and got home by 2, after a delightful 10 miles of exploration of the desert, to make secure arrangements for an early start next day.

Flinders summarises their trip:

20–27 February 1898

Beiram feast coming on made all our men feverish to get away. So though Beiram was not until the 23rd, they all went off by 19th–20th. This made an admirable break for my getting away, as Hilda was in good condition for it, we tried to get off, but owing to difficulty in getting fit donkeys here we walked some way to start and then had to return. I sent off Ali to get some good donkeys and he brought three fair ones. So then we set off next day. ... we reached Marasdeh 12 miles W. of Dendereh where we pitched under a group of big tamarisks by the roadside. ...

The next day we went on westward and began the great cemetery region at Semaineh, which no one has yet described I believe or hardly even visited. The start of it is at a modern cemetery with some large domed tombs, one white. It was the great feast day of Beiram as kept locally (really a day wrong) and there were hundreds of people thronging the cemetery, where there were all sorts of diversions going on, reputable and disreputable, pious and impious. The affair was on the wane and a stream of people was drifting homewards on donkeys, when the grateful variety of two foreigners on donkeys came up to give new interest, and we were at once the centre of hundreds of folks who ran before behind and before and were whacked by guards and scampered and staded and made a dust, squabbled and squeezed up as close as they could whenever we halted to look at the cemetery. The tombs were XVIII dyn and prehistoric (New Race). Thousands stood open, plundered in recent years, but evidently there were many more not yet attacked, all the way along the desert edge to Sheikh Ali.

5 March 1898

[H.P. writes]

The last few days have been taken up chiefly with indoor work of various sorts. F. writes letters, works at the general plan, and I plot mastabas, large numbers of which are roughly sketched and carefully measured, and waiting to get planned to scale. Also F. has been sawing down mastaba cornices to manageable thickness, and we have been mending the broken ones with tapioca, till their hieroglyphs are pieced together satisfactorily.

This hot weather never stayed with us completely. Afternoons are hot; it is 70° and sometimes up to 85° in my hut. But the mornings are quite cold. We sat out in the strong wind this morning on the Gebel outside our courtyard, F. making a copy of some of the columns on our great Beb sarcophagus lid, and I correcting MSS.[1]

Various visitors took up yesterday afternoon. Miss Brodrick[2] and Miss Anderson-Morton turned up from a dahabiyeh, on donkeys, and spent an hour looking round things, and having the site explained to them from the tunnel-tops, and after they had gone, in came Prof. Sayce to have a long talk with F. and to sit and hobnob over our best finds.

Sunset

F. and I have been off across the plain, to measure in whatever mastabas have given us fresh names in the last few days. Beb and Beba occur in about half of them! the number of Zantas and Antefs and Mer names confuses one

---

[1] Manuscripts.

[2] May Brodrick had been one of Petrie's first students at University College.

much. We begin to get many interesting inscriptions now – not only the Suten-du-hotep formula, and religious invocations that are customary but delightful descriptions of the private people, with details of their boats of 4 and 5 oars, and their sycomores in their forests and fields, and how many oxen and asses they had. And their quaint children make them offerings, each named above their heads, and in the corner is the servant, stooping over bread-making!

Lord Northampton turned up again today, in the coloured Bedawy head-dress, and was duly impressed by the sight of our mastabas, and the strange new one, the galleried sand-pit, in particular. He is on his way down, now that the river is running lower.

The sunsets are very magnificent sometimes: we have not had such wonderful ones lately, but an ordinary sunset here in its clear amber, and brilliant flood of light, equals a more than ordinary sunset at home. If it is a yellowish sunset, and the horizon is a distant one, one sees the 'green ray'. Just as the sun is disappearing into the desert, there is a strong bluish-green tinge over the disk of the sun, an instant before the last of it altogether sinks out of sight.

13 March 1898

[H.P. writes]

Various things of interest keep turning up. Yesterday we were summoned down into a dark hot cavernous hole to see several sandstone sarcophagi, one of them inscribed all along one side: this F. decided must be sawn off, and as one of the saws here could do such a job, a great saw 90 inches long was constructed this morning, whose teeth consisted of large French nails, with even their heads left on, which we found would rake up and down tough sandstone and make huge grooves satisfactorily: F. invented this saw, one former year. The lid however is full of enormous flints, so there are fresh difficulties to withstand. The side will cut up into 4 nice panels.

Today came news of a gigantic inscribed stela, down in the pit of a distant mastaba. Men came to fetch tent-poles, and the long wooden Cradle, and we left our Beb-copying and followed, to see that the lifting was carefully done. Half-a-dozen men were down in the pit holding the stone on end, under Ali's directions, and a dozen above were keeping it in position with ropes. It was let down slowly on to the cradle, and hauled with many Arab shouts and ejaculations up a slope, and all across a mile of desert home, F. and I going in front, and flinging stones out of the way, to smooth the path, and several boys with turyahs[1] making it level also. It came soon into the pathway of

---

[1] Hoes.

Prince Beb's coffin lid, and was brought home in triumph, with monotonous refrains and responses all the way. Salli' Allah, pray upon it, as before, and a number of new ones.

Flinders and I spent much of today at the back of the huts, where all our large false doors are laid, leaning over respective halves of Beb's sarcophagus lid, getting on with a facsimile copy of the inscription; for the last part of the day, we had a blanket spread across two tent-poles.

Today is the hottest day we have had, 85° in my hut. The Khamsin was blowing, a hot wind from the south-east, with sand blowing along disagreeably, and everything indoors getting covered with sand. It grew fiercer in the afternoon, but fell as the wind changed west-ward, and this very short spell of it is now over. We have had attempts at it before, once or twice, when columns of sand rose 1000 ft. into the air, and it was wonderful to see the sand lifting like smoke! Today the sandiness obscured the desert-cliffs – our mountains are scarcely discernable at all, and we could only see the foot-hills.

A few days ago, the tunnels which we thought were played out, produced several things of interest – the animal catacombs namely, with which we began the season. In the part dedicated to the sacred hawks, in a corner of a tunnel lay a crumbling old box, and at the top of it, Flinders picked out some small bronzes – a figure of Horus, seated, figure of Ra, seated and a Horus-hawk. There were various mummied hawks as well, and one gorgeous to behold, a stately hawk-mummy cased in stucco covered with gold foil, with figures and inscriptions in relief on it, all very freshly glittering: the whole was past preservation unfortunately, and crumbled away immediately.

The mastabas to plan are innumerable. I get on with about half a dozen daily, but we are always measuring in more.

There are 4 men here now: besides ourselves Mr McIver is at work measuring skulls and bones, and seems to be working out some interesting details of measurement. The skulls stacked outside here are numbered by hundreds now, and there is one whole mummy among them. We have not had such a spell of Ptolemaic mummies lately, but are digging mainly VIth – XIIth.

One mastaba yesterday turned out some nice XVIIIth dynasty pots of various shapes with slender necks, and a nice round pottery bowl or basin, with pierced work, and a procession of cows round the top – small images at intervals along the rum. We daily mend portions of broken stone cornice with tapioca, to get the inscriptions complete. And then F. has a photographic morning and gets them arranged in their order and photographed off. A very thin knife, a fine flint implement was found the other day in the corridor of the great sand-pit mentioned last week, which is a sort of cloister (with several archways of rough cutting, leading into a square courtyard) whence a

Southern tombs east of Cairo

The Citadel, Cairo from the west

Mosque (El Ashraf?)

Excavating a tomb-shaft (Meydum?)

Akhenaten tomb

Palm tree,
Tell el Amarna

Tell el Amarna

Denderah 1897–98

Hu from the dig huts in the cemetery

Mosque in the Hu cemetery

Dig house at Hu

Hu, Upper Egypt

A house on the desert edge

A sheikh's waly

Landscape

Looking across the Nile Valley to the western hills

long passage runs inward with lateral openings: there are several separate burials, but the place is not wholly worked out yet.

A pretty little figure turned up yesterday, 1½ inches high, of a woman holding a child seated on her hip. It is in ivory, end of XIIth dynasty date.

20 March 1898
Dendera, Keneh

[H.P. writes]

We have had another short spell of khamsin,[1] ending in a blustering wind yesterday afternoon; and now we have cold north wind, and mornings are sharp.

We were out yesterday morning before sunrise to go down to the works and measure up the said XI dynasty gallery of tombs, popularly known as the sandpit. It is intolerable to stay long in it when the 4 men are at work in it, they make such a dust, and so we had it all to ourselves, by going at 5.30 we lit a candle, and F. measured each passage and pit, I recording, and then by these measurements we scored the plan on the desert surface above, and marked out the angles with stones, so as to look for a mastaba, or cenotaph belonging to the burials below. Then we got home to breakfast about 7, and spent the rest of the day at Beb. F. is at the great coffin lid, and I am at the side piece of the coffin. They lie behind our huts, and for the sunniest part of the day, we stretch a blanket over tent-poles, and work under it. The mountains on either side of us are lovely to look at, at intervals in the drawing. The range this side looks quite close, its great jutting promontories look a mile off, though really they are 5 miles away. The others, across the Nile, though they appear so close, are 12 and 20 miles away. A hundred XIIth dynasty skulls with their bones are lying peaceably spread out on the ground beside us, very white and neat. The main collection is round the corner, hundreds piled on each other.

Two mornings lately I have devoted to clothes washing. I bring it round to the back, and work beside the stone copying and do them alternately, so as to alternate the back-aches connected with each employment! I had collected all the paraphernalia the other day and watched over a certain pan of water on the stove with tender solicitude for at least half-an-hour and was at last just beginning to set to work, when Muhammed the cook boy rushed down upon me, and snatched my hot water from me, so that I had to begin preparations all over again. It was the rice for the midday meal that he was rescuing!

On the weekly holiday, the men (M. Mac I and D) generally go off to the river in the afternoon and get a bathe. Last Thursday, while we were at our

---

[1] A hot, dusty wind.

copying, an excited crowd of Arabs came up from the village, and stood gesticulating near our huts. We gathered it had to do with the Khawagas' bathing: and found that it was a deputation imploring that the Khawagas would not swim so recklessly in mid-Nile, or would anyhow not get drowned opposite their village, or they would all get hanged for it. They had threatened and expostulated with the bathers themselves, and dragged them out of the water apparently! It was rather an amusing incident.

Another amusing thing was a conversation one of them had with the effendi[1] who strolls lazily about our works and professes to keep watch over all that goes on, but in reality never sees anything that is found. He described how he was for a year in England, and the things that he most admired in England were the Mile End Road and Poplar Station! He had been to a music hall every evening and thought them fine.

The flies tease us dreadfully while we are copying, we have to cover everything with powder, including a handkerchief over one's head. Often Flinders has taken to a veil in self-defence.

Today is a day of wondrously enormous white clouds. They are not only larger than any clouds at home, but are the desert clouds, in that all their under-surface reflects the yellowish-brown of the sand below, so that they look very curious indeed. On cloudy days this is always seen in every part except the strip of sky-cloud which overhangs the cultivation and is a pure white without desert reflection.

The morning before last at 7 a.m. something phenomenal happened. It rained for 5 minutes, raindrops very few and far between. Rainfall, according to F. was one drop to the square foot. It is a comfort it does not rain here, as our finds could not possibly be all under shelter: our own roof is not of course rain-proof, and it is well that there is never a shower.

The railway runs all the way to Qena, and there are trains three times weekly, so we get our letters more quickly than before. And when we leave, we shall be able to get down to Cairo in 14 hours, independently of lengthy camel or boat travelling. Train costs 38 PT, 3rd. Cook now offers a 20 PT passage, including bread all the way, 1lb of meat and 13 cigarettes! But people persist in taking the train.

2 April 1898
Hotel du Nil, Cairo

[H.P. to her sister]

My dearest Amy,

We arrived from the Desert at 10 this morning, after an all-night journey: it is so strange to be in civilisation once more. English shoes are

---

[1] Educated Egyptian townsman.

uncomfortable, and I hardly know myself in stockings: they are so stuffy and irritable: I put them on as we were nearing Cairo. And as for Flinders, he looks quite strange in a collar and tie, socks and a black hat and dark tight trousers. And on the strangeness of a tablecloth, and butter, and European bread! and furniture! The Quibells and Miss Pirie all got out of the same train, so we are at the same hotel, and have spent the afternoon looking at their wondrous finds, both in sculpture and in solid gold workmanship, and in seeing drawings of all the invoices and curios: it has been a wonderful year for Q. at Hierakonpolis.

There has been no journal lately because we have been so busy, in spite of intense heat, in finishing Beb's sarcophagus facsimile (VIIth dynasty), in final surveying, and in packing. A wooden box remains at Deir al Bahari (Hat-y's place!) with half my things, and cabin box returns in June. Just to show you how hot it has been, I will candidly inform you that it has been my practice lately, to wear out of doors, 6–10 a.m. and 4–6 p.m. *no* underclothes whatever! only a skirt and shirt, cap and slippers and indoors 10–4 p.m. *no* clothes whatever!

The following letter was written on the return journey, at the end of the season, to James Breasted, the head of the Oriental Institute of Chicago which was helping to finance the work.

12 April 1898
Naples

My dearest Breasted,

Many thanks for your letters of 6 Dec. and 20 Dec. which I have left till I could tell you of our winter's work. Dendera cemetery was a large mouthful, but with my wife writing down all my survey work, and drawing all the plans, Mace to clear out tombs and work the men, Davies to copy and to do the Ptolemaic tombs, and MacIver to measure the hundreds of skulls and skeletons, we have succeeded in getting all the main points settled in three months. The whole place is nearly a mile long and half a mile wide, full of tombs; but we have searched every part and opened nearly half the area of the ground.

[continues in H.P.'s writing]

It proves to be a little of IV (3 or 4 mastabas) much of VI–XI, one tomb of XVIII, a few of XXV–XXX, and much Ptolemaic and scattered graves of Roman. The total absence of names of XII – not an Ameni or Amenemhat or Usertesen – is strange, and seems to shew that the rise of Koptos and Thebes had destroyed the life of Dendera. We have a series, in sequence of position and architectural development. The main inscription is the sarcophagus or Beb from which I have copied about 12,000 or 15,000 signs, though a good deal is lost. ...

The architectural results are very good. The brick mastabas are nobly built with great arches and vaulting, that remind one of Roman brickwork, and they form a connected series of development of form in the VI–VII dynasties. ... All large tombs were completely plundered, and only a few of the poorer ones have yielded any objects. But the harvest of stone slabs and steles has repaid our work. I have photographed all of clear condition to scale ¹/₈ and shall publish in collotype. ... I much hope that I may hear from you soon, as to what support you may be able to find for the E.R.A.[1]

[in F.P.'s writing]

My wife has written off this so far, and I can accept all your good wishes for our joint life and work as being in course of fulfilment. All our ways and thoughts and interests are so closely in common that we neither of us have to change anything in placing our lives together. Antiquities, geology and many tastes of my own are also my wife's for years past. So you see that the Egyptian work will be reinforced and not in the least hindered by the recent change.

When shall we see you and Mrs Breasted over in England? I should like to shew you our pretty village of Brasted in Kent whence your family must have come. I shall be in England from April 25 till 12 Nov.

Yours ever sincerely,

W. M. Flinders Petrie

If you want slides for lecturing let me know how many (I have about 150 plates this year besides Quibell's) and whether you wish for films glass or prints.

[Reproduced with the kind permission of the Oriental Institute of Chicago]

The following winter (1898) Mace and MacIver were with Petrie again and Hilda had two companions, her friend Beatrice Orme and Miss Lawes, one of Petrie's students. They set up camp on the south bank of the river, first at Abadiyeh and then a few miles further on at Hu, in both of which places extensive cemeteries yielded important finds.

December 1898
Abadiyeh (Hu)

[H.P.writes]

We have dug a well for our own use in a little ravine behind the huts; we cut through a bed of fine ash at about 8ft down, with all the sand burnt red for a foot below it, shewing a long contained heat, but not any mere rubbish or dwelling waste in it. I think it is one of the burning places where the prehistoric folks burnt offerings before putting the ashes in jars in their tombs.

---

[1] Egyptian Research Account.

We began on a cemetery close before our huts but found it all totally plundered, only a few poor XVIII burials on top of it. Then ½ mile south, we struck a fair prehistoric cemetery. In 6 days we have got out a fair quantity of stuff, many clay toys and models quite new to me... Many good flint lances and fine hardstone vases, good slates, mace heads.

1 December 1898

[H.P.writes]

Rooms in our huts 80° in daytime always.

[pages of drawings of grave goods and plans of graves]

The huts have just the same appearance as last year, except that Ali has added himself a hut at the back close to our courtyard entrance, with a fantastic fence made of bus,[1] durra stalks, plastered with mud, and its waving leafage at the top looks so quaint. Our men are close to us, within those old walls that we discovered on last year's donkey-trip; they have heightened the walls, but put on no roofs. Ali's wife has turned up, and Ali Jedullah's mother; our 5 or 6 turkeys walk about the premises, and the horse stands about on the desert, hobbled, with a small red leather prayer book hung around his neck! *[register of grave contents]*. ...

Hyenas howling and whining in the evening.

18 December 1898

[H.P. writes]

F. indoors, because of ankle. Ali got to worrying the men, because they idled, being on a day-work, not piece. So Hassan Osman and ¾ of the men all struck and came up to the house demanding who was their master. F. said, you are under me, so they all trooped back again. However F. was meaning to make changes, and they resulted thus. Ali himself and the men who had not struck were moved away to better work, the 4 elder men were put on to huge dull metre-digging, without chance of bakshish, and their boys split from them, and next day half of them were dismissed, until we begin to work at How in a few weeks' time.

18 December 1898

[H.P. writes]

Prof. Sayce[2] came to see us.

---

[1] Straw.

[2] Professor A. H. Sayce, orientalist and professor of Assyriology, was an old friend of Petrie's.

19 December 1898

[H.P. writes]

Market Day. B. O.[1] and I on the horse, and Ali, to market at Waqf, 12 of the workmen with us, all in blue overalls and white head-shawls. Our road was a high dusty embankment, with camel and donkey traffic, overlooking a low plain of cultivation brilliantly green with stretches of sugar cane and beans and durra. We heard the saqqiehs, and songs of the fellahin, and watched the reaping of the fields of Aalu.[2] Every large gamus[3] that passed us shied at the horse. ... I cantered along the desert edge. Ali showed us a rough mud-built sugarcrushing place, where by saqqiehs worked by oxen, they press the sugar-cane. Market only for sugar-cane, and a little tobacco, however the horse had crimson leather anklets stitched on him, so we waited 1½ hours in the gaze of 200 people, who crushed and mobbed us, amid flies and airlessness, pressing to get closer view of us, 2 village guards valiantly flogging everyone at intervals, to give us a moments peace and air. ...

The horse now has, besides his red prayer-book, a scarlet embroidered saddle and crimson leggings! he goes fast, and has once bolted with me, but is very mild and tame withal. Rides to and from the mastaba with F., who has now sprained his ankle 5 times.

Hussein Osman, one of our boatmen, bought 5 turkeys in Waqf market today. As he was carrying them away, with a boy, the Qadi of the village came by, and eyeing 5 turkeys in the hands of a stranger, determined to have one. So he went to Hussein and claimed two of them as having been stolen from himself. They disputed and then went with the village guards to the Omdeh or chief sheikh. The Omdeh told the Qadi he could not claim to know his turkeys from all others. But the Qadi insisted they were his, and at last said "Let them be sent to my house because my wife will know if they are mine." So the Qadi led Hussein and the turkeys to his house. Once inside, he said "I shall keep one of these turkeys but you may have the others." Hussein protested that he had paid for all the turkeys. "Oh son of a dog" said the Qadi "Get out of this place or I will accuse you of having stolen them from me." Finding words were of no use, Hussein left with his 4 turkeys, and had to let the Qadi keep the 5th. That evening (we heard) the Qadi feasted on the turkey, the dearest dinner probably that he ever ate. In 2 days, F. sent to Dickens and wrote to the chief of police, complaining of the theft. The police being in the matter would make plenty of trouble, so we only demanded 14 PT. and an apology. Next morning arrives a fine fat turkey from the Qadi,

---

[1] Beatrice Orme.
[2] The fields which the dead were expected to cultivate in the afterlife.
[3] Water buffalo.

with request for receipt! F. is going to inform one of the judges in Cairo of the conduct of the Qadi of Semaineh.

23 December 1898

[H.P. writes]

This week has brought us nearer the close of our work here. The place I am now finishing is a group of 2 big mastabas with pit tombs round them. One mastaba (D5) had all the carved stone smashed and removed in Roman times. But we recovered a piece of an entirely new architectural feature, a cornice representing projecting poles. This ran all along the recess of the doorway, as we know from the number  of hemi-cylinders knocked off in retrimming the stones. The poles were just a palm each in width (3in) and 7 of them to a cubit that we found intact.

The funeral chamber of this mastaba is lined with fine stone. It was all plundered in antiquity, and 10ft depth of its well entirely filled with loose bones and skulls of a pile of reburials of the XVIIIth dynasty. At the bottom of the well was a hyena's skull. ...

At Abadiyeh now we have finished the prehistoric cemeteries and also this patch of VIth dynasty. Both mastabas had been plundered, and re-used for a large mass of mixed bones of the XVIIIth dyn. From one alone we took about 100 perfect skulls, besides many others broken up. With these were many ox bones, an ibex head with five horns, and a horse's head complete. This last is valuable, as the only early historic horse skull from Egypt. The carpenter has been at boxes for a week or two; 65 for pottery and 25 for skeletons. Next ten days spent in packing small objects found, photographing and registering all the stone vases, slates, beads etc. for publication, so as to be independent of what might be kept in Egypt.

Snake tracks found outside the men's huts, 4 in. across.

Modern Egypt. The camels carry 2 baskets, when out sebakh-digging, with caps on the bottom, which are removed to empty them, and the basket left on the camel.

Bread-making. In a large mud oven *forn*. Oven blown clean, then saltpetre and water mixed in red pan. Box of flour poured in, (pan dirty) paste kneaded, 10 mins, with one hand, Mrs Ali picked up *bus* in her toes and fed the fire. Then on a bigger box lid, sprinkled flour, rubbed hard with her camel's hair shawl, rolled out a lump of paste very thin, poked into oven, rolling round rolling-pin, laid out there. Fire put out by *bus* down chimney, and oven cleaned by wet rag twisted round stick. Bread done in a few seconds. Large flap, 1 foot across, $1/3$ inch thick, two layers. Thrown out onto lap to be dusted with dress from cinders, and salt picked off.

Ali brought back glowing accounts of an Englishman at Luxor with carriage and pair 'second only to the king', melek. Also news of a cow with 6 legs he had seen at Dechneh.

Our new huts are built up against the great east wall of the temple enclosure, a mile south of Hou, on the desert edge. We are perched on a narrow ledge under the wall, and in front of us is a steep slope of Roman house rubbish and potsherds innumerable covering all, descending to a little wady forking from the cemetery, a modern one. Every day we hear chanted as follows:-

La illa-ha il-la Al-la-hu Mohammed rasul Al-lah.

The Arabs, in procession bearing a bier covered with a red shawl, come up from funerals here, sometimes under our very huts, chanting this all the way from How. ... 50 donkeys.

8 January 1899
Abadiyeh (Hu)

[H.P. writes]

At Hou, Diospolis, F. began on the temple enclosure, and tombs outside of it, but in a few hours was stopped by the guards of the Omdeh, on the ground that they had not received any authorization to let us work. We telegraphed to Cairo, but Brugsch would do nothing but send on to Loret. We were stuck for 1½ days, and then allowed to go on only on sebakhin ground by the Omdeh. Whenever they tried to bully us about the business F. retorted worrying them over certain heaps of stone which had been illegally removed from the ruins. So the Omdeh wished to be quit of the matter. At last due warrant was sent by Loret, and we are clear to go freely ahead.

The temenos here proved to be not before late Ptolemaic, and there is no trace of earlier things inside. All over the ground beneath it is Ptolemaic cemetery. I have found the site of two temples in it, one of which has many blocks of sculpture left in it. There is also a brick building of very fine work, which I suspect to be the basilica of the Roman camp here.

[Detailed report of discoveries].

9 January 1899

We hear that last night there were 5 robbers in Hou, armed and on horseback. 24 village guards were clever enough to take them unawares at night, surround them and imprison them. They found that each man had 25 cartridges, with fire-arms and three knives apiece.

17 January 1899

This morning, a wonderful sight: a party of some dozens of women, in long black draperies, perched on camels, going over the bridge and along our desert edge to the Coptic cemetery, wailing. 15 camels first with 2 women apiece in rope bags hung on poles, then as many with 3 women each, on blankets or carpets. All in black, with discs of mud smeared on their head, hands blue-black with blk lead? Wailing chromatic from Do to Mi. Words Nusrani.[1] They returned after an hour there, wails and shrieks continued still.

Today the wall of Mohammed Derwish's hut fell down. He only remarked "Robbina kerim. Iza kan fil lel, ana tahtu." What a philosopher. "Our Lord is bountiful. Had it been in the night, I should have been crushed."

The day before yesterday, a procession of women came up the embankment from Hou, in long black garments, with sound as of drum. When they reached the shekh's tomb at the beginning of the cemetery, they stopped and closed in, about 50 of them, in a closely packed group, left off their wails and shrieks, and holding aloft 2 tambourines (whose noise we had heard) beaten by several with open palms, they began a performance of slow rhythmical dancing up and down from one leg to the other, exactly like the ancient Egyptians in XIXth dynasty wall frescoes. The accompaniment was fast but the hopping slow and measured. They continued this curious performance at intervals of every 4 or 5 minutes many times  on their way up to the cemetery, slowly and ecstatically, and one old blacky woman in particular seemed in raptures. Tho' we were not far off, only in our own doorways across the narrow wady, and could see plainly, we looked through the telescope by turns so as to miss no detail. About 20 minutes later, a large funeral came up. All went back together at sunset. It was for this that I had heard so much wailing at Hou the previous night.

In the evening, our men held a derwish meeting by moonlight in the wady. These are always on moonlight nights, and originate probably in moon-worship. Their name is zikr. We attended it, and found it very interesting and weird. First they all assembled together, and sat cross-legged on the ground; and bent forward all together, chanting ALLAH with great energy, in monotone, and next likewise chanted Illahaha for some time; then 2 men sang a tune beginning with a very long note, and going off into a sad minor with accompaniment of grunting exactly like pigs, and a chorus of grunts between every bar or two. The grunts led the time, which rapidly increased, till tune and grunting and clapping of hands grew so fast, they at last stopped for want of breath, I think, almost choking. After a short relapse into talking

---

[1] Christian.

and laughing, they worked themselves up again by yet another chorus, *aleh* Allah, *aleh* Allah, etc. again swaying backwards and forwards in an ecstasy and groaning it in a frenzied exaltation of "seeing Allah". This was followed by another swaying and bowing chorus which sounded like OY or HOYA, continued with clapping of hands. It culminated in a strange chorus of heavy breathing in and out, frantically kept up for some time, just like dogs out of breath and nothing human. Then Dahshur's companion sang several times: there was one song accompanied all through with assents and groans, and another sung very quickly, with grunts throughout, which left off when the chorus seemed tired out. Then there was laughter and talking. Lastly a long refrain beginning Sul-lul-la, and ending (Moh)hamed. The zikr here ended.

   [Description of burials, mostly Middle Kingdom].
   [Notation of threshing tunes, funeral tunes, worktime tunes].
   [Description of "pan-graves"].

During Ramadan, the Petries took a short holiday in Luxor, giving Hilda her first sight of the Theban tombs and temples. Returning to Hou, on February 22nd work on the pangraves continues. Hilda notes, three days later,

... the howling women, mourners, have come to the cemetery in a company, dancing to tambourines, while they wave red, orange and green kerchiefs and slap their cheeks, and also sing and shriek. Their song going up was

       er ghet khai-I fil fassagi, ya yini
       (from the field, my brother, to the tomb, oh we have come)
       and coming down
       ib-khi alek ya aini bil hamaran
       (weep for thee, oh my eyes, to reddening)
       anzil el khawia wahedi, banzil el khawia qoddam
       (bury the brother alone, bury the brother before (us).

   [She notes further funeral songs].

Everything has been of XIIth dyn. which was found with the Pan. deposits or in Pan-graves.

   F. sees in the thick dishes of Kahun with incised patterns, XIIth, the descent of Libyan incised pottery: certainly those dishes are not connected to anything Egyptian in origin.

   F. began to work on the old temple site of Hu, but was unjustly stopped. Claims to private property. The Mudir of Qena will not specify govt. land, and F. will report in Cairo, and get register looked into by surveyor. ...

In March, Flinders took another short break with Hilda and Ali; he was anxious to see what a French archaeologist, M. Emile Amélineau, was finding at el Araba, the site of the ancient city Abydos, downstream from Nag Hammadi. Horrified by what he found in the cemetery of Umm el Qa'ab, Petrie realised that the Frenchman was not competent to excavate what were clearly early tombs of the utmost importance, he resolved to make the site his next objective. Amélineau's permit had not expired, but he did not appear to be interested in returning; Gaston Maspero, who had replaced Loret as Director of Antiquities, granted Petrie the concession. Petrie began work at Abydos at the end of 1899; it was to be one of his most rewarding excavations. The vast cemetery of Umm el Qa'ab (Mother of Pots) contained burials from prehistoric to Roman date and here Petrie found the tombs of the earliest pharaohs surrounded by their courtiers, and a rich harvest of grave goods which the previous excavators had failed to preserve or record. Petrie found that what he had heard of the Frenchman's methods was true and went on to prove that there was much that Amélineau had missed.

Petrie writes from Abydos:

12 February 1899

It is a scandalously long time since I sent any journal, but every evening is so occupied with drawing that I never seem to have a minute to spare. Most of my time is taken up in dealing with the things, only part of each day being spent on the work. First there is the sorting over the vase fragments: each kind of stone to be put together, then each lot of one kind to be spread out and every possibility of fitting tried: at last to ends by ¾ of the pieces being lotted up in paper packets, each packet holding the bits of one vase. It is seldom that we get even ¼ of a vase from the pieces, yet there is often enough to show the whole outline, from which I can draw it. There were enormous piles of alabaster and slate fragments, which it is hopeless to match together, but all the other stones are thus sorted, the classes being porphyry, grantie, diorite, basalt, breccia, metamorphic limestones, metamorphic volcanic ash, serpentine, white marble, blue-black veins very hard, saccharine marbles, shelly marbles, limestones, buff, pink, black, grey and white. As I have done about 10,000 or 12,000 pieces from the two tombs of Mersekha and Qa and secured every possible fit among them all, this may be allowed to occupy a few mornings work.

There is also the drawing of pottery to be done; over a hundred outlines are finished, but there is about as much waiting. Then the clay sealings have to be carefully copied. Among hundreds of fragments of sealing, all the pieces of one have to be collected. These are then laid out and the inscription made out; then must be traced how many repetitions there were around the cylinder seal, 2, 3, 4, 6 or 8, detected by minute differences in the arrangement. Lastly a facsimile drawing of the whole sealing is patched together, often getting only a single sign from one sealing and never more than ¼ or ⅔ of the whole impression. If I finish one seal in an evening I am satisfied. There are now 17 drawings of these seals finished, but still more than these are waiting.

I have also drawn many dozens of marks on jars giving the names of kings or names of palaces and tombs. But Hilda has done hundreds of signs from jars and yet many more hundreds are waiting.

Then there are the plans of the tombs which have to be kept up to date every day as the work goes on; and when each great tomb is finished Hilda plans the whole of it in fair copy.

Besides this the photographing often demands a morning's work and an evening developing after it.

So I hope that friends won't put it down to laziness or indifference if they do not get a weekly journal. My aim is to be able to get out a first volume on the royal tombs as soon as possible after I return, without waiting to issue the later inscriptions found here.

Mace and MacIver are going on well. The XII dyn. temple is finished and gives most of the plan. The pyramid is not yet entered, and Mace is now tunneling under the rock underneath it. The cemeteries are flourishing and Garstang is doing finely, paying more for bakshish than for wages. This is the place that Amélineau left last year as exhausted and told me that all the fellahin knew that the royal tombs were finished and nothing could have been found by them there after he had left!

December 1899

... In Cairo the dealer from Keneh turned up, and I bought a large lot from him. ... On reaching Girgeh we had 12 miles to ride. Hilda did well on the horse, but I found donkey almost too much strain for so long, and had to get off and rest on the way.

We found that Mace had not plastered our rooms, and so were moved about from one to another while plastering went on. In this work someone stole my watch from a room. I was sorry to lose one I had constantly had for 10 years. After 3 days of arranging and settling in, I began work about the temple just by the house merely to fill a day or two and get things in train. We have 80 men and boys from Coptos, all living in huts just behind our house. The first day in the temple we found a batch of cooking pots etc. of bronze, buried together: unfortunately very brittle being corroded by damp. ... Then after market day we started regular work on the cemetery. I have identified the royal tombs, partly by finds, partly by what the effendi here tells me. He is a capital man and seems to be quite our friend. I knew him 15 years ago, as Maspero's servant. ...

The first day we tried a triple line of chambers E. of "Osiris", but found they had been wholly cleared by Amélineau. ... The ground is thickly covered with pieces of stone vases, all thrown out by Am's workmen. In one afternoon my men collected about 2 or 3 cwt of pieces, including many of rock crystal, and some pieces with the name of Azab.

I picked up myself pieces of sealing of Za and Den at their tombs, which are also thickly strewn with pieces of vases. There does not seem to have been any attempt to secure the pieces in Amélineau's digging. We hear many tales of the way in which he was robbed wholesale of the things; and he was paying about 4 or 6 times the proper price for things he bought in the village, food, boxes, etc. ...

11–25 December 1899

Journal has fallen into arrear owing to the many other things which needed time.

We have had to get our rooms into order: arranging many things so as to last permanently – stores to be put by, shelves and cupboards to be made up, two doors to the dining room and one to the lock-up store room to be fitted with hinges and locks.

The work has been active, and kept us all busy. The royal tomb Mersed has been more than half turned over again and the remains left behind by Amélineau quite justify us in working over again all the stuff that he threw out from the tombs. ...

We have – from only one part of one tomb – over a dozen pieces of inscribed stone vases. ... The inscribed pieces are but a small fraction of the plain pieces of stone vases, of which we have about 1 cwt of variegated stones and several cwt of fragments of alabaster and slate. Of course we cannot hope to do anything with the latter, but bring the pieces which shew the form well; but we shall try to keep and join up as far as possible all the fine stone pieces. ...

It is important not to talk about these results for the next few months, as Amélineau's permit does not expire till 1 June, and if he knew how much he had left behind he might claim to go on there again. He merely worked by an ignorant gang, driven on by the lash, and not paying anything for results. He got hardly any of the minute results and was grossly robbed of what was found. With trained men, well paid for every inscribed chip, the case is altogether different. ...

After ten days on Mersed I withdrew most of the men from there to try some great mounds. We hear that Amélineau may turn up and demand to go on this season, so we are rushing on to various classes of work in order not to leave any obviously good thing unclaimed before Am. comes. ...

There are [...] some great mound tombs, plundered of old and attacked by Amélineau, at the foot of the hills to the south. These we are leaving for the present, just putting a couple of men on to enter a claim in case Am. turns up.

... The great enclosure of the Osiris temple, and the Old Kingdom town, in which we live and where the complete 1st(?) dyn. tomb was found, I am reserving for another year. It will need to be exhaustively turned over. It is about 300 × 250 metres = 75,000 area, and about 3 or 4 deep = 300,000. This would cost £1500 or £2000 and even if we do only the most promising parts I ought to have £600 or £800 in hand, and nothing else to do. It will well keep for another year. ...

Maspero came the other day. He was genuinely pleased with things, and seemed very happy that I was here to clear up matters. Of course I shewed him everything we had found and discussed it with him. ...

We have had Francis Galton[1] and his niece Miss Biggs staying here for a week, much interested in all our proceedings and especially in the skeletons. Lieblein[2] and his wife have also come to Abydos for two days and twice looked in on us. ...

Petrie was always afraid of the danger that his finds might be snapped up by dealers in antiquities who hung about on the fringes of an excavation in the hope of bribing the workmen. His concerns are revealed in a letter to Francis Galton.

[Letter to Francis Galton from Flinders Petrie]

23 December 1899
Arabah, Baliana

My dear Sir,

We shall be delighted to meet you and your niece on the 5th Jan. at Baliana and bring your wife over here. But we still hope that you will see your way to doing without a Luxor boy. We see the cloven hoof in all such, and avoid having any such outsiders about the place or the work. My wife will attend to anything about the premises that you want, and our horse boy, a vivacious little negro, will be at your service all day in and out. We find the need of keeping our work and discoveries as dark as possible in this country. The

---

[1] Geneticist at University College, London, later Sir Francis Galton; a great traveller and cousin of Charles Darwin.

[2] Norwegian Egyptologist.

dealers – especially from Luxor – stick at nothing if they see a chance of robbery. Such [are] the difficulties that all our workers are drawn from a village 50 miles away, and no man of the plunderers and dealers here is allowed about the place. If a Luxor spy was found prowling in the desert our men would catch and thrash him. In this state of siege, which generally prevails about our excavations, you will perhaps see in what light a Luxor boy would be looked on about our premises. So I hope he is not indispensable to you. If he took care of himself he would live in the village and tell people of our work and finds. All our workmen live behind our house, and are forbidden to go to the village on pain of dismissal, so needful is it to keep our business to ourselves.

This system which we have had to make is, of course, so unusual that you could not anticipate it, or see beforehand what antipathy we have here to the sophisticated native.

We will undertake that you shall have as many good boys to run about as you can use; and my wife or Miss Johnson will always be at hand. So the wily Luxorian would be needless as well as dangerous.

Hoping to see you all well on Jany. 5

Believe me

yours very sincerely,

W. M. Flinders Petrie

November 1900
El Arabah, Baliana

[H.P. writes]

It seems impossible to write any letters this winter, there is too much to tell. And then with heavy arrears of work constantly before one, one can never allow oneself to write letters, go [for] walks, read or sketch. Half a day's excavation brings in fragments enough to take three of us several days' time to mark up, classify, draw, photograph, and otherwise work over. It takes much of each day to group and sort these fragments: the fitting is often a great puzzle. We have two great rough tables in the courtyard, for sorting specimens, one supported on bricks which I built together, the other on two great prehistoric pottery tubs.

Our dining room and store rooms and the men's 4 rooms look on to a large square of courtyard filled with pre-hist. and XVIIIth dyn. pottery. There are diagonal paths, and two ropes slung on high (supported where they cross each other by a tent pole) on which we daily hang our blankets to air, and on market day our washing. At the corner by the gateway we have a hut for the cook-boy Mohammed, and a hut for photographing, and outside the gate is Ali's square hut, with a yard of bus, and a mud mastaba, and a mud oven where his wife bakes our bread.

She is a rather pleasant little girl who wears a great deal of Arab jewellery, bakes very good bread, and sits sewing a teqieh (embroidered skull-cap) all day long. We have short talks often, but she talks very provincial Arabic, or perhaps it is women's talk, so we don't understand each other very well. Ali is as delightful as ever. He has been very wandering in his work, so has dug in a good many interesting places and out of the way, but not got much luck or bakshish up to the present. He is now in a full place in cemetery E where plenty of good XII–XVIII things are turning up and is very useful in working with 4 gangs of men at once, and training new recruits from Quft. When the holiday was over, and our 130 men returned from Quft, we had 60 new workmen on, mostly brothers and friends of the old men, as Mr Garstang is digging some good ground for the Egyptian Research Account, and needed plenty of men for XIIth dynasty pits.

I am in the thick of a quantity of work, far more than I can possibly get through. To begin with, there are endless inscriptions of which I have to make facsimile copies – long columns of Hieroglyphs on XXXth dyn. stone sarcophagi, XVIIth dyn. statues and lintels etc. and also innumerable wooden coffins, and ragged cartonnage. Also we shall have a grand series of 1st dynasty pot-marks to publish, as we have four or five piles of shuqf[1] in the courtyard with interesting marks on them, all of which I am copying by slow degrees. Then also there is the marking-up of everyday's finds, which is particularly laborious as it consists of labelling many hundreds of smashings of ivory often, and small flints, beads, pottery shuqf etc. Mr Wilkin[2] helps in this considerably.

One is sorry to hear of so much illness at home. Even in the desert we are not entirely free ourselves. All of us have had colds or coughs – this cold weather lately is hard on one's throat. Perhaps you could hardly call it cold, for it has not been below 60° lately in the day, and is sometimes at 67°. But nights are cold and I find I cannot do with less than five blankets. ...

I broke off from describing the huts, and meant to tell you further about them. All I have hitherto mentioned is this year's addition to the usual plan, but we have, beside these storerooms, and square courtyard, the usual row of small huts, all in line, and narrow corridor in front of them. 3 spare rooms, F.'s large hut and mine, and the dining-room make as imposing a row as usual – the huts being twice the usual size. They are very comfortable, and we have a lot of new arrangements, mostly F.'s contrivance, most useful cupboards and racks for things roughly manufactured. We are much tidier and more civilized than before.

---

[1] Potsherds.
[2] A young assistant.

9 December 1900
El Arabah, Baliana, Upper Egypt

[H.P. writes]

A very hot morning. I rode up south two miles this morning into the bay of the hills to Umm el Qaab (Mother of Pots) as usual 4 days ago. At the beginning of our week, we began to dig here, and F. put on 50 men in groups of 4 and 6, on purpose to work through these great royal mounds covered with potsherds, as (in spite of ancient plunderers and the plunderer recently at work here) there are plenty of remains of interest even in the most despoiled of these tombs. This large mound, on which I am sitting, besides producing the magnificent shabtis before mentioned, and other XVIII dynasty stuff, will most likely prove to be another early king's tomb: it is a little detached from the rest, northerly. One mile further north, Mr Mace[1] is working the Shunet es Zebib (raisin magazine) a huge VIth dynasty (?) fortress of immensely thick sun-dried brick masonry, standing up, four square, higher and larger than the temples further on. ... Next ½ mile further east, towards the temples, stand the high brick walls of the ancient temple-site. In this great enclosure, in the north-west corner we have built our row of mud-huts. We have 8 good-sized huts with high slanting roof, six of them constantly occupied. In the spare rooms we have already had 2 Americans, Goodspeed and another, and next week we expect the Galtons, and next night the von Hügels. So our camp will be completely full most of the winter.

F. and I have huts at one end of the building as usual, and the spare rooms come next: then Miss Johnson. The dining room has a real door and a real window facing east, which we shall use when the heat begins, meanwhile we use a south door, warmer these cold evenings. Both doors are very strong, set in strong frames, and possessed of handles and locks. We had great fun with Mohammed the first day they were up, we shut the door, and he could not think of any knack for opening it for some time, not knowing that handles should be turned. The bedrooms have grass-mats as usual hung over the doorway. We have only taken to doors for the dining hut and our store-room. The dining-hut is squarer than usual, and far more civilized. The rope-ladders are banished, and we have, besides the petroleum stove on a box, a cupboard with our sideboard on it, also a side-table, also a long dresser with stores on shelves below, and crockery at a convenient level above. All these pieces of furniture are contrived solely with deal boxes, and a few planks. F. has made a long table with X legs, with room for 5 each side. And altogether we feel more civilised than usual, and are contriving to keep everything tidier and

---

[1] Arthur Mace, beginning a long and distinguished career in Egyptology.

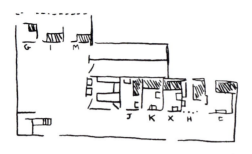

Plan of the dig house at Abydos.

cleaner. We have some capital new things in our stores this year – enamelled boiling pots (for bread, rice, lentils etc.), drawing boards, lids for water-jugs, felt-covered flasks, bridles, girths etc. enamelled dishes with covers for food, and other innovations. Now that we have two big store rooms F's room and the courtyard will be more free of antikas, and all our extra stores are neatly on shelves there.

We are all getting on very well, and harmoniously. Our daily things run quite smoothly. Everything in our present arrangements makes for cleanness and tidiness. Native food is a little difficult to get, as the markets are poorly provided, and to get anything in Arabah needs much bargaining, as Amélineau paid four and six times the right prices. The donkey boys here are used to demanding shillings instead of piastres, so we have some trouble with them whenever a visitor arrives.

The cold winds have ceased, and today is very hot. The great bay of hills encircling Umm el Qaab, several miles across, seems to close me in here, and the cliff-tops which look a few minutes' climbing from here, it would take many hours to reach. It is almost too hot to sit writing here.

Every second day Miss Johnson goes into Baliana, 7 miles off, to post letters and get any small things we want, generally riding, sometimes walking. She likes any amount of exercise, and never tires of Baliana (though she doesn't know much Arabic yet), so she makes herself very useful. The horse is stronger, fatter, and much improved in his paces, since last year, and tamer than ever. He bears a new name, Mursi, and wears a new red leather prayer book.

Afternoon.

In the pit of Mersed's tomb half a dozen men are working over all Amélineau's rubbish on the flanks of it – a mountain of stuff. 3 of our best men are between me and them working down in to small bricklined graves which are untouched and look promising. Ali has come upon the usual fragments of vases of rock-crystal slate etc. and also two bits of inscribed limestone [...] Mer-hes; these are graves of dependents of Mersed. Basket loads of fragments come in daily from this mound, and we are getting sundry inscribed bits of pottery, Horus-names etc. and portions of rock-crystal vases, but all ruthlessly smashed. The havoc made everywhere here is lamentable.

I wish I could paint Ali[1] now as he works. His slim little figure is so active, and he looks so picturesque. He wears a white skull-cap, blue duster twisted round it and a red and white hdkf. twisted round that; a white cotton sort of shirt, a green-and-orange striped waistcoat with red buttons, bright blue bags to the knee, with a scarlet rope and tassels; and a white string fishing net twisted many times round his waist. Copper coloured legs and arms, bare. To go in to market, he wears a long striped cassock and slippers and head-shawl.

13 January 1901
El Arabah, Baliana. Upper Egypt.

[H.P. writes]

We are going on well here. Ramadan is nearly over, and Beiram close upon us, when the workmen take 4 days' holiday. For us, we are not going away anywhere, and it will serve to lessen our arrears of work here. There is an immense amount of accumulations of stone-bowl-fragments to sort out, from tombs of Den, Zer, Perabsen, and Khasekhamui. Flinders works half his day at the final sorting (with a magnifier) of the stones of Den, preparatory to our hunting for fits in the fragments, and, the remainder of the day, he does 15 or 20 photographs, to different scales, and draws the said stone vases when the scanty portions of them are put together. He works this by means of a home-made apparatus of deal and bamboo, with a floor of concentric circles and a moveable central rod centred on a square of deal bees'-waxed, so that with the minutest fragments of bowl-bottom stuck to this, and a mere scrap of brim propped on its circle, the diameter and angle of curve of every vessel can be ascertained, seen in position and drawn. 270 are finished and this will form a valuable corpus of all the forms of stone vases. One of the spare huts is set apart as a little study for this manipulating of the fragments and drawing the vases. Besides this, he is spelling out all the sealings and drawing them, as last year. ...

1 February 1901

[H.P. writes]

We had the disaster of 30 hours rain here, never known before. It soaked everything but our beds; and MacIver and Garstang had not even dry beds or clothes. Our walls are soft mud along the tops, and I have got a bad cold with the damp, and have been in bed two days. A few things were damaged, as clay sealings, and bad stone steles.

---

[1] Ali es Suefi.

4 February 1901

[H.P. writes]

My sister Amy sorts out fragments of special bowls, takes them under her wing, and spends days in her hut piecing them together, and finally seccotining into shape, ready for Flinders to draw. She also marks the pottery etc. outside with the letter of the tomb indelibly, and I make pottery stacks behind the house, ranged according to form ready for Flinders to draw.

Mace is up at the tombs all day superintending the workmen, about 100 Quftis and 40 local boys who do the carrying. B. Orme (who was out here *Hu* year) draws all the potmarks, inks in all Flinders' sealings and vase-drawings, develops all his photographs in the evenings, sorts and pieces, and does a quantity of odd jobs. Besides photographing and violin practising.

For my own part, I do all the plan-drawing, some sorting and piecing of carved slate, copying of inscriptions, arranging of stores and antikas, keeping the courtyard in order, and the drawing of all the 1st dynasty hieroglyphics. The latter I am doing on a uniform scale from all ivories, steles, clay-sealings etc. that come in. ...

17–20 February 1901
El Arabah, Baliana Upper Egypt

[H.P. writes]

Saturday to Wednesday last, 5 days, were taken up in an exhaustive search along the desert northward for cemeteries and early buildings etc. including a run down to Monfalut, 100 miles north, to explore the remains of a pyramid which turned out to be a late fort.

We started early on a Saturday morning – as early as the packing and loading would allow – and rode to Mahasna, 8 miles, during the morning. Flinders and I, and Ali, rode donkeys from the village, some without bridles, some without stirrups! F. had on rather Bohemian working-clothes, I went in a galabiyeh, the native dress, and Ali had a long striped green Quftan or cassock with a huge headshawl of soft ornamental muslin. We were innocent of collars, ties, or stockings but met no Europeans, so they were not expected of us. The camel was laden with two cases of our blankets and food-tins, and our two small tents wrapped in grass mats to make a floor. We started along the cultivation edge to Mahasna, called in at Garstang's[1] hut at midday to look over his alabasters and sealings, and then proceeded across a great stretch of open desert to his king's tomb. ... the huge mastaba-pyramid of Neter-kha or Khet, about the end of the IInd. dynasty. It is an enormous mass of masonry,

---

[1] John Garstang had been excavating in Egypt since 1900.

lying by the foothills and almost rivalling them in height, far back under the high gebel. G's workmen have built a row of huts under its wall, and a camel brings them water three times a day. We pitched our tent behind the mastaba, and had a lovely quiet night and dawn there. ... in the morning we clambered under a portcullis, and F. took a photo of the brick vaulting of the passage leading between arched doorways, by tying back the camera button with his watch-cord for 10 minutes' exposure. A smaller mastaba there has a perilous descent of 40 ft. down, which it was great fun to scramble down, and we ducked under props into small chambers, and turned corners in the dark, and had to swing ourselves up the slope in the shaft with a rope. From thence we rode to Raqaqnah, and looked over a mound with some small mastabas of early date, not yet disturbed, and along a bit of cemetery scattered 18 plunderers who were busy rifling Coptic graves which they left strewn round with red and yellow grave-clothes with decorative borders, V–VIth century. Thence we struck right across the desert some miles back, thinking we saw just such a dark mass of building as Neter-khet's, but it turned out to be a platform of natural rock jutting from the foothills, so we took our way to Kawamil, a straggly village on the desert edge, where men were weaving in the side alleys. While Ali had the camel unloaded and tent pitched, F. and I went off exploring to the cliff-face of the high gebel which here projects to the cultivation, and discovered a ruined Coptic monastery under the precipitous headland which was itself the home of many other brethren formerly, as all the natural caves and all the rock-cut Egyptian tombs had been used by Coptic hermits and monastics. The face of the rock was riddled with rows of small square openings, the tomb-doorways being hewn out with a lintel above: there were thirty or more in each row! We climbed up about 250 ft. to the tombs, and just got down by sunset. F left his purse under a large stone, in case any convict might be lurking in the caves. By the time we got back to the tents, the 50 or so inhabitants eager for a sight of our camp had melted away and we were left in quiet.

1903–1922
Excavating across Egypt and the War Years

Refused permission to dig at Saqqara, Petrie's second choice, Herakleopolis, modern Ehnasya or Ahnas al Medina, was granted in November 1903. The Petries were joined by Edward Ayrton and a zoologist Leonard Loat.

30 November 1903
Ehnasiyeh

This place is very different to all our desert homes. We are a few feet above the inundation. Our floors are never dry, all black damp earth. Our walls drying very slowly, even after a fortnight half dark with wet. Mists on most mornings, and our clothes clammy and chill with damp every morning. The swamp of wet round us has nearly gone now, though the fields are too soft yet to walk across. All this is a shivery, snuffly, contrast to the dry desert where we have been 10 years past. How much we shall manage to do here is not clear. The mounds are immense and all disgustingly late; even Roman is a cheerful relief to Byzantine and Arab and anything dynastic is welcome. Ramessu seems quite archaic and our highest hopes are to get back to the Xth dynasty.

The temple of which Naville found the front has still to be searched below the XIXth level; and probably we shall find earlier stuff below. But the water has been up to the XIXth floor; it is now 30 ins. below that, and falling 20 ins. a month. So by the middle of February we may get down 6 ft. under the XIXth and that ought to take us down to the VIth dynasty. The earliest temple here, Ist dyn. is probably hopelessly under water. ...

15 January 1904

[H.P. continues]

We are perched on dusty Roman mounds, acres of ruins of the once great city of Herakleopolis; 5 minutes off us lies the big temple of Hershef, where our workmen have excavated a hall of columns, far behind the façade which is figured in 'Ahnas', and are descending to XIIth dynasty pavement on all sides. The remains of the city lie mainly between this temple and our huts;

many of the houses were burnt down and these we have now excavated and searched for papyri but in vain. We have however interesting small scraps of well-dated houses, II to IV centuries – lamps, coins, pottery, scraps of decorative work, mosaic etc. terracottas and iron tools (saws, knives, sickles, keys, locks, mallets, hooks and nails). The pottery has all been drawn by Flinders and he has photographed all the terracottas. The tools I have drawn, and built up one complete plate for lithograph. This excavating of burnt Roman houses occupied our first 2 or 3 weeks here. Stuff to draw began to turn up at once, and I was occupied with Ptolemaic inscribed blocks built into a stone cellar upside-down in one of the Roman houses. Sitting copying in the deep pit of this cellar one day, I heard the well-known roar of falling earth, and was immediately buried up to the waist with cartloads of earth and bricks. One of our Arabs near rushed up to help and I made him pick the bricks off me and shovel the earth away. Their first instinct is to drag one out straightaway. ...

Aly Suefy, our former friend and chief digger has turned up again, for Illahun is his home. So he has once more joined the work and is invaluable. Mr Loat who has many years' experience of natives both here and in neighbouring countries, says he never met anyone of such acuteness and forethought. He also says he never knew such first rate hands as our better trained men. Aly Suefy came over [...] with Currelly:[1] it was quite nice to see him again. He did not leave us in disgrace, three years ago, only from momentary foolishness and impracticable behaviour, so we have no reason against taking him on again. Currelly has built some huts at Illahun, and they have work at full swing there. ... Ayrton[2] is the one who is working with us here, most of the season, and running the workmen and local carrying boys, in the big temple-work. He spends all his day out there, directing them and measuring their pits, and follows the archaeology very keenly. All his spare moments he seems to be seeing to workmen, medicine, letters and all their other needs, does all their accounts, and is working very systematically. He takes in hand the developing of all F.'s photographs and has drawn the plans of the Roman houses.

We are a small party of 3 here generally. For about a month of the time we have been 4, as Mrs Milne[3] was with us. She was very bright and cheery, adapting herself well to mud huts and everything Egyptian. Fortunately for us she was here just during the Roman digging, so she daily took all the Roman things in hand, washed and brushed and marked them and mended

---

[1] A Canadian who had been with Petrie at Abydos in 1902.

[2] Edward Ayrton had first worked at Abydos in 1902; he went on to excavate for the Egypt Exploration Society.

[3] Wife of the archaeologist J. Grafton Milne.

fragments. She used to go round the excavations each day, helped me about mending sheets and often went to post for us. She has now left us for seeing Luxor before she returns to England.

The people of Ehnasieh, the village here, seem very quiet and orderly and do not resent our intrusion. We have had several dealings with the village officials here, the Omdeh (head sheykh) and the sheykh of the guards, and found them very civil. The Omdeh had put up Ayrton for the night in his dingy audience room, and the S. of the G. had lent me a mattress when Currelly and I were in a state of no bedding or roof, the first night or two. So we thought them clean, tidy folk, and at the feast we presented the O. with an old deck-chair which he admired, carpentered up by Flinders to the level of bakshish, and gave the S. 5 yds of twilled calico to make a galabiyeh. The O. has since sent us some cakes. Mrs Milne and I set forth just before sunset today therefore to pay our respects to his harim, expecting some superior quarters and get-up, but to our astonishment we were greeted by quite a dirty village woman in a dirty courtyard, and inveigled up a stone staircase with pigeon-holes, into a fearful room where they whisked about a dirty blanket and matting and worried us to sit on them on the floor. The place was so unspeakable that we did not stay for coffee, but after palavering for ten minutes we fled. Happily Mrs Milne had a very short skirt, and I had only a brown holland galabieh and high riding-boots to the knee, but twenty fleas were discovered thereon, and this was a small part of the total number. We made up our minds we would never pay visits promiscuously again!

In December 1904 Petrie set off with a small party to Sinai, where he planned to excavate in the region of the ancient mines in the Wady Maghara. He left his wife with three women friends copying reliefs in the mastaba tombs of the Old Kingdom at Saqqara. Hilda however was determined to join him. When she heard that the excavating party had moved south to Serabit al Khadem, she set out with her friend Miss Lina Eckenstein; their journey, which took them six days on camel-back, she described in an article for a women's magazine.[1] It is worth quoting in its entirety.

> With what strength of purpose and high hopes we start to join an expedition which has no less in view than the complete copying in facsimile of an ancient but hitherto neglected site. But when this is combined with travel of a lengthy and primitive sort across little known country, and one is let loose to pursue after adventure among weird uninhabited landscapes where all the conditions are different to anything one has experienced before.

---

[1] The Queen, November 25th 1905, entitled 'On camel-back to Sinai'.

21 January 1905

We started at 6.30 in the morning, at a slow dignified pace which was never quickened throughout the 6 days' journey. We first traversed a flat desert near the sea, into hills to the east of us and this fell gradually into the head of a shallow valley; winding through this there are 4 parallel camel-tracks, some of which occasionally branch and split into two; there were generally 5 tracks on this first part of the way down. The Red Sea was visible all along to westward, deep blue in the early morning and changing then to a brilliant green, flecked with foam. Behind it lay the barrier of high desert cliffs, forming the boundary of Egypt proper.

Pinkish-brown and lighter-coloured strata alternated in the higher levels, but in the early morning light the whole range appeared a warm greyish-purple. The surface of the desert was all white with salt under the lee of the browner humps of sand, and sparkling also with faces of crystals of selenite. The way sloped gently down to the first oasis, Ayun Musa (the wells of Moses), where we dismounted on a sand slope between two enclosures of palm trees, and watched the feeding and unloading of our camels. The palms grow in three or four plantations edged with tamarisk, and eight or ten ramshackle buildings are scattered nearby. There suddenly appeared a thin featured Bedawy lithe in figure, wearing a thick white sheepskin on his back. After we had exchanged greetings, and he had answered a few words of enquiry on the conditions of the place, he produced from his leathern pouch four turquoises and a pebble of turquoise matrix; and tendered them with quiet reserve, showing no zeal for commerce; and as we were bound for the region of the turquoise mines, we refrained from dealings with him. Our halt was in a tree-y hollow, facing a small line of Arab graves. The four Bedawy take some flour from a sack, and mix it in a basin of hammered copper, then make a fire of palm branches and bake some *ruqa–q*, thin flaps of unleavened bread. They then produce a black hairy goatskin with thick honey (*asal*) in it, and mix some honey and oil in a bottle. The flaps are then transferred to a small wooden bowl, and honey and oil are mixed in with the bread (*goddah*). This was our only opportunity of seeing at leisure our companions' morning feed, as after the first day we never halted en route. The camels kept steadily on from sunrise to sunset and their only means of refreshment was by hurrying on in advance to feed and smoke till they were overtaken once more and left in the rear.

As we moved on south, the desert became more undulating and diversified in its character: each *wady* seemed scored out by denudation, and large stones were strewn over the surface of the desert which was covered with shingle in some parts. To the east were some low sanddunes, with greyish tufts of vegetation scattered about, and behind were brown foothills, flat-topped and scooped away here and there to the level of the dunes. Behind the foothills rose the pinkish-brown escarpment of the *gebel*, the table-land of Sinai. This escarpment runs on southwards and, as far as the eye can reach, recedes somewhat, and an isolated group of peaks stands out, Sinn a-Bisha, and the Gebel Raha. The steep counter-range of Egypt glittered in sunlight towards midday, all its serrations and groovings glowed in lurid colours, for a storm was raging, the sea darkened to a deep grayish-blue, a wind howled from the north-west, and thick layers of rain-clouds filled the eastern sky.

Our desert path now looked more frequented as the parallel track had grown to eighteen in number. Amid the camel tracks of this pilgrim route we passed the heaped-up grave of a *hajji* or pilgrim; our camel-men thought it might date from 20 or 30 years ago, but they always end such surmises by saying 'Who knows?' Morasa lay in the distance, the spot where our expedition had camped on the first night down; we ourselves pushed on considerably further, as we had started our journey several hours earlier in the day. Presently the sun came out, the sea grew a brighter blue, and the foothills shone again. The range of Egypt assumed many greyish purples, marking out four different cranes of distance, and gradually the hill ranges of Asia and Africa diverged, and the sea between them widened. Our camels still jogged on; we crossed one shallow *wady* after another, and rose to slightly higher ground strewn with pebbles and covered sparsely with scrub, and here the desert is scored out by many small stream-courses. Towards sunset, the sea softens to a lighter green, the mountains slowly disappear in the evening mist; the Gebel Raha is bathed in purple glow. Reaching the Wady Kurdiyeh, where we are intending to camp for the night, we dismount, and the camels are turned loose. We unpack and pitch the tent, undo the rolls of blanket and arrange our food, then, leaving Yusuf on guard outside, wander off into solitary desert; the open expanse about us is wide and flat and covered with pebbles; beyond this area, ranges of cliffs form the horizon in all directions. We select a slope under the shelter of some broken ground, as the Bedawyn are always afraid of a low bottom becoming swamped in sudden rains, and the higher places are more exposed to wind and cold. Our landscape is bounded by Ras Lethatha (to the east) and the great Gebel Sudr.

The first experience of nightfall in the Sinai desert is one that is calculated to remain always in one's memory. Several years of winter evenings in the Egyptian desert had accustomed one to a certain amount of spaciousness, freedom, air, and to the sense of a primitive return to nature. In Egypt one has the undulating flats of low desert, the steep lines of escarpment above, the unhidden vault of clear sky filled with such brilliancy of stars as in northern climes can scarcely be imagined. But in Sinai we have this and far more – a sense of vastness, of unfilled chapters in its history, of travelling towards Arabia, towards sunrise, making one's way through an unknown land where anything may happen. ...

22 January 1905
We took the road next morning early, and proceeded across a fresh expanse of desert; the camel tracks curved winding over this, and skirted the Gebel er Raha. The great Gebel et Tih, the central plateau of northern Sinai, lay on our left eastward, and we had it continuously in view for this part of the journey down. Conical hills like pyramids stood about, detached from the plateau and probably owing their origin to more indurated portions of the limestone withstanding the general denudation. The surface of the desert here was

covered with black flints, angularly broken. Towards noon we first saw vegetation of a larger sort than the glaucous-grey tufts of the more northern piece of desert we had traversed. Here the tall bushes of *retem* appeared, a sort of *planta genista* or broom, whose long angular switches looked strong and wiry and were pleasantly green, but still unclothed by the wealth of white papilionaceous blossoms which covered them two months later when we were retracing our footsteps across Sinai back to Europe. This *retem* is the bush whose name is mistranslated as Juniper in the Old Testament. It is stated of the prophet Elijah that 'he himself went a day's journey into the wilderness, and came and sat down under a *retem*' (2 Kings, XIX,5) before he 'went forty days and forty nights into Horeb.' Job also mentions the solitary 'fleeing into the wilderness... who cut up... *retem* roots for their meat.' In one of the Songs of Degrees (Ps. CXX,4) 'sharp arrows of the mighty, and coals of *retem*' are pronounced as the punishment for a false tongue.

Charcoal burning is still one of the few industries of Sinai, and large quantities of the small timber which the peninsula affords, are brought down on camel back to the various centres. ...

A storm came up and gathered overhead about mid-day, and the dark clouds cast their shadows hither and thither over the waste. We chose to dismount and walk a few miles, and consumed our mid-day rations under the shelter of a bush during a shower, while we were waiting for the camels to overtake us. And now began the daily fight of words, which we had been spared the first day, but which we had to undergo today, and each of the subsequent days, from noon till the hour of three. For when the sun got high above us, the Bedawyn world always begin fidgeting about the time, and then they required to be joked and have their attention distracted; about two o'clock they grew importunate and saw urgent need for dismounting and encamping – the sun was just going to set!

Suwedeh, who had the appearance of belonging to a primitive race, would dance up and down like a monkey under my camel's head, in an agony of entreaty to be allowed to have the guiding-rope delivered to him, for if once the camel driver has this in possession, it is he and no longer the rider who dominates the camel. So soon as one bestrides a camel, one realizes this, and therefore while one remains in possession of one's faculties, one remains of necessity in possession of the rein; if it should inadvertently slip from one's grasp, one promptly reaches forward and hooks it up with the handle of one's hunting-crop, before the less nimble Arab realizes the situation and takes the opportunity of securing it for himself. Argument being silenced by a peremptory refusal, one remained inexorable until 4.30, when with a sudden acquiescence as to sunset, one stopped the caravan. As the day wore on, our Journey had progressed steadily; the only physical feature that was especially noticeable had been the abundance of water-courses hereabouts – indeed the small river-beds which we constantly crossed in this part of the desert were the only places of temporary shelter in the *wady*, but they were unsafe for camping in, as change had set in, and we were now entered upon a spell of stormy weather, with only intermittent bursts of sunshine.

Perhaps I may now give some further idea of the Bedawyn of Sinai, if I describe our following. Most of the men wore thick white sheepskins on their backs, and sandals on their feet. All of them carried weapons, and were heavily armed. They bore across their back horizontally a blunderbuss five feet long, were girt with a long curved sword, and had a brass-handled dagger in their belt.

The two brothers, Abu Sihu, were owners of my camel, and the postcamel which joined our caravan. They were thin, lithe, aquiline-nosed men. Salim had a sedate and modest bearing, was slow in gait, and appeared to be always pondering. His head was bent, and eyes invariably cast on the ground, he walked with his hands before him, crossed upon his breast, and seemed to pass along his way in a gentle even tenor of meditation, unmoved by the ambitious schemings and socialities which swayed his fellows. His appearance was that of an ascetic; his air was more than reserved, it was dignified, and he looked a very Baptist in the Wilderness. He had an oval face, lean featured, olive complexion and dark eyes near together, a long aquiline nose, and a trace of thin black moustache, and slight fringe of hair below the chin. His head was swathed in the usual Bedawy head-cloth whose sparse folds stood out squarely round his temples, kept in position by the black woollen head-rope, *'awqa–l*, which is known in Sinai by the name of *mereiry*. This, he told me, was made by his wife, some sheep's wool is twisted into a stout rope which goes twice round the head; the ends are finished off with an ornamental tail of copper ending in a terminal knob; four strands of copper are wound into a spiral loop, with copper knobs twice repeated, and finally a larger plaited knob. Salim wore an under-garment of white cotton, long-sleeved and reaching to the knee, and above this a dark blue drapery much patched and stitched about with white threads. Over all attached across his shoulders, and hanging down his back, was the brown furry skin of an antelope (*teytal*). He gave me a description of one of his feats of the last year, the killing of this creature "with lead", *bil rusas*, and shewed his gun, a long spindly weapon of an antiquated pattern which hung level across his back. Slung around him was the fringed bandolier, *rakhera*, of plaited leather, black and greasy with age, which had six brass-bound powder-holders lashed to it at intervals. His equipment was completed by a leathern pounch containing flint and steel, a hanging leather purse, *sofe–n*, and a dagger *khusa* with a curved steel blade and brass handle with incised cross-lines; his sword, *seif*, was an old one – "the sword of his father"; when I enquired of its former history, he could only reply "Who knows?". It was slung by a plaited cord of black and white sheep's wool.

The other of the Abu Sihu, Suleyman, was yet more picturesque in his appearance. In face he resembled his brother, but his features were less regular; he had a broader brow, and eyes wider apart, which gave him a less sanctimonious air, but he was yet strangely mysterious, and had a secretive manner, and a habit of silently brooding over whatever took possession of his mind. Suleyman's white linen head-shawl had a white fringe, and was ornamented by two small red tassels hanging from red strings; it was worn much as his brother's, in a fold round the face and chin, and was held in place by a brown head-rope of goat's hair, over which a large black and crimson chequered shawl was draped. He wore an inner garment of white cotton, which had sleeve-peaks to the knee, and over this a second cotton garment which had originally been white, but which was stained reddish-brown from constant wear; all white stuffs in Sinai become gradually of the same colour as the rock, a pale ruddy brown, like terra-cotta. His long coat was of cotton, of a Venetian red colour, striped with yellow, black and green in strips of varying sizes; there were narrow black stripes in the front, the back was adorned with stripes of all colours, and the sides had wide stripes of alternate green and red.

Our first sight of the women of Sinai was at Esh Shatt, where, after glancing at the shanty for camel stores on the flat desert, we pottered round to a little group of mud cabins which appeared to constitute a native village at the boundary between civilization and the wilderness. Here in this modest cluster of dwellings, we saw several specimens of the Sinaitic women, small and ugly creatures, made grotesque by a peak of greasy black hair, trained into a projecting horn over the forehead. The face was veiled, and the whole upper person hung with sequins and amulets.

The head-ropes of the Bedawyn the leading-ropes, bridles and saddle-bags of their camels, are the handywork of the Bedawy women, so far as I could ascertain. On enquiring as to their industries, I learned that the wife lived at home, in her tent, in the dwelling-place of so many weeks' standing, and pursued her home arts in the intervals between household removals.

When we ourselves came across women, however, in the journey down, it was always in their capacity of tending flocks or herds. Whether the property of the household were owned by the mistress, and she was fulfilling her own peculiar duties, aided by her child or children, I did not happen to find out, or whether she was set to the task by her male relatives, but certainly the management of the livestock is a considerable feature in her life and must from time immemorial have been one of her chief occupations. Two or three times, as we had occasion to pass down some wide reach of *wady*, where a little scanty herbage subsisted, we caught sight of a herd of shaggy black goats grazing precariously in the wilderness, and amongst them, standing motionless, or urging them on with gestures, a figure draped in black, sometimes alone, sometimes accompanied by a small boy who, stick in hand, helped her to keep the herd from straggling. On our approach, the woman always hastened to veil herself from our gaze, or shrank behind a stunted tree with a timid air, or with the precautionary instinct of hiding from a stranger.

CAMELS

The camel in Sinai is a very different animal from that of Egypt. Anyone who has lived in Egypt and is accustomed to the long trains of baggage camels, gaunt bare-skinned beasts of a dark and dingy hue, and grotesque shape, would appreciate the delicate, soft-furred animals of beautiful proportions which day after day pace the long waterless stretches of the wilderness, tardily indeed, but with apparent ease. This camel is in many ways a smaller animal, it is thinner and inferior in carrying power, it is true – all beasts and men are thin in Sinai. Some can scarcely carry 3 *kanta–rs* (300 lb) and the drivers are always anxious to keep loads as light as possible, to one's frequent inconvenience; but judging merely from appearance, the Sinai camel is the nobler beast and always looks beautiful in this landscape which especially fits him. I saw many different colours, among them, brown, fawn, grey, and most striking of all – a delicate ivory colour, a sort of glaucous white. Not all of them are quiet in action.

One hardly realises till one lives in Sinai that the camel is a creature of the mountains. He belongs, no less than the chamois and the goat, to mountain scenery. When not in active work, he is sent up each morning from the *wady* to graze upon the plateau, and has to climb by narrow zigzags up the face of the precipice till he reaches the flat saddles and flat amphitheatres of rock where he can pick up a precarious living among the grey tufts of vegetation which grow sparsely here and there. He picks his way along dizzy edges and stands pausing in a meditative way on some slippery edge. As, from the wady bottom, one looks up the face of the stratified cliffs, one sees him, in silent dignity in the foreground against the skyline, the only sign of life in a barren landscape that might otherwise belong to the country of the moon.

On January 31st 1905 Petrie wrote home from Serabit al Khadem, where he was recording a temple of the Middle Kingdom and many inscriptions including those in a proto-alphabet,

Hilda and Miss Eckenstein have come over from Saqqara all well, and are hard at copying, as well as the rest of the party. We go up about 250 feet out of our valley, the steep sides of which are like a flight of steps weathered out of the sandstone strata. Then we cross another valley about 150 feet deep, and go on about a mile and a half to the temple. ... the winds here have been strong and cold, and on that bleak hill copying was hard to manage. Wielding a flimsy sheet of wide paper in a high wind gives occasion for spiritual discipline when it crumples up many times in succession. And fingers numbed through with the cold can hardly grip anything or manage a pencil. It freezes every night, and blows pretty well most days.

The following winter (1905–6) the Petries chose a Delta site for their excavations: Tell el Yahudiyeh, some twenty miles north-east of Cairo. This site was a huge fortified camp of the Hyksos period, later the site of a town of the New Kingdom. The name 'Mound of the Jew' derives from a Jewish temple built there during the Ptolemaic period. The pilgrim route to Mecca ran nearby.

17 December 1905
Poste Restante, Cairo

[H.P. writes]

We arrived in Cairo towards the end of November and had several days there for doing necessary business. Two of our men[1] were with us all the way from Naples, full of questions and anxious to learn, so our hours were very full. We also had daily Arabic lessons going on. The third man[2] joined us just after we had encamped at Tell el Yahudiyeh. Cairo was delightful, in hot sunshine, and so brilliant in Oriental colour. We had a long morning at the museum, and saw very much, and spent the rest of our time in work, and seeing people. Fortunately places of business are not shut during *Beyram*, and we got everything wound up in 4 days, and a dozen of our best Arabs collected, and joined us to come on to Shibin, by the 1st of December.

Four of us, and one first instalment of men, came down by the first train to Shibin, on the eastern side of the Delta, reached Shibin at 9 a.m. and proceeded to pick up all our store boxes and tents and canteen from Suez, which were already awaiting us. We four walked across a couple of miles of cultivation to a high sandy mound or *Tell* with many acres of ruins and potsherds, lying around it. We put [up] tents, and got unpacked and settled in, that afternoon, and eventually we erected a small hut, for Flinders and myself and the best of the antiquities, and the men built two or three single rooms for themselves. Nights here are cold and windy, and we live in perpetual draughts. The dews are very heavy, and our first three hours of every day, till the sunshine begins to tell, are very cold and damp. In the warm weather of the first week or two, mosquitoes from the innumerable small ponds and water-logged holes plagued us at night, and sleep was very difficult. Now we are so bitterly cold, the mosquitoes have disappeared, and we sleep better.

Work began on a small scale, with twenty men, the morning after our arrival. A line of men, turning back stuff as they went, began on the eastern edge of the early temple site, and have turned over a considerable portion of it. ... I am now drawing the small things all day long scarabs... cylinders, beads, seals etc. to scale 2:1. There are also flints, pot-marks, pottery fish, copper tools and fragments of pottery with Cypriote patterns, all of which are drawn and inked in daily, as they come in. This keeps me busy all day long, and soon I hope to begin plotting the plans, as the survey is in course of preparation, and we are only waiting for the store of large paper to arrive.

---

[1] T. Butler-Stoney and C. Gilbart-Smith, students.
[2] The Rev. T. Garrow Duncan, an old friend.

Butler-Stoney[1] remains with us, and helps in sundry things; he is out at his oil-painting most of the day, and often goes in to Shibin for us. Some Scotch missionaries at Shibin come out to call on us occasionally, and have offered us storage, and various attentions. Others are at Bilbeys, and friendly with our camp there. They have supplied me with St. John in very well-printed Arabic, and I hope to work up a little more Arabic during the winter.

We are pitched against the slope of a sand wall, but it does not afford much shelter: the clean sand serves for good flooring however. The tall mound gives us a fine view across the green delta and in the far distance, S.W. we can see the citadel of Cairo, and the tops of the two great pyramids. Below the mound lies the large square area of tumbled heaps of potsherds between little pits and watery hollows; this is all that remains of the early town and temple site, and ground below the dug-out palace of Rameses III. One group of our men has been turning over this last-named, and a small amount of tiles and rosettes characteristic of this place has come in. The town east of the mound still has walls up-standing, in mud-brick, and lines of streets showing. A large party of Bedawyn and easterners are encamped on part of the ruins, with little brown tents facing east, inhabited by wild but pleasant-spoken women and packs of brown goats and sheep, and business-like children who tend the beasts and cook the lunch. The sole furniture is the big cooking-pot, and the grinding stone, and a pack-saddle. The men remind me of the Tawarij Arabs of Sinai, they are wild but gentle. One of them, a scraggy shaggy man in a head-rope and short draperies, sitting over his fire, talked to me about the place down there: he knew Ayun Musa and Wady Gharandel, but preferred the flesh-pots of Egypt. They drive their flocks all over the waste ground here, and pasture them about everywhere. One very wild looking old woman drives a hundred sheep, and donkeys and goats right across our work at sunset every day, and we pick up the conversation each day from where we left off the night before. Her talk alternates between questions as to how we live and what we do, and personal compliments to me.

We are not hearing much that is of interest about the neighbourhood, sites seem few and far between. One or two elderly people tell us how the ground used to be, and point out where the walls ran, the local dealers seem friendly and bring us what they have, which is not much. The missionaries tell us what they can. *Sebakhin*, the earth-diggers, seem to have been destructively at work here for many years, till everything is down to a low level, and only the heaps of potsherds, the insoluble residue, tell of what once stood here. A few months more of such work would have destroyed all the plans that Flinders

---

[1] An artist who joined them.

is working out. We are only just in time to catch the last evidence of former buildings here. There are the usual Arab reports of wonderful sites and wonderful finds, but they do not come to much. Yesterday we got a glowing description of a magnificent golden cup of large size: the natives who described it had not been allowed to see it. We followed this up, and eventually it turned out to be a very shabby electrotype, almost past recognition, of the Vapheio gold cup![1]

The high road from Shibin passes our camping ground, and turns the corner of the *tell* beyond us. Between it and us runs a little line of Delta light railway, and several little trains pass every day, and an occasional trolley. Natives and flocks of animals are passing down the road all day long, and sundry Greeks and Italians, and it is even wide enough for an arabiyah,[2] so that the tumble-down country carriage occasionally rumbles past. Within a stone's throw of us, and all along west of us, are great stacks of maize, and the women are picking and sorting the cobs all day, and shrieking to each other, and the people sleep in the maize by night to protect them. Twenty or thirty grey buffaloes have been tethered among the stacks to feed there, so our immediate neighbourhood is lively. The people are well-behaved, and only among us trying to sneak into our well, and fill their pots there, as it is a little nearer for them than the canal.

Market day is Sunday here, and then our men take the day off to do washing and mending, play single-sticks, shop in the big market beyond Shibin, eat sugar-cane, and get their letters written by our one scribe. I have been down to market one morning, and bought a few draperies of a Delta sort, different from the up-country ones, and two rolls of brown woollen stuff after much bargaining. Our men find things dearer here, and food is so much dearer that we are allowing every man 7 P.T. a week for bread-money, over and above wages and bakshish. The Bedawyn drive in a great train of about 50 camels to the camel market each week, and the remainder return next day. One day some natives rushed in to us to borrow a large knife – a camel had fallen down, and was so much injured that it was necessary to kill him. Another day two men carried by a dead wolf, to sell to the Bedawyn for food! Altogether, being encamped on a populous highway we see much of native life here, but we shall not be remaining on this site for very much longer.

---

[1] A treasure of Bronze Age Greece in the Athens Museum.
[2] Horse-carriage.

17 January 1906
Kassassin, Lower Egypt
[Hilda writes to her friends]

Many thanks to all for letters received in the past fortnight. They are received with gratitude, in this wild out-of-the-way place where we only have a few Bedawyn, and a few little farm-holders to share this narrow strip of country. The Wady Tumilat, leading from the Delta to the Suez region is very narrow and bounded by sand; clean rolling desert on both sides, and this mound, the *Tell el Retabeh,* is a large square enclosure of clean sand surrounded by sand-dunes and a few bushes and isolated palm-trees. The scenery reminds one of Ayun Musa and the northern part of Sinai. The *tell* lies between the main canal and a small branch canal, and east of us lies Malesameh and west of us Kassassin and small wayside stations on the line from Cairo to Port Said, merely railway-sheds on the open desert. Behind our canal is the strip of cultivation, green fields with an occasional small ezbeh or farm. This formerly was part of the land of Goshen, and its capital lies on one side of it, and Pithom the store-city is the other, some miles distant. The country is very sparsely populated here, labour is difficult to get, and food is dear. The limits of the cultivation are so narrow that the feeding of the animals is difficult here, all products are dearer and scarcer than in the Delta itself. For corn and food in bulk, we have to send a man in to Zagazig (Bubastis).

The local people are polite, and curious: they seem interested in us, and well-meaning. It is however impossible to get boys to work here. Workers are scarce, some of the lads seem to be earning far higher wages than we should care to give for unskilled carrying, and many of the people have the Bedawy distaste for work. The *tell* looks promising, as it is a large enclosure filled deep with desert sand, but our pits descend to various traces of large building; scraps of hard stone, quartzite and granite, are scattered about the surface, and the natives mention great inscribed stones, and heavy building stones buried in the place. Part of the lower ground eastward is probably a temple site and the town runs westward. The former was not built over later, and nothing of late times occupied the ground. ...

We hear of two other *tells* in the neighbourhood, which may be interesting, as they are not known hitherto. Altogether there are probably enough sites in this region to occupy us for some weeks to come. The natives of this region seem particularly unsophisticated. They scarcely know what an antika is, and there is neither buying nor selling of them hereabouts. We have not had more than 3 piastres' worth offered us here, and they do not supply any other market outside. The only digging hereabouts previously was that of M. Naville, who sank a few trial pits in various parts of this *tell*, and then went away disheartened.

It is a delightfully dry healthy place, with a fresh breeze generally blowing, and clean gebel[1] sand round about us. It is so pleasant living on the desert once more, after the damp mound at Shibin surrounded by cultivation, And so far we have had no rain, since we arrived, so the conditions are far better here than in the Delta, and remind one of the Said.[2]

At first we camped in a couple of tents just outside the south wall of the enclosure, and close to the small canal. It is useful to live near a good supply of clear water, and we get frequent bathes in it also. It is rather muddy and shallow, but clear in the middle of the stream, and the banks are steep and lined with rushes and flowering plants. By degrees all our baggage has arrived on camel-back from the station, and the camp is assuming larger proportions. So soon as the huts are ready, we shall strike tents and live permanently under galvanized roofing, and more spaciously. The little mud huts are running up quite fast now. Smith[3] and the workmen did nothing towards building, the first two days they were here. They never searched for the old 17-inch bricks, so found nothing to build with. Directly on arriving, we had to search down a foot underground and there got enough bricks out for building. The plan of them is thus:

We are building up against a sort of cliff-face of ancient wall, as at Hu, and have taken down the rotten edge, and added 4 layers of bricks above, and banked up the running sand with a mastaba to keep the face of the wall from falling.

Here is Yusuf coming up, he still wears the little blue jacket, of a Well Road[4] blue, and has the short indigo kilt, and his spare legs beneath, and a great twisted turban. In the tents at night, I hear long accounts of what happened "last year", always recurring, and the others listen with respect. There is perpetually something to say about "last year". The men who were in Sinai have a sort of prestige among the older men and small boys whom we did not take there.

Our off-day is Saturday, when we stop digging and the workmen go in to Qassassin to market. The first market-day I went with them to see the scope of the provisioning there, and to pick up anything interesting that I might

---

[1] Desert.
[2] Upper Egypt.
[3] George Smith, a student who had been sent ahead of the Petries.
[4] The name of the Petries' road in London.

buy. Kassassin is nothing of a place. Three mud ezbehs[1] stand near the small station-house on the open desert, and a lock to the canal makes the place accessible from distant farms, so everyone troops in on donkey-back, and there are great stores of lentils and grains, and pottery and copper vessels spread out, and little depots of stuffs and gay haberdasheries laid out in rows on the sand. Many Badawyn come to buy and sell. The only outside diversions were that of a man dancing to a tambourine and two tumblers, till suddenly it was announced that the paraphernalia of the Mecca pilgrimage would be passing through immediately to Suez, and the next train that came slowly across the desert there, was indeed a highly ornamental series of cars with triumphal arches and flags, and the great camel lying down in an open truck gaily decorated. The greater part of the carriages were filled with a body of soldiers, and the procession looked very brilliant and festal. Our men told me that the clothing of the Prophet himself was there, and that the soldiery was safeguarding it, lest anyone should take it. Hundreds of people ran from the market to line the banks and get a view of the train and everyone seemed much impressed. At the station I had a conversation with a little under-official who knew English, and stood blushing and saying "Yes, Sir" till I left. Two of them came over for a lesson in archaeology next day, and they write in English letters in answer to my Arabic ones, and are very obliging in procuring bread for us.

We shall probably remain here for 4 or 5 weeks, and the remainder of our party may join us later on, when they have finished their second site. At the end of February we shall (F and I) return to Tell el Yehudiyeh (Shibin el Kanatir) for ten days, for money and final digging when the water is lower, and shall work there in the interval between two Cairo lectures. People in Cairo [...] seem Mabsut[2] about a British School of Archaeology here, and E.R.A.[3] is taking well. The lectures will serve to bring the tourists as well as the residents more in touch with the work.

[*List of sixteen recipients to whom the letter is to be sent in turn*]

22 February 1906

[H.P. writes]

I think I have already described the Wady Tumilat somewhat, its rolling desert and sand-dunes, and the scarcity of scattered farms, where food supplies are very insufficient. Weekly market on the open desert a few miles from this *tell* supplies most of our needs, but when our men want their staple

---

[1] Villages.
[2] Satisfied.
[3] Egyptian Research Account.

food, they have to fetch it in sacks all the way from Zagazig. What small population there is in this wady is mostly Bedawy, part of it nomadic and part settled in houses. The people have not much taste for work, and we can get very little local help. They are polite however and give us no trouble, and there are no antika professionals. We have rain-storms and gales frequently, and all this district, all the way to Cairo, was invaded last week by a mighty hurricane; which blew for many hours during the night, and necessitated our standing 3 hours at a stretch with arms uplifted, holding our iron roofing down, which threatend to fly off and blow away. We got some hundred weights of limestone and brick overlaying it, but the danger of it going altogether kept us active most of the night. We lost 3 or 4 pieces periodically, but got them hastily put back each time. Sheets of sand blew in on us all the time.

Flinders spent a day at Pithom (Tell el Maskhuteh) lately, and took a wet squeeze of an enormous stele of Darius, found there for the Egyptian Research Account last season. It weighs several tons, and is of granite, broken into several pieces. Pithom which was in our possession has suddenly been wrested from us and handed over to a Frenchman; this stele however stands on the desert edge. I am now occupied in pricking off this squeeze on to innumerable sheets of paper upside down, and drawing it out on these. Many parts are indistinct, but it will make a fine body of inscription. ...

Flinders has had several other long exploring tramps, looking over *tells*, and stretches of desert for Hyksos and other cemeteries. We had an 18-mile walk last week, starting from Tell el Kebir, the sandy rise of desert where the battle was fought, and got down to the desert to find a mile of Roman potsherds, the remains of a town site, and kept along westwards till we struck Tell es Suleyman, a worn-out site, and thence up to Abu Hammâd, where we took [the] train, and got an evening walk home from Qassassin. The natives were very polite, frequently inviting us to coffee, and even to sleep the night. Another day, F. struck the cemetery of Saft el Henneh, the capital of Goshen, and now our students are at work there. We saw the place and our antiquities on the way back from Cairo yesterday. There is some of the prettiest Delta country there that I have seen. Even the town site has scattered trees and an old sheykh's dome upon it, and the canal with its grassy banks and sailing barges, and a profusion of trees and crops, is as charming as any English river scenery, with an added wealth of Oriental colour.

We leave Tell el Retabeh in a few days. Flinders is busy with his survey and plan of the place, which comes out very different to look at from the superficial aspect of the site. I am finishing the drawing of pottery and the facsimile copies of the inscribed stones, including the temple front of

Rameses II, which has a scene of the King smiting a kneeling captive, before the figure of Atmu the god of Succoth.

[Postscript] Address Poste Restante, Cairo.

We shall be leaving this district of Mahsameh and Qassassin in a few days, and shall be wandering from one site to another about the Delta, so the above (Cairo) will be our only settled address after this. Letters will be forwarded wherever we go. But posts are very uncertain. Letters sometimes remain in our present postoffice for 9 days, and Mr. Griffiths' last letter, tho' very distinctly addressed, went to Massurah and stuck there for three weeks! Several letters have been lost altogether.

In the Autumn of 1906 Hilda found that she was pregnant with their first child. John Flinders Petrie was born on the 26th April 1907. Hilda remained in England with their small son whilst Flinders returned to Egypt to begin work at Memphis in 1907– 1908 .

8 November 1907
Cairo

[Flinders Petrie writes to Hilda in England]

Building a 'dig house'

Went to Saqqara with Schuler and Ward; looked after site for house at Memphis, and found a good place, only one tree to come into the courtyard, but four or five in a row just south to shade the roof. The soil is all dusty *sebakh*, but that can't be helped there. Contracted with the Museum guard to see to bricks being made at 2 P.T at 1000. Left 15 with Quibell,[1] to be given out £5 for each 40,000 made. And when 120,000 are done it will be time for our party to come down and begin building. The bricks cannot be begun yet as the good soil is all under water still. The Nile is held up late, being poor, and all the country is still inundated. So I saw Memphis at the worst, and fixed the house quite safe above the highest flood. Rats swarm there at present being drowned elsewhere. We shall have to keep an ichneumon[2] to kill them off.

20 December 1907
Sohag

It has come on cold here, 52° and a high wind. I could not do anything out yesterday, the sand got in my eyes so. We have now inked in all the pencilled sheets, and I shall join, and send to Gruggs direct from here. So the Athribis

---

[1] James Quibell, who had worked with Petrie previously, was now an official in the Cairo Museum.

[2] Mongoose.

Petrie excavating at Memphis, 1908.

plates will be done by the time I return. Ward and Mackay[1] can both ink evenly. Schuler is excellent, so quiet (non-smoker) hard working and studying. He longs to come to England, and I have asked him to stay with us. Oppe is useless, and does not want archaeology, he is to go in a week and shift for himself. ...

The following extracts from letters written to Hilda from Egypt show Petrie's dealings with some of his staff and his exasperation at the incompetence of some members.

3 January 1908

I expect to get to Memphis by 16th and to have all finished by 1 Feb. Ward and the men are now on the spot to begin building.

8 January 1908
Sohag

... We have just had a hot wind, the earliest I remember. It seemed warm all day, but when I went to my room at sunset it was 77°, and must have been far over 80° all day – a hotter day than we had all last year. ... The VIth [dynasty]

---

[1] Edwin Ward and Ernest Mackay.

tombs here well cut and of good work, and nearly perfect. Mackay has taken to inking in and does it very delicately and smoothly. I am inking and joining sheets of the zodiac tomb every evening. ...

11 January 1908

We had it up to 89° on 9 Jan. the hottest I ever knew in the winter, hotter than anything in March last year. Then came the burst down to 60° and it has been a gale all yesterday with sand driving over all the ground. But though strong N below, there is a SW wind above, shewing that the cyclone has not yet past.

15 January 1908

I expect to get away from here by about the 22nd or 25th so all future letters should be directed to Bedrachein, as the post spell it. Schuler and Ward have finished the large visitors' room on the ground, which will serve them to live in *protem* and are beginning the arch floor rooms, but they can hardly be ready for me to get into till 25 Jan. Aly Suefy is with them, chafering in his old way and glorying in running things.

22 January 1908

Wainwright[1] was 5 days late by bad weather, but is here at last. He had hardly any sleep for three nights, owing to noise in town and cold at Bedrasheyn. So he slept with hardly a break from 1 p.m. yesterday to 7 a.m. today and is set up. I am going to the VIth tombs today to copy, with him to ransack round, and look at all likely places for more.

Our rock temple promises. We have now a square cutting into the rock 8ft. high and built stone against it. As the doorway is probably 15 to 25ft down, this is as promising as we can yet expect. The house is going on at Memphis and will be done about 1st–5th Feb. By then I hope to know about this temple and be able to leave here with a clear notion of what there is to do still and whether to come back to go on. I reckon on taking Dec–Jan on a south site each year, till water is down at Memphis. ...

30 January 1908
Bedrashen

... I got here two days ago, found beastly muddle and mess. After laying out the plan of the site I said, Schuler and Ward had neglected every detail and direction that I had written down and told them. They had never roofed any rooms, built 10 days ago, though all the iron roofing was lying aground useless. They had left everything out in drenching rain, wood, tools, bricks and all; exactly contrary to what I said. Schuler had thrown up all my directions and made immense arches instead of low ones, and so all the rooms are 2ft. too high. Then they complain that the walls are too weak (because so high) and

---

[1] Gerald Wainwright, whom Petrie had met in Bristol the previous year and invited to Egypt. He proved to be a most competent and reliable assistant.

build double thickness. I reckon that £10 of brick labour and wood have been thrown away, and the work is not ¹/₃ done in 3 weeks, which ought to have finished it. They could not have muddled worse. It took me all yesterday to pull things round, clear up the ground (covered with piles of loose bricks trampled to pieces in the wet) and get things genuinely into shape. Not a single thing wrong would have gone so had they done as I directed. It throws us back a fortnight all this bungling.

Now I have Aly and all the men wrangling outside and must take charge of the building.

Your own, F.

8 February 1908

All is well here, but I am in a scrimmage of shelves, doors, etc. beside general direction of men all day. Ward does the accounts and measuring, but I have to settle where to dig. ...

10 February 1908
Bedreshen

... We are now fairly settled in and only some plastering is to be done. The house seems to be comfortable, and good for hot weather in which we shall mainly want it. The verandah will do well to sit out entirely when it is hot; and having a high wall 7ft. outside, 3ft. inside, they are quite private and self-contained. The front one 5ft. wide and 50ft. long will be a grand run for John[1] when he comes out; and it serves to hold all our store boxes along the side, where they make tables and seats. The rooms are rather dark from the door owing to the low verandah roofs; but each has a window enough not to leave any corner unlighted. The room next to mine which will be yours and nurse's are for Schuler and Wainwright who do not smoke, so they will not get nasty. The smokers are all to be kept to the south verandah. The court at the backs of the rooms is 32ft. square, it serves already for the rough antikas and pottery, spare wood and roofing, the rough stone we found which is worth a good deal for building, and the stock of petroleum.

This is far the most serious house we have ever built, and looks as if it would last well for a lifetime. The position is the best we can get, but it will be damp and foggy till February always.

I anticipate coming here the 1st week of Feb. each year and doing short work elsewhere in Dec. and Jan.

There are scattered palms all round the house, giving a slight shade and in every direction the view is half blocked with palm stems. On the north we look through palms across the wide space of the Ptah temple. We have now traced the great wall of Ptah all along the south, half the west (all that remains) and turned to the east. We cannot do more on Ptah till the water is lower. So I have begun on what is most promising. A great lintel of a pylon was found

---

[1] Their son, John Flinders, had been born in April 1907.

in place last year deep in mounds just south-east of the Ptah temenos; it is of Merenptah, and around it I picked up many handles of archaic Greek amphorae. All this fits to its being the foreign Aphrodite, in the traders' quarter said to be south of the temple of Ptah (due south is blocked by the Serapeum) and built about the time of Trojan war. If this be the foreign temple it is grand to work at, as the site is clear of any great mounds, high and dry, and we can work it early. This is the most important temple of all for history, and, if we have found it really, it will be great for us. I shall say nothing public till we see further.

In front of our house I have made a wide courtyard, built at the sides, but loose in front. The loose bricks will serve to block the doors when we go, and removing them will prevent anyone herding goats in the court.

There are corner gates left and at the S.E. toward the men's huts is our own well, so the water supply is quite safe and so close to the kitchen K that there is no water carrying. The kitchen K and cook's hut C are just at the side of our steps, so as to guard the place.

It keeps very cold; I have had 48° in my room and it has scarcely ever been up to 60°. It is only 53° at present, and I must get into bed to keep warm. The boys of the place are beginning to come on to the work and seem willing and active. They are better on the whole than the Abydos lot, more intelligent and friendly. The omdeh and the museum guards are cordial, so all seems well as to people. The whole tone here is submissive, begging us not to ruin trees or bury crops; and I think we shall be able to negotiate all we want about land without any obstinacy. The line is "do whatever you like so long as we are not damaged." ...

Plenty of small stuff, of amulets, green gods etc. comes in, there is a pottery Horus which is closely Buddhist in pose and drapery, and struck Schuler at once as Indian before I saw it. We may at last get the Buddhist link here, the foreign quarter of Memphis (where this was found) is exactly the most likely place for such a find.

7 March 1908

Aly has got his wives here. I found him bent zealously on it, so let him build a hut apart and they appeared. M.[1] had been to Quft to see his son (just born) and when he came here, I said that the hut was Aly's. "Lakin fi niswan hinak" *[But there are women there]* said he. "Eywa, beta'u" *[Yes, his (women)]*. "U enteh khallitum gai" *[And you let them come]* said M. disgusted. "Eywa, izakan humma mush heneh yumkin gaad fil beled." *[Yes, if they were not here, he would probably live in the village]*. "Ah, entaref esh shoghul" *[Ah, you know the work]* with a sort of siding up air, satisfied that I did not invite them. M. is very good this year, efficient and thoughtful. We have a tidy hut for him, about 7 × 4ft. next to the cooking hut but at the foot of the steps. The men say our house is "Zay wahed Locanda" *[Like a hotel]* and are impressed with its dignity.

---

[1] Muhammad, the cook.

11 March 1908

We have today at last got the bedroom jugs that I have tried for since we began here. They hold about a gallon each, and basins will not go out to be filled. Each room has one, a bucket, so all goes on smoothly thus. I have an extra room for the Qufti men, and they shift one room every three days so that each room of the 12 gets left bare to air in 6 weeks. They quite like the plan and it makes them entirely clean out each 6 weeks.

I am getting more from the dealers here. It is quite like Abydos for small stuff. Today a man brought a camel load of inscribed stones from Saqqara, and I took half a dozen, all worth having. I keep 3 and 3 go to Bristol.

Wainwright is very nice. Keen for reading and learning all he can. He is quick by nature, but liable probably to be superficial. I make him see the point and use of being thorough, and he has enough sense to wish to be so, and to try to do well. He is better fit to take up my line of work than anyone I have yet had, though Weigall was the nearest before. But Wainwright will I think study, do field work, lecture, and probably write. He and Mackay are each to give a couple of lectures on return to Bristol. B wants to push them on and imitate Liverpool. So all this is excellent for me, as I have helpers really wanting to be as fit as possible. ...

Muh[amma]d is most pious. Very attentive, and has lately brought up boxes of 25lbs and about 50lbs on his head from the station rather than take a beast.

The Petries in Thebes 1908.
Brian Hatton was a young artist, a protegé of G. F. Watts, who joined the Petries in Thebes as an assistant in December 1908. One of his letters to his mother (quoted by Celia Davies in Brian Hatton 1887–1916 T. Dalton Ltd. Lavenham Suffolk, 1978) tells of his experiences working with the Petries.

He travelled out to Cairo with the Petries and their assistants for the season, G. Wainwright and Ernest Mackay. They spent a week in Cairo and he did the usual round of sight-seeing. "I like the P's very much" he wrote, "they have been very decent to me all the time; they are certainly somewhat unconventional, especially Mrs, but she is very decent and kind all the same. The other two are quite good sorts too, and very wrapped up in their work. Apparently the party is complete. There may be some visitors later on but we shall be at Thebes for a couple of months first. I find the coinage frightfully muddling." He was also intrigued by the rapid sunsets: "The sunset does not last long, but it gives a beautiful rose madder tinge to everything just before the sun goes down; while the sun is actually sinking an inch or so off the horizon, everything seems to be in shadow, which is somewhat strange to me as the sun is still visible."

They went by train to Luxor and spent a few days seeing the temples, before crossing the river to the Petries' camp, in the mouth of a wady under the cliffs. Hatton spent his days in sketching the workmen and children and made one or two sketches of the Petries. "Mrs P. is a regular corker. She makes a point of being extremely independent and won't accept help from anyone (suits me all right!) She is of course a hot suffragette! tho' not militant. Her costume out here takes the biscuit. Usually a blue native gown, such as the poorer class men wear, and a sort of small motor cap, plenty of bare throat and ditto leg, no stockings of course!... I am doing a sketch of Mrs P. in the evenings now. I have done one of the Prof. too, but he is too busy to pose and I could only catch him for a few minutes while talking and digesting after dinner. Mrs P. wants me to do as many as I can of him. He won't sit for his portrait at home. He did once when Mrs Watts asked him to, but the result wasn't up to Mrs P.'s expectations!"[1] ... "I probably walk 5 to 8 miles a day and occasionally go tramping 10 to 12 at least. The other day I went up the Farshut pass over the hills behind us. It brings one out on the peak of the highest hill after two hours steady climb and pretty rough going... I don't know how camels and donkeys manage it but they do. From the top one gets a magnificent view up and down the Nile valley, of which I did a little sketch. I walked a couple of miles along the desert which is undulating and covered for the most part with black flints, many of these chipped by neolithic and palaeolithic man. I brought down a pocketful. ..."

Hilda had returned to Egypt with her husband at the end of 1908 leaving their young son with his nurse.

19 January 1909
Western Thebes

[Hilda writes to her family]

After the visit to Memphis, and looking over the sites of last year's excavations there, we remained 3 or 4 days longer in Cairo, with time enough to spend 3 mornings at the Museum, and see dealers' wares in the afternoons. I also went to the top of the Great Pyramid, with the hand of two Arabs, and part way only one, and found it a very easy climb though the steps are very high. The view from the top is indescribably impressive, across the flats of desert and river to the mountain cliffs on both sides. We visited Gizeh village on the way and a wealth of antiquities there.

Flinders and I took day-train up the country, passing all the well-known places, very interesting to glance at on the way – Medum, Illahun, Tell el Amarna, Assyut, Sohag, Abydos and finally reached Luxor at night (13 hours) and slept at a small Swiss locanda opposite the station, which has neat bare rooms and a shady open loggia. Thence next morning we passed on to spend 2 days in the Inspectorate where Weigall[2] is in residence (and found comfort there, and an English baby). I paid two visits to Luxor temple, and three to

---

[1] There is a portrait by G.F. Watts in the National Portrait Gallery.
[2] Arthur Weigall.

the temples of Karnak, besides seeing dealers. Twice at Karnak, it was evening by full moon as clear as daylight. The great pylons and obelisks looked so stupendous, and the halls of columns. The approaches by long avenues of ram-headed sphinxes also looked most impressive. The newest feature there is a small dark temple, containing statues of Ptah and Sekhmet in position; a small staircase leads on to the roof. One of the great pylons gives a fine view also. About the 3rd day, we met several of our Arabs, and had news that the huts were complete, and all was ready for us across the river, so we went across at once, and had a hard spell of unpacking, getting out food and necessaries, and rigging of shelving, and disposal of furniture in the small premises. One little hut makes our dining room, and each young man has a smaller hut. We ourselves settled into a square limestone cave or rock-tomb, in the cliff above the huts, which required little preparation for use, as no door is necessary, but the men scraped a path to it, a very steep approach. It is a rock-tomb of the XIth or XIIth dynasty, and has a high recessed bench at the end of it, beyond two square pillars (on this bench I have my bunk, and climb up there for the night).

Our Arabs swarmed up from Quft next day, those that were written for, and the excavations began the following morning. The majority of the men were put on to some early cemetery ground to the east of us, and some were sent up a wady behind, to dig along all the places likely for a large tomb, as some of the earlier royal tombs may still exist unknown, among these smaller valleys contiguous to the Valley of the Kings. We worked at flat cemetery ground, extending towards the river, for about a fortnight or 3 weeks and worked out cemetery A, XIth dynasty and cemetery B, XIth dynasty, continuing to XVIIIth or much reused down to that time, and found all considerably plundered. The remains were mostly pottery, and I was occupied for a fortnight in drawing pots to scale 1:4, about fifty each day, so we have a good *corpus* of XIth pottery to publish, and early pottery is not known much from Thebes. ...

Work continued in the wadys behind, but with no result of any large tomb. One burial was found under the cliffs, that of a sarcophagus, feather-patterned, with an interesting arrangement of pots in nets, and some decorative toilet objects. These things took five hours to secure in proper order, and preservation; after being planned and photographed in position, and treated with preservatives, they were carried at dark to the hut, and photographed singly next day. Then work began on the south side of the beaten road, and we excavated several of the painted tomb-chambers of Dra'a-abul-Negga. From frescoed walls of these chambers, I have copied in tracing for subsequent colours-work, seven plates for the coming volume, and we have been repaid for our digging, by finding a very good statuette. ...

Flinders has done much photographing, and some diagram drawing, and an elaborate sketch map survey of all the mountains and valleys hereabouts, going [for] long desert tramps over the tops of the gebel with instruments, and drawing in contours. He has measured all the skulls, done much comparisons of pottery, and superintendance of workmen who are under

Mackay's charge.[1] Mackay is out all day with the men. Wainwright had workmen at first, up the wadys (but now confines himself to special work among certain tombs), and is just leaving us for Memphis, where work begins on a small scale this week. It is a hard-working sort of place, we breakfast at sunrise, work hard all day, and have no interruptions. Even Beyram festival was not a delay to the work, as the men gave back on market-days, the days they took for the feast. (A few workers, a few scholars, a few subscribers have looked us up, Carter, Tyndall, Davies, Jones, are all stationed within reach of us, so we have an occasional visitor at sunset. Weigall inspects us). We are fortunate to be on the cool northern side of the place, and away from the native villages and the noise of dogs. Their barking is only distant. Jackals often trot past here, or a fox, on their way in the evening, and sometimes a hyaena whines for an hour or more, but we are singularly little troubled here by anything, and there are no insects at all.

After only a few weeks Hilda discovered she was again pregnant and returned to England. Their second child Ann was born in August 1909. At the end of 1909 Petrie returned to Meydum, where he had excavated in 1890, to resolve unanswered questions and investigate the many tombs that were being plundered. By February 1910 he had moved to Bedrashen leaving Wainwright to continue work at Meydum. Hilda stayed in England.

2 December 1909

[F.P. to Hilda]

Off by 9.30 for Rikkeh. Got a boy to carry my sack, and shouldered saddlebag myself. He reckoned that I could then be screwed into taking his donkey, but I would not. So he rode with the sack and I tramped about 4 miles. The road is very zigzag by canals and ditches, and lastly I had to wade knee-deep in mud, where the donkey could never go. Our men then carried me over the last canal. I found 4 bedrooms and dining room finished, but as we may be six of us here we started two more rooms next day. It is hot here, 75° in rooms; and Mackay is rather upset, and I had to keep him lying down today, 3rd. My old holes here have not sanded up, and I can resume the work of 18 years ago almost straight. All our men have now come, and we begin the work tomorrow 4th. They all enquire for you particularly. I expect Wainwright in two days, Fletcher and Westrop about 10 days hence, and perhaps Makin. ...

[At the end of the letter Flinders writes]
My dear John,
    Here I am at a pyramid again, which Mammy will show you the pictures of that I did long ago. And I am going to dig holes all about it with a hundred men to work, and see what we can find about the people who built it. ...
    Your own Daddy.

---

[1] Ernest Mackay was to become one of Petrie's most trusted assistants.

[No date. To Hilda]

On the S.W. of the pyramid we have found that the deep hole is the rock cutting for a sepulchral chamber, probably of a queen, now all destroyed except the entrance. But next to it is apparently another chamber complete; I have seen part of the top and we have found part of the roofing passage, and are trying for the entrance. If unopened it would be a huge prize; but anyhow we must find our way in. ... I will report all this properly for people, as soon as we know for certain.

Turkeys are cheap here, 30 PT so we have had two.

[At the end of the letter Flinders writes]

Dear John,

We have had little mice running about the rooms all night. They dig holes under our walls and throw out heaps of earth. I have to put our bread in a basin of water so that they cannot get at it. And we get bread once a week and it is very dry at the end. Kiss Ann for me, and help Mammy all you can.

Your own Daddy.

4 December 1909

As Mackay was unwell I went out and started all the men on the work. There are six main divisions each put under one principal man. (1) The East face of the pyramid cleared down to ground in order to tunnel to the central mastaba. Huseyn Osman. (2) The temple site (?) at the foot of the causeway. Hasan Osman. (3) The big mastaba, of which no entrance can be found, and in which I got the lining wall of the central pit of the chamber, 15ft. below the ground outside. Aly a.r. Rahim and the above are Wainwright's lot, with two fellows tomb hunting. (4) The deep ruins south of the pyramid, probably catacombs of royal family, with rock cutting and tunnel found before. Shehad Ahd. ...

We have about 100 men and boys, after two or three day's work, about 40 being locals. Just found lower part of a building with 5 big courses over the sloping entrance, another pyramid or a big mastaba.

Meydum n.d. written on Christmas Eve

Fletcher has been here ten days or so; he can draw very well, has painted much the last three years in Egypt with fine colouring, and he has taken keenly to all our pot and vase drawing. He is a thorough gentleman, accustomed to good society, and has done much on boys' clubs and living, about East End. I much hope to keep him about our camp in future. Westrop arrived yesterday. He is a fit man, and knows how to take things: walked over by guess and crossed ditches wading, and turned up at sunset, his bags to be fetched today.

This latest addition to the staff did not last long; Petrie's diary for January 1st 1910 reads: 'W. queer; Jan 2nd W. worse and Jan 5 Westrop left for Thebes'. In Petrie's autobiography, 'Seventy Years in Archaeology' Westrop's sudden departure is explained: his strange behaviour attributed to drug-taking, he was sent by Petrie to Luxor, and thence to Cairo on the advice of the hotel doctor; he ended sadly in a mental home.

10 March 1910
Bedrasheyn

The work at Meydum is not yet finished, as the removal and packing of the sculptured tombs there is a long work. Rahotep is now in the Cairo Museum, Nefermaat is being packed. Atet is nearly packed and is coming altogther to England, beside the remaining portion of Nefert. The state of the stone is bad, in much of it, being fissured and sealed, but capable of repair. There are however several blocks in good state with all the inlay perfect. It will be a most interesting and valuable asset to us, as there are no other tombs of this work, in inlayed coloured pastes. As there is altogether about 30 feet length of it, 10 feet high, there will be enough for several museums.

Beside removing the sculptures, we have been searching for the chamber of Nefermaat. No pit could be found, so we dug out the whole depth of the mastaba behind each of the false doors and also in the middle, down to native rock, which is quite undisturbed. We then tunnelled in different directions along the rock, but cannot find any trace of a chamber. Now we are trying for a pit outside of the mastaba.

The tunnel through the pyramid is continuing in search of a possible *ka* chamber. We have gone about 100 feet, mostly through solid stone and are now close to the face where we shall get our answer, yes or no.

At Memphis we have been doing a good deal on the palace. The great court seems to have been a gigantic work of Apries or Psamtek entirely. The walls of it and the foundations for the columns go down over 40 feet; and as the walls were 42ft. high, there must have been sheer walls of over 80ft. high. This is the greatest black-brick walling known. ...

This year water is short on the temple site owing to the new irrigation. So we began moving again about getting land. We went to the Omdah, and he said he would help – we could have any of his land. So we discussed – mostly Mackay's affair – and it was all settled and I went to sign a contract for the hire of it for two years, on the forms which we had ready printed two years ago. Then I found a new clause put in that I was to pay £300 an acre if the government wished to take over any of the site! That was too exacting by far, as £150 to £250 an acre is full value. So we sadly gave it up.

But there had always been two parties in the village and we had suffered much worry from one party because we dealt with the other. So finding our party had tried to screw us we boldly went to the other. Immediately the other rival notable took up the matter, made agreement for ½ acre of his land, and got another man to do the same, and now a third, without any stipulation about our paying total value for the land. There is an intense rivalry in the village now, as the election for Omdah, or chief Sheykh, is soon coming off, and the most popular man will win. The old Omdah, whom we first dealt with, thought to be popular by screwing terms on us. The rival has tried the opposite course of taking our terms and being the kind friend to landowners to write their contracts and help them – and us also. We met the old Omdah today and he was quite civil and friendly, and *congratulated* me on having begun work!! though it was through his rival. All the owners are now dancing attendance on the rival to get him to make good terms for them with me. So we have profited after all by the village squabbles. Our friend in the matter owns about 1000 acres, or is worth about £150,000. But he took care to get all he could screw for his bit of land and now recommends lower terms for others. We can afford to laugh about it now with 1½ acres secured for two years, and every prospect of getting in all we want. I am paying £40 an acre for the use for two years and the right to all antiquities we can find. It costs about £250 an acre or more to dig it over, a little more or less to the owner does not matter. And I am offering ⅕ down as earnest money to anyone who will make a contract to let me work at any two years in future. If this succeeds I shall be able to lay out the work regularly so that it follows conveniently; and I shall have an unassailable legal position of right to continue excavations. We have 55 men and 110 boys now on the Ptah temple.

When war broke out in 1914 the Petries began a four-year enforced break from Egypt. Flinders occupied his time in studying, lecturing and publishing material from his excavations. He also helped establish the British School of Archaeology in Jerusalem and saw John Garstang appointed as its first Director. When war was over, the Petries were keen to return to Egypt. A permit was sought and granted for them to resume work at Lahun and they returned in the winter of 1919–1920.

18 January 1920
Lahun

[H.P. to Ann, aged 10]

> ... Here it is what we call very cold. There is a strong wind blowing up at lunch-time and raging in on us for several hours. That means that a lot of sand and grit blows into all our food through the open doorway, and covers our wooden plant shelves and linoleum-covered table with a grey dust. And at night, our galvanized iron roofing clatters up and down a little, towards the windy corner. It is getting very near bed-time, and as I am very cold I must

get to bed early tonight. Tomorrow I shall find very tiring, as I am going to arrange for the Engelbachs[1] to go out all day, to see Hawara pyramid, just as we did a week ago, and that means that I shall be minding their little girl all day. She is a funny active little thing and races about all the time, getting too near the paraffin tins, or the boiling pots, or pails or water, or the donkey which brings water up, and losing teaspoons in the sand floor, if one does not keep an eye on her. ... We send to post every day, except Fridays, but it is of no use to write oftener than once a week to any one person, as the mails to England do not go as frequently as they did before the war. ...

17 February 1920
Lahun

[H.P. to Ann]

Today we could not have church, nor tomorrow, because the Christians in this country belong to a different church – not a branch of the Catholic church like us, and so all the fasts and feast-days come at different times to ours, and their Xmas was on 6th January, 12th night, and I cannot remember when their Easter is. You would like the trotting jackals with their long tails, and the desert foxes, and I wish you had been with me when I was walking on a high terrace or ledge of rock, high up, back in the hills, and a great grey wolf, such a handsome lively beast, trotted round the corner and along my ledge towards me. I stood quite still, and he went on trotting till he got quite close, when he suddenly caught sight of my long blue qalabieh,[2] and he turned round and trotted back, ever so fast. 5 minutes later, he was on the top of the ridge looking down on me, and wondering how he could get past me to seek his business.

I wanted to look for his den, and presently the others came back, and they had found it, so I went off to see it. We walked 10 minutes westward to a coomb in the hills, and climbed up some rocks, and there above us was a snug hole in the rock, with a long curved entrance leading down into warm darkness, and on the steep slopes of sand to the valley below about 100 bones lay whitening in the sun, in all directions! Untidy fellow! Well – he comes down some miles, for a chicken or a kid, for there is no food in the desert, and he often passes close to these huts, even by broad day-light. Another animal here is a sweet little hopping jerboa, yellow and furry with bright eyes and little paws held up. One hopped into our dining-hut last week. They burrow in the sand and play about, in the desert.

---

[1] Reginald Engelbach was helping Petrie that winter. He was subsequently made Chief Inspector of the Antiquities Service and Keeper of the Cairo Museum.
[2] The native dress which Hilda usually wore on the dig.

17 February 1920
Lahun

[H.P. to John]

... Nights are very cold, and it is all one can manage, with many blankets, to sleep a goodish part of each night. Then at dawn we get up, and as soon as I have had my bath and dressed, the workmen come to the wall, for pick axes, ropes, rope-ladders, sledge hammers, and crowbars. Then the bell rings and a little after sunrise, we get on to breakfast. Tea and coffee, and eggs, which are 1d. each, here. Mr Brunton[1] is off with the workmen at sunrise, but comes in to have his breakfast before we have done. Then each person goes to their place, some to the workmen, some down a pit to take measurements, some to sort or wash potsherds, and find joins in fragments of inscriptions, Daddy off either to continue his general plan, with box-sextant and compass etc. or to photograph things in our courtyard. We all meet again at 12 for lunch, (tinned food, or market meat and rice and jam). Then people draw in their huts or keep quiet, and anyone can rest for an hour, if needful – then a smiling boy with brilliant white teeth, and a blue frock, called Selim, appears at the wall, every second day, and goes with a saddle bag to the village and post. We scatter at our work for the afternoon and reappear for a cup of tea at 4. There are plenty of small home jobs, connected with the antiquities, the workmen, the huts, the food, the tools, the planks, and straw, and pots and petroleum stove, carpentering, and cleaning of objects. We hang our blankets in the sun on a rope – someone daily: and someone's washing is washed each morning. At sunset, the men come in with their basketfuls, and return the tools, and we give them eye-wash, or someone asks for quinine. The water-donkey carries to and fro, at intervals all day. We sit round the long table drawing, in the evenings, and get to bed early. Open doorways, and only a grass mat hanging up at night.

25 February 1920
Lahun, Fayum

[H.P. to John and Ann]

... What do you think we have had today? Some violent rain storms, and our clothes getting soaked through in the courtyard. One of my jobs now is to go round all our work, every morning about 8 – (we have breakfast at 7) – and take a roll-call of all the names of the locals. Seven long pages of names of men from Lahun, and little Lahuny boys, and as I shout "Ahmed Muhammed" or "Ma'awad Taha", each boy sings out "here am I", or his companion calls "aho." They bring all their aches and bleeding fingers, and toothaches and sore toes to us at mid-day, and there is a dispensing of boracic or hot water or bandage, or eye-wash at the courtyard wall – then at sunset we blow a whistle, and they all run shouting home, their rags waving in the wind.

---

[1] Guy Brunton, Petrie's assistant on many excavations.

But our own men[1] and *their* little boys, in blue and white, come to the wall with their potsherds and their pick axes, and then go off to their little pots of lentil soup, and tuck in to their little dug-outs near by. ...

27 February 1920
Lahun, Fayum

[H.P. to Ann]

It is just getting too dark to go on drawing my plan, with its small fore-court and 4 pillars, and now I can begin a letter to you – the pick-axes having come in. We wash and go to supper at 6 o'clock, and then sit round the table to draw, and sometimes Daddy goes off to the store-room, and sits in the dark and develops the photographs he has taken that day.

A workman who was ill went into Medineh today to see our friend the American doctor, and get his medicine, and he has brought us back a few extra things, such as lamp-glasses and wicks, a bag of flour, and some very sweet oil-food, called sim-sim because it is made of sesame oil and sugar. Yesterday and today I have been out by the pyramid at 8 in the morning, calling over the names of all the Lahuny boys: some of them have such long names, such Abdullah Awadullah, and Abd el Latif Abd el Aziz.

A few days ago, just as we were going to have lunch, someone said – here is a reverend gentleman arriving on his donkey and I went out and found a very ancient wrinkled old man in a white turban and a long black cloak, who jumped in an agile manner off the red leather saddle, bowed low and kissed my hand many times with prayers and kisses and many greetings. He did the same to Daddy, and they talked about 32 years ago, when he was lock-keeper at the canal gates at Lahun. Daddy says he looked very ancient then, and he told us his age was now 120! – but natives very seldom know their own age correctly; he may have been about 60 then, and may be about 90 now. We put a low chair for him near our gateway, and gave him soft meat and rice to eat, as he was quite toothless and he enjoyed it so immensely that he stopped every now and then to roll his head from side to side, and gave long fearful groans like a camel, ending in a long-drawn ah! and thanks and blessings. He must be half starved on the rocky native bread, which is all they have, as a rule. Then when he rose, I was running forward to un-hobble his donkey, when he seized me politely by the arm, he couldn't let your excellency stoop to do that, and he rushed and did it, sprang on to our brick wall, and from that astride his saddle, so his 120 – or even merely 90 – years do not stop him from athletics. Daddy says he was the most honest and straight man in Lahun, 32 years ago, a character to be admired for his integrity. ...

We get bread in round brown cakes, very flat, and hard, sent in by train twice a week from Medinet-el-Fayum. One of us goes across the desert to the little halt, and shouts "aish, aish" when the train stops. Aish is the Arabic for bread. The guard on the little train, not to be outdone, shouts "bread, bread"

---

[1] i.e. the Quftis.

and hands it out, tied up in string. We then transfer to a saddle-bag and carry home just in time for tea.

We still have sudden rains, and furious winds blowing, and it is cold enough to wear one's thickest shirts and coats. Not so bad as Jerusalem, where Mr Mackay describes 2 feet of snow, snow-drifts 6 feet, and 3 feet length of icicles.

We have caught, and been able to examine for a few moments before releasing several creatures here. A bat – bats have such curious short frilled noses and a mouth full of teeth; there are hundreds in some underground passages here. An owl, such a great yellow-brown fluffy dear, blinked at us, and swooped a little way off on strong wings, and then sat looking at us – A scorpion, very large and greenish-gray, tail up aloft – a Locust, flew on to a doorway and lived there – 3 drab well-marked lizards, two live on our store room floor, and come over the still into my bedroom. A jerboa hopped into the mess-hut one evening. The jackals and hyaenas we sometimes see on the prowl, and my friend the grey wolf, but do not cultivate acquaintance with them. ...

In the winter of 1920–1921 they returned to the Fayum, camping for a short while at Gurob, and then revisiting the site of Sedment and the cemetery of Ahnas where Petrie had previously excavated in 1904.

17 December 1921
Lahun, Fayum, Egypt

[Letter from F.P. to his children]

My dear John and Ann,

Though I date this Lahun, I am about 10 miles south of that, and my letters will be sent on. If you look at a map of Egypt you will see the stream running into the Fayum; I am now on the little neck of land about 9 miles south, between the fayum and the Nile. M. Bach is with me, and the rest of the party with Mammy are still at Ghurob.

This is one of the queerest places I have lived in, on a slight ridge of desert sloping down about 100 feet for a mile to the Nile Valley, and about the same to the Fayum. There is no shelter for tents in any valley, and we could not cook, or perhaps keep a tent up, if there was a gale here. But I found two great pits, where big tombs had been opened and filled with sand half up. One pit is about 30 feet across and 9 feet deep; the other about 40 feet wide.

In the 30-foot pit we have pitched three tents, rather loosely for there is no room to stretch them. One is mine, one for cooking and cook. Down in our pit there is no wind, and on one can come about the tents without coming down the slope or stairway before our doors. It is the safest place of all, as good as a house. The larger pit is for our men who have built up rough stone walling to support the iron roofing leaning from the top. We are so snug that no one can see us by day or night unless they come up to the edge of the pit.

Our men who went down to get water at our well a mile away, came up in full moonlight and walked past us a few yards away, on toward the Fayum, and had to be called back. Tonight again they missed us on the other side, though we have bright light in the tent. This is good for us as we are much less likely to be troubled by prowlers or thieves if we are so hard to find. Whether the party will put tents in the open, or live in some smaller pits and chambers like rabbits I do not yet know. If we have high winds I expect all will get into pits.

5 January 1921

[H.P. to Ann]

This is the first day I can use my thumb which I cut with a big jam tin lid, and so I am going to sit and write to you under our cliff face in the shade, facing the 3 tents, (ours, the dining tent and the kitchen), where we shall soon be having tea. The petroleum has just come from Sedment, 3 or 4 miles away, by donkey, and yesterday we managed to get 6 long loaves of bread from the Fayum, so we are set up once more. Postcards we cannot manage to get as we are not near any p.o. but Mr Miller[1] will bring us some in a week, when he gets back from Cairo. Yesterday I walked across a piece of desert to look down into a deep hole, and I saw a long staircase cut in this hole by people of the Ist or IInd dynasty (7,000 years ago), and I went down the staircase, and peeped into a chamber, from which our men had taken down a great portcullis of stone, and behind that I saw all the lovely alabaster vases lying grouped on a wooden tray (as big as a study table) flat on the ground. Nearest the cuddled up body of the early man lay his copper basin and spouted jug, and some beautiful stone vases near by. It was one of the most interesting places we have dug.

6 January 1921

[H.P. to Ann]

This is 12th night, or Epiphany with you, but here it is Xtmas Day, and if I had not had a lot of work to do and rather a headache all day, I meant to have gone off at 7p.m., like I did last year at Kahun (from Lahun) and spent part of the evening in the Xtmas service 8–12p.m. There was also a morning service 8–11, and a Copt brought over a donkey for me, but I was busy with workmen's accounts and also had to be down for an hour, with my head bad, so I never went. It is as warm as August today, 70° in the morning and 80° at midday. We have breakfast and supper 7a.m. and 6p.m. in the tent because of the cold, and lunch and tea (12 noon and 3.30 or 4p.m.) outside in the pit because of the great heat. Nights are very cold.

At breakfast time, I give out ropes, and candles, and tools, and rope ladders. Muhammed brings in coffee and eggs, and sometimes there is bread, but always lentils and jam. Then we all scatter to our 4 diggings on the hills around. I go round 3 of them, and mark off the names of all the "locals", the

---

[1] Captain Eustace Miller.

people who come up every morning from a farm-village on the desert edge. 20 are men with picks, 5 are little girls with pink trousers and gold earrings, 18 are little boys in blue or white; all the children have a basket each, and they pick them up and carry them to a dump heap outside each cutting, and empty them, and return them quickly to the men. But one of the 'men' is a quick lively woman named Amina Nakhla which means Amen Palmtree and she is a good worker, and shouts at her boy if he doesn't bustle back.

Then I come in, and see to the camp, and send out men to the Nile Valley to fetch washing water or to the Fayum for drinking water, or a boy for petroleum, or a man to railway for letters. And open tins, and settle lunch and dinner, and air blankets, or begin a drawing, or count eggs, or put feet of shabtis on to bodies, 200 of them lying on our pit-slope to be fitted. Or a desert sheykh calls in for his cup of coffee and a few remarks and blessings. The old Bedawy sheikh of the Arab village comes on his donkey in white woollen wrap and has a great old pistol mounted in chased silver and gold. The police-officer comes in khaki with fine leggings, on a prancing horse. He is a Captain and talks some English, and his brother quoted a lot of Shakespeare to me, while I sat and drank tea with the wife and 2 untidy children, in a drawing room very like a station waiting room, after morning church. The priest wears a black turban and long black robes, and has a silk scarf, and an ivory-headed ebony walking stick. He talks to me about church festivals. In church he wears beautiful simple embroidered vestments, and swings a censer and looks like Aaron. They make me stand in the very middle in front of the altar (for 3 hours), back to the lectern, and he blesses us all, at the end, with the water with which he has cleaned the paten (or vessel for bread). It is a church with several white domes, dedicated to St George, and we can see it from here, 4 miles away, with the white buildings of the police station near it, and a mud Muhammedan village behind it. A lovely winding canal, the Bahr Yusuf, with white-sailed boats, makes this village a very pretty place. ...

10 January 1921
P.O. Cairo

[H.P. to John]

... It is a lovely January day, and it was nice to have lunch in the "sky parlour" once more. Daddy's little after-lunch rest is over, and Muhammed has climbed down in to the pit, to fold up the morning's washing and put a kettle on. A small boy calls out "candle" with a sort of lisp, and we throw a paraffin candle up from under my bed. Many of the shafts have run deep, and the men are working in underground chambers with small lamp or candle. They also have to send round whenever they want a pick, or sieve, or rope. I give out ropes and rope ladders, candles and matches before breakfast each morning, and the 3 or 4 men on doses come round to be dosed 3 times daily, but Major Hynes does the medical department this year, which lightens my work. He is the man who has been in the Indian army all his time, and his people in India for many generations. He knows so much about natives, and camping, and such things that he is one of the best helpers we have ever had. All his Hindustany words come in useful, and the many other Eastern words he knows... Mr Neilson knows a lot about natives and tribes, and shooting, and camps, and carpentry, and dies and weaving, and is a botanist and fisherman. Both men can shoe horses and do a hundred other things! So they are very handy in this camp, and do their own surveying; and there is always a lot of interesting talk on technical things going on, and Daddy has such a lot to tell them also. You would enjoy to see all that is going on – the brushing, fitting, mending, finding joints, the smoothing down of bits of papyri, the copying of shabti texts, the scraping of plaster from a plain stone to find an inscription and scenes underneath, the sorting of a hundred legs to a hundred heads (red pottery shabtis), and piecing fragments of alabaster. ...

14 January 1921
P.O. Cairo (from Lahun)

[H.P. to John and Ann]

I was very pleased this evening when the camels came up from Fayyum, with 20 food boxes, to find that there were letters forwarded from Cairo. ... Today has been a very domestic day, as it was market day, i.e. the workmen's day of rest. It took all the morning to sit on a box in the desert, and recite the workmen's accounts to them in Arabic. After that, they all trooped off to Sedment to buy their food and ours – they live on bread and onions and lentils, and a little meat sometimes. They buy us meat and bread and coffee and tomatoes, and lentils and rice, and sugar, and suet, and mallow-spinach, and potatoes, and yams, and sometimes dates, and methylated spirit and petroleum.

I tidied, and did house-keeping accounts, and aired 2 beds thoroughly (blankets all out to sun in the desert), and washed some clothes, and laid a new sand floor, and was about tired out, when suddenly the chief police officer, in khaki, and a sheykh in draperies, came to call on horse and donkey back, and had tea and much talk. We showed them some of the annual volumes, and the chief of police has borrowed one to read, as he knows some English! In return, I tried his horse, an Australian one with a very humpy uncomfortable trot. When they went off, the camels arrived, and it is always nice about twice a week, to get our post in. ...

Such a lovely great fox ran across our desert this evening, and a hyaena prowled round here last night. I forgot to tell you that before I gave the men their a/cs this morning, I told them all to turn out their huts, tidy the ground (covered with litter of onion skins and sugar cane rubbish), sun their clothes, and re-sand their floors, and then I put on top boots, and held a sanitary inspection. ...

We still live in a well, drawing; we live on jam, not treacle.[1] All we can see

---

[1] As in Lewis Carroll's *Alice in Wonderland.*

is the sky. Do you remember the view from the top of Arundel park right across the weald from S. Downs to N. Downs? We see a view like that, westward, from the top of our pit, right across the Fayyum about 30 miles, to distant mountains. And if we turn round, we see another view, almost as large, across the Nile valley to the mountains behind Beny Suef, 20 miles or so. And such gorgeous colouring – the pinks and blues of desert hill very bright, and blue gleaming of canals. Then the green of the clover and beans and other crops is a brilliant green, brighter than any greens at home.

Friday morning: a rabble of people came up this morning to see if there was work, and wasted my time clearing them out. We already have 60 nice men, and boys and girls from 2 villages and that is enough. Since then, we have unpacked some of this year's stores, and had a first sight of unaccustomed things such as dish-cloths, treacle, ginger, lemon-juice, photographic chemicals, biscuits, and carbolic soap. Now I am off to the roll-call in the various big pits of the two hills where we are at work, and shall soon discover if any odd boy has tried to get into this week's work without coming up to be selected by me first. That did happen once, and he got cleared off after an hour or two, without thanks or pay. One must have the choice of whom one employs.

Daddy is tightening the tent-ropes and making this tent seem double the size, and a better shape. Two of our men have gone further off this morning with workmen, so we have a lot extra to do at H.Q. When I am going round the work, I shall pick out a small boy of our own to go off to the Fayum to post. ...

20 January 1921
P.O. Cairo, From Lahun

[H.P. to John and Ann]

It is only 80° today in this mess tent, so I can sit and write, on the shady half of our little table, and box extension which serves the 6 of us for meals. A strong wind blows, so we are not using the sky-parlour today, except between meals. The day before yesterday, the woman on our work rushed up, almost in tears, to say that her little boy down on the cultivation edge grazing a goat had been struck on the face by Arab people and the goat stolen away. She came up to ask leave to follow up, and when I gave it she thanked me with many blessings and picked up her black skirts (she is a Copt), and ran 1½ mile like a hare, after which I could see no further, but she was back in the work later in the afternoon, and triumphant, she had rescued her goat! She is a poor widow, Amina, with 6 children, and her husband was a Copt named Makha'in (Michael). I wouldn't have the little boy in the work, he was too small and weakly, but a sturdy little girl Shafya comes with her, and does her basketing, she herself wielding a hoe like all our men. There is another little Copt in the work, Sab-ha Girgis, by her name. St Michael and St George figure in all the churches, brightly coloured horsemen combating dragons and their names are common among Copts.

Yesterday was a festival, the Aid el Ghatsa, which by counting up the days
from Old Xtmas day I found to be the Epiphany, and the Coptic priest with
3 of his chief church people came up and called (on their donkeys) on the way
to the Fayyum, where they were going to hold a service in a village there,
probably in an upper room like the early Xtians did. He brought the holy
bread over with him, covered with little crosses, and gave me some.

The old Sheykh Abdullah and his chief man called the same morning; they
were on their way to look after their buffaloes in the Fayyum, and called in for
talk and cups of tea! so we all 3 sat sipping tea and conversing, at 9a.m. on 3
chairs in the desert. He was very pleased that I did not smoke – tho' he
smokes plenty, himself! and he was very pleased to hear about you both and
that you could both write letters! He used a good many words I do not know,
but the conversation did not drag at all. When it is going to, I generally ask to
have a look at his silver and gold-mounted pistol. His donkey has no name;
isn't it a pity they don't trouble to give them any? He would only say it was
just "donkey". The loss and recovery of Amina's goat gave me plenty to talk
about, both with the old 'Arab sheykh, and the Coptic people; when we say
'Arab here (rather a nasal a) we mean Bedawin, either wandering, or settled
into a village, and they are as distinct from the ordinary villagers, fellahin,
these latter are from the Copts. Our own men are upper class fellahin,
cultivators of the soil. One of them who has an 'Arab mother is called "the
Bedawy". And among the locals we have mostly fellahin, and just a few Copts.
They all three seem to know and like each other in this district, and they are all
very polite to us. The work people come early and work late, and are quick to
do as they are bid, and they like and trust our Upper Egyptians[1] so we are all
a happy family together. Next week, I will count up and tell you how many we
are in number. (Jan. 22) I have to finish this letter and post it quickly, as our
oldest man is ill and going in to Fayum to see the doctor, who will keep him in
a native hospital, or send him home to the upper country.

23 January 1921
Gebel Sedment

[H.P. to John and Ann]

... The jackals are beginning to whine, and Muhammed is beginning to snore
in the kitchen tent; I am sitting on the ground in my bed tent, and now I am
going to tumble into bed, for my arms and legs are like ice, and I have been
writing all the evening, while Daddy develops in the dark in the mess-tent.

28 January 1921

[H.P. to John and Ann]

I am again in my light tent, bitterly cold, while Daddy develops in dark tent.
Each market man has come to the top of the pit, and shouted down in the

---

[1] i.e. the Quftis.

dark what each of the other men took from him in the market yesterday some 1/-, some 2/-, some 3/6d, and so on, to buy their lentils, rice, and onions for the week's food, and those I have to list up, and then place against their names next week, as so much less in their banking account with us. Now I have done all my evening's a/cs, I can scribble a few words to you, before I go to bed. ...Muhammed who rushed down the rock stair case to the kitchen tent 3 minutes ago is already snoring! We were all out at dawn this morning, Friday being the beginning of the new week, and I was marshalling "locals" – grouping dozens of shouting people, taking all names, and sorting them out to new work. It was such a tangle, but I made them squat in groups of desirable old, less desirable old, new (very undesirable), and told them off to our men to the S. work, the N. work, and the E. work. Then we came in, frozen through, to our breakfast.

18 February 1921

[H.P. to John and Ann (Postcard)]

More settled weather since the big sandstorm here, and we are all working very hard. The Bruntons[1] have left Lahun, passed us and are now settled in a rock hewn mansion 4 miles south of us, where one of our men has gone to joint them and dig.

As I sit over my [...] I see across 70 miles of country, yellow rolling deserts, and such a gorgeous sight of green lands, all brilliant with clover and beans of a brighter green than you can ever see at home. We had a magnificent sunset last night, and all the sky got flecked with scraps of crimson and part got as if on fire and there were, down west, little pink and fiery islands of cloud such as Fra Angelico's angels stand on.

The sheykhs and chief officials still come to talk and coffee sometimes, and then the Arabic flows. Some came on trotting camels, armed, the other day, and one in a robe of hot reddish purple. I am going to buy a goose from a Coptic girl in the work this morning. Eggs flow in from various girls and boys; they have come down to 8 for 5d. What a pity I can't cook you some! I have been doing all the cooking for 3 days, custard pudding for Daddy and an invalid workman, and boiling water etc.

20 February 1921

[H.P. to John]

... and all round, neatly arranged are all our tinned foods, and books, and tools, hurricane-lamp, rice-pail, stocks of water, dozens of alabaster vases, 2 boxes statues, another and an immense tomb-stone, my box of clothes, table and larder foods, camera and photographic, supply of dates, bread pan, lamp, drug box, post-tray, sugar stocks, rolls of paper, eggs, my top boots, ink, bottles, biscuit tins, paraffin wax, canteen, and telescopes!

---

[1] Guy and Winifred Brunton.

10 March 1921

[H.P. to John (Postcard)]

I am very busy doing last drawings, and planning breaking up camp. I went in to mess-tent just now, 12 oc. to pick up a knife lying on table in sunshine and found it too hot to touch! Looked at therm. and found it 97° in shade, so took off some of my winter clo's which were so necessary this morning, and will be at night again. I am stopping letters being forwarded to this desert, and shall call for them next week at P.O. Cairo and Khedivial Hotel.

Hilda left England for Egypt on November 1st 1921, visiting Italy en route for Egypt. Flinders left England two days later. By the end of the year the Petries were back at Abydos where they had excavated from 1899–1904. They were accompanied by Gertrude Caton-Thompson who was interested in collecting Egyptian flints. After two months they moved on to Behnesa (Oxyrhynchus) a site Petrie had previously visited in 1896.

11 December 1921
Baliana, Upper Egypt

[H.P. to Ann]

Now that I am settled down, I am able to get at ink and sit down and write you a letter, and if you could see our enclosure we live in, you would indeed marvel at it. Imagine a big wall of brown mud brick, as tall as the house you are in, and thicker than a castle wall; it encloses a space larger than the Grange gardens (3 or 4 acres), all tumbled sand and brick, and potsherd, and we have piled a long terrace of sand on which our 8 tents are pitched. At the 2 ends are two little gaps for gateways, one east, one south, and at the north-east, and west (northerly) corners are two guarded gateways with guard-rooms, and in 3 of these our workmen are planted, with their roofs of plank and maize straw, so they act as a guard for us. Through these gaps we have lovely views of pinkish mountain cliffs, of palm trees, of desert. The wonderful part of it is that this is the ruin of a great fortress of the IInd dynasty, built not long after Mena himself, and belonging to 5,000 B.C. – long before the Pyramids were built. There are 2 such fortresses here, and traces of a third. The other stands near by, and I went into it this morning when I went to church, because it is now become a Coptic village, and an old Coptic church stands in it. The priest in a purple cope was reading a very long second lesson when I went in, and I stood in my riding or land suit, in top boots, as everyone was probably very dirty, in front of him, all the service, while all the men squatted barefoot in front of me, and all the women in long black draperies squatted behind me. There were many responses, and a good many long recitals like creeds, but the only things I could join in were "kyrie eleison" and the frequent "Amen".

Now, as I write, the sky turns purple and pink, and a superb sunset begins. As the workmen come in, I sing out the names of 4, and they each seize a big water-jar and run off ten minutes away to the priest's well and water wheel slung with pots which draw up the water, as a cow or buffalo walks round. ...

11 December 1921
Baliana, Upper Egypt

[H.P. to John]

... I pushed up country by night train, and got to Luqsor, where I had a most enchanting fortnight, a week with Engelbach on the eastern bank, Luqsor and Karnak and a week with the American excavator, Winlock,[1] and his party, on the western bank, Deir el Bahri, Medinet Habu, Deir el Medineh, the XVIIIth dynasty painted tombs, Qurneh, Tombs of the Kings, and Tombs of the Queens. All that there is to see on the bank where there are no habitations or hotels, so it is a tiring business crossing by boat and donkey, and spending single days there, and I found it a great boon to live in the American excavations. ... I have sent Ann a long description of our ancient enclosure in which we live. I forgot to say that this IInd dynasty fortress is now called the "Shunet ez Zebib" which means magazine or storehouse of Raisins, and that these two Shuneh's are quite near to the ancient temple of Osiris, at Abydos where Daddy dug ten layers of temples in 1901–2 and 1902–3. A little further along Abydos, there is a painted temple of Rameses II, and a very large sculptured temple of Sety I. Up in a bay of the hills, a mile from here, lie all the royal tombs of the 1st dynasty, and those we dug in 1899–1900, and 1900–1, for we lived here 4 years altogether. Abydos is much improved. The wicked old sheykh and his son are gone. A very good sheykh or omdeh has taken his place. The thieving is less, and there is a police station now, and a made road and telegraph poles all the way from Baliana, 7 miles.

All the workmen ask after you and Ann, and are so pleased when we tell them you are both well, and both large and strong. We have about 35 Qufty men and boys here, and are employing only 15 local boys, at the start. 50 seems a mere handful, but we have only dug 2 days, and shall take a big lot of locals on, in a day or two, I expect. Our party is almost complete now, for the Bruntons do not arrive till January, and Baird telegraphs he cannot join us this year. We are 2 selves, Guinevere Morton, and 3 "khawagas". And in a day or two, Miss Caton-Thompson[2] will join us from Luqsor where we left her, hunting flints, and she will take up flints here. Abydos was always a great place for flints. ...

---

[1] Herbert E. Winlock was excavating in Thebes for the Metropolitan Museum in New York.

[2] Gertrude Caton-Thompson, her first archaeological experience in Egypt.

17 December 1921
Baliana, Upper Egypt

[H.P to John]

... Today we found something of a fair size, and which needs facsimile copying, so we were all very happy – Daddy to get it, I to copy it, and the men to feel they were doing well. It was a hot day, and Miss C.T. came back from the top desert quite hot and tired. She laid out all her flints (of the first 3 days, on top) and made a chart or schedule of them. I went off this morning to see our northern dig, a mile off, from which some very interesting copper weapons have come. I also called at the Coptic village, the other IInd dynasty fortress, and left a message for the Coptic priest to come and have coffee with us, but instead of the black-bearded man coming, who officiated on Sunday, a very very old man came on a donkey, who was rather deaf, the chief of the 4 priests, and we had not much to say to each other, but he was very pious and cheerful, and went soon after the coffee. This evening it was warm, and the men all sang songs. We went round and listened, it was mostly very slow monotonous minor singing, like plain-song, but with a little warbling in parts. It was mostly love songs they sang. Then I brought 3 little boys round to sing, and they warbled away, just the same little songs, in minor key, and looked so solemn, squatting on the tumbled ground in dark over-surplices, and great white turbans.

It is 8.30 and I must stop now, as everyone else has been in bed for some time, and Daddy says it is very late! Last night it was cold, and seven grown-up people all went to bed at 7p.m.! We have b'fast at 6.30, and are in the sun and wind all day, and by the time we have had 6 o'c. supper and talked a little, or done accounts or some other work, we are quite ready at 7.30 to turn in, bed being the only warm place, and everyone sleepy.

18 December 1921

[H.P. to John and Ann]

The Sheykh of the village night guards has just been up to pay a call, with the two usual requests, that we should take a friend of his on to the work, and that we should cure someone who has been suffering from something for 6 years (probably incurable) and one isn't sure what. He had his cup of coffee, sitting on a packing case in our enclosure – (our enclosure is only one brick high) no one had time to converse much, as it is 8a.m. and we are all busy. Daddy is finishing an article for "Discovery". Miss C. T. is sorting flints, the young men are skurrying to and from the digging with survey instruments, Miss Morton is washing her head. I am finishing this letter to you, before I go on with my copying of a long inscription. ...

3 January 1922
Baliana, Upper Egypt

[H.P. to John and Ann]

It is very hot in the sun, walking across the desert, and about 80° or 84° in mess tent about 10 a.m., but cool by lunchtime as our tents are under the shelter of the great fortification wall. In front of us, in the enclosure of about 4 acres lies the palace of the king, walls 18in. high (IInd dyn.) and the guardhouse of his guards, and besides the 2 entrances there are 2 lesser sally posts. Our men sleep in 3 of these, and we guard the remaining one ourselves, so we are fairly safe against marauding and night thieving, and hardly any village dogs venture in either, though, half a mile away, hundreds of village dogs bark all night. Night sounds here are chiefly the hooting of the owls, and by day there is a humming of thousands of bees, building in the walls.

Today we had a visitation from all the great men of the district, the mamur, head of police, and two ma'ouns, under him, and a local omdeh of our nearest village, who had already come here for a previous tea and talk. Three were trousered and in khaki with a fez, and capable of some English and Fr. and 2 were in dignified robes and spoke only Arabic.

Arabah is not quite such a noisy unmanageable place as we found it 22 years ago.[1] At least we had some trouble at first, with the population which came up to seek work each morning, and later, guards were turned on, to police it, but I have to do a good deal of shouting orders and policing myself, as well as picking out all the more likely youths, marshalling the groups and booking their names. One day, the folk did break into our work, and we ejected them with difficulty. One of our men had a pick stolen, but we marched him off to the omdeh with a complaint, who gave him another, and has given orders to the whole neighbourhood, so that I have a much more disciplined crowd to deal with now. The boys wish us "that our days may be like milk". This is the work before b'fast. There is no giving out here of tools and ropes, as last year. At sunrise, the men start for their pits, none very far. Glorious sun rises seen behind a precipice of "gebel" through the broken-down sallyport. After b'fast, one sees to water-supply, or airing of blankets, a man brings up eggs and some milk, the cookboy does his boiling, also rice for lunch, and some washing of clothes. Each person hurries off to the men under their charge. Morning work is various: I look after men and the basketing, or else copy inscriptions on stone stelas, or begin some plotting of a plan. At 12 we whistle off the men, and all 7 of us come in to lunch. Some of us get a rest and a cool down, afterwards, or one goes on copying in the shade. Changing shoes and washing feet is of great consequence out here. Early tea helps also on hot days. On Monday afernoons I go round the work and pay all the local men and boys in their pits. At sunset, all the workmen come in with their basket loads, and hand in all the finds, and have their value assessed and booked. I send several men with the great water-jars to a

---

[1] See p. 155–165.

neighbouring Coptic well. There is often a superb sunset, seen through the other sallyport behind our tents, fiery and opal, and green, or else all flaming pink in ripples on the bluest of skies. Pottery, any skulls, stones etc. are ranged on the sand below our sand terrace, and marked in ink next morning. More delicate finds, wood, ivory, flint, beads and other objects are put by under canvas, and sorted into tins or parcels later on. We get supper, I give out names for water-carrying at sunrise; after he has washed up the boy brings back the hurricane lamp, and most nights people retire to bed, to avoid the cold. Warmer nights we may write letters, draw, or do a/cs. On Tuesdays, the workmen take the market-day for holiday, and the morning is very busy with our Quftis' accounts, and various archaeological jobs. It is sometimes the busiest day of the week, as all very large things, and many small things are reserved for its peaceful hours. Occasionally we go off on some excursion, to temples, or with our lunch to the top desert, but that is only early in the season before work accumulates. In the afternoon, market stuff comes in, the week's supply of rice and lentils, coffee, some meat, a sugar loaf, potatoes, cabbage or lettuce, occasional oranges, tomatoes, soap and methylated. The workmen bring their grouped market accounts. They cook by their little fires, plait baskets, and come to have something cut by scissors, or sawn with our saw. They sing monotonous plaintive minor songs all the evening, in unison, with refrains – mostly love songs, or have athletic sports, or do a zikr,[1] a swaying back and forwards to chanting of "Allah", in the moonlight.

On Fridays there is a good chance of letters from England. On Sunday morning, I get across the ruins of a second fortress to a third one, which still stands as a Coptic deir, and is entered by a great heavy wooden gate in the wall. There in the old church of many mud domes, service is going on from 8 till about 11, the Coptic priest reads the lessons in Coptic and Arabic, and entones the long communion service in a sort of plain song. There is incense and there are cymbals, and there is a great square altar hidden in the holy place, and tiny acolytes hold candles, and a cross. The congregation join loudly, with many a long response and canticle, and many amens, and kyrie eleisons. The men stand or crouch on matting all round the reading desk, and the women all sit along the back wall with small children. I have to stand fronting the altar, and I go in, and slip out, to suit my own hours. ...

20 January 1922
Baliana

[H.P. to John and Ann]

... We have been much busier the last week or fortnight, and much to tell of course but must tell on my return. It takes all day to copy inscribed stuff and make outline drawings of things, and in the evenings I am very busy inking in. Yesterday morning was an All Souls day in the C. Church, and hundreds of people went to the cemetery nearby, between 5 and 8 in the morning. Daddy

---

[1] See p. 62–3, 153–4.

had things waiting to be photographed, pits with unusual arrangements of bones, so we safeguard these by lying at each end of a long trench for 1½ hours of starlight, and when the sun got up, got the photographs and came in to breakfast. We have some beautiful sunrises here, and still better sunsets. ...

17 February 1922
Behnesa, Beni Mazar, Upper Egypt

[H.P. to John and Ann]

... I am afraid I haven't written so much lately, but I have been quite over-worked with a big household removal, packing boxes, and beds and kitchen stuff, and all our things, and despatching several camel-loads on various days. We got off about 15 boxes and beds and bath and buckets, a week ago, followed by 5 more boxes and 2 more beds 3 days later; then we came away 8 miles donkey, 4 hours train, a night in a Greek inn at Asyut, and 5 hours train again, and 11 miles donkey back to Behnesa, the former capital of a nome, Oxyrhynkos. The tents and blankets by passenger train never came to time, so we had to do without bedding and sleep in our clothes in the new hut, the first night. The ground was very hard and chilly. Fortunately there were plenty of food stores, and here we can get tiny broad beans, and the (1st dynasty) NAR fish, from the Bahur Yusuf. We live across a great bridge, but donkeys cannot cross it, as one steps from sleeper to sleeper with a yawning gulf of water between each step. None of the sleepers are equi-distant, and many are not even parallel. However one can go quite fast by practice, and there are 185 of them.[1] Here our little huts (3) look towards bridge and Bahr Yusuf, and the tents are all in a circle, under the palm trees. In the middle, which is bare clean earth with stems of half a dozen great trees, we shall be able to have lunch and tea in the shade. It is penned in, away from river, but very shady, and with inland views of ruined town stuff and potsherds, many camels and donkeys passing, sheykh's domes. We miss the desert sand and mountains. Here a dusty earth blows and there are many flies. The water is dusty too. It is a place for papyri, things are of Greek and Roman age, but the river and the palms are nice. I have not had time to go into Behnesa town yet. We are on the outskirts of it. The Omdeh is to call on us tomorrow. Aly Swefy is here, one of our best old hands. Being a fisherman, he has a little rough boat below here, and rushes off sometimes to catch a fish. ... Try to imagine walking along a railway from sleeper to sleeper, but with no ground between – just a blank, with water 30ft. below you. It takes sometime to get across 185 of them, at a steady tramp. The bridge opens occasionally, to let feluccas through, the rough boats with a long yard and 3-cornered sail. Across the rails, a wild untidy garden lies, enclosed with 4 walls. The man has brought me a large rusty key, and I am to take vegetables when I like. I went in yesterday, and picked a bundle of spinach-like mallow. The other vegetables there are onions

---

[1] Crossing this bridge was a twice-daily ordeal for the Petries' assistants, see G. Caton-Thompson's autobiography *Mixed Memoirs* (Paradigm Press 1983).

and clover. A man came up, with a big bath towel round his shoulders (and fleas visible) this evening, and brought some papyri to our wall. Boys come and ask for work, and we shall begin to employ some tomorrow. The workmen began to dig yesterday (at papyri), when they had made their own dug-outs, and helped us to pitch tents.

I much regretted leaving Abydos, after spending a fifth winter there, in addition to 1899–1903. The scenery of the mountain cliffs and gorges, standing round in a great semi-circle, is so splendid, and then the early forts, and the XIXdyn. temples make the place very interesting. Here there is only distant desert and that quite flat, merely getting rather hilly 6 or 7 miles away. Jackals, foxes, wolves, we have none, but tiresomely present dogs and cats, and townspeople and Bedawin, all too near. There is said to be a police station here and 6 English engineers, but we have seen nothing of them yet. I must tell you more about Aly's boat and fishing. I crossed in it yesterday when I found the bridge "up".

I hope, now, that all the packing and unpacking is over, I shall be able to get back to ordinary work. The "sebakh" dust, the mosquitoes, the muddy water, and the fierce barking of dogs, are going to be drawbacks here, but one cannot live on the edge of a native town, without an uproar of dogs at night, and by day town smells, and many flies.

Hundreds of camels and donkeys with little boys to drive them, are passing our courtyard daily, to fetch "sebakh", the dusty-earth from city mounds; it is the sebakh diggers who find papyri, and dig down the mounds, partly destroying what we want, but also getting them down to the levels where we can go on digging, so they do good as well as harm.

We are digging in papyrus levels now, ourselves. Until we begin to find anything that wants drawing, I shall ink in the many sheets of drawings I made at Abydos. Egypt is very interesting, one never gets tired of the people, the scenery, and the various sorts of work. Our helpers will be coming back tomorrow. I wonder how they will like the circle of tents in our palm-grove. ...

22 February 1922
Behnesa, Beni Mazar

[H.P. to John]

We are now settled in here, and have had our first market day. Yesterday D and I went a very long expedition, starting by moonlight across our openwork bridge, catching a light-R. train about 6, then tramping from B. Mazar to the Nile, crossing with 70 natives and 15 donkeys and then a very long hot tramp to foothills. I got a donkey the last part of the way. We hunted through many cliff caves (quarries) for inscrips. and at last had a good find. Ferried and journeyed back and made acquaintance with an interesting old magnate in train. I bought veg. and bread in the town, and some gay dusters. Some rock broke under me while on the foothills, and let me down with a crash, barehead on to hard rock, also my back, so at present I cannot turn my head sideways, or lift anything. D. and I were out at 6 this morning choosing men and boys.

Mr Wainwright has come down to inspect this district, and has put his tents in our compound. We are about 200 miles from Abydos. This is Oxyrhynkos, where the Logia, the "Sayings of Jesus" were found. Daddy's tent was in this palm-grove and then he left Grenfell and Hunt here, because of papyri, and he himself went on to Deshasheh, where he got that fine early painted statue, now in Brit.Mus.

25 February 1922
Behnesa, Beni Mazar

[H.P. to John and Ann]

... I have told you of the new features in this very different place. It was a delightful change to find shady trees and running water here, namely a straggling palm grove and the great Bahr Yusuf canal. The long yards and sails of the vessels (as the one-maylim stamp) are always before us, and the boats lade and unlade all day and pass through the turn bridge at noon. I am quite used, now, to stepping from sleeper to sleeper across the big bridge, and even to running across. Some people do not like seeing the water below, between each sleeper, and the ferry and shipping. Beasts have to cross by ferry. Our palm-grove is the one in Daddy's sunset sketch of his tent here, 26 years ago. He found nothing but papyri here, handed it over to Grenfell and Hunt and moved on. The tents are in a circle under the palms and we have lunch and tea out there daily. The mess-hut has a low door and a kitchen-hatch and a square window of wire mesh. The long coffin-lid from Lahun, (brought from there by boat with our rope-ladders and food boxes) serves us a third season for our dining table. The mess-hut and, later on, our antiquities, are guarded at the inner end by my small hut alongside, and at the outer end by the kitchen hut in which Muhammed sleeps, and his again by a lean-to of corrugated iron in which 3 men sleep. Our tents are flanked by Mr Wainwright's two, and they lead on to Aly Swefy's two, and beyond is a lean-to, with the remainder of our men, and a village guard minds the approach, as there are many Bedawin in this district. Another guard minds the bridge and challenges passers, and we have to see that the two do not get together and talk. Twice over, Bedawyn have tried to camp between us and the rail alongside us, but we clear them out. Today some arrived from the oasis some days' journey west of us. They of course had many camels, and wore white woollen draperies and head ropes. They bore great basket-work parcels of dates, very weighty, and some large basket trays but had high notions of their value. They exchanged these for other commodities in the village, and departed.

It took nearly a week to unpack my camp stuff and settle in, as I was single-handed – all our staff away at Luqsor – but on the second or third day of it, we began digging, so there has been little loss of time in moving. The men had travelled down by night, and we overtook them after a few hours' sleep at Assyut. We rode over here by donkey, 11 miles, to save time. Light railway reaches 3 times daily, and post at noon daily. At first the natives were very curious as to our things, and used to swarm on the railway line to overlook us, but now they take us more as a matter of course, always civil. The tourist is unknown here.

We have had one very pleasant and adventurous market-day. Started across the bridge by moonlight, got to Sandafa at 6 and Beni Maz. at 7.15, and the edge of the Arabian desert at 8 or 9, after crossing the Nile with a sailing boat, which punted and tacked, as both stream and wind were against us. Such a crowd, 70 people and 15 donkeys. Towards the foot-hills I secured a donkey, and a sheykh of Arabs accompanied us and Aly to a row of caves, many of which we searched for inscriptions. We only found one, in the top of the cliff, but that was a prize, for it had a great many inscriptions of a language hardly known here – Aramaic – the dialect talked by the apostles. Now we are getting an Aramaic scholar on to them.

We spread in various directions, and each hunted. My line of caves was very sultry, and when I climbed down and was going to mount, I had quite a nasty fall on what looked like a plain ledge. It crashed, and my head crashed, and back, on hard rock and I found everything difficult for 3 days. I quite enjoyed the journey back, by desert, and sugar cane, and a village market, and the Nile, and I bought vegetables in Beni Mazar, and made friends with a fine Coptic magnate who lives by the bridge here, and came to coffee next day, after sending me butter and cream cheese from his farms. It makes a nice change from tinned jam. Yesterday 3 of us were obliged to go and lunch with him and his 2 sons, and talk a great deal of Arabic. In a squalid mud village with lanes almost impassable for flies, we found a large house with courtyard and portico and benches, and a plain dining room, doors on 4 sides and through draughts. Little sitting room all chairs and divans round, all doors and windows, quite cool on a hot day and not a fly. While we ate, a dear little mongoose or ichneumon ran about the floor and fed out of our hands. Qattas Bibawy was dressed in the long black drapery of a Copt, and a striped silk cassock under it. Thin rolls of white muslin round his head, hiding the red skull-cap and blue tassel. A massive man with a kindly face. You will see his grandson next year, who is coming over to London to learn medicine. He is named after S. Mark, Murgos, and his 2nd name is his father's 1st name, Ibrahym.

There is no high desert here – one sees square-looking chunks of hill about 6 or 7 miles off, and all is low here, with rolling miles of tumbled mounds of dusty earth, covered with potsherds. The landscape is rather diversified with here and there a hillock with a white dome on it, and there is also a fine old ruined mosque, and a hollow with columns standing in it; perhaps this was the cathedral at the time when Oxyrhynkos was a great Coptic city as large as Alexandria. We are finding something that may be a monastery further afield, and some undug mounds elsewhere which look important.

One of our people has just brought in a jerboa, asleep, curled up. He has a soft little coat, is much prettier than a mouse with little bright eyes and a long tail, and hops high. One used to hop round the mess-hut every night, at one place, I remember.

Aly has a small boat here, and one market-day, I hope to take an hour off work, and go out fishing with him. He catches the *nar* fish, after whose name a king of the time of Mena, was named. There is a very ancient Coptic church some miles from here, which I hope to see, if I can get free of work long enough to ride there. Sandafa, here, has 1,000 Coptic population, and our friend Qattas has promised to build them a church.

Behnesa is an entirely Muslim place, and has some fine scraps of ruined architecture of mosques about it and some tiny shops in which only Greek soap, tobacco, and dusters can be bought. There is only one plastered house and that belongs to the Omdeh[1] who called in state on us when we arrived.

I copied a large Greek inscrip. yesterday, bold incised letters painted red. Scraps of glass and of papyri turn up daily. I am also busy with all the workmen's a/cs.

26 February 1922
Behnesa, Beni Mazar, Upper Egypt

[H.P. to Ann]

We have a grey day which is very unusual, and dust blowing off the great mounds today, a good deal of wind. My Coptic friend came to tea and we had a long talk about the Coptic and English churches, and he sent his servant across to fetch butter, bread and cream-cheese for us. He came in his boat as he does not appreciate the openwork bridge. Today we have brought back a darling jerboa from the desert. It sits up on its hind-paws to eat bread and has long whiskers and a very long tail. It is lovely yellow sand colour and has bright black eyes. Quite happy in a tiny house of potsherds in a large box of yellow sand, which is our table for lunch and tea in the palm-grove.

4 March 1922

[H.P. to John and Ann]

There has been so much to do, getting all the camp and the work running, and seeing to all the local men and boys we employ, that I have had no time to write lately. I have been late at night over accounts too, and we have been many here, coming and going. Miss C. T. and Miss Norton have left us this morning, to spend a fortnight at Helwan, where the former hopes to examine flints. Mr W. and Mr N.[2] have joined us from Abydos, now the packing is finished there. Daddy has gone away on donkey-back for 2 days, or 3 to search for sites. It is the first time I have not accompanied him. Mr Wainwright was travelling over the same parts of the desert, so he went with Mr W's tents and arrangements; I expect him back today. I have to go the round of very scattered work twice a day while D. is away. My boat sails on 23rd, so I shall be home this month. ...

---

[1] Mayor.

[2] G. W. H. Walker and Montgomerie Neilson.

16 March 1922
Behnesa

[H.P. to John and Ann]

    ... I am only able to scribble this roughly, tired out, after a long 3 days' expedition into the eastern desert. I took 3 of our own men, and had ½ dozen Bedawyn up in the hills. The young chief and his henchman came and slept outside the door of my cave, and we dug out one pit and filled in two, in 2 caves high up. I brought back a brass flute and some Bedawy songs, and made some plans of underground chambers. The air was so strong and bracing, and the cave so snug to live in, but I am quite worn out with the work, and with racing up and down rope ladders. ... The desert on the Arabian side of the Nile was so beautiful, and clear and clean, and high – the moon golden and full, the daylight so airy and bright. I enjoyed that caravan life so much. Here it is all dust, and mosquitoes, and dogs barking all night, but it is very interesting here too, though not so beautiful or so healthy. Go on writing to Daddy, as he continues here, after I leave. ...

1926–1935
Excavating in Palestine

In the summer of 1926, after some forty years of excavating, Flinders Petrie decided that the time had come to leave Egypt: after the war, severe conditions imposed on excavations by the authorities in Cairo, and a prospect of new discoveries in "Egypt over the Border" led him to transfer his work to Palestine. He chose as his first site Tell Jemmeh, a great mound in the Wady Ghazzeh (now Wady Besor), one of a line of ancient fortresses built to keep out invaders; when the Egyptians had conquered Palestine, they became military strongholds in the Pharaonic system of occupation. The Petries were joined by a number of people: James Starkey had worked with Petrie at Qau; Gerald Harding had been a student of Margaret Murray at University College; Dr Parker joined the team as a volunteer and proved invaluable. So too did the Risdons, a retired naval commander and his wife.

30 November 1926
Gaza

[H.P. writes]

The last day in Egypt was spent partly in the Museum, partly at Gizeh 2–4, and there we sat under the Great Pyramid for lunch, and went all round the (newly excavated) Sphinx. Got back by 5 to catch the 6 o'c. night train to Palestine, after a hotel tea. The 4 of us had carriage to ourselves all night. Impossibly jolty line, all through bare rolling desert. I cdnt. sleep much, so watched the desert and its little tufts of vegn. most of the night, with great joy. Very uncomfortable journey. Starkey and the men had gone on, 24 hrs earlier, but by mistake didn't send down to meet us. So we waited fr. 4½ (till 6½ or 7a.m.) in the starlight, partly in a small shed which called itself the station. Desert single line never has a station or a platform. The first native I saw had a Bedawy head-rope and cartridges, and the second a great white sheepskin coat. Many of them are in full Bedawy dress, a few have sheepskins, others are in striped caftans, or in tarbush and caftans, or in galabiehs. The turbans are gayer than in Egypt, being mostly red or orange, and some are yellow and white. Stripes predominate. Many wear the thick straight abayeh of wide brown and white stripes, like a sack with 2 armholes.

26 November 1926

[H.P. writes]

At last I got F. to go up to the town[1] and find the rest-house and send down
the men for our baggage. We had a suitcase and a kit-bag each, and had
managed them all thro' the journey, but now there was no need, and the town
was ¼ mile off on a hill, stone houses, trees and minarets, all very picturesque
in the dawn and early sunlight. Down they came, in their Upper Egyptian
dress so different from anything here – Hasan Osman, Umbarak and Sultan
Bakhit, Ahmed Aly, Muhammed Sayd, Hofny Ibrahim, and one boy, (the son
of Nasr-ed-Din).[2] They took us across desert and a Muslim cemetery, and up
through a narrow stone-built street, and thro' a great gate down into ¼ acre
garden full of tall weeping "pepper trees", and a stone-flagged terrace, thro' a
mediaeval gateway (the men sleep on one side, and our dining-hall is on the
other), and so into a marble-paved court, with small palace or fortress
surrounding it on all sides, 2 outer staircases, and a large ancient gnarled tree
called "sub-sa'af" of unknown sort, weeping, in the middle, under a blazing
blue sky. 4 rooms are apportioned to us; the 8 men's at the entrance and the
Starkeys' upstairs. Harding has one in the corner with a Syrian carved doming,
which Parker will share when he comes, (we left him in Cairo with Mrs
Harrison), and then we have one like a church along the south side, have
blocked the channel off with store-cases, for Risdon, and F. and I have the
nave – plenty of doors and windows double ogee with capitals. There are
pointed arches to every recess and window, and groined vaulting everywhere
with occasional Arab decorative carving and marbles. Walls over 3ft. thick, so
very warm at night and cool in the day. Marble pavements make bare feet or
nailed boots impossible, also the reverberation in the dining room makes
single sentences, words, or orders quite useless, but we manage to converse
at table. F. is in fine form at meals, his table talk, especially of adventures and
topography, S. Palestine. He is walking across deserts, reconnoitring, all day
now and every day, and it thoroughly agrees with him.

Part of our fortress is 600 years old, and a small corner, bombed, was
rebuilt. It belonged to 7 brothers. The ogees and small domings in the dining
hall are very nice. An occasional official turns up to use a room, or get a meal,
but we see little of them. There is a lovely bath on the roof, but no water! I go
up there often, to look at the black-headed birds, of thrush and finch sizes,
which settle in our trees, and the front room also commands the garden, a
blaze of bougainvillea, and part of some large things like lumps of stone,

---

[1] Gaza.
[2] Quftis.

turned out to be huge bulbs – bassul (bulbs or onions) they call them. Further on, many of these had sprouted 3 inches and looked like well-to-do hyacinths, and there were a lot of clumps of sword-leaves like daffodils, all sparsely sprinkled on the desert, so the desert which is so bare and pinky-brown lifeless now will evidently be blossoming later on. After some miles we came upon a bare wady by a wooden (military?) bridge to the village of Bet-Hamun, on a slope. Very narrow clean streets between clean mud-houses with flat mud roofs – Muslim but surprisingly clean and neat. The little fields are surrounded by hideous grotesque cactus. Many men in turbans saluted us, the women were Syrian-dressed with embroidery and sequins, and the children wore tarbushes.

The fish-goddess was very coy. No sign of any temple or fish-ponds, or anything, anywhere. We transversed the desert home by noon or so, got a good rest in the afternoon.

I wandered about Gaza later, and saw many Bedawin, some with the immense red leather boots, very hand-sewn, others with great long curved sabres; all with head-ropes, some very thick, of black hair or brown, others with the metal coils at intervals: the headshawl is white or sometimes orange. One Bedawy sheykh was very gorgeously dressed, and had a handsome inlaid sword, but was in a Ford car!

28 November 1926

[H.P. writes]

We all 5 tramped parts of the town and cemetery early, 7–9, and later F. got the place where we are now digging, the great north sur or wall. Bells of a Franciscan chapel were ringing. There are thousands of Muslims here, and a few Jews, and about 200 Christians. They have Arabic services in a chapel in the grounds of the C.M.S. Hospital. Later in the day, F. and I called on the matron, the only English person of them, and found a parson and his wife from Jaffa, who come over once a month for services, there, in Arabic and one in English. I wished I could have motored back with them next morning to Jaffa, to see it, but couldn't ask them. Next month, I shall have to go in on business probably.

29 November 1926

[H.P. writes]

F. took a whole day's tramp over the NW dunes towards the sea, and exam-ground to N. and finished with Beit Hanun, this time locating a site worth examining further. He took R. and H., and one man, with him, and their lunch and water. At 4p.m. I motored up to the bridge near Hanun and picked them all up. The bulbs were greener on the desert, and the low-lying sunshine on the expanse of rolling distance was a wonderful sight, pinkish and brilliant, as only Holman Hunt knew how to paint. ...

9 December 1926
Gaza, Palestine

[H.P. to John – Posted the evening of December 12th]

My dear John,

I am afraid I have missed a good many days, but we all had a touch of Cairo 'flu and I was in bed 2 days and didn't want to write at all! It came after several days too busy to write, so there must have seemed a huge gap! From now onward, I will try to keep you more informed. Please post this on to Ann. ... Go and see her as soon as you are able to be in town, but meanwhile post this at once, as she hasn't heard either.

10 December 1926

[H.P. writes]

Today the post wagon caught fire at El Arish, so the mails are delayed. No events lately. We have been the victims of Cairo 'flu, one by one, but are all well again now. I crawled in to a meal again on Tues. Ev. and spent an active Wednesday. We motored to the edge of the Wady Ghazza that morn. and F. got an hour's prospecting. In spite of the forlorn desert expanse, the chauffeur raised an uncle and an orange grove in half a minute, so during the hour's wait, I ate oranges for a cure: there was a sandstorm raging. The way led out by a nursery of almond trees, from cactus hedge into the plain desert. The ravine of this wady leads down from the "tell" which we retreat to, in a few days, to begin work.[1] We keep a good deal in our courtyard, these days of sand. The 2 men are working at various points of the Gaza walls, very near at hand. The remainder of the workmen (5) have already gone to the tell, and as soon as they have finished the huts, we remove thither, a good many camel loads.

11 December 1926

[H.P. writes]

Fourth day of sandstorm. The district of Gaza still keeps free of rain, but has this other visitation. News of heavy rain, with wash-outs, comes in today from Jerusalem, from Jaffa and from Lydd. It has kept Garstang[2] from

---

[1] Tell Jemmeh, 9 miles southeast of Gaza, on the Wady Ghazzeh (now Wady Besor).
[2] John Garstang, then Director of Antiquities in Palestine.

coming down to us. The day of the deliverance of Jerusalem was kept here as a government holiday. I went to tea with the Municipal engineer, and collected from him the names of the tribes of Bedawyn with whom we shall have to deal and heard a good deal of the desert politics.

The last few days have been mostly taken up with calling on various officials, on behalf of the School Arch. Eg. and eliciting information of all sorts – Governorate, Head of Police, 2nd. ditto, the Surveyors in their tents in an orange grove. From two of the latter I learnt of two inscriptions; one in Greek F. followed up a ladder to a roof, and made facsimile copy. The large Byzantine one, used as a doorsill, I shall do in facsimile tomorrow. The survey party, and wives, all came to tea with us. It was very nice making friends with them, in spite of the fact that we were just packing, in our courtyard, for camel convoy to the tell. And on the morrow, the convoy left (5th). When the police so named it, it consisted of but one camel, but the buying of a huge sack of flour for the men, and the removal of all their belongings, necessitated a second camel, and as I got police protection for this, to make a favourable impression on the Bedawyn of the tell, and we had our Bedawy guard in addition, we made a fine cavalcade. The Ford car, with advance party (Starkey and Harding), self, and the Bedawy, reached the tell many hours before the camel convoy, the five Egyptians, and the mounted police. After settling my party, and exploring the tell, I returned by car, with a handful of Canaanite and Greek potsherds. The road there and back was no road, it was pathless waste, with limitless desert in all directions. From places one got a fine view of the Palestinian range, Hebron to Jerusalem, all blue, in the east. And about the expanse, one saw various little black hair tents of the Bedawyn making the loneliness look more lonely. When we made a wild rush for the scarp of a wady, Starkey was out of the car in a twinkling rather than rush it – so we all got out and it was a marvellous sight to see the car dash down and climb up the other bank. I had much the same, returning sole, a few hours later.

The tell is a fine sight, rising artificially from the plateau. The scarp of it, where cut back by the Wady Ghazza, is all stratified and striped. One sycamore fig stands below, and behind it is a ramshackle collection of tents, each with a camel. The little lithe dark Bedawyn in their striped coats came up on the tell to greet us, and offered *our* Bedawy coffee. I acquired a cheap glory by guessing the no. of their tents, and left them pleased and curious. On return to Gaza, 9 miles, I called in and fetched Mrs St. and Dr P. and took them both to the sea. A new road runs straight, 3 miles across the sand dunes. Blue sea, some boats on the beach, and small bivalves, and that straight straight coastline, featureless. After that, I fetched a box from the station, in car.

Going about the town of Gaza, by day or night, one sees everywhere this strong eastern architecture in the Syrian style, everywhere fortress-like. The lanes are very tortuous and narrow, clean also. All the decoration, mushrabiyas[1] etc. were looted by the Turks, and the town suffered badly in the bombardment, so that there are parts of every street laid waste, but a few good buildings have been preserved – the great old high decorated palace (now the police station) and our own fortress-palace, also the Greek church of S. or Abba Porphyrius 425 A.D. (where he died 450 A.D.). This has an apse and some ancient pillars and is arched right across in one. One bazaar street is stone-vaulted all the way, and very picturesque at night, deserted and no shops reinstated. The great church of the Crusaders escaped the shells in part. It is now a mosque and is being restored by the engineers. Some of the decoration is very beautiful and rich; it is a dignified building of great size and simplicity. Beyond it, and in line with the narrow native bazaars, lies a wide street with open cafes where the Bedawyn and others are always thronging; beyond this again, the English hospital. Large Muslim cemeteries occupy every slope on the edges of the town.

In the newer piece of town across the railway line one sees a more Arab population and denser bazaars. Here the weavers are working black hair and brown, and the cloths in coloured stripes, with large looms. Dyers are also at work, and carpenters at their rough ploughs, and smiths. There are shops of glass necklaces, and of swords and sabres. The great white fleeces are made into sheepskin coats for the Bedawyn. Some Aleppo carpets find their way here and are cheap. The Bedawy carpets are very dear. The quarter is called Saggariyeh, "of the trees", but there are none. I followed a native funeral along. First, the women were dancing in a circle and slapping their cheeks; then the men came in procession after banners and great palm-branches, decorated.

Today a procession went round the town, for rain. There were fine banners, covered with Arabic texts, and green flags, and two large flat drums. They do it for the latter rains, in March, also. But the rain does not come, though the rest of the country is getting deluged, especially Haifa flooded out.

In a few days the assizes will be held here, and the Lord Chief Justice of Palestine and his wife and a judge are coming to this rest-house. Murderers are tried once a year; the second of police came to call and told us. A police petrol goes down past our camp 3 times a week, he says, and we are in his district. So we shall have some connection with the outside world. Mr Stark the engineer has promised to come and see us down there, but we cannot

---

[1] Window lattices.

expect anyone else to leap the wady or find a path to reach us. The tell is called Tell Jemmu, and was lived in by Abraham and Isaac; (Gerar) and its king was Abimelech. Its pottery ranges from 2000 B.C. Canaanite down to 300 B.C., very fine Greek. The Romans never used the site. Later when the rains are over, we may move on to a larger tell, 17 miles from Gaza, towards Beersheba.

The great Bedawy sheykh whom I saw last week, dressed gorgeously and with good weapons, is a well-known character here. He is lord of Transjordan, and like his predecessor Mesha King of Moab, is a 'sheep-master'. He tried to get 1,000 sheep through without paying customs, and brought himself under the police here: the dues now have to be paid. Meanwhile, he nearly eluded them over 700 camels in transit. These are feeding in the neighbourhood here, as we saw when we viewed the district from the roof of the old palace or governorate (now police).

The vegetation in or round about Gaza is most of fig and olive, tamarisk, sycomore fig, pepper-tree and another weeping tree, with banana and pomegranate; scarcely any date palms. Orange groves here and more towards Jaffa; towards the sea, crimson-black iris will appear later and the common flowers are the big red anemone and the tulip.

Today, in a levelling expedition, 7 to 10a.m. with mirror levelling tube, we examined all the sites we have dug round Gaza; these are finished now, and the 2 men have gone to join the 5 others at the tell.

Under the north face of the mound of Gaza, and overlooking rolling desert partly grown with olive and sycomore fig, there is a concave reach of cliff of reddish brown earth which on close view seems to be brick walling. This Canaanite fortification wall of grey and brown bricks is 10ft. high (bricks 18 × 12 × 6); eastward it lies on native earth; further is covered by 2 courses of stone paving and probably a gateway. An upper wall, 17ft. high, is composed of reddish brown bricks, an Egyptian cubit in length (dimensions 20.4 × 10.2 × 5.1). It probably dates from XVIIIth dynasty. Encircles a field with a few gnarled olives, and leafless figs; cliff face of cactus. Plump grey birds with black head and tail and yellow rump, make a great noise here. Under a huge tamarisk, a saqqieh[1] creaks: banana trees lashed by the wind. In a gully running down west between two Muslim cemeteries, we dig and find a stone pavement parallel to road above. A little further, two lumps of hill divided by a road, seem to be part of Alexander's great siege mound, which was 250ft. high and ¼ mile across. We found the top of the deliberately piled stuff, and tumbled yellow earth, not native ground. At the corner, under a large tamarisk is the wely (tomb) of the Sheykh Salim and near it Sheykh

---

[1] Water-wheel.

Saba'a. Little lanterns hang from wooden cross-bars above their tombs.

The excavations of the last week or so have determined these several points. The most promising site is built over by a large new school close here; gold and antiquities were found. Opposite is the traditional tomb of Samson, now overbuilt by some sheykh's tomb: I crawled in but there was nothing much. ...

11 December 1926

[Letter from H.P. to John]

> We have had a long enforced wait in Gaza, but got a 'move on' on Sunday last (Dec. 5) when we decided we should begin our operations at Tell Jemmu, about 9 miles across the desert, south. I went over with Starkey and Harding in a Ford car across weird tracks and ploughed land and pathless desert, and as the crow flies, across a whole ravine, and behold a great reddish 'tell' came in sight, and when ½ hour later we arrived at the next ravine or watercourse below it, we dismounted and the 2 Khawagat[1] were left there to fight the battle of making us a home there. I have sent you a p.c. today, lest Xmas come suddenly, and have told you that the home is by now half built. They manage to get large stones and mud and we are having corrugated roofing sent down from Jaffa. Next Friday 17th will see us, probably, going over to settle in. It is a romantic and lonely spot, very rough and exposed and the rains, which are 3 weeks delayed, will be on us by then. So there are only a few more days remaining to us in this Syrian fortress. Gaza is a picturesque little city but there isn't much to do here; the bazaars are dark, noisy and picturesque: the weavers, dyers, carpenters, interesting to watch. Half the houses are waist hight since the bombardment. Some of the tiny lanes are very tortuous and very clean. ... After we move off to the Tell, about 18th we shall send in an Egyptian, or ditto – camel, for post and for market food. He will do the 18 miles shopping and be back by sunset. I should think this will be twice a week.
>
> ... Your letters are coming regularly. It is *so* nice to get letters here, when one is tired and bored with mosquitoes and cold gales and lacking so many things. It isn't easy getting along in this particular place, but I am grateful for the inconveniences here, when one considers what the tell will be like! I am much looking forward to Gerar and Abimelech all the same. I wish you could see the Oriental jostle of Gaza. Now I must get a drink of our thin blue water. There isn't going to be much water at the tell, as we shall have to fetch it by camel 3 miles and very saline at that, I hear. Daddy talks astronomy and travel, various sciences, with amazing energy here, and was wielded a hammer and chisel all day. He is in top spirits, always up by 6a.m. and working hard.

---

[1] Europeans.

11 December 1926

[Letter from F.P. to John]

My dear John,

You will have had all our main news from Mammy, so I will not go over that. Six days ago Mr Starkey and Harding went off to build huts for us, nine miles south at Tell Jemmu.[1] This is believed to be the Gerar of Abraham and Isaac history. It is a great tell going back to 2000 B.C., so a first rate place to work in relation to Egypt, as well as Biblical. If we can get any tablet letters of Abimelech the prize will be great.

The country all round here accords with the phrase in Acts, "the way to Gaza which is desert." All around, as far as one can see, the rolling country is dusty brown with no trace of green; only around Gaza are some sycamore fig trees and horrid cactus hedges. We are waiting for the rains, and bulbs all over the land are pushing up shoots in readiness. We have had a few light showers at night, and furious gales from S.W. for four days, while all the rain has fallen northward, deluges at Jaffa and Jerusalem, roads washed away, and so forth. Yesterday there was a procession for rain here, with three large banners and drums going. If rain comes the roads and paths will be so slippery with mud that going is difficult, especially for camels. So it is well for us that the rains are three weeks late this year. We hope to move down to Jemmu and begin work in about a week or more.

We looked in at the great church this morning, an early building, roofed by a single open arching. It commemorates St Porphyrius, Archbishop of Gaza in 425. You will find about him, doubtless, in the Dict. Xn. Biog. in the study. The iconostasis, etc. was all obviously new, since the war. The Turks looted and destroyed everything in Gaza from houses etc. before they left. Most of the town is in ruins still, and pop. only 15,000 instead of 40,000. The Turkish destruction has drawn the wrath of the populace, and there does not seem to be any resentment at our shelling of the town to drive the Turks out. All over the country there are bits of shells, and duds lying about. I saw one cottage with 27 shells stacked together like bottles for a good corner foundation. Mazes of barbed wire lie about the landscape rolled up. The land is well policed by English officers. There used to be 10 or 20 raids of Bedawy in the year, over the district. They were cut back by wireless and mounted police till last year there was only one raid, and this year none. All the south of this region is only occupied by nomad Arabs. There are many at Jemmu, but quite quiet and friendly. ...

I have been hunting potsherds around Gaza, and found a bit of the early wall, 27 ft. high in two periods, probably Canaanite and Egyptian. The clearing up of our old stores, sorting boxes, and getting ready to settle to work takes much time, while waiting for huts.

Love to Ann, who should have this.

Your own Daddy.

---

[1] Now thought to be Yerzaa.

12 December 1926

[H.P. to Ann]

... I wish you could see the long brown reaches of desert out here, which roll away endlessly. There are such funny large bulbs lying about, with nice liliaceous leafage several inches up. They say that, after the rains, the ground is covered with great masses of red and purple large anemones, and many tulips. Towards the sand dunes here, crimson-black iris come up. In the desert there are going to be many foxes, so no doubt Samson had no trouble in getting his. Where is Samson, and where are the gates? We are close to him, but one is never allowed to dig anywhere near a 'holy man'. Successive towns have grown up here, till Samson's level is 30ft. below us.

Muhammed[1] sends you his best sala'ams. Today he was cleaning and making reminiscences as to my best old milk-can of afore-time, and reminded me it belonged to "Dendera-time" that is 1897 (when he came into my service at the age of 14). His son is now table-servant in the America work. He was terribly worried when Daddy cut his finger a few days ago. He much enjoys his daily shopping in the town, having never had that oftener than once a week, any other year. The tell will be a very different thing: he will only have the little weird Bedawyn to speak to, and our own 7 Egyptians. No shoppings, not even on market days, 9 miles of dreary desert back of beyond. ... One of our party was at Ramleh lately, and the air force have promised to take air-photographs of our 2 "tells" for us.

Christmas Eve 1926
Tell Jemmeh

[H.P. writes]

Blaze of sunshine, the dusty wind having subsided. The desert is not very hilly, but ends in a near cliff and some distant serrated cliffs and we see a goodish way, the tell standing steeply behind us. I am sitting in the sunshine on my door-sill. We live in a neat row of huts, F.'s and mine at one end, as always, and next to our 2 doors come, in order, Risdon, the Starkeys, the mess-hut, the kitchen (with hatch between) Dr Parker, Harding. At the far end, an empty hut juts forward, still not roofed; will do for stores, or antikas, or a visitor. It blocks our 4 foot terrace: below the little wall of that lie 2 great plots ready for pottery etc. with a garden path running down fr. mess-hut to the only gate. A dwarf wall surrounds the whole. The 6 balalis, water jars, stand on a bench and another bench stands outside the gates, for sheykhs and others.

The dining table is composed of 4 planks on 4 corner boxes. A plank shelf runs round the room. F. and I sit at the 2 ends nearest the door as usual. The tins of food, the drawing boards and big tools are stacked against the walls. The

---

[1] Muhammed Osman el Kreti, their Egyptian cook.

Excavations at Tell Jemmeh, Palestine.

stone walls of the huts are concealed in their dried mud mortar and coatings, so tone with the landscape which is all mud colour. A lonely landscape rises and falls in all directions and winds away indefinitely. Across it go herds of camels, or a flock of sheep, or a few Bedawyn with black headropes and wearing an orange abbayeh.[1] Today, 300 of the camels of the recalcitrant sheep-master of Transjordan loomed along, towards the Egyptian border.

Christmas Day 1926

[H.P. writes]

The plan of the tell progresses. The Basha[2] has it tied in at all points, and it begins to look like the top here, with its narrow neck, and anchor-like arms; and blue streamcourses show the hollows. The various walls and circular pits of the city of Gerar begin to appear. This morning, I was up early to give out pick axes etc. and we chose some fresh locals from a friendly crowd who awaited us. We have now, therefore, 64 locals working on our hill, making a total of 71. There was a stormy appearance in the sky, and a rainbow, and we got in, much in want of b'fast. I made clearances in my hut, and in the mess-

---

[1] Cloak.
[2] 'The Pasha', i.e. Petrie.

hut and courtyard, and all is getting into order. Then we saw a car in the distance, and behold the 3 Stacks and their dog, bringing with them Mrs Risdon, who is youthful and pleasant. Our party is now complete, 8 in all, with 2 Starkeys, 2 Risdons, Parker and Harding. My house a/cs, personal, and Jerusalem a/cs, and the men's a/cs worked out successfully. All the afternoon F. and I were on the tell with a tape-measure and rods and sextant, and got the various chambers and granaries (?) and walls that have appeared, settled into a fresh plan. This I am beginning to draw tonight. It is 1:100, with all the smaller detail.

I also went the round of the 71 workmen. Got the names of each one, and the name of their provenance. Can now build their a/c book and get all registered, before next pay day.

I told the party I should expect them to a fancy dress dinner tonight, and they all came most gorgeous and effective. I had bought 4 dresses in Jerusalem, so F. appeared in a blk. robe trimmed with gold, Mrs Starkey in my Bethlehem dress with a tall headdress, Starkey in a caftan, shawl and turban, Mrs Risdon in something shimmery and Turkish, Risdon in my abbayeh, Harding in a sheet and a blanket, Sinai Bedawy to the life, with a local headrope and dagger, Mr Parker in his white hospital coat, and self in a blue abbayeh, headshawl and headrope. We all looked very gay and had much dessert after a grand stew and veg. and Dr Parker produced some mince pies! I couldn't get them to sing carols as we discussed haematite weights, and the maps I brought fr. Jerusalem, but Harding and the Bedawy guards made music in the desert by turns. Since then proofs and now it is bedtime.

Tomorrow, Garstang may turn up, as he is over fr. Jerusalem and dining with the Stacks at Gaza, so we get letters ready in the hope of posting.

26 December 1926
Tell Jemmeh, Gaza

[H.P. writes]

Journal 5 and letters sent off this morning. I went the doctor's rounds of his 2 or 3 patients for small ailments, acting as interpreter. Dr Parker proves a most valuable member in camp. He is very genial and well-informed, and reminds me rather of my father. He busies himself with the workmen and helps the students with them, and sometimes he does surprising things, as when he wandered off into the loneliness of the desert – we thought we were 9 miles from anywhere – and discovered a solitary hut which proved to be a shop, selling lemons, matches, oranges, radishes etc. Another day, he actually walked to Gaza and back, 18 miles of rough desert, though by no means young. This weather threatens to break at last, and we have had 2 heavy showers, at 5 and at 8: the roofs held well, and rain only got in at one point.

Police patrol visits us twice weekly. A sergeant in a Bedawy headdress appeared on a nice chestnut (sic) and while he sat on our mastaba and drank coffee, I put on my top boots and went round our work on his horse, a heavy trotter but good at a canter. The sergeant rode away at a fine gallop. We also saw a car today, but it only contained a native official who climbed our hill and visited the digging. Mrs Starkey found half of a Hyksos scarab today, went back to the place and discovered the remaining half. Altogether ½ dozen scarabs have turned up, bought and found.

Small drab lizards, and one large one, run about on the desert here, but we have seen and heard none of the reported hyenas, jackals and foxes, neither have gazelles come our way.

Camels, donkeys, flocks of sheep and goats are always in view, or passing. The Bedawy dogs bark all the evening, and a cat visits our mess hut nightly. Quite a good crop of grass blades is springing up on my walls, from the damp of the mortar scarcely yet dried, all round my hut inside. We send 3 miles for water, and it is brackish, and made me rather ill at first. Before I arrived, they had a very bad time, and no-one could drink it for 2 days. Two police came to settle terms for us, and the eight of them arriving made the woman of the well throw down two sackfuls of contraband salt into it, to hide the purchase. I found it still painfully salt and ghastly to drink, but it is improving a little. Today, we sent a camel in to Gaza and have had the slightly brackish water from there, a great boon. We try to disguise it with orange, lemon, soup or tea, but the tea is extraordinarily nasty.

By taking on 11 more boys this morning, before b'fast, we have increased to 76 strong and 7 Quftis.

The tell here is 100ft. or more in height, and very precipitous; it reaches 200ft. above sea level, the natural mound being capped by 50ft. of town strata. It is anchor-shaped and 500ft. long. The hollows at the sides may have been enclosures for cattle in case of raids. At the top is Greek pottery of VIth cent., but nothing later. Hyksos remains occur, and we are *hoping* for buildings and objects, temp. Abraham and Abi-melech, Isaac and Rebekah. All distinctive potsherds are kept and levelled. From the top of the tell, one sees the dusty plain rolling away in all directions, cut by water courses, Wady Ghazzeh and Wady Sheri'a. When the rain comes, all will be cultivated.

I am beginning to draw the pottery, scale ¼ now that several whole ones have come in, and to draw a plan of the buildings 1:100, as we have some chambers, and walls, and two large circular buildings. Some haematite weights have come in of 2, 3 and 4 Babylonian shekels. We are evidently working the most important end of the town. Nothing turned up on the plain around, so far. Insha'allah there may be found some traces of all Rebekah's damsels and her old nurse Deborah!

Muhammad has been suffering from the cold, and has been in the Dr's charge, but the boy Sadiq has carried on, and Muh. is now right again. If, at half the season, we should move on by camel to Tell esh Sheria, our address will still remain Gaza. It is a larger city than this but looks, on the surface, less interesting.

28 December 1926

[H.P. writes]

Early morning. We are sending in to Gaza this morning, so I send to post. The men are asking for advances of wage to send it to Egypt, and buy seed while it is cheap; their relations will get on with their sowing. The Qufti who works with Harding will be called off to work, and make a day of it, and I shall incidentally get bread, greens and potatoes replenished here. I hope to be back on biscuit and tinned veg. as seldom as possible here. Everyone is very merry over their meals, so far. B'fast, tea and coffee, porridge, tinned milk, eggs, br. butter and jams. Lunch, tinned meats and huge bowl of rice: golden syrup and jams. Dinner ditto, plus lentil soup. We have plenty of oranges and tomatoes and tinned fruits and odd tins to make variety. Tea – br. and butter and jam is a very popular meal, as soon as the whistle sounds, the locals disperse and the Quftis come down with their antikas and pickaxes to hand in.

A lot of flying ants have come about, but we are singularly free of small fry here. The Bedawy village is right the other side of the tell (5 or 10 mins. to go round to it) 15 hair tents which supply many of our work boys, and in all directions is a wide and clean waste of landscape. It will not look a waste, 2 months hence, but will all be green, they say. Two of the Bedawy women came up yesterday to offer milk. It is not leben here, but "halib". I went out and bargained with them, cow's milk to be milked straight into my milk-can, and this morning it has come, $^2/_3$ full. I commandeered Mrs S. and Mrs R. and we had a grand cleansing and re-arrangement of the mess-hut.

Beautiful sky by day and by night. The stars are as brilliant as in Egypt, and the sun-rise exquisite, facing us. We are about at dawn and have this gorgeous expanse all day, without need to move out of the hosh;[1] but from the top of the tell we have a very extensive view, the sea out to NW, the long line of the mountains of Judaea (from Beersheba past Hebron and Jerusalem to the north) all along E. and to S. we see Sinai itself. With good glasses, F. made out the highest of the range there to be Mount Serbal, the chief "jebel" of our Sinai campaign.

---

[1] Courtyard.

We are expecting some roofing soon, for the extra hut at the end of the little row, and then if Commr. Trumper comes up from Port Said, we can put him up for a day or two if he brings his blankets. We are also telling Yeivin,[1] in case he passes near on his way from Beisan (Bethshan) where he is digging with Rowe. Garstang passed through Gaza at Xmas, but was not able to look us up: he dined with the Stacks on Christmas Day. The High Commissioner and Lady Plumer are to be in Gaza next week. He lives in his railway saloon when he travels.

Our Bedawy guard is longing for a gun, and the G. police say he can have one, but we don't see any occasion, and fear he would be popping at dogs all night. I don't feel inclined to pay for his licence, and he looks more than picturesque already without one! Muhammed is washing our clo's in the hosh this morning, the camel man is bringing in water. F. is rushing round with his big camera, and all is active. The doctor has no patients and has gone up aloft to help the students.

F.'s first lot of photographs were spoilt by the Jemmu water, so last night he developed with Gaza water, and got the usual excellent results: the mess was given up to this cause last night, and folks retired to write letters. Starkey and I gave up the evening to the complicated a/cs of the Quftis, their weekly wage modified by advances for travel, and for marketing weekly, and increased by bread-money till we bought flour, and by backsheesh, earned for finds: we had to allow for extra days of work, and for the building, and various individual differences. I have also worked up the a/cs of the 70 locals, mostly Bedawyn, into book form, and notified as to their local groups: these groups are massed for payment by 100-piastre notes. The Egyptian currency holds here, till Palestine gets its own currency. Every afternoon, I go the round of the whole work, up on the tell, and down on the plain, and do the roll-call of the locals. Yesterday, list of absents only 3.

Hofny has now come down from the tell, to walk in to Gaza, and we shall hope for letters from all of you.

A happy New Year or as we say here

Kull es sana enteh tayyib!

All the year (with) you well.

Many thanks for all letters received.

---

[1] Samuel Yeivin, archaeologist.

31 December 1926
Tell Jemmu, Palestine
[H.P. to John]

> While the camel goes to a brackish well in the desert to fetch our water, I hastily jot down a few lines: the camel will then proceed to Gaza for better water and for food and post. ... We are well settled in at the tell of Abimelech, and enjoy the brown rolling plain of desert on all sides of us – the views from the top are beatiful – Mediterranean to N.W. Sinai mountains to S. the Judean hills to E (Beersheba, Hebron, Bethlehem). We cannot see up to Jerusalem.
>
> We are a very happy party. I think you know the Starkeys and Harding, and have seen Risdon. Mrs Risdon has joined us now, and is lively and youthful and very accommodating. Dr Parker is a great acquisition, he joined us by sea, in Cairo. He is intellectual and talks interestingly, helps the young men with natives and potsherds, and doses our Egyptians and our local boys; he is very enterprising and walked to and from Gaza, 18 miles very rough ground, one day lately. We have just seen off the Starkeys and Harding with their toothbrushes and the ukelele,[1] all in ties, collars, and breast-pocket handkerchiefs, and clean boots! They are walking to Gaza and sleeping there for New Year's Eve, returning to be back by 7.15 by car, to put the workmen on, tomorrow morning.

16 January 1927
Tell Jemmeh (Gerar)
[H.P. writes. Postal address Gaza, Palestine]

I have been unable to send any journal for more than a fortnight, owing to being down with a bout of high fever, and, after that was over, was out of action again with 3 days' toothache. Police patrol calling, a few days ago, I was able to have a horse to ride round the tell to the work, so resumed roll-call once more and have carried on for several days. Today a horse again. There have not been any events and work goes on much the same daily. Before sunrise we have waking bell rung, and then b'fast bell. Starkey acts as overseer to all the work: Risdon and Harding have each their gang. The men number about 120 now, and our 8 Egyptians here, and the Bedawi guard in black headrope, smart blue jacket, and dagger. Mrs Starkey and Mrs Risdon attend to the stacks of broken pottery that are sent down in baskets, and brush and sort it. The Dr helps on the hill and is much beset with patients – our own staff, often out of sorts from the queer water with salts and magnesia in it, also the Bedawy work-boys who come down to have eyes, or head, or a tooth, attended to. He also mends our Quftis with quinine or boracic water, and indeed has quite a reputation in all the neighbourhood now, so that

---

[1] A small stringed instrument, popular in the 1930s.

women and babies and old men turn up at unwanted moments (some easily relieved and some less curable) when I act as interpreter. We all have lunch at 12, when the whistle sounds and then some of us rest. I try to keep the camp quiet until 2 or so, by circumventing water-camels, old women with eggs, police-patrol, and would-be patients of all sorts: I am getting them all trained to better hours by degrees. The young men get up on the hill about 1 o'c and ourselves about 2 o'c. I go round the entire hill-top, and the work on the plain below, as well, see it archaeologically, drive forward the workers, and get every man, girl and boy marked in my lists (pinned to a drawing-board and secured with wound string because of the high winds). F. and I get an early tea about 4: the others a heavier one later, when the work has ceased. The pickaxes are brought in, and a few patients linger about: it is such a relief to have doctor to see to them, and never attend to the boracic and the quinine oneself! I write out the roll-call at teatime. People wash and tidy up: the warmth turns to cold. Beautiful still moonlight nights, all blue and silver, and a blaze of stars. Sirius very bluish above and Canopus very twinkling below. Dinner at 6.30.

We had actual rain, for almost the first time, lately and it showered all night: perhaps an inch or 1–2 of rain. We now send for a dark brown sandy water to the wady near at hand, 2 miles and drink it with joy (boiled). We need 12 jars per day, and the water-camel makes 3 journeys daily.

A few nights ago, the village of black hair tents behind the "tell" held a fantasiyeh, close to us, all the evening. The lines of men stood swaying and chanting, in great ecstasy, while a woman, in the usual black garments, pranced to and fro with swinging vigour, brandishing a naked sword which gleamed in the moonlight. It is derived from ceremonies for the incitement to raids and is very impressive. 1926 is the first year in which raids have not taken place in the Gaza district, and 4 raids have only lately been suppressed in the adjoining Beersheba district, so we are not very far removed from them.

Nights are bitterly cold: we hear the sand-grouse and the owls at night, and have occasional trouble with the barking of the Bedawy dogs.

I have begun plan-drawing here, and hope to begin pot-drawing as soon as my temp. can be depended upon. We haven't seen much of the neighbourhood yet, but the guard tells me there are Roman pavements, "pictures", at Umm Jerar nearby, a Roman site that is the daughter city of Tell Jemmeh, and I shall get there by donkey one market-day soon. Dr Parker has time and energy for long walks, and he has visited Deir al Balah, a sea-coast village in the railway, and has walked to Gaza and back.

16 January 1927

Tell Jemmeh, Gaza Palestine (9 miles southeast of Gaza)

We are perched here at the foot of the great mound of Gerar, the city of Abimelech, and are steadily clearing out the rooms of the later levels, hoping to get through the fifty feet of successive buildings and reach the earliest city.

At first we had but few men, beside the 7 Egyptians whom we brought as skilled excavators. After a month, our gang of men, boys and a few girls came to about 120, and our current expenses to over 50 a week for labour. We shall need even more workers, if we are to clear the most important end of the city by May. Happily there is no Ro[man] or late G[ree]k layer, and we begin work in stuff of 500–600 B.C. in the filling up of earlier buildings of probably 800 B.C. or before that. There has been great denudation of the mound; one edge is left, of great circular granaries 35ft. diam[eter] on the top of a ridge; the rest of the circle would have been over ground now 30ft. deeper. Moreover these granaries must have been 50ft. or more in height, but only three ft. of one edge is left. This sweeping clearance has taken away the outer edges of the city, but we hope to get some early remains in the central parts.

The people are nearly all settled Bedawy, who have been here a few years, cultivating the ground, but mostly still living in the open-sided low tent of their ancestors. I am surprised to see how well they work, thou' not equal to Egyptians; also how amenable they are, and ready to be friendly. Raids, which used to be common here, have died away owing to good police work; there have been 4 attempts on Beersheba in the year, but none reached out to this region. The posts of wireless at points in the wilderness give notice of movements, in time for the mounted police to save the position. Three times in the week two police come round here to see that all is quiet, either from Gaza or Beersheba. They also act as our postmen.

Our position is all the stronger, owing to the drought. The lateness and scantiness of the rains threaten to stop most of the cultivation, so that the people are largely dependent on our wages to keep them for the season. In other years the whole face of the rolling plain should be full green with barley and wheat. But only two inches of rain have come and that in the last few days, and all is bare brown for many miles, up to about a dozen inches to the north where rains have fallen. Until we got some rain the wind – often a gale – used to fill the air with fine dust, in which one could not see a hundred yards. We have a well two miles away, too brackish with magnesia to drink or wash satisfactorily. So we send a camel 9 miles to Gaza for that water, but even that is enough to upset nearly all the party. So we had even to get bottled water for drinking, until the rain came and filled pools in the valley. When those are dry we shall be back on Gaza water. Thus in various ways we are rather near the limits of practicable work on a large scale. We have to bring the water 2 miles for all our workmen.

We are gradually learning the history of past conditions here. It was a great region for grain about 600 B.C. shown by the many enormous granaries, circular buildings 17 or 35 feet diameter, and probably 50ft. or more high in proportion. Then in Roman times the land was crowded with villages, proving close cultivation. In 1500 B.C. the Egyptians reaped great crops out of Palestine. In 1800 B.C. Isaac "sowed in that land and received in the same year an hundredfold." The position seems to have been that Abimelech the Philistine had pushed up the Gaza valley, as far as he was still in sight of the sea, and got control of the corn production, for export to Crete. He relied on Syrian troops, as his general was named "the Syrian", Phi-chol, Pa-khalu. The Bedawy Isaac came settling in the region, and was moved off because his herds ate up the grain supply, and did not leave enough for export. The climate must have been closely like the present, when flocks depend largely on wells in the dry season, and wells were always squabbled over. So we can begin to realise how the history worked out. It might seem contradictory that Abimelech from his palace could see into the camp of Isaac close enough to observe actions. But we now see that the entrances of the city were to the S. and the great buildings were along a precipitous N. face, below which the Bedawy now camp, so that every movement in the tents can be seen clearly from that position. We have cleared down about 6 or 8 ft. already, and every wall is planned and levelled; and all the pottery is searched, and every distinctive piece is kept and marked with ch[ambe]r level and letter. There are very few scraps of Greek red-figure vases, (after 480 B.C.) but more of black-figure, and the great loop handles of vases for carrying from a pole, are common, of about 600 B.C. One scrap of vase – black-figure – has Oedipus and the sphinx. There is also Cypriote pottery, of about 800 B.C., after a burning of the town. Gradually successive events of rebuilding and burning are being gathered, and placed in order.

All our party are working well together; Starkey mainly ganging men, Risdon and Harding watching different parts of the work. Mrs Risdon and Mrs Starkey sorting and cleaning pottery, my wife keeping all the accounts of men and market, and my share is the surveying and photographing, with general planning out of the ways and means of work. Dr Parker looks after all the ailment of ourselves and the workmen, and is most active in going about.

As if the water was not salt enough already, the wife of the engine man took fright on seeing two policemen about, and shot off two sackfuls of contraband salt down the well to prevent its being found, which would have entailed a heavy fine. So for two days no one could drink any of the water, until it was all pumped out. Such is life on the border land.

16 January 1927

[H.P. to John]

... Times have been very busy. I was up on my hill-top before sunrise as usual, but I am unable to fag all day on my feet this week, and have to sit a little each day, I find. As I have plenty of proofs and of a/cs that keeps me sitting a bit. There are a good many difficulties which have to be squared up to and they involve a certain amount of work, and odd carpentering. Being away 3 days has disintegrated a good many things. The new breakfast lamp and my new hot water can have died the death! someone smokes in the dining-room! spills are not wiped up! shut doors are left open! locked doors are left unlocked! someone's puppy tears everything and eats all my cats' food, the servants' food is in peril! a cricket chirps where not wanted! several people have drifted unpunctual! tools left all night in the damp. Lights left on into the night! A few days' overwork, and a little too much lifting about of things will get all the abuses down in about 4 days, as I know by experience.

17 January 1927
Gaza Palestine. From Tell Jemmeh

[H.P. to John]

... Daddy is very active and lively. He is first up of all of us, in the morning, and is tearing about on the tell, supervising the Bedawyn, the Egyptians, and our own 3 "khawagat". He spells out the history, day by day, of all the cross-walks, at varying angles, and the granaries, the fort, the burnt houses, a staircase, etc. and will work out the various periods, as we descend through them in depth. On still days, especially if a market day, he carries his camera aloft. He also prospects in the neighbourhood on foot. He does a lot of drawing, and plan-drawing, and develops the photographs some evenings. Now that I have left off my vile fever, and the toothache, and have got back to work, I am occupied with the men's accounts, the house accounts, the daily roll-call, the weekly pay day, some pot-drawing, some plan-drawing, and a lot of general direction and supervision. ... You should hear how the camels groan out here: they are most disturbing and disturbed. The Bedawyn too are so strange: very amenable, and some very handsome however, among the full-grown men. Some youths well-set-up, and others so spindly and elfish, with long wavy looks which have *never* been combed. Weapons good.

25 January 1927
Tell Jemmeh

We have only 1¼ jars of drinking water left, so must send in to Gaza tomorrow for 4 jars, as the supply of good water which ran in the wady, 2 miles from here, ceased to run after 8 days, and we are back on the saline 'saqqiyeh' water once more. We revelled in the rain water from the wady those few days, for though it was dark brown and looked queer to drink, it had no salts or magnesia in it.

Nothing much has happened since I wrote last, on 17th. We now have about 200 men and boys in the work, and among them a dozen little Bedawy girls, with names like Fatma, Amina, Dalamiyeh, Farliana, Miriam, Salma, Safia, Zayna etc. Some of the lads are good-looking, and a great many of the men look like minor prophets. We are confronted with a mouse in the huts, and in the evening a great many moths; free of vermin, but worried by dogs at night. A night of showers, 10 days ago, has made the Bedawyn plough many acres of desert ground here, each Bedawy with his camel and the Roman plough. Some ground in the near distance has corn coming up, with a haze of green colour, faint but widespread. The ploughing and sowing will be wasted however, unless we can get more rain.

Half a dozen officials came over to see us the other day, in 2 cars, on their way from Beersheba to Deir el Balah. They were the District Commissioner of Beersheba, and the D.S.P. (police), with no less a personage than the Governor of South Palestine, and a Drought Commissioner, and an official who is going to make a road somewhere in the district, to whom we mentioned rate of wages.

Starkey, our chief assistant, was laid up for some days and the others halved his work. He is quietly about again now, mending pots etc. but not up with the gangs on our exposed hill-top. Risdon is getting out of action today: we seem to take it in turns. Happily we are getting more acclimatised lately to our 2 sources of drinking water, and avoid the saqqiyeh except for washing: it does not even do for photography. ...

The new week began (Saturday morning) with so howling a gale that all excavation was stopped till it abated about noon. We sent round to the Bedawy tents behind the tell, and to all the odd workmen sheltering in corners, to proclaim that in an hour (12 noon) a half day's work would begin.

I have been drawing scarabs (scale 2:1) most of today, and inked them in, with the original in hand. I go the whole round of the work every day 2½–3½ with roll-call, and seeing to the mechanical detail of the work. Then in to an early tea, with Prof. and Dr. and any students who are at hand. Superintendents of the gangs have theirs, when the whistle sounds and everyone disperses. A gorgeous sunset usually finished our day's work – the words at the gate with workboys, patients, or a camel-man – "a stupendous pavilion of Oriental glories."

Through the open hatchway of the kitchen, a sound of peaceful snoring comes – Muhammed rolled up in his quilt – and reminds me I must go to bed.

One of us brought in a darling little tame unfrightened quail the other day, caught by a Bedawy: it found its way into the desert again. Three snakes, 3ft. long, of two different species, have turned up in the rubbish mound of the city, and one hole produced 18 scorpions.

The doctor has, besides his in-patients, more out-patients than ever. Tonight, an eye, a finger, a cough, a toe, and a head were all at the gate at sunset, and the mud mastaba,[1] built to entertain sheykhs with coffee, is taken up every day with odd incurables, or the workboys suffering from small ailments.

We are getting 20 great jars of water by camel, per day, now, as we have to supply all the work people as well as ourselves, so a local boy is constantly at the gate, through the day, to refill a (cleaned out) petroleum tin and carry it up to the digging. Each group sends down, to supply the gangs: 7 pickaxes go out every morning with the Quftis, in addition to their *turiyas,*[2] for the ground is very hard in parts and requires hewing: I have just left off dealing them out, and Harding goes it instead, and starts the work on the hill before he comes in to b'fast.

We made a find, a few days ago, which was not archaeol. but was more akin to "Swiss Family R." We were down in an ancient granary and we came upon 5 of the black rotund water-jars, modern Arab, of a rather different pattern to our own sixteen, so we use them for the workmen and it saves us buying more. We have 4 camel-men now, with running a/cs, and water-camels that do not run but proceed very sedately and with heart-rending groans: the well gave out yesterday, but the pumping apparatus has been mended, or else the stale cistern water was even less to be commended than the other.

When dust-storms are on, everything gets unrecognisable in the huts, from a deep layer covering all. In the landscape, we see the great swirling columns of dust, ascending sprially and stalking across the country, "jinns" (the genii of one's youth). The powdery dust here is not so bearable as the clean sand in Egypt, though it is less stinging in one's face and less gritty in one's food.

26 January 1927

Two camels have come in, laden with water from the "bir", and as one of them now ambles off to Gaza, I must close this for post.

31 January 1927
Tell Jemmeh

We had a great scene a week or 10 days ago, of the inoculation of our workpeople. The municipal hospital doctor came over – the one who pays us constant malaria visits – with his assistant and they managed to inoculate 422 in about 2½ hours or less. Our 2 native villages were rounded up and all our workmen as well. Then 3 days ago, he came again for the 2nd half dose, and

---

[1] Bench.
[2] Hoes.

"firsted" about 50 people more – also doing all this camp, both khawagas and house-boys. I went into it, that there should not be a single being missing, and suffered considerably for 2 days after it.

4 February 1927

Then two days ago he came again for second treatments of the second batch, and has given 497 inoculations twice over – just on a thousand!

Today when the pay for the week was over there was a general break-up and packing, and most of our khawagas went off. I wish all of them could have gone, as it would make a nice change for them, and a lovely empty camp for us: however some linger through the workmen's Bayram. Market day and 3 festival days gives us 4 days when we really hope to have the camp without noise and fusses – if we can only have this, it means a chance of getting on to all sorts of records, reports, a/cs and other careful work which have had to be postponed for weeks. Publicity begun. A "Times" letter ought to come out, now, somewhere about today, on the first phase of the work. Shall be glad to hear the date of it. Weather is cold and stormy here, grey leaden skies. We have just had a night of furious downpour and it hindered half the work for a Ramadan morning, as the tell is exposed towards the sea, 100ft. high. Now to describe my loose-box. It is about 7 × 12ft. Two feet along its north wall, you step over a sill, or threshold of grey cement two feet wide, down on to a grey cement floor. Sill is chamfered and a cement wainscot runs all round. Let in, is a white cross as pavement. Bed with blue blanket occupies S. side. Tin jugs, candlestick, mugs, even to my books and pencils, are the same lovely blue. The walls are bare, whitewashed. On the long one hang my Bedawy headrope and dagger and camel-sceptres and brass stirrups. My new furniture, picked up for a few shillings (from Customs Officer leaving Gaza) consists of a deal table, and white painted cupboard with plain deal top, a deal basin box 9 in. square, a green office stool, plain deal top, a tiny rush bottom footstool, a deal bootshelf, 4-storeyed, with white medicine chest above, a canvas armchair, a deal towel rail slung from my long shelf. The latter has water jugs, soap and sponge, a few books, helmet, and candlesticks (old brass ones for our annual communion). A white shelf, a tin medicine chest, a hunting crop, and a coloured bed-mat finish the inventory. Purr-box lies tethered in doorway and looks at me lovingly and purrs. Papers, a/cs. and School business live in card trays and boxes. The door is contrived from a double thickness of green grass mat with leather thong to fasten. The upper foot has a glass window, opening sideways and shut on cold nights. On colder nights I barricade it with 2 large box lids and a frill of chair-canvas. Am called at 5.45. Sun comes in all day and wind.

8 February 1927
Tell Jemmeh

[H.P. writes]

The famine conditions continue very seriously here and, as a consequence, hundreds of Bedawy families are on the move, trekking northwards along the great desert track that runs from Egypt into Palestine. The trains of camels all loaded with the tents and possessions, the flocks of sheep, men, women and children all pass along to seek pastures and food elsewhere. Half the population of Khan Yunis has migrated, in search of better conditions. This road passes within sight of our hut doors, and the moving creatures in file appear as in perpetual cinematograph.

Rain comes in small occasional showers, but not enough to do any good.

I had occasion to see after some special business for the School about a week ago, and thought I should have to journey to Jaffa; however, when it came to the day, Gaza did instead. I started about 9a.m. on a very small yellowish camel, a hagin, gaily caparisoned, and got there before noon. I took no camel man, but had the Bedawy ghafir,[1] Salim, along with me. He held on the camel's tail. It was a fierce morning, with a gale blowing, bitterly cold, but I wore a thick top coat and leather jerkin over landsuit, same top boots, and Mrs Starkey saw to my chinstrap and buttons before I started. Rug, and pillow, and hunting crop, saddle-bags full of soda water bottles as bakshish for the clinic, the pot-bag, all the messages, emergency rations, shoes and gaiters in case I left my boots to be mended, all this and more I took along. And first I met a carpenter riding his donkey to come out and make wooden ploughs, and later saw two donkeys, and single camels, ploughing, but the desert was mostly solitary. Swi grew all along, bluebell-like in its sword leaves and fleshy spikes, perhaps a sort of asphodel, and salamun, the tulip-like bulbs that they all call "onion". Hollows in the ground betoken digging for dyes for the camel tassels and other coloured gear. To the west, the sea appeared, beyond Tell el Mudr'a, Tell Ajjul and el Gid. The track runs along a narrow water-shed and crosses the Wady Nahabir. The jebel eastward is Towq el-Shayir, lastly Jebel Baras. I saw swallows and goldfinches. The new aerodrome is finished: Sir Samuel Hoare[2] expected again, in a day or two.

At Gaza, I amused myself with Mrs Stack and a cup of tea, after sending cable, getting post, and seeing to water supply. The train never arrived till 3 hrs. late, so, to see my client, I had to give up returning that day. I sent off the water camel with 4 jars, and sent the Bedawy home on my camel, with the medicines and stores, then lunched with Dr and Mrs Johnson at the hospital,

---

[1] Watchman, guard.
[2] British Secretary of State for Air.

shopped in the native bazaars and bought kitchen canteen and a blue silk headrope, had tea with the D. S. P. Major Partridge, where I met the Stacks, the Atkinsens, and others (Gaza) and Miss Dixon, Mrs Taylor, Mr FitzGerald again (Jerusalem). ... and finally I dined with the Partridges, who have turned our bare looking Rest-House into a most charming private house. ... Major P. saw me back to the hospital, where I slept in a very plain little bedroom, which seemed very pampered with its good pillow and real jug and basin, and a floor and a door to it. Mr H. Bowman, Director of Education in Palestine, was the Johnson's other guest, and it was kind of them to put me up on the spur of the moment, there being no rest-house for the nonce – when it became necessary for me to sleep in Gaza. ... At 9 Mr Bowman with 2 inspectors was starting for Khan Yunis,[1] and wanted to visit our excavations in the afternoon, so I got him to take me along. We had much rain in the night – Gaza only, locally, not the Tell – and the desert tracks were mostly mud, across which we skidded fearfully but we got out. ... We motored to Khan Yunis by 10.30 and then, with the 2 native inspectors visited schools till lunchtime. It was intensely interesting seeing a girls' school, in this small provincial place (only a glorified mud village), and run by a thoroughly native and Muslim young lady in the usual black draperies and black face-veil. 50 little girls sat on forms with their clean little hands folded on their desks: they went through their singing, reading aloud from an illustrated reader etc. and answered questions intelligently. The few elder ones at the back of the room had face veils, the small ones dress in black cotton, with white limp collars or capes, and their hair done up in a black net. The rooms, with wide open doors and windows, opened on to a half-outdoor room and that on to a garden with verandeh, and the teacher's bedroom in the far corner of it. We inspected the needlework, too much of English fancy work and I recommended several things which became instant instructions! The drawing also, in the boys' school, had no native ideas but was exotic. Education, as a whole, is splendidly run in the this country, on lines much an improvement on Egypt. Mr Bowman has been in both countries many years, and it is well for Palestine that the direction is in his hands. I knew the native inspector who has been often in the Gaza resthouse while we lived there, and the young man showed me round Khan Yunis. In the bazaars I bought a huge cabbage and 2 bundles of spinach, all opportunities of buying vegetables being only too rare.

At 12.30 we went to the large native house of the Reis el Belediyeh,[2] and I had quite a nice talk with the harim and all the young sons and nephews there. The "drawing-room" had a long diwan, running the length of the

---

[1] The most southerly town in Palestine.
[2] Mayor.

room, a table draped at one end, with showy lamps and gew-gaws and paper flowers. The walls were hung with cheap rugs, pin cushions, toys and waxwork rubbish, a 4-poster and an elegant cradle stood in the further corner and a cheap modern wardrobe. The young Sitt[1] – there was only one – was very smiling, in an ordinary black figured muslin dress, but covered with necklaces, bracelets and rings. She put a foot on the chair next to me and proceeded to draw on a blue silk stocking, ditto other foot, and patent leather shoes! then stood before me, respect forbidding her to sit. The youths conversed in Arabic, and also knew some English – all scholars in the native schools. The great man appeared, a quiet old fellow in purely native draperies and turban, and I had some tea. I had previously had coffee with him alone in state in the village council chamber surrounded by greybeards.

We then adjoined to the half out-door room, and sat down to 14 hot dishes, cut with knives and forks – stuffed leg of lamb, chickens, pigeons, a preparation of rice, qara vegetable marrow, everything rather spicy and stuffed, lastly oranges and the usual Oriental finale of the hammered metal basin and the spouted jug poured over the hands. After the coffee we adjourned, and the greybeards, chief villagers, sat down in our places, and fell to, on the remainder of the food. We walked back up the narrow land, to the council chamber of the Reis el Belediyeh, and then packed into the car, and came on across the desert to Tell Jemmeh. It is about an hour, but took us 1½ hours, as we kept getting to impassable places and having to make detours. The best running was across acres of plough land, which no motorist in his senses would consider it possible to cross, at home. Along the furrows was queer, athwart was queerer, but crossing them at right angles was unspeakable.

Another educational effort in this country, besides the teaching of girls, is that of teaching the Bedawyn. As some of them are more or less settled, and till the ground, it is possible to build a little school house on the desert near their tents! We visited one such building on our way. It stands on a hilly ridge within sight of the tell, but is only just built and has not come into use yet. I made sure that the Bedawy girls are to be treated the same as the boys, and taught with them. In the villages and small towns, they have to keep quite separate and taught by teachers of their own sex, but in the desert this does not apply. The chief idea is not to Europeanise or denationalise them. As we got nearer the tell, it became very difficult to cross the wady and we had to go a long way round. We got here about 4 o'clock and all looked quite strange, for though I had only been one night away, it seemed like a week, and after a long sojourn in the desert, it had seemed quite strange to see trees and houses again.

---

[1] Mistress, lady.

We have had trouble with an epidemic for the first time in our lives. The doctor spotted mumps among our workboys, and two boys were sacked. They got once or twice into the take-on after that, but we kept clear of them. Then a 3rd was sacked and shortly after that, one of our own men Ahmed came out with it. A small tent being to spare, I started him on an expanse of desert exactly in front of our huts. ... and no one can go near him. It is a funny little isolation hospital, and he sat here all day like a caged bird, no person but me to take him food or drink. We gave him a blanket and a large mug, and there he was for a week. He is now doing isolated digging, miles from the others, with the first of the mumpy boys, now recovered, to help him. He is still of course in his own tent, and I will carry him the morning and evening food.

The animals have been dying in this province, for want of water and of pasture. The Government have offered to give free transport for flocks to grassy country, and some of the Bedawys are accepting this and shepherding them, but others don't take advantage of the offer. We saw in a London paper how lambs were sold for 3d in Beersheba. Hebron district is the worst, where they threaten to close the hospital. At Gaza the hospital is going strong. We now send there twice a week for distilled water for F. The rest of us and the photography depend on Gaza water. And the local well, 2½ miles off, provides for our thirsty 270 souls in the digging. Boys come down all day long with petroleum tins to fetch water from the 16 jars in our courtyard. When our 2 camel men would not carry more than 4 jars per camel, we got in a rival who carries 6, and now we have 3 camels plying, and the brothers have accepted that 6 is the right load, so we are served better than we were.

The higher levels off the site, up aloft, are now disappearing and giving place to a more interesting stratum belonging to an earlier period. We are now: staff 8, Egyptians 8, ghafir 1, local 274 = 291 in Tell Jemmeh.

[Journal ends here]

22 February 1927
Tell Jemmeh

[H.P. to John and Ann]

> I know it is a very long time since I have written, but we have been through such storms of rain and gale, and terrible weather, it has been impossible to settle down to writing civilised letters. Our roofs kept collapsing, in dining hut all one night through the fury of the gale, and we were up and doing, but now we have writed them and can stand a good deal. The storms – during a whole week – meant that two raging rivers separated us from Gaza – no one could cross them for many days. Yesterday we had warmth and brilliant sunshine once more, and about 300 on the work, but today it is raining hard and

blowing, and I am persuading a camel to slither in to Gaza, because we are entirely out of bread, salt, tea, and lettuces, and nearing the end of our condensed milk. I do not suppose we shall start home till the beginning of May. ... Now the camel has come and I must stop. Don't think we have perished, if you do not hear. Merely imagine that the two rushing rivers, 130ft. wide, 5ft. deep or more, and pelting 8 miles an hour, are cutting us off from our base!

8 March 1927

[H.P. to John and Ann]

... I know it was a long interval, but the violent storm weather lasted more than a week and I was so sciatic and had such a return of my aches that somehow I didn't get any writing done. ... There is no news here. All goes on as usual. I wish you could see our Bedawyn. They are amazingly picturesque. Last week I had 380 men, women, boys and girls. Some are more or less townspeople from the large distant villages, but the majority live in black hair tents and wear headropes. It is Ramadan, and everyone is fasting, which is very inconvenient. We stop work at 3.30 therefore, 2 hours before we ought, and do other work, when the workmen are dismissed, each day. The mornings get earlier and earlier. No chance of our coming via Italy, or coming early. It won't be till the middle of May as it is a lengthy job we have here. A woman came with a sack slung on 2 sticks today. It was a portable cradle with a 3-day old baby in it! The people who came to sell eggs today had spindles with them, and wore masses of beads, amulets, and enough coins to fill a coin-chest, as all these women do.

Our doctor has now left us, and we miss him very much. He was elderly but a wonderful walker, and thought nothing of 18 miles of rough desert path, into Gaza and back. He had an enormous following of Bedawy patients to whom he talked English hard, and they didn't understand a word he said! We are only 7 now. The large storeroom we built lately is getting crowded with antiquities and pottery. The huts, being partly of stones, stood the bad weather very well. We have run into a spell of summer weather at last. 84° today at the hottest time: flies beginning to be troublesome. Two swallows flew into the mess tent today. Several hundred pelicans flew across us from the direction of Egypt. They looked so lovely wheeling in the sunlight, with black bars across their white wings: they circled round for a long time: they have come to settle in the cultivation, but that is barely 2 in. high as yet.

4 April 1927
Tell Jemmeh

[H.P. to Ann and John]

... No news, as 1 day, for things continue very much the same here. Highish winds, and cold at morn. and ev. but about 75° or 80° at mid-day. Our natives are very much pleased that Ramadan, and all their fasting, is over, and the feast Beyram is on, so they take 2 days off, but they worked all market day so we only lose 1 day. We saw a quaint fantasiyeh today, where the women made a square of clothing – 3 in a row holding up a cloth, so as not to be seen, and then all chanting monotonous chants by the hour. Then a women dressed with much embroidery walked slowly about with a big girl standing on her shoulders, very brilliantly apparelled, and waving a decorated belt – such an extraordinary feat, and so blazing with colour. These 2 days give us time for putting antiquities in order, and much drawing etc.

Twice, we have had the chief expert in Palestine archaeology, Pere Vincent, from the Dominicans in Jerusalem. Several other people have come by car from Jerusalem (75 miles away) and returned in the day. Once such a car took Daddy and me off, last week, and we spent 5 days staying with the Bishop (MacInnes) in St George's Close. Daddy was in bed 1½ days, but saw a very good doctor, and we planned how we should have better nourishment here, and avoid all water by having distilled only.

For ourselves, the wady water has ceased, and even the big Roman cistern has begun to run dry, so we are back now on sending a camel to Gaza every 2 days, to fetch stuff that we can drink. Local supply still does for washing. My leg is troublesome for a small part of every day, but on the whole I manage to keep fairly well, in spite of the roughness here, the uncertainties of the weather and the trying work.

19 April 1927
Tell Jemmeh

[H.P. to John]

... It has been a very interesting year out here, on the whole, and Daddy has some splendid plans of all the periods of the Tell, also a very good series of drawings of all the objects. I think the history of the place, and the variety of the objects will arouse interest at home. The "Daily Life" or "Daily Use" volume is just coming out – the last proofs being returned to Holzhausen. I am now beginning to think of the journey home. ...

The following winter the Petries moved their camp to another mound further along the Wady Ghazzeh, Tell el Fara, which Flinders was inclined to identify with the biblical Beth Pelet.[1]

2 December 1930
Tell Fara

[H.P. writes]

We are now working at full swing at last. Time drifted on and at last I arranged that we should go over, 4 miles or 5, to Tell Ajjul and hold a council

---

[1] Possibly Sharuhen.

as to immediate plans for the future. If Tell Ajjul were to remain unworked till the heavy rains should come, and the mosquitoes be washed away, it was very necessary to concentrate on Tell Jemmeh (Gerar) or Beth Pelet, Tell Fara, at once and get some digging done. Having told us that T.J. was reported to be feverish, so we planned for Tell Fara, got the concession, and ordered a ton truck to bring out us and our belongings. F.P. and Mrs Benson seated in the cab of it, and Richmond Brown[1] and I mounted on the summit of the baggage behind – suitcases, boxes of water, 2 mattresses, a vast mousetrap, my Gaza purchased canteen, garden chairs, a lamp, water jugs, drawing boards, medicines, overcoats, tools, a large melon, a bath, tin of petroleum, 6 pails with vegetables in them, and hosts of things besides. The journey round by Tell Ajjul and on to Khan Yunis and inland across the desert was 27 miles. We only once stuck and furbished up, just under Sheikh Nuran, the *wely* of the local saint. Arrived about 1 or 2 o'clock, having started to load up at 8 o'c. The promised white cat fell through at the last minute: the little shopman would not part with him. All Gaza crowded up, over this, then another cat was sought, paid for and packed, but the payment indignantly placed on the bonnet of the lorry and the cat withdrawn. We now have only a mouse-trap which measures 12 × 8 ins. still I feel prepared, in case the rats and mice reported at Beersheba descend on us. It has already caught 2 desert mice and a jerboa; the jerboa we carried ½ mile along the work and released.

Perching on the lorry was rather like riding on a camel; we bowled along at a good pace along an atrocious road; the desert track of the last dozen miles was still queerer and more precarious. Muhd Osman in white squatted behind me, a little Palestinian in striped quftan, and a lout belonging to the lorry. I was glad of top boots.

We found the old Tell Fara huts reroofed in part, by Harding and Scott who had tented here 3 days, and sideboard boxes and table (3 planks), and some camp beds erected. ... I started 11 men and boys our very next day, on work, and on first day of week (Saturday) we rose to 54, today 16 more making 70, so have increased quickly in the three days since we came.

No-one is allowed inside the hosh or enclosure except Muhammed. The men, boys and girls come many miles each day for the most part. A few are in a tent near the huts and water camel, but we have 2 huts we shall roof for the girls and some of the boys. ...

We are 20 miles from anywhere. The tell is a grandly precipitous place, most striking as to scenery. The Egn. governor's residency with the paved courtyard, and the great walls of Ramses III and of Shishak are very imposing.

---

[1] A new recruit to the expedition. Other newcomers were Norman Scott and John Vernon.

I have given 69 lectures on them and raised about £350 by it,[1] and love to meet them. I find the steep hills and the climate very trying and of course I am out of practice with all the odd building and carpentering jobs I have to do: yesterday I got hold of a fine-looking Bedawy to make mud-mortaring for me, and together we filled open windows with stones and muddled them in, I inside with trowel and he outside. The shelves are mostly up now. F. and I get up when the bell rings at dawn and 2 of the 3 boys – the other comes an hour later to b'fast. They alternate. Before sunrise 2 of us get on the hill. In 5 days we have had 2 multitudes awaiting selection. I go out and place them in a long row sitting, faces to light. Then the boys come out to see how it is managed – the choice by face, the taking of names and villages – the separating from the crowd. One takes them up the hill, while I disperse the crowd. The last few hangers-about need much scorn and severity at intervals of a few minutes (between tidyings, tooth-cleaning, cups of tea etc.) from me and pieces of his mind from Muhammed, and then they disappear, and we are at peace. I go up the hill 3 times a day, to inspect 4 pits of workmen and the Hyksos trench with 30 more at work. The rounds of them in turns, – with one or two of the 3 students, to adjust the basket-boys and explain all the innumerable ins and outs of adjustment. Also all the interpretation at present, and getting them to list up the commoner words, Brown, Scott and Vernon. It isn't so much the archaeology as the technicalities of gangwork, and the treatment of individual cases of work that need expounding. They are all 3 so anxious to learn that it is a pleasure to teach them.

We are looking for a large building on the top of the *tell* at the northern end, of which many evidences remain in the shape of large sandstone blocks of masonry, stuccoed, which have been thrown down below. There are 4 pits in progress now in the area where an acropolis temple might be found. We are also continuing a search for tombs in the vast depth of the Hyksos trench, by bucketing out its sand filling, at the point where we left off.

Last night, I spent an hour or two reading aloud Beth-Pelet I to the 3 students and going over the plates with them, illustrating the Hyksos part with accounts of the 2 Hyksos diggings in the Delta; they seemed to pick up a lot and were very pleased, so it was a success.

F. has got a little table for writing and drawing in the corner of the mess-hut, and a little window to light it.

We send a man 20 miles into Gaza twice a week and he gets back by camel or donkey next day. At the end of this week I go in myself, and have a long list of foods and outfit to buy in Gaza. The doctor will probably fetch me in his two-seater and return to me, as I am to open the sale of work at the

---

[1] Lectures given in England and Jerusalem.

Hospital, on 5th. I am not sure what day, but can pack in two minutes.

At any time between now and the New Year, the great rain may come, when the dry stony bed of the winding Wady Ghuzzeh will become a torrent, and we shall long for guttering to our huts. When it has well washed down to the mouth of the Wady 4 miles west of Gaza, the mosquito trouble will be overcome and Tell Ajjul will be fit for work on a large scale. At present 3 Starkeys, Tufnell and Harding and a handful of Bedawyn hold on there, with small work. The huts are ready to receive us all. Dr Parker joins the expedition after Christmas. Mr Royds[1] joins us earlier (9th) and comes up here at once. He was 14 years on land registration in Iraq, so knows Arabic well, and dealings with natives.

Our box has never arrived yet, but fortunately I have landsuit and boots and have acquired – since first day with a touch of the sun which laid me up – an English straw sun-helmet which stands the worst mid-days. We rush around till we whistle off at 12 for lunch. B'fast is 6. At 1 o'c one man whistles on, while the others all stay on a bit. The last b'faster gets the early aftn. work. Dinner 7. Bed any time from 8 on. I am writing at 11 p.m. but must now turn in. Muhd. stirs early and I get up when he does.

In 1931 the Petries moved to another great tell, Tell el Ajjul, an imposing mound six miles south of modern Gaza.

19 November 1931
Tell el Ajjul

[H.P. writes]

Arrived yesterday, about 10 a.m. at the Tell, in Mr Reading's car and it will take us a week to settle in, at least.

It is a merry hive of semi-townspeople and Bedawi folk – the children, boys and girls and a little nigger boy – run backward and forward with sand and shells and lime and mud and water and stones. The kitchen has moved into the store room and the kitchen is to have a hard floor and some cement dado, and white tiles on the mastaba part of it, and whitewashed walls, so it will be really modern and up-to-date and no longer muddly and Arabic. Muhammed[2] is entranced. The dining hut has had the next room (double suite) thrown into it and the roofing much heightened, and today it is all being whitewashed. It now has 2 doors and about 4 windows, mostly at the back and against the slope of the tell.

---

[1] G. F. Royds.
[2] Muhammad Osman el Kreti, the Petrie's cook.

Pay day at Tell el 'Ajjul

The 6 new bedrooms make a long street running north, and approached thro' the corner of the quad. (N.W.). They have a parquet wall of their own, and the doors face inward towards a long public hall, which will have 4 pillars and a roof, and will be our store room, and room for plan-drawing. The antikas will all live here.

The roofings are yet to come, and the smooth plastering is going on meanwhile, preparatory to plastering. The latter is a new plan, to prevent mosquitoes settling on the walls. The old gray-brown mud colour was so soothing and comforting for the eyes, in both senses, but a mosquito will lurk on brown, and will not on white, where it can be seen. The chatter and the mud-pie and all the activities are quite pleasant, and the sun blazes away, so delightfully.

Prof. and I have 3 active members of the family, all rushing round in shirts and shorts – Royds, Harding and O'Brien. 2 more are away getting roofing etc. in Jerusalem and Jaffa and have not been seen for 4 days – Starkey and Richmond Brown. So we are a family of 7 at present. Everything is very picknicky, but we have a rather grand new table, white wood, very long, 4 thin legs.

Nothing can be unpacked yet, as there is nowhere to put anything, till the rooms are readjusted: I have 6 zinc-lined boxes being made by a new carpenter and then can unpack blankets, and fixed stores, in a week's time. It is too hot to wear a shirt under my crash tunic, and my breeches end in bare legs. We all clothe our shins at night, however, but the mosquitoes appear to be *nil*, none seen in the last 30 hours. Harding is as lively as possible, Brown went down since, but we hope is rejoining us from Jerusalem at once.

The camel that walks into the courtyard every 2 hours is accompanied by a lovely little baby camel. Its back is many inches deep in fur and it makes delightful faces and bleats a good deal. My last year's cat, the tabby named Shatra, is installed here, having been caught with much difficulty, and daily re-tamed in Gaza while we waited there 4 days. Now Harding goes in to buy wire and post this. The right wiring is very difficult to raise. I will write again in a few days.

The Petries' final site in Palestine was Tell el Ajjul, a huge mound overlooking the Wady Ghazzeh some six miles from the city of Gaza. They named it ancient Gaza. Mackay went ahead to build the house for the excavation party on the usual plan (huts around a courtyard). Muhammad the cook came as usual from Quft, and the Petries moved in.

21 November 1931
Tell el Ajjul, Gaza

[H.P. writes]

I think it must be the 21st; it is certainly a Saturday, and just as we had finished b'fast this morning, Olga[1] turned up, very healthy and cheerful, on a Gaza donkey. She came in and got some food at once and then repaired to my hut with hot water and had a wash – then proceeded to spend the morning in arranging her bed and unpacking, I had got most of her necessaries ready. Even at the roughest, one has to have basin, etc. jug, candle, candlestick, lamp, matches, shelves, chair, bed and mattress, towels, water, all clean and in working order. Lunch, 11.30, is just over and most people have repaired to their huts. We are now 8 people, as we came over, to Harding, ourselves bringing Royds and O'Brien. ... I have just written to the Warren Hastings and to Dr S. Johnson to tell them, at Luqsor and Jerusalem respectively, that I shall be ready for them on 28th so we now have a week in which to finish the whitewashing of the new roofed bedrooms and build the reading room and roof the pillared store room. The courtyard is a mere builders' yard at present. The dining room is getting whitewashed daily, as we eat! and the kitchen is being marvellously got up, with hard floor, cementing, whitewashing, and a white-tiled mastaba. I shall reorganize the shelving and cupboards etc.

---

[1] Olga Tufnell, Hilda Petrie's secretary and assistant at the British School of Archaeology in Egypt.

It is warm weather here, about 80°. Very cool before sunrise and getting hot by about 8 or 9 – then fatiguing at midday and cooling off to spring time at sunset. The evenings are very warm and very starry.

My best cat is very pleased to be stroked, but lonely at any other time. ...

I have not seen a single mosquito, nor heard one, ever since I arrived on 18th. We consider ourselves swept up and cleared of them. We do not expect any future malaria.

Rains came, they say, a week ago, and last night it rained hard for an hour. ... the whole countryside is probably saved therefore, and all the landscape is pale green with inches of barley. The great green melons, a foot and more in diameter, are nearly over, but a dozen or two have been saved for us. We have Hebron grapes and plenty of bananas. ...

Flinders Petrie photographing at Tell el 'Ajjul.

24 November 1931
Tell Ajjul

[H.P. writes]

I am writing in the shade, in the front seat of the 2-ton truck, in the open courtyard of the police station. It is a fine old building with Arab decoration and Napoleon once slept in the Pol. Commrs. room. Brown is having a test, and a med. inspection for his driving licence. H.P. drove the truck in today (without a licence) to the confines of the town, spinning along the very twisted rutty roads, crossing railway line twice, open ditches on both sides, and many camels, donkeys and natives, the Gaza – Khan Yunis high road isn't much better than the Ajjul side road. I was said to steer with consummate skill. The lives imperilled were Starkey, Browne, a child with swollen wrist and her mother our washerwoman, and a small survey boy with eye trouble, Royds' companion to hold tapes. My cargo going back are the same 2, and the same hospital patients and 2 boxes of carrot and turnip roots given me by Mrs Lash who is leaving Gaza, and 270 workmen's baskets rescued from the railway goods yard. Starkey is now driving a bargain to buy a special sort of hoe for the digging, so I do not expect him or Brown till I see them. If they come at once we shall only be 2½ hours late for lunch.

9 April 1932

[To an unknown applicant for a place in the Gaza 'dig']

Dear Madam,

  Your letter will be duly considered when we make up plans for next winter's work. At present we have closed for this season, and shall be in London May to October.

  The work in camp begins with breakfast ½hr before sunrise, out at sunrise on to the men. Shut down at 6 p.m. to one's room or to study. It is an active life, doing as much as is compatible with health. No frills, but work all day to a definite end. It does not fit with much of customary life, as we must keep to Arab hours and ways. So there are many folks whom it does not suit. I will write again in July.

  Yours sincerely,

  Flinders Petrie

Refused a permit to continue digging at Tell el Ajjul by the British Director of Antiquities (on the grounds that his lists of finds were inadequate) Petrie decided to prospect for a site in Syria then under a French mandate. They found a promising site on the Syrian coast, but were refused permission to dig by the French Director of Antiquities: North Syria, he told them, was reserved for excavation by the British Museum. Not defeated, the Petries began looking for a site over the Egyptian border in Sinai. In March they set off from Jerusalem to begin their reconnaisance. Hilda's letters and journal entries describe their expedition into Sinai.

March–May 1935
Sinai Expedition

[H.P. writes]

... On March 6th we were off to Sinai, driving bus 3 sides of a square (Gaza, Beersheba, Asluj, Kosseimeh) and sleeping on way. We had Ellis and Pape[1] with us, and a new Xtian Arab chauffeur – not as clever as the former, but he did wash up and do what cooking there was, as on sand dunes one never drives unless obliged! We spent much of March in El Arish, in resthouse in the Governor's garden, preparing for our Sinai expedition. Went across to our site often, in the Government sand-cart, and set Pape to build at Sheykh ez Zoweyid. Dr Murray[2] joined us for a spell, then on to work at Ajjul and at Jerm.[3] We got a great brick fortress of the time of Solomon, with a great fortress under it with apron of brick, all stepped, and below will come other

---

[1] Jack Ellis and Carl Pape.
[2] Margaret Murray, Petrie's old colleague from University College, London.
[3] Jerusalem.

Jack Ellis excavating at Sheikh Zoweyd.

buildings of earlier dates when we go down and down in November. For this I shall want money. The natives were pleasant, but poor diggers. We got in some old hands to encourage them. The huts are L-shaped, flanked by 2 square tents. We also use a good room in the little police post, opposite to which we have planted ourselves. The life was v. rough. A mud village supplied eggs and bread precariously. Sometimes the water tank on the rail line played out, as they would clean it and deprive us of the key for long. Then water came from a well that was brackish. The sand marches daily, you can see it march. The depths are too great for balloon tyres even, and Ellis had to rush to Cairo to buy a Ford with aero tyres. The bus sat at El Arish 20 miles off, as no bus could plunge down precipices of sand, even with A tyres. It got hotter and hotter. We stayed on the last fortnight at 117° in the shade (in tent 120°) but all the birds – warblers and redstarts – took refuge for hours at a time in our hut, their beaks open, gasping, and stood or sat dazed. They perched on our hands and feet and knees, and one even sat for a long time on F.'s head! They hardly knew how to drink, and we forced them into baths. Many died about the place. We shall find it cooler November to March and the sun won't be so outrageously early. We always had to get up at 4, cook eggs, b'fast at 4.40 and out on work 4.10–15 when the sun rushed up. The hour at midday had to be changed to 2 and more as heat increased. Bedtime was absurdly early of course.

12 February 1935
Sheykh ez Zoweyid

[F.P. and H.P. to Ann]

My Dear Anne,

Your would have been amazed at today's storm. It has lasted 24 hours now, and rages but not quite so totally. It was furious 3 to 5 a.m. I defied it by staying in bed ½ hour longer. That still enables me to have a fair b'fast 20 mins instead of the ceremonial 40, choose boys, and get up to the top of the *tell* before sunrise. I'd no intention of giving up this morn. I chose 7 boys in the teeth of the gale, and Ellis appeared 1 hour later. The thoroughly disagreeable suddenly became thoroughly impossible, and the workers trooped to tents or village. We have each hugged our hut and only appeared at meals, to be eaten under lids, and tea drunk with the saucer on the cup almost! Cooking remained impossible. I had grand accounts, packing, listing, tidying my drugs and listing them and a dozen quiet employments so that I got no lie-down but am going to bed early. I have 2 alarms now – a fat little Blk. Forest cheap clock, and a superior watch in case with illuminated hands and a gentle aristocratic voice, expensive. The dining hut alarm goes to the earliest riser each night, and another cheap but effective one goes home with Hoseyn. It doesn't always get obeyed, but I have ceased to light earliest kettle, whatever the dismay, and poor Pape lights his own if H. is ½ hour late. We now turn in to a rattling night, exactly like board ship at its windiest. The 10 loaves have come late and are perched all round me to cool, before I pack them in bread tin, so I am in dining-hut for first time to write, to see that dogs don't visit them while they air. The wowies[1] made a tremendous wailing last night, but fortunately did not incite the village dogs. There is one naughty boy here without the pale successfully. There is also the cook's sister Fatma Nasr, who gets in once a week, with eyes veiled and a different name every time. Feeling ill and unobservant one day, I put her in myself as Zahariya 'Abid'!! but when I called over I shouted "Fatma Nasr" very quickly, and she of course said "Na'am", and I fell on her with wrath, to be very dramatic before the large audience! she has not reappeared – idle brat. The particular houseboy – hush! deadly secret, gave us the 'flu', so we are not enamoured of that family. He leaned with his head on the primus, lighted or unlighted, and cooked naught. The present one goes home, for 1 hour, and stays 3 hrs., but when here is cheerful and willing, and cooks quite nicely. No particular news. We tried a new tin called Oxford brawn the other day, slightly spiced, very like tongue and ½ the price. Daddy has "Klim" every night with excellent effect and is not too thin. He has boundless activity and spirits; and no obstruction will ever stop him, I am sure. He laughs at intriguers, as he laughed a few years ago at Colt and Co (winking at me, so that I didn't catch his eye!).

---

[1]Jackals.

The governor[1] was over the other day, went all over the work, was impressed, and came back to a long drawn-out tea. He brought an enormous crate of vegetables. Gardening is his hobby – vegetables and 2 *grass* lawns at El Arish. I have not been to El A. this season, as it is no longer our post-town or shopping centre. The road is so impossible, a wildly sandy 20 miles, and at one place a precipice, down wh. you rush. You know I don't care what I do – I gloried in the awful Kerak road almost an impossibility in twists among precipices – but this one is a real leap. So we do K.Y.[2] instead, though some miles of it are an adventure.

Mrs. Jarvis is not come out, so I have brought my velour 3-corner in vain. Nothing is needed here but a helmet, tunic, breeches, fieldboots, and occasionally 2 overcoats or a jerkin. Funny history to your Bedford cords; knees want patching, left them with tailor at Gaza. Fortnight later called: a strike, in sympathy with Syria forsooth, couldn't get them. Another fortnight, fetched and found one patch unmended. Another fortnight, took them again. Another week, forgot them on way back from Jersum. Another week, called and they were not there, hunted the shop, they asseverated they hadn't had them, tho' I watched the chauffeur deliver them as I thought. Dismayed, best breeches lost for ever, yours moreover, and I am going all through winter in summer ones. When perambulating Gaza, a boy rushed at me and begged me to enter his shop. I went, and found it was a tailor. They were longing to return them beautifully patched. So today I shall stem the gale in Bedford cords and shall sleep in them, in case the roof goes in the night. Inshallah, we shall have less dirty weather tomorrow and shall make up for a lost day. You will find Williams[3] a jolly girl when she comes back. She has experience of many digs and was supervisor at her latest. At the moment, she is up at Jerusalem, and returns in 5 days. The doctors were named Teasdale, they did us well, clever at medicine and knowledgeable travellers, old Indians. Their remedies were not hackneyed, were to the point, and suited me. ...

When the bread was cold, and put away, I came back to my room, bed warmer to sit on, and bus table beside it (white American cloth) it was as golden brown to my sand floor.

I only found 1 ant tonight. The first month here, we were overrun with enormous ants, double-size, who were on and in everything.

Last night I slept till 3, then woke hungry and could not sleep again. I grudged that hour fr. 3 till 4. I always wake at 4 or 4.20. There had been some wind in the night, several bangs, but from 3 till 7 it simply raged, every iron dancing. It is only comparable to shipboard in a storm, when everything here dances or blows away, even petroleum tins, the kitchen door frame, pots, and light boxes move across the hosh (courtyard). You can see the sand scouring across the landscape all the time, like steam from a boiling kettle. I did not get

---

[1] Major Claude S. Jarvis, Governor of the Sinai Peninsula 1923-36.

[2] Khan Yunis. The most southerly town in Palestine.

[3] Dr Veronica Seton-Williams. For her memories of life in a Petrie camp, see her *The Road to El Aguzein* (London, Kegan Paul 1988).

up till 5 therefore, got some breakfast in case I had to go up left. F.'s coffee and 2 boiled eggs ready, went out and chose 7 boys, and Ellis went up. ... In an hour, he was down again. The storm had broken on us.

12 April 1935
El Arish, Sinai

[H.P. to B.O. Tufnell]

... This morning I had a stiff time. I ran beside a good trotting donkey for a kilometre along line of rail and ran all the way back too – this was at 5.45. I had the key of a huge railway tank of good water instituted for us and had to initiate the ceremony and see it done hygenically. Hoped for b'fast on return, but no such luck. A posse of Bedawy men and boys arrived on my return, and I had a scrum taking all their names and prices – then got Pape to take them to the dig and at last got tea and an egg at 7.30, two hours hot and spent. We have next sprinted in car to Gaza for this repair, as I had to go to Khan Yunis on business. We are now 1 p.m. on way to Ajjul where we pick up our stuff at camp, and shall have the picnic lunch which I always carry in car as emergency rations.

Sheikh Zoweyd was the Petries' last dig. They had hoped to return to Tell el 'Ajjul, but their camp there was wrecked by bandits. Aged 86, Flinders resigned himself to living in Jerusalem and completing books which were already in the making. He died in hospital in July 1942. Hilda lived to complete the publication of several volumes and to wind up the affairs of the British School of Archaeology; she was the guest of honour at University College in 1953 at the celebration of the centenary of Flinders Petrie's birth.

Postscript

'On travelling' was written by Hilda Petrie, most probably for a magazine or journal. Although there is no indication of the date it was composed, it reflects Hilda's desire to escape the trappings of modern life and roam freely among Egypt's ruins.

On travelling

Sometimes one is filled with a vague longing to wander in untrodden country, to cease frequenting the company of civilized men, and to share the existence of the wild creatures, and one is driven to avoid the haunts of all those who in kindliness to their own profit, minister to the needs and luxurious habits of the ordinary traveller. I once knew an old man of the gypsy or tramp class who condescended to wage-earning and submitted to the duties of a gardener, but now and again the old propensities grew strong in him, and periodically he threw up his work, and disappeared for a few days, over-mastered by his desire to "scatter on the mountains".

We may habitually eschew the wagon-lit express, the station-omnibus, and the tourist hotel, and may travel and feed with the natives, and go about on foot, but we occasionally feel our instincts rebel against the mild comforts of the flagged floor and coarse linen, and amid the flesh-pots we sigh for the wilderness.

Perhaps one of the easiest trips of the less civilised sort that can be made is a wandering along the length of Egypt, partly by donkey, partly by omnibus-train, partly on foot with an attendant donkey to carry the baggage. One naturally chooses sites of archaeological interest, and visits temples, tombs and other remains, and one intersperses visits to the larger towns, where one can see native life, and go shopping in the bazaars, and therefore one's nights may be alternately spent in rock-tombs and other such shelter, and small Greek inns. To be entirely independent, it is best to have an unsophisticated native boy with one, and carry a small tent. A couple of old socks will contain all the tinned provisions and stock of biscuits necessary for two people for a few weeks, and water-boiling apparatus must be at hand. The oldest clothes, strong boots, a stick, and stirrups or a rope, complete one's equipment.

Index